COUNSELOR SUPERVISION

Approaches
Preparation
Practices

John D. Boyd, Ph.D.
Counselor Education Department
School of Education
University of Virginia
Charlottesville, Virginia

Contributors

Roger F. Aubrey, Ed.D.
Daniel J. Delaney, Ph.D.
Neil A. Gunter, Ed.D.
John T. Hardin, Ph.D.
Harold A. Moses, Ph.D.

Endorsed by Association For Counselor
Education And Supervision

Accelerated Development Inc.
P. O. Box 667
Muncie, IN 47305
Tel. (317) 284-7511

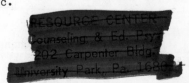

Library of Congress Catalog Card Number: LC 78-53069

International Standard Book Number: 0-915202-15-8

Corporate Editor: Linda K. Davis
Book Editor: Rita McKee

Graphic Artist: Mary J. Blizzard

Printed in the United States of America
      April, 1978
      December, 1978

For additional copies order from

 Accelerated Development Inc.
2515 West Jackson Street
P. O. Box 667
Muncie, IN 47305
Tel. (317) 284-7511

Cost: $12.45 plus postage and handling
                -in U.S. and Canada add 50 cents
                -in other countries, postage depends upon
                     prevailing rates

Price is subject to change without notice.

To my father

FOREWORD

It is both a personal and professional pleasure to accept
the invitation to write a few introductory remarks to this
significant work in counselor supervision. The development
of this book has a long history and the Association for Counselor Education and Supervision (ACES) is proud to have been
associated with it. The original undertaking was commissioned
by the ACES Publications Committee, and its subsequent
publication has the endorsement of the Association.

This book will contribute measurably to filling a gap in
our literature for the number of significant treatments of
counselor supervision is limited. This text is one of--if not,
the most comprehensive treatments of counselor supervision
available. It identifies four major approaches (psychotherapeutic, behavioral, integrative, and systems), moves to
a discussion of the preparation of supervisors for counselors,
and concludes with critiques of the practice of supervision
in four different settings--elementary and secondary schools,
university graduate programs in counselor education, state
departments of education, and agencies.

Anecdotes and examples from John Boyd's personal and
extensive experiences with supervision are liberally sprinkled
throughout the book. In addition, there are numerous charts,
rating forms, and how-to-do-it materials. The book attempts
to blend theory and action not only through a critical
assessment of the state of our available knowledge, but also
by a presentation of practical suggestions and forms for
using what we know. In Chapter 6, Boyd synthesizes the different methodologies of supervision and offers suggestions on how
to establish supervision programs. The chapters contributed
by Roger Aubrey, Daniel Delaney, Neil Gunter, and Harold Moses
and John Hardin all complement and extend Boyd's efforts to
comment authoritatively on the status of counselor supervision.

The importance of supervision to the helping profession is highlighted early and underscored throughout the text. This work should prove useful to counselor educators as well as practicing supervisors in schools and agencies. Boyd not only works hard at integrating theory and practice but also presents material that will enable the reader to gain new insights in the process of supervision.

Chris D. Kehas
Professor
Boston University

January 1, 1978   President, ACES

TABLE OF CONTENTS

LIST OF FIGURES

PREFACE

Becoming a counselor, whether conceptualized as a growth experience or a learning process, is a long and complex journey which begins with early personality development. Of the many factors affecting this journey, counselor supervision is considered to be one of the most influential. The importance accorded supervision was illustrated in 1969 by the ACES Committee on Counselor Effectivenss. Charged with studying counselor effectiveness with an eye toward improvement of counselor preparation, and being forced to limit study to a single variable, the committee chose supervision as its target. A nationwide survey of counselor supervisors was conducted and the results were presented in a report (ACES, 1969) which added enlightenment to a topic inadequately understood. Frequent reference is made throughout this text to the ACES report

Counselor supervision has a unique and strategic relationship to counselor development by spanning both preparation and practice. Supervision has always been considered a crucial component in counselor education programs. Standards for the preparation of counselors usually include explicit criteria for evaluating the quality of supervised experience (American Personnel and Guidance Association, 1967; American Psychological Association, 1963). Supervised practice has been given pivotal significance in the education of school counselors (Hansen, 1965), and supervised practicum courses are considered culminating points in counselor education programs (Hansen & Stevic, 1967). Internships and other arrangements in which counseling experience takes place in field settings also rely on competent supervision for their effectiveness (Batdorf, 1973; Boy & Pine, 1966; Hansen & Moore, 1966; Segrist & Nelson, 1972). Although on-the-job supervision has not received as much attention as that done by counselor educators, this is also a vital consideration for improving the quality of counselor performance (Kehas, 1976). As stated by the ACES

Committee on Counselor Effectiveness (ACES, 1969) "In view of the increasing pressures and demands being placed on counselors, it seems essential to implement continuing supervision if competent counseling skills are to be maintained, refined, revised, and integrated with new knowledge." (p. 13)

As the profession of counseling and guidance enters an era when more attention can be given to the quality of counselors rather than just to the satisfaction of quantitative demands, the time is right for further development and refinement of supervision. Steps in this direction require comprehensive and clear articulation of supervisory purposes and activities. When counselors say they are counseling, an individual at least has a generally accurate perception of what these counselors are doing. However, when counselor supervisors say they are supervising, one must guess what kind of procedure or activity is being performed. This difference highlights the need for greater clarification of what is involved in counselor supervision.

Another supervision need, demonstrated by the literature on the subject, is for more cohesion and synthesis. What is known about counselor supervision appears in scattered articles in professional periodicals, a few text chapters (Dellis & Stone, 1960; Eckstein & Wallerstein, 1958; Evraiff, 1963; Finn & Brown, 1959; Kell & Mueller, 1966), and even fewer major texts (Hendrickson & Krause, 1972; Mueller & Kell, 1972). Adequate treatment of the subject requires that information and ideas in the sources be pulled together so that theories, approaches, and strategies of counselor supervision may be compared, analyzed, and converged into an operational methodology.

This volume has been prepared with the foregoing supervision needs in mind. Hopefully the material herein will contribute to improvement and an increase in supervisor preparation, effective supervisory practice, and supervision research and evaluation.

John D. Boyd

February, 1978

xiv

REFERENCES FOR PREFACE

American Personnel and Guidance Association. Standards for the preparation of secondary school counselors--1967. *Personnel and Guidance Journal*, 1967, 46, 97-106.

American Psychological Association, Division of Counseling Psychology. The role of psychology in the preparation of rehabilitation counselors. Unpublished manuscript, 1963.

Association for Counselor Education and Supervision, Committee on Counselor Effectiveness. Commitment To Action In Supervision: Report of a National Survey of Counselor Supervision, 1969.

Batdorf, R. L. A proposed internship model for students in counselor education or supervision. *Counselor Education and Supervision*, 1973, 12, 271-277.

Boy, A. V., & Pine, G. J. Strengthening the off-campus practicum. *Counselor Education and Supervision*, 1966, 6, 40-43.

Dellis, N. P., & Stone, H. K. *The Training of Psychotherapists: A Multidisciplinary Approach*. Louisiana: Louisiana State University Press, 1960.

Ekstein, R., & Wallerstein, R. S. *The Teaching and Learning of Psychotherapy*. New York: Basic Books, 1958.

Evraiff, W. *Helping Counselors Grow Professionally: A Casebook for School Counselors*. Englewood Cliffs, N. J.: Prentice-Hall, 1963.

Finn, M. H., & Brown, F. *Training for Clinical Psychology*. New York: International Universities Press, 1959.

Hansen, J. C., & Moore, G. The off-campus practicum. *Counselor Education and Supervision*, 1966, 6, 32-39.

Hansen, J. C., & Stevic, R. Practicum in supervision: A proposal. Counselor Education and Supervision, 1967, 6, 205-206.

Hansen, J. C. Trainee's expectations of supervision in the counseling practicum. Counselor Education and Supervision, 1965, 4, 75-80.

Hendrickson, D. E., & Krause, F. H. Counseling and Psychotherapy: Training and Supervision. Columbus, O.: Charles E. Merrill, 1972.

Kehas, C. D. From the editor. Counselor Education and Supervision, 1976, 15(3), 164-165.

Kell, B. L., & Mueller, W. J. Impact and Change: A Study of Counseling Relationships. New York: Appleton-Century-Crofts, 1966.

Mueller, W. J., & Kell, B. L. Coping with Conflict. New York: Appleton-Century-Crofts, 1972.

Segrist, A. E., & Nelson, R. C. A model for on-site supervision of the school counselor. Counselor Education and Supervision, 1972, 12, 144-149.

SECTION ONE

Introductory Perspectives

John D. Boyd

John D. Boyd (Ph.D.) has an interest in counselor supervision which began during his doctoral studies (1968-71) at
Ohio State University. The tutelage and clinical experience
received at this early career point influenced him to make
counselor supervision a professional specialty. He has
followed this specialty in an academic position at the University of Virginia (1971-78) by coordinating a laboratory-
practicum facility, teaching a course on supervision, and
supervising many counselors as they complete practicums and
internships. Another reflection of his involvement in supervision and counseling has been numerous presentations at
national conventions and articles in professional journals.

As a counseling psychologist in private practice Dr.
Boyd has acted as a supervisory-consultant to schools, industry,
and helping-service organizations. In this capacity, as in his
university-based supervision, he has pursued the mission of
human resource development which is stressed throughout this
text. Through supervision, Dr. Boyd believes that counselors
can become persons of greater self-direction and professional
capability.

SECTION ONE

COUNSELOR SUPERVISION: INTRODUCTORY PERSPECTIVES

OVERVIEW

Section One sets forth a conceptual structure for counselor supervision which will be followed in Sections Two and Three. The conceptualization was formulated through an analysis and synthesis of information which has previously been published on counselor supervision, in addition to the author's ideas borne of supervision experience. Included in the structure is a description of the supervisor, the purposes of supervision, and the activities which comprise the supervision function. This definitive treatment of counselor supervision enables its approaches and techniques (Section Two) to be applied within purposeful activities, thus creating an operational methodology.

Chapter **1**

A

DEFINITIVE CONCEPTUALIZATION

OF

COUNSELOR SUPERVISION

John D. Boyd

A DEFINITIVE CONCEPTUALIZATION OF COUNSELOR SUPERVISION

John D. Boyd

Counselor supervision is a term which can be found throughout counseling literature, particularly in association with the topics of counselor education, counselor preparation, and leadership in the helping professions. The term "supervision" appears in the title of one of the strongest divisions of the American Personnel and Guidance Association, i.e., Association for Counselor Education and Supervision. Yet, despite this accepted use of the term, "counselor supervision" does not have a standard definition. This text on counselor supervision therefore appropriately will begin with the establishment of an operational definition. The report of the ACES Committee On Counselor Effectiveness (ACES, 1969) was the basis for development of a three-part definition which identifies who a supervisor is, what supervision seeks to achieve and what constitutes supervision.

COUNSELOR SUPERVISION . . .

> is performed by experienced, successful counselors (supervisors) who have been prepared in the methodology of supervision.

> facilitates the counselor's personal and professional development, promotes counselor competencies, and promotes accountable counseling and guidance services and programs.

> is the purposeful function of overseeing the work of counselor trainees or practicing counselors (supervisees) through a set of supervisory activities which include consultation, counseling, training and instruction, and evaluation.

THE SUPERVISOR

Every profession includes master practitioners who can guide and direct less-experienced colleagues and pre-service trainees. Master practitioners function within apprenticeships and internships by promoting a transfer of learning from instructional settings to the actual environment where the profession is practiced. Moreover, these individuals are key factors in continued personal/professional development which extends throughout a professional's career.

In the helping services and specifically in counseling and guidance, these master practitioners often are called "supervisors." They also are known by other labels, such as director of guidance, head counselor, chief psychologist, and/or pupil personnel services director. Whatever the official title, the criterion for being a supervisor is that an individual performs the function of counselor supervision. Supervisors are responsible for supervising the work of student-counselors and/or a staff of practicing counselors.

To estimate the total number of counselor supervisors in the Nation is difficult. Undoubtedly the number is greater than the membership of the Association for Counselor Education and Supervision, because supervisors are scattered through numerous other disciplines. Relatively little identifying information on supervisors is available, although their academic preparation and background experiences have been investiaged by Riccio (1961, 1966) and the ACES survey (1969). Results from these studies indicate that nearly all supervisors in colleges and universities have attained doctoral degrees and the majority of supervisors in field settings (i.e., agencies, state departments, and schools) have gained a significant level of education beyond the master's degree. Despite these high levels of educational attainment, the alarming fact remains that only a token number of supervisors, regardless of work setting, have received specific preparation for supervision.

Moreover, the majority of agency and state department supervisors sampled in the national ACES survey (1969) had not completed a counseling practicum. A reasonable assumption is that supervisors in the ACES sample and counselor supervisors in general achieved their supervisory positions on the basis of educational level, tenure, and successful counseling experiences. However, counseling experience and an accumulation of academic credits must be viewed as insufficient qualifications, by themselves, for supervisors of counselors. Preparation in supervision methodology (see Section Three) must become an entrance criteria if supervision practice is to be validated.

8

Other demographic data from the ACES (1969) study are rather predictable. Undergraduate preparation of supervisors is usually in the fields of education and psychology, while graduate preparation and advanced academic work are in guidance and counseling or other helping service disciplines. Supervisors tend to be situation oriented; they gain counseling experience in a particular setting and are likely to remain there for supervisory practice.

Information concerning personality attributes of supervisors is scarce. This is unfortunate because such data would have potential for improving selection of supervisors by answering some interesting questions, i.e., what kinds of people are supervisors? What are their beliefs, attitudes, and values? What are the personal characteristics of successful supervisors? Research has not been directed at such questions but the literature on supervision and supervisory job functions generates logical assumptions. The supervisor is and must be a serious, committed professional who has chosen counseling and supervision as a long-term career. This assumption implies that the supervisor is energetic and ambitious, but not in an egotistical or opportunistic manner. The supervisor is committed to and ambitious about developing and maintaining accountable helping services.

Competence and success with a broad range of helping activities are essential criteria for the selection of supervisors, although realistically the supervisor cannot be expected to be omnipotent; skills and expertise will be unevenly distributed. In addition to such professionally demonstratable qualities, a supervisor must possess confidence and professional assurance. A hesitant, unsure supervisor cannot offer the kind of leadership that is needed in supervisory positions. In a profession where nurturance is sometimes more prevalent than ego strength, those in leadership roles must be self assured. This fact is particularly true in schools where counselors are subordinate to principals and other administrators. The supervisor must be confident and strong when working with those who have administrative power over counselors, as well as when grappling with the difficult decisions that arise in supervision.

A supervisor should have both the professional and the personal respect of colleagues and associates in the work environment. Professional respect is founded in competence and ability, first as a good counselor and then as a capable supervisor. Personal respect relates to whether the supervisor is totally accepted as a person by his or her associates and is based upon values, attitudes, ethics, and other moral indices that are reflected through professional behavior.

Finally, the supervisor must have the characteristic of advocacy--the ability to serve as an advocate for counselors. All individuals need reinforcement, and counselors as a group suffer from a lack of professional affirmation. Supervisees need to feel that the supervisor believes in their ability or potential to be capable counselors.

To summarize, the supervisor of counselors is a well-prepared individual who has entered the supervisory position after a successful tenure as a counselor. The supervisor is regarded as a capable professional from whom other counselors can learn and is respected as a person of exemplary character. The supervisor is an advocate for counselors and is dedicated to their personal and professional development.

THE PURPOSE OF COUNSELOR SUPERVISION

A purpose is that which is set before as a general goal to be attained. Statements of purpose characteristically are overlapping, but these statements are extremely important because they register intent and set direction. From purposes may come objectives.

Counselor supervision has three main purposes

1. facilitation of the counselor's personal and professional development,

2. promotion of counselor competencies, and

3. promotion of accountable counseling and guidance services and programs.

Singularly and collectively, these purposes provide a rationale for the work of supervisors.

Personal and Professional Development

The first purpose of supervision is a dual one--to facilitate personal and professional development of counselors. Gilbert Wrenn's (1962, p. 168) strong statement provides a rationale for the personal development aspect of this dual-faced purpose.

The counselor as a person is the most important single factor in counseling. He needs to understand himself psychologically in order to be effective in helping others.

Another statement by Wrenn (1973, p. 272) also adds support to the rationale.

10

A professional must be forever at the job of learning.
I am proposing that to learn about one's self and the
/noncounseling/ world around one is as important as it
is to read new texts and attend summer school. Perhaps
it is more important.

Assuming agreement that facilitation of counselors' personal development should be a purpose of supervision the next
questions are how much and what kind of emphasis to place on
personal development? Answers to these questions are a matter
for conjecture, but the following guidelines may be helpful
in arriving at a partial resolution.

1. Generally, counselor supervision should not attempt
   to intrude on the personal development of counselors.
   Supervision should offer the counselor an optimal
   opportunity for self-initiated personal development,
   and encourage the counselor to take advantage of the
   opportunity.

2. Supervisory intervention into the counselor's personal
   development should be undertaken only when psychological
   distress is obviously and deleteriously affecting the
   counselor's performance. "Facilitation" of personal
   development is, however, a continuing supervisory
   effort.

3. The counselor's personal and professional development
   are interrrelated concepts. Damage to or facilitation
   of one of these concepts has a reciprocal effect on the
   other. Furthermore, facilitating personal development
   can be construed as contributing indirectly to all
   purposes of supervision.

4. The foremost purposes of counselor supervision are
   facilitating professional development, increasing
   competencies, and promoting accountability in guidance
   and counseling. An assumption is that selection and
   preparation have produced well-adjusted counselors,
   thus allowing the facilitation of personal development
   to become a second priority purpose of supervision.

Since the concept of personal development inherently is
vague, the supervisor must be able to put the concept into
concrete terms so that supervisory techniques and strategies
can be applied. No attempt is made here to give the concept
tangibility because personal development is being treated as a
general purpose. In Section Two, Chapter 2, the "psychotherapeutic approach" to supervision will treat the concept more
concretely. At this point to affirm facilitation of the

the counselor's psychological development as one general purpose of supervision.

Professional development, an interrelated part of the dual purpose of supervision, is a concept that must be clearly defined if the supervisor is to functionalize its intent. In a broad sense, professional development encompasses all that makes the counselor a professional--including increasing and improving competencies. In the context of this presentation, however, a more narrow definition is used, since competency improvement is designated as a separate supervisory purpose. Professional development, as here defined, refers to four tasks which have been adapted from Becker and Carper, 1956; Hart and France, 1970; Zerface and Cox, 1971; and Stefflre, 1964:

1. The counselor must accept the name and image of the profession as part of his or her self concept. This task causes problems for counselors because their preparation may lead to a wide variety of positions, each with a different job or professional person title (e.g., guidance counselor, school counselor, child/adult development specialist, psychologist, or counseling psychologist).

2. One must have a commitment to, and a clear perception of, the professional role and function. Counselors do not typically enter positions where their role and function have already been established. In fact, establishing this operational base is one of the most important and difficult functions of the newly-employed counselor (Hart and Prince, 1970). Occasionally, situational conditions can be so restrictive that the environment is unfit for good professional practice (Zerface and Cox, 1971).

   A frequently slighted facet of the counselor's role and function is support of the profession and contribution to its growth and strength. Counselors are in dire need of professional affirmation but, ironically, the only way to receive this affirmation is to produce it! Participation in local, state, and national professional associations is a start.

3. The counselor must be committed to goals of the institution in which counseling and guidance services are performed. This commitment does not preclude the counselor's influence on establishment or alteration of institutional goals.

4. The counselor will recognize and appreciate significance of the profession for individuals, groups, institutions, and society as a whole. A true profession exists to meet the needs of society, and professional accountability begins with recognition of these needs, understanding how the profession meets them, and an assessment of the profession's impact.

12

An integral component in the supervisory purpose to facilitate personal and professional development is the assumption of responsibility by both the counselor and the supervisor for achieving this development. As Ekstein and Wallerstein (1958) have noted, counselor preparation should help the counselor separate himself from formal preparation and carry on a continuous process of independent learning. Responsible self development (Arnold, 1962) is a theme permeating the purposes of supervision.

Competency Development

The second purpose of supervision, to increase counselor competencies, incorporates helping the counselor acquire, improve, and refine the skills required by the counselor's role and function. This purpose unfortunately has become associated more with counselor education programs than with in-service supervision because field supervisors often are reluctant to accept responsibility for colleagues' competency development. Before entering the position of supervisor the master counselor was responsible only for self improvement, and to monitor a colleague's skill level would have been presumptuous. Upon entering the supervisory role, however, the responsibility for supervisee competency development must be accepted, and here the personal characteristics discussed earlier in the Chapter become crucial. Does the supervisor feel confident enough to help others with their skills? Is the supervisor respected as a capable counselor who has something to offer?

Another reason for field supervisors to be uncomfortable with responsibility for supervisee competency development is that most of them have not been prepared in the methodology of supervision. Although supervisors in counselor education programs likewise lack formal supervisory preparation, they have the advantages of modeling the supervisory behavior of colleagues, being encouraged by eager students to assume a supervisor role, and the controlled conditions of a laboratory setting or a counseling center.

Still another reason why competency development has been almost exclusively associated with formal preparation programs is the assumed existence of a competency ceiling--a point at which the counselor has "learned it all." Such a terminal point is often perceived to be a graduate degree or state certification. A different perspective is needed by both supervisor and supervisee if competency is to be received as something to be upgraded throughout one's professional career. As symbolized in Figure 1.1, the development of counselor competency can be conceptualized as a continual process with several distinguishable levels.

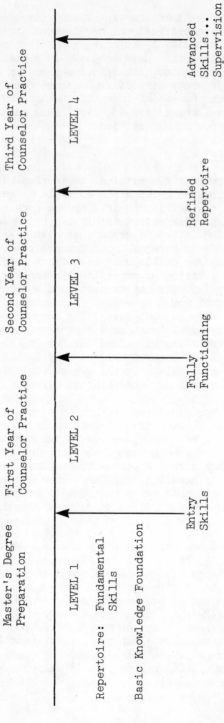

Figure 1.1. Continuum of Counselor Competencies.

14

Four finite developmental levels of competence and one infinite level are shown on the continuum. Level 1 represents the skill level which is reached through a master's degree counselor education program. Although such programs (most of which are completed in one academic year) strive for the ideal of producing a fully-functioning counselor, more realistically Level 1 may be described as consisting of a repertoire of fundamental skills and a basic foundation of knowledge that extends beyond entry skill boundaries. The repertoire of entry skills are those that the profession and the preparing institution have identified as necessary for competent counselor performance. Attainment and demonstration of these skills should be criteria for awarding a professional degree in counseling.

The basic foundation of knowledge at Level 1 provides a background of understanding that enables the counselor to broaden the repertoire of entry skills via experience and supervision. Progress would lead to the Level 2 goal of a "fully-functioning counselor" defined, for example, as a school counselor who can capably perform the 44 functions incorporated in ASCA role statements (Herr, 1969).

Level 3 on the continuum is devoted to refinement of the fully-functioning repertoire of skills. At Level 2 the competency dimension of quantity (i.e., the number of skills) was the target, but at Level 3, the focus is on quality. The counselor achieves Level 3 by improving existing competencies and moving toward the goal of a repertoire of refined and polished skills.

Advanced skills are the goal at Level 4 of the competency continuum. This level is achieved, after several years of experience, advanced preparation, and supervision by a small percentage of counselors who may be called "master practitioners." The work of the "master practitioners" is outstanding in all respects. These individuals possess and perform advanced skills that would be unethical for the neophyte to attempt. Other professionals use such persons as models and depend on them for guidance and leadership because of their demonstrated effectiveness. One of the competencies that may be gained at this level is counselor supervision.

Beyond Level 4 is a continual process of competency development. The neophyte at Level 1 may think that the supervisor, who always seems to know what to do, has reached the ceiling of competency development. However, this is a misconception and perhaps the supervisor should share the truth-- that despite advanced preparation, successful performance, and the professional prestige of being a master counselor, always more is to be learned, for the process of competency development never stops.

Promotion of Accountability

To say that the helping professions, and particularly
guidance and counseling, are presently in an "age of accountability" would be an understatement. Accountability is being
demanded by the public that funds these enterprises (Humes,
1972; Pulvino & Sanborn, 1972), and personnel in these professions are trying to demonstrate accountability to that public
(and perhaps to themselves). The consequence of not being able
to satisfy public expectation could be disastrous for the
helping professions. Counseling and guidance is most vulnerable
because this field always has been forced to fight for federal,
state, and local dollars and lack of demonstrated effectiveness
could reduce or redirect funding, thus changing the support
structure of the profession.

To ignore the realities of jeopardized funding and the
popularity (however faddish) of accountability would be
irresponsible but these forces should not be the motivation
for helping services and programs to respond to the need for
demonstrating accountability. Such forces from outside the
profession may serve as cues to raise serious questions about
effectiveness, but the motivation for demonstrating accountability must come from within. A profession emerges in response
to the needs of society and exists for the purpose of meeting
those needs. Accountability is the profession's index of
validity--evidence that the profession is meeting society's
needs. The profession's obligation, not society's, is to
establish accountability.

As a term, accountability has been given many definitions
(Lessinger, 1970), but the core concept relates to accomplishment of purposes and goals which a person or institution has
contracted or promised to accomplish. Glass (1972, p. 636)
compared this core element of meaning to "the simple economic
relationship of vendor and buyer." The public served by
helping services is the buyer and counselors are the vendors.
An accountable relationship between these two parties would
involve

1. complete disclosure concerning the service being sold,

2. a testing of the effectiveness of the service, and

3. a redress if the service is found by the public to be
   ineffective or falsely advertised.

According to this vendor-buyer paradigm, counselors are accountable to their employers--the public. Counselors must openly
and honestly explain their functions and what their services
can do. Counselors must test and evaluate their services and

16

share the findings with the public. Lastly, counselors must be responsible for the consequences (good and bad) of their work and make adjustments where their work is ineffective.

Counselor supervision is a means for promoting accountability in services, programs, and relationships between helping services and the public. Supervised assistance to an individual counselor improves that person's accountability, while supervision applied to a staff of counselors involved in program development, management, and evaluation is a route to program accountability. In both cases, a special set of skills --a technical expertise--is needed by the supervisor if accountability is to be achieved.

THE ACTIVITIES OF COUNSELOR SUPERVISION

So far in this Chapter two parts of a definition of counselor supervision have been covered. The person who performs supervision has been described and the purposes of supervision have been discussed. The third part of the definition states that counselor supervision is the purposeful function of overseeing the work of counselor trainees or less experienced counselors (supervisees) through a set of supervisory activities which include

1. consultation,
2. counseling,
3. training and instruction, and
4. evaluation.

This "nuts-and-bolts" definition has two key phrases, the first of which is "purposeful function of overseeing." To this author the concept of function seems the most logical and understandable way of dealing with counselor supervision. A function (noun) is the "action for which a person or thing is specially fitted or used or for which a thing exists" (Webster, 1974, p. 465). In terms of this definition, supervision as a function is the characteristic action or activity involved in implementing a purpose. The word which best describes the characteristic actions and activities of supervision is overseeing--the act of "watching over." Whatever diverse activities comprise the work of counselor supervision, they are subsumed under the principal supervisory function of being aware of and monitoring the work (and development) of counselors.

The second key phrase in this part of the definition of counselor supervision is "through a set of supervisory activities." This phrase indicates that the purposeful function of overseeing is implemented through a number of activities. In contrast to the idea that counselor supervision is a singular entity or activity, it is defined here as a function consisting of at least four main activities: consultation, counseling, training and instruction, and evaluation. Each of these activities will be discussed, but mention should be made of one activity which has been omitted from the list. A review of literature on supervision reveals that administrative activities frequently have been linked to, or considered a part of, the supervisor's role (ACES, 1969, p. 14). Despite this fact, administration is not herein considered a primary supervisory activity. Recognition is made that the supervisor will engage in some administrative duties, one example being organization and management of helping service programs, but such duties are seen as being incorporated into the four activities which have been mentioned.

Hays (1971, p. 124) supports the position that administration should not be undesirably emphasized in functions of a counselor supervisor. Hays posits that organizational structure should separate administrative and supervisory positions.

The individual (in the position of supervisor) should not be involved with administration or management but only with the improvement of the skill for which he is supervising. A counselor supervisor should be concerned only with the improvement of the counseling skills of the counselors within the system. He does administer to the extent that he plans his own activities and organizes his own time. Within the organizational framework he would not manage, appraise, or control any portion of the program. He is free to provide a service beneficial to the personnel within the system.

Although Hays' supervisory role is restricted to the one activity of skill development, a stance which conflicts with the conceptualization being presented, his recommendation for organizational structure is consistent with the author's ideas because this action relieves the supervisor of unnecessary administrative duties. This recommendation is admittedly an idealistic one, but a deserving one in view of the fact that the supervisory function presently exists as one of many functions comprising broad roles. A recent survey of guidance directors (Biggers & Mangusso, 1972) illustrates this point. Results indicated that the majority of guidance directors sampled were performing supervision, but only as one of twenty-eight frequent duties! That greater delimitation of function would be desirable if supervisory responsibilities are to be discharged at an optional level is apparent.

A reality is that in a multi-faceted role the supervisory function could suffer from the competition that administrative

18

duties make upon the supervisor's time. Even administration that is related to the supervisory function can monopolize the supervisor's time and energy. Results from the national ACES survey (ACES, 1969) indicated that the majority of school, state, and agency supervisors sampled spent more time on administrative activities (i.e., placement, orientation, supervision program evaluation, public relations, certification, and licensing) than on any other supervisory activity!

For all of the foregoing reasons, administration has not been given the status of a primary supervisory activity, but the importance of certain administrative skills that have a direct bearing on the supervisory function should not be overlooked. The "Systems Approach" to supervision described in Section Two, Chapter 5, is closely related to administration.

Having defined counselor supervision as the function of overseeing the work counselors via a set of four activities (see Figure 1.2) some rationale should exist for selective employment of the activities. In other words, when does the supervisor use what? This question represents a major epistemological weakness in counselor supervision, because a rationale for selection and use of supervisory activities is lacking (Walz & Roeber, 1962; ACES, 1969). In the next portion of this Chapter an explanation of the four supervisory activities are given, along with a suggested rationale for their selection and employment.

Depicted in Figure 1.2 are four supervisory activities through which the counselor supervision function is exercised. Consultation is the principal activity and stance of the supervisor, with training and instruction, counseling, and evaluation completing the list. In the following pages a rationale is offered for selecting and employing each supervisory activity.

Counselor Supervision: Consultation

Consultation is performed in many contexts, in each of which its implementation may be somewhat different. Consultation as an activity to carry out the function of counselor supervision is quite different, for example, from mental health consultation. Identifying characteristics and an implied rationale for supervisory consultation are included in the following items:

1. The consulting supervisor is an authority in his/her respective helping profession--a master counselor who is experienced in performing the counselor's work.

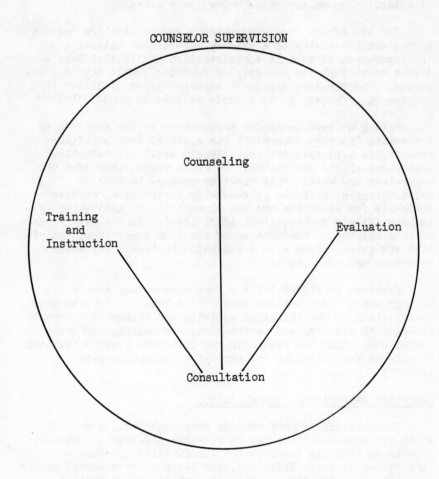

Figure 1.2. Activities Comprising The Counselor
Supervision Function.

2. If consultees are practicing or post-degree counselors, they are accepted as able professionals by the consulting supervisor. Presumably a selection process has been applied before employment and counselors have been judged competent and must be accepted as such. If counselors are still in a counselor preparation program they are accepted as potentially capable counselors. In either case, if the supervisor cannot accept the consultee in the manner described, supervision will be impaired.

3. A compatible and complementary relationship must exist between roles of the supervisor and the counselor if consultation is to succeed. The role of the consulting supervisor is to help the counselor with personal and professional development, competency development, and establishment and maintenance of accountable services and programs. The role of the counselor is to seek and capitalize upon the supervisor's assistance in the achievement of responsible self development. Development through supervision is a joint responsibility, but the central obligation is on the counselor, since self development is the goal. Sometimes, however, the supervisor may need to establish the environment and the attitudinal framework for self development before the supervisory relationship can be effective. If motivation for self development is dormant and the supervisor must assume all the responsibility for direction of the supervisory process, the activity becomes akin to autocratic instruction and cannot be called supervisory consultation.

4. Consultation in the context of counselor supervision should lead to objectives which are mutually agreed upon by supervisor and counselor. Objectives tend to fall into the four categories of

   a. personal problems which are interfering with the counselor's work,

   b. concerns about professional development,

   c. acquisition of new skills or improvement of existing competencies, and

   d. program development, maintenance, and evaluation.

   To determine which objectives of supervisory consultation are pertinent to a given situation, some type of preliminary assessment will be needed. Self assessment by the counselor or cooperative assessment by counselor and supervisor are the preferred types if self development is to be encouraged.

21

5. To accomplish objectives in supervisory consultation. effective strategies must be applied. Some strategies allow the supervisor to remain in the consulting role. In other strategies the supervisor may need to conduct training sessions and other forms of instruction or render appropriate conditions to shift into counseling. Strategies which lead the supervisor out of the consultation activity and into other supervisory activities should be regarded as acceptable but temporary aberrations. A return to consultation should be later accomplished, thus reaffirming consultation as the dominant activity of supervision.

6. Evaluation has been designated as a supervisory activity separate from consultation, and evaluation will be discussed in that context at a later time. While on the topic of consultation, however, its interrelationship with evaluation should be clarified. The two aspects of supervision are frequently considered antithetical, with consultation being viewed as a threat-free and non-evaluative working relationship with a counselor (Johnston & Gysbers, 1967). As employed within supervision, though, rarely is the consulting activity completely nonevaluative. Supervision, as previously stated, is the function of overseeing the counselor's work. Evaluation is implied in the overseeing function, and is obviously a necessity for accomplishment of the purposes of supervision. Evaluation can and should be used in conjunction with supervisory consultation without raising the counselor's anxiety level enough to hamper supervision.

Whether the supervisor should evaluate the counselor's performance is a practical rather than just a theoretical question. How can the supervisor nurture counselor self-development while concurrently assuring that supervisory purposes are being achieved? If an autocratic or directive stance, which excludes counselor input is adopted, the objective of self-development is sacrificed. If the supervisor is totally nonevaluative in the relationship with a counselor, the situation may be too benign to be effective. An imperfect but realistic compromise is for the consulting supervisor to encourage counselor self-evaluation, to generate cooperative evaluation wherever efficacious, and to judiciously apply some evaluatory procedures on a unilateral basis.

As depicted in Figure 2.1, consultation should be the predominant stance and activity of the counselor supervisor. Consultation is the most viable activity of those to be reviewed, and it provides an orientation that allows the supervisor to act immediately when situations call for supervisory action.

Counselor Supervision: Counseling

Several areas of conjecture have already been touched
upon in this Chapter, and the activity of counseling raises
another. The question is, "Should the counselor supervisor
provide counseling to the supervisee?" Material in Chapter 2
presents a school of thought which views counselor supervision
as a counseling-like, therapeutic process, however, this viewpoint seems to obfuscate the issue. The question is not how to
supervise, but whether supervision should be permitted to
revert to counseling, thereby abandoning for the time being
the predominant activity of supervisory consultation.

The issue of whether supervisory consultation should be
permitted to revert to counseling may be dealt with in the
context of two related questions. Question one is, "Does the
counselor (supervisee) ever need counseling, and/or could the
counselor profit from counseling?" Clearly, the rationale
upon which counseling is founded gives an affirmative answer
to this question. Counseling exists to help individuals with
the developmental tasks, stages, and personal adjustment
concerns that beset everyone (Blocher, 1966; Kell & Burow,
1970; Sprinthall, 1971). The professional counselor may at
times be facing quite stressful events in his or her life
which affect job performance, and particularly then the counselor can profit from counseling.

Question two is, "Who should provide counseling to the
counselor and in what situation?" With few exceptions, the
supervisor (a master counselor) is the most qualified person
in the counselor's professional environment to provide counseling. Furthermore, the supervisory relationship is by
definition the right context for facilitating personal development. In the author's opinion, the issue is not whether to
include counseling in the set of supervisory activities but
when and how the supervisor should utilize counseling?

Typically, the supervisor will be engaged in the consulting
activity with the counselor when cues emerge from the counselor
which indicate that he/she wishes to discuss a particular concern. When such cues become apparent, the supervisor can follow
the counselor's lead. No abrupt changes need to occur in the
supervisor-counselor relationship because establishment of a
positive, interpersonal relationship has already been accomplished in consultation. Gradually, the interaction focuses on
a concern that is more personal to the counselor and which is
outside the defined objectives of consultation, and counseling
ensues. Several counseling sessions may be devoted to the concern, or, if extensive treatment is needed, the supervisor can
make a referral to another agency or counselor. Assuming that
extensive treatment is not usually needed, counseling will be

short term in duration and the transition back into consultation can be achieved through the supervisor's adept management of the interaction.

Counselor Supervision: Training and Instruction

Training and instructional activities are the most common supervisory procedures (other than administration) in actual practice (ACES, 1969). A listing of these activities will be presented in Chapter 3 under the topic of the "Behavioral Approach," but at this point discussion will be limited to why and how they are used.

The variety of supervisory procedures and disagreement over approaches to supervision led Hosford (ACES, 1969, p. 26) to state that "the only area of agreement, and that for which some research is available, is the consensus that the supervisory process is a learning experience in which the principles of learning apply." This single area of agreement could explain the wide application of training and instruction as a supervisory activity. The point may be that supervisors believe the supervisee should be learning something during supervision, so they tend to apply training and instructional methodology. However, a question may exist about how well the principles of learning are employed in this methodology. Findings from Walz and Roeber's (1962) descriptive investigation of counseling supervision among supervisors in North Central Association of Counselor Educators and Supervisors (NCACES) revealed a response style which was cognitive, informative, and evaluative. Supervisors in the national ACES sample (ACES, 1969) were reported as depending more on lectures and discussions than on other instructional modes, such as critiquing taped performance and demonstration. This evidence suggests that when supervisors use training and instruction they are likely to apply techniques which are traditional and unimaginative in nature--probably reflective of approaches experienced during their preparation as counselors or supervisors.

A rationale for effective use of training and instructional activities in the context of supervision should begin with the setting of objectives for these activities within the total framework of supervisory consultation. Strategies would then be selected or constructed to reach the objectives, and they would be of two types:

1. self-managed learning programs, and

2. those involving the supervisor as an active trainer.

In a self-managed training program the supervisor remains in a consultative stance and assists the counselor in progressing through the program, whereas strategies of active instruction and training put the supervisor outside the consultation activity. The differentiating criterion between the consultative stance and that of active trainer is counselor input. A shared responsibility for learning, with maximal input from the counselor, characterizes consultation. Conversely, the supervisor, when functioning as an active trainer, carries most of the responsibility, with the flow of information and direction being principally from supervisor to counselor, and with counselor input at a minimum.

When engaged in consultation, the supervisor can digress to engage temporarily in active training and then return to consultation, just as was done with the counseling activity. One can also feasibly be engaged in the consulting activity with a number of individual counselors while concurrently conducting an in-service training program for the group. Determining when and how to use instruction and training versus consultation is a matter of professional judgment. As an alternative to choosing one or the other, the supervisor can alter the character of an instructional program and incorporate some of the advantages of consultation. Counselors' input can be solicited by letting them select instructional goals, by including counselors as peer trainers, and by using counselors' own tapes and cases as instructional material.

Counselor Supervision: Evaluation

The importance of evaluation to the supervisory function has already been stressed. Evaluation is essential for accountable supervision and for accountable counseling. Potential roadblocks in the path of evaluation include lack of skills in performing evaluation, confusion about the compatibility of supervision and evaluation, and anxiety-evoking qualities attributed to evaluation. The first two roadblocks mentioned are easier to overcome than the third. Skills can be acquired through training; a conceptualization of the appropriate relationship between supervisory consultation and evaluation can be clarified, but the debilitating fear associated with evaluation is the most pervasive roadblock. This fear has led to the anti-evaluation syndrome of those who think that more learning and performance can take place if evaluation and its accompanying threat are removed from learning/performance situations. An oversight in anti-evaluation reasoning however is that evaluation itself need not be anxiety-evoking. Rather, the real antecedents of fear are misperceptions about evaluation.

Evaluation was never intended to be a fearful activity. To the contrary, evaluation was meant to be an eagerly sought activity that answers the basic accountability question that should be asked by every professional, "Am I accomplishing my objectives?" The coup in supervision is to manage the evaluation so that perceptions of those being evaluated create positive motivation rather than anxiety.

Several conditions prerequisite for low-threat evaluation are inherent in the consulting guidelines that were proposed previously. The foremost condition is that the targets for evaluation are known to both supervisor and counselor, and the counselor has input into selection of these targets. This condition does more to relieve anxiety than any other. Another condition is that the counselor is aware of the evaluative procedures being conducted, and performs some of them (self-evaluations). In a nutshell, evaluation in conjunction with consultation by the supervisor should be performed cooperatively whenever possible. Finally, the goal of evaluation should be perceived as documentation of success in obtaining objectives and the identification of areas for improvement. Evaluation is proactive rather than being aimed at punishing counselors whose work is not reaching objectives.

Current supervisory practice deviates somewhat from the views presented in this Chapter regarding evaluation as a conjunctive activity with supervisory consultation. As indicated in the ACES survey (ACES, 1969), a balance exists in the use of direct appraisal, indirect appraisal, self evaluation, and peer evaluation. Probably counselor participation is present to a significant degree only in self evaluation.

Whatever evaluative methods the supervisor employs, three things need to be evaluated: the work of each supervisee, helping service programs, and supervision itself. The scope of this task is beyond the capability of any one supervisor, a condition which provides another reason for sharing evaluation with counselors.

Evaluation of each counselor's progress toward objectives is completed most ethically in individual sessions; program evaluation is performed most efficiently by a division of labor among a counseling staff; and evaluation of supervision can be done by the supervisor with feedback from supervisees and superiors. In each of these areas, evaluation is incorporated into the general planning operation. The supervisor and counseling staff plan a program of services geared toward criterion-referenced objectives, and the supervisor prepares a planned program of supervisory activities. Evaluation thus permeates most of the supervisor's work.

SUMMARY

Counselor supervision has been defined as the function of overseeing the counselor's work for the purpose of facilitating personal and professional development, improving competencies, and promoting accountability in services and programs. To accomplish these purposes the supervisor engages in the four activites of consultation, counseling, training and instruction, and evaluation. Consultation includes establishment of the objective and strategies of supervision and is the supervisor's predominant activity. Strategies for consultation may allow the supervisor to remain consistently in the consulting activity, or they may involve the activities of counseling and training/instruction, during which the supervisor digresses temporarily from the consultant stance. Evaluation is another major activity of supervision that is often a companion to consulting and training/instruction.

Counselor supervision has been presented as a professional specialty with a methodology requiring highly developed skills. Successful counseling experience is a necessary but insufficient prerequisite for supervision, and should be supplemented with advanced preparation in supervisory methods.

The importance of supervision to the future of helpgiving services should again be stressed. Counselor supervision is an indispensable component of counselor preparation programs. Coupled with the counselor's self-development process, counselor supervision is a key to accountable helping services and attainment of a counselor's professional potential. Saying that counselor supervision can be one of the most instrumental factors affecting future development of the helping service professions is not an exaggeration. Furthermore, counselor supervision can have a similarly facilitative effect on counselor-offered services in other disciplines.

REFERENCES

Arnold, D. L. Counselor education as responsible self develop-
    ment. Counselor Education and Supervision, 1962, 1, 185-
    192.

Association for Counselor Education and Supervision, Committee
    on Counselor Effectiveness. Commitment to Action in Super-
    vision: Report of a National Survey of Counselor Super-
    vision, 1969.

Becker, H. S., & Carper, J. W. Development of identification
    with an occupation. American Journal of Sociology, 1956,
    41, 289-298.

Biggers, J. L., & Mangusso, D. J. The work of the guidance
    administrator. Counselor Education and Supervision, 1972,
    12 (2), 130-136.

Blocher, D. H. Developmental Counseling. New York: Ronald
    Press Company, 1966.

Ekstein, R., & Wallerstein, R. S. The Teaching and Learning of
    Psychotherapy. New York: Basic Books, 1958.

Glass, G. V. The many faces of educational accountability.
    Phi Delta Kappan, 1972, 10, 636-639.

Hart, D. H., & Prince, D. J. Role conflict for school coun-
    selors: Training versus job demands. Personnel and
    Guidance Journal, 1970, 48, 374-380.

Hays, D. G. Administrator, director, supervisor--Would you
    accept chief? Counselor Education and Supervision, 1971,
    11, 119-128.

Hendrickson, D. E., & Krause, F. H. Counseling and Psycho-
    therapy: Training and Supervision. Columbus, Ohio:
    Charles E. Merrill, 1972.

Herr, E. L. The perceptions of state supervisors of guidance of appropriateness of counselor function, the function of counselors, and counselor preparation. Counselor Education and Supervision, 1969, 8, 241-257.

Humes, C. W. Accountability: A boon to guidance. Personnel and Guidance Journal, 1972, 51, 21-26.

Johnston, J. A., & Gysbers, N. C. Essential characteristics of a supervisory relationship in counseling practicum. Counselor Education and Supervision, 1967, 6, 335-340.

Kell, B. L., & Burow, J. M. Developmental Counseling and Therapy. Boston: Houghton Mifflin Company, 1970.

Lessinger, L. M. Every Kid a Winner: Accountability in Education. New York: Simon and Schuster, Publishers, 1970.

Pulvino, D. J., & Sanborn, M. P. Feedback and accountability. Personnel and Guidance Journal, 1972, 51, 15-20.

Riccio, A. C. The counselor educator and the guidance supervisor: Graduate training and occupational mobility. Counselor Education and Supervision, 1961, 1, 10-17.

_____. Counselor educators and guidance supervisors: A second look at graduate training. Counselor Education and Supervision, 1966, 5, 73-79.

Sprinthall, N. A. Guidance for Human Growth. New York: Van Nostrand Reinhold Company, 1971.

Stefflre, B. What price professionalism? Personnel and Guidance Journal, 1964, 42, 654-659.

Walz, G. R., & Roeber, E. C. Supervisor's reactions to a counseling interview. Counselor Education and Supervision, 1962, 2, 2-7.

Webster's New Collegiate Dictionary. Springfield, Mass.: G. & C. Merriam Company, 1974.

Wrenn, C. G. The Counselor in a Changing World. American Personnel and Guidance Journal, 1962.

_____. The World of the Contemporary Counselor. Boston: Houghton Mifflin Company, 1973.

Zerface, J. P., & Cox, W. H. School counselors, leave home. Personnel and Guidance Journal, 1971, 49, 371-375.

SECTION TWO

Differentiated Approaches

SECTION TWO

DIFFERENTIATED APPROACHES TO COUNSELOR SUPERVISION

OVERVIEW

Counselor supervision is a relatively immature function,
since it is not based on tested theoretical and pragmatic
foundations. Supervision always has been a slighted function
in counselor education, and an even smaller degree of attention
has come from practicing counselors. Yet, during the last two
decades, a steady dribble of literature on supervision has come
from an interested minority. Because so many of these writers
have been counselor educators involved with supervision of
counseling within practicum courses, the literature is replete
with treatises on counseling supervision. As a consequence,
counselor supervision (i.e., overseeing all of the counselor's
work) appears as a rather insignificant topic which often is
considered synonymous with supervision of the counseling
activity. Because of this misconception, counseling supervision
has had a confounding effect upon the topic of counselor
supervision. In Section Two an attempt is made to avoid this
error by treating counselor supervision as a function which
subsumes counseling supervision. Counseling supervision is
theoretically and methodologically the most well developed
aspect of counselor supervision, and it has much to offer in
the construction of counselor supervision approaches. Nevertheless, counselor supervision should not overshadow all other
activities which comprise the supervisory function. This
Section will capitalize on the literature of counseling supervision, as well as on that of counselor education in general,
and extract from the literature four differentiated approaches
to counselor supervision. Although each approach has distinctive features and a special contribution to make to counselor
supervision, one would make an oversight to assume that the
four have no interrelationships. Rather, the approaches may
be viewed as compatible methodologies, perhaps even complimen-
tary means, for performing supervisory activities. Readers are

33

therefore encouraged to ingeniously apply techniques and strategies from the four supervision approaches (psychotherapeutic, behavioral, integrative, and systems) to the supervisory activities of consultation, counseling, training and instruction, and evaluation.

Chapter **2**

THE

PSYCHOTHERAPEUTIC APPROACH

TO

COUNSELOR SUPERVISION

John D. Boyd

THE PSYCHOTHERAPEUTIC APPROACH TO COUNSELOR SUPERVISION

John D. Boyd

The psychotherapeutic approach to counselor supervision is a synthesis and extension of views that conceptualize supervision as being similar to counseling and psychotherapy (Altucher, 1967; Arbuckle, 1965; Ekstein, 1964; Ekstein & Wallerstein, 1958; Kell & Mueller, 1966; Lister, 1966; Moore, 1969, Mueller & Kell, 1972; Patterson, 1964; Rogers, 1957). According to this approach, counselor supervision is a therapeutic process focusing on the intrapersonal and interpersonal dynamics in the counselor's relationships with clients, supervisors, colleagues, and others.

Of the four supervisory approaches to be covered the psychotherapeutic approach is ranked first in seniority. This approach was the first to be advocated and has always had a large following, although its proponents have never been in total theoretical accord. Historically, the training model for psychoanalysis, with its required analysis for trainees, probably had an early influence on other schools of psychotherapy and the upstart profession of counseling. Those who prepared counselors discovered and promulgated an important principle. As stated by Altucher (1967, p. 165) "learning to be a counselor is both an emotional and intellectual experience, and of the two, the emotional part is the most crucial."

FOCUS ON DYNAMICS

The psychotherapeutic approach to counselor supervision could well be called a "dynamic approach" because interpersonal and intrapersonal dynamics are its focus and modus operandi. An individual's dynamics are considered a criterion of psychological adjustment, and the dynamic interplay between helper and helpee is the instrument for therapeutically induced change. The counselor must be aware fully of these dynamics and use them for the other's benefit. Psychotherapeutic supervision aims at helping counselors attain this awareness and acquire skill in utilizing dynamics.

Conceptualizing psychotherapeutic supervision is difficult
because writers have described the approach in piecemeal fashion and have often failed to explicate underlying theory.
Thus some writers and practitioners explain how dynamics
operate in supervision from a psychoanalytic viewpoint; others
may treat dynamics from a phenomenological perspective. At the
end of this Chapter a case study from the cognitive theory of
supervisory dynamics is presented, and Chapter 11 is devoted
to a conceptualization of dynamics based on Robert Carkhuff's
(1969) theory of helpgiving. Presently, however, the psychotherapeutic approach to counselor supervision will be explained
from a somewhat atheoretical model of dynamics, and readers
can apply their own theoretical orientations to this model.

To gain an overall perspective of the psychotherapeutic
approach and to facilitate explanation, Figure 2.1 has been
drawn to depict focal dynamics in the supervisory situation.
As illustrated, the dynamics which are examined in supervision
are provided by three people: the counselor, the person
(helpee) who is interacting with the counselor, and the supervisor. The numbers in Figure 2.1 identify the dynamics occurring among and within these three parties, and these are the
focal points of psychotherapeutic supervision. Numbers, 1, 2,
and 3 depict <u>interpersonal</u> dynamics, and <u>intrapersonal</u>
dynamics are identified by numbers 4, 5, and 6.

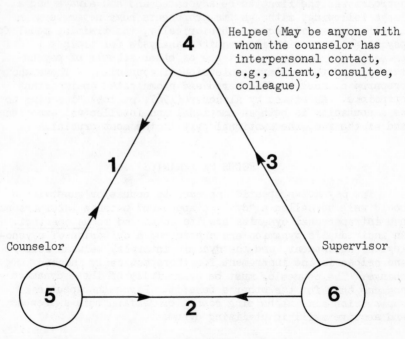

Figure 2.1. Counselor Supervision Dynamics.

Interpersonal Dynamics

The interpersonal dynamics which occur between the counselor and helpee are a primary focus in psychotherapeutic supervision (Figure 2.1, dynamic 1). Communication travels by non-verbal as well as verbal interpersonal behavior. Obviously, the counselor is responsible for being a sensitive receiver of both explicit and implied communication and a sender of communication that will have a beneficial effect upon the one being counseled. Supervision should help the counselor to be an effective interpersonal communicator.

Interpersonal dynamics between counselor and supervisor (Figure 2.1, dynamic 2) are a second focus which has much in common with the counselor-client interaction. Within the supervisory process the supervisor has the same responsibility toward the counselor as does the counselor to the client in counseling. The supervisor is responsible for dealing with received and sent interpersonal dynamics in such a manner that the counselor learns how to interact effectively. Counselor learning takes place as the supervisor is accepted as a model of interpersonal behavior within supervision.

The third set of interpersonal dynamics in Figure 2.1 relates to the supervisor's responsibility for the quality of the psychological contact with the helpee. Concerning this responsibility, Altucher (1967) has noted that the supervisor's first commitment is to the counselor, and that a consequence of allowing neophyte counselors to work with clients is less adequate service. Patterson (1964) agreed, but suggested that an adequately trained (but neophyte) counselor will rarely damage the client irreparably in a single interview before the supervisor can intervene. Supervisors have a three-fold responsibility of allowing only adequately-prepared counselors to do supervised practice, of monitoring their performance closely, and supervising without taking responsibility away from them. A supervisor's ethical responsibility to protect the welfare of those who are being counseled need not be compromised unduly by the "less adequate" service of trainees. Although less adequate than the service of experienced counselors, supervisee performance can and must be competent.

Intrapersonal Dynamics

Intrapersonal dynamics consist of covert behaviors and sensory processes such as feelings, thoughts, and perceptions. Included in the intrapersonal realm are attitudes and beliefs--cognitive routines for attributing meaning to stimuli. Many other terms are used to refer to intrapersonal dynamics. From a phenomenological foundation, Rogers (1951) might refer to intrapersonal activity as organismic functioning: perceptions,

thoughts, and feelings that could be clustered into aspects of
the self. Another common term associated with the intrapersonal realm is "experiencing" (Lister, 1966; Hansen & Barker,
1964). Experiencing can be defined as a sensory awareness of
psychologically influenced physiological activity.

Terminology used to describe intrapersonal dynamics in
scholarly discourse can be confusing, but this difficulty may
not be as prevalent or significant in supervisory practice.
Terminology is relatively unimportant as long as the supervisor
and counselor can communicate clearly.

Within the psychotherapeutic approach, nature and amount
of supervisory attention given to intrapersonal dynamics varies,
depending upon the counselor, supervisor, and situation. Some
counselors pay less attention to intrapersonal aspects than
do others, and the same is true for supervisors who vary on
their particular style of supervision. The degree of attention
given to intrapersonal dynamics is also a function of how
appropriate such a focus would be in the situation under study.
For example, when supervising an educational counseling session,
fewer opportunities would exist for fruitful intrapersonal focus
than would be present in supervising a counselor who is resolving a personal conflict with a colleague.

Of the three sources of intrapersonal activity with which
the psychotherapeutic supervisor can grapple (Figure 2.1,
dynamics 4, 5, 6), the least threatening for the counselor and
supervisor is the intrapersonal realm of the helpee (dynamic 4).
The supervisor's main task in respect to these dynamics, which
will be discussed later in this Chapter, is to help the
counselor understand the other person's internalized responses
and the influences on his or her overt behavior.

Counselors' intrapersonal dynamics (Figure 2.1, dynamic 5)
are often very threatening to them, and, consequently, may be
well guarded by resistive defenses which are difficult to handle
in supervision (Bauman, 1972; Guttman, 1972). Ironically
though, the counselor's anxiety surrounding these dynamics
may offer a cue to the supervisor, indicating which ones need
supervisory attention (Mueller & Kell, 1972).

Psychotherapeutic supervision must "zero in" on the counselor's intrapersonal dynamics, particularly those which
evoke anxiety, because these covert elements are a direct and
powerful influence on the counselor's interpersonal behavior.
Therapeutic utilization of one's interpersonal dynamics in a
counseling relationship is virtually impossible if corresponding awareness and control of covert dynamics are not present.

Another intrapersonal focus in psychotherapeutic supervision is the supervisor (Figure 2.1, dynamic 6). The supervi-

40

sor's overt behavior is influenced by intrapersonal dynamics, and professional control (not to be confused with supression or repression) must be maintained in both realms. If uncontrolled and unconscious intrapersonal dynamics are primary antecedents for the supervisor's conduct, supervision will become a freewheeling relationship in which both counselor and supervisor are striving to satisfy their own needs. Instead, professional intent should guide the supervisor toward behaving (supervision methodology) in a way that will be optimally beneficial to the supervisee.

Dynamic Interactions and Patterns

Although the foregoing discussion has treated the six dynamic foci of psychotherapeutic supervision as discrete elements, operationally they are expressed in patterns. Patterns develop when a number of dynamics have contingencies which link them together. A specific pattern may be somewhat characteristic of an individual's typical interactions, or it may be idiosyncratic to the immediate human relationship. In the former case, a dynamic pattern, if recognized, is a particularly revealing clue that guides efforts of the counselor or supervisor. Identification of and intervention in patterned dynamics is the essence of therapeutic supervision methodology.

Patterning may be illustrated in the case of an insecure beginning counselor interacting with a defensive client. The counselor attempts to perform capably, but the client does not respond in a reinforcing manner. Many of the client's statements and mannerisms may be perceived by the counselor as indicating that he/she is doing a poor job of counseling. These perceptions, some of which may be unrealistic or exaggerated, cause the counselor's anxiety to rise, thus further inhibiting effective performance.

The pattern may become even more of a problem if the client begins to act in a way that capitalizes upon the counselor's insecurity. For example, if the client were threatened by the counselor, an aggressive reaction might be to say something about the counselor's neophytic status or lack of helpfulness. This action would thwart the counselor, and effectively safeguard the client from being confronted with any more threatening material. Just such a client confrontation would be necessary for therapeutic counseling to be effective, and good results would occur only if the dynamic pattern were broken.

Another common illustration of a dynamic pattern occurs when counselors express incapability and dependence, causing the supervisor to accept his/her responsibility. In this case the counselors' intrapersonal dynamics are expressed inter-

the supervisor, whose nurturance needs are tapped, and the supervisor's overt response is one of helpgiving. This pattern would undermine supervision because the counselor would never be given the opportunity to gain competence and self-confidence.

Mueller and Kell (1972) have described several other dynamic patterns that frequently arise in their work. One pattern is for the client, particularly a female client, to present herself as fragile and easily hurt. When the counselor approaches the client's anxiety-laden material, she may cry, and the counselor then concludes that he/she has erred in following this direction. If the counselor thereupon becomes guilty and apologetic, the client may shortly attack the counselor for being ineffective. In this pattern, the client's behavior initially fends off the counselor, then administers punishment for not helping. For the dynamically naive counselor, such a turn of events would create an impasse in the counseling process.

Another common pattern is when an angry, hostile client attacks the counselor, who responds with a counter attack. This deadlock of reciprocal hostility probably would lead to termination of the counseling session unless the counselor could gain insight into his or her own dynamics and then begin to understand how the client elicited hostility.

"Parallel reenactment" is one of the most interesting dynamic patterns in therapeutic supervision. This pattern consists of the supervisee replaying, within the supervisory setting, significant dynamics of the helping relationship. The counselor will act toward the supervisor just as the helpee was perceived to have acted toward him/her. Frequent instances are (1) the helpee expresses dependence on the counselor and the counselor expresses dependence on the supervisor, (2) the helpee becomes angry with the counselor and the counselor becomes angry with the supervisor, and (3) the helpee dominates the counselor and the counselor tries to dominate the supervisor.

Why parallel reenactment occurs is open to debate. Perhaps the occurance is just happenstance, since the main dynamic dimensions of human relationships are few and universal, and possibilities exist that a certain percentage of instances would illustrate similar dimensions that could be interpreted as dynamic parallelism. A contrary hypothesis by Mueller and Kell (1972) is that the counselor actually experiences conflicts which are perceived as paralleling those of the helpee. This feeling or perception may be the motivation, not necessarily conscious, that is responsible for reenactment.

GOALS OF THERAPEUTIC SUPERVISION

Discussion of dynamic points and patterns in psychotherapeutic supervision identifies foci but does not define
what the supervisor should try to accomplish. What are the
goals of psychotherapeutic supervision?

Mueller and Kell (1972) have offered a two-part goal for
dynamically oriented supervisors, a goal that should be acceptable to most theoretical persuasions. Their supervisory
process goal is for the counselor to learn what is therapeutic,
and the product goal is for the counselor to behave in a manner
that has a therapeutic affect on the client or other party.
Relating this two-part goal to the dynamic triangle of Figure 1,
at least four sequential subgoals exist that the supervisor
attempts to accomplish: dynamic awareness, understanding dynamic contingencies, change in dynamics, and therapeutic utilization of dynamics.

Dynamic Awareness

Learning what is therapeutic begins with discovering
(becoming aware of) interpersonal and intrapersonal dynamics.
This first subgoal, which opens the counselor's eye to the
existence of dynamics, is low fidelity in nature and is
followed by learning that dynamics influence human relationships. Through such awareness the counselor learns that everyone has a covert world of thoughts, feelings, and attitudes
and that human interaction, by its nature, involves interpersonal pathways of communicatory behavior.

Awareness is basic to power--power to change or prevent
change during counseling (May, 1971, p. 99). Awareness is the
first step in gaining personal control of the dynamics in a
helping relationship and in using them therapeutically.

Understanding Dynamic Contingencies

After awareness of dynamics has been achieved, the next
step is understanding the operations of these dynamics within
helpgiving and supervision. Understanding comes about through
assessment of dynamics within two contingencies: (1) the
influence of intrapersonal dynamics on interpersonal behavior,
and (2) the influence of interpersonal behavior on intrapersonal dynamics. Using the counselor-client dyad from Figure 2.1
as an illustration, assessment would involve the following
questions:

   1. How does the counselor's intrapersonal behavior (#5)
      influence his/her interpersonal behavior (#1) toward
      the helpee?

2. How does the interpersonal behavior of the counselor
   (#1) influence the helpee's intrapersonal dynamics
   (#4)?

3. How do the helpee's intrapersonal dynamics (#4)
   influence his/her interpersonal behavior (#1) toward
   the counselor?

Answers to these questions would unravel the patterns of
interacting dynamics in the counselor-client relationship.
Similar questions and answers pertaining to the supervisor-
counselor dyad would provide a helpful diagnostic picture at
that level. Assessment and diagnostic unraveling of this kind
constitutes a large portion of the methodology of therapeutic
supervision. To the supervisor unacquainted with the therapeutic approach, too much emphasis may seem to be placed on the
goal of understanding dynamics, and too much time may seem to
be spent in examining the dynamics of the supervisory triangle
(Figure 2.1). However, the supervisor must comprehend the
theoretical rationale underlying the goal and methodology of
psychotherapeutic supervision if an appreciation of the approach
is to be attained and if skill in application of its principles
is to be acquired. Numerous writers, such as Cashdan (1973)
and Leary (1957), have offered a dynamics-oriented theory for
psychotherapy. Kell and Mueller (1966), Kell and Burow (1970),
and Mueller and Kell (1972) have provided a theoretical rationale for dynamically oriented supervision, with support from
Altucher (1967) and Moore (1969). Briefly, and with the
author's interpretation, their position is that interpersonal
and intrapersonal dynamics are subject to the general principles
of social learning theory. The dynamics which an individual
has developed through past learning experiences tend to be
reasserted in future situations, particularly when conditions
are perceived to be similar to those of the original learning
situations. Research by Heller, Myers, and Kline (1963),
Mueller (1969), Raush, Dittman, and Taylor (1959), and Raush
(1965) have supported this theoretical contention.

Thus, when a client demonstrates certain dynamics in the
helping relationship, the counselor can hypothesize that
these are indicative of at least a part of the individual's
dynamic make-up, established through time. The performance
tells the counselor how the client is likely to react dynamically in other relationships. For the client to hide dynamic
difficulties from a competent counselor is impossible, because
the dynamics played out in the counseling relationship relate
to the client's problems outside the counseling relationship.
Kell and Burow (1972, p. 15) suggested that "clients present
most of their problems in a compacted, cryptic form in the
first interview." If the counselor identifies the client's
problematic dynamics as they occur in helpgiving, this diagnos-

tic knowledge can guide the counselor in utilizing dynamics within the helping relationship.

Correspondingly, dynamic difficulties in the counselor's helping efforts can be found in the helpgiving and supervisory relationship. These difficulties will hinder supervision and the counselor's future helpgiving, if not resolved. In summary, focusing on intrapersonal and interpersonal dynamics is a way for the counselor to unlock others' problems, and in parallel fashion, the same approach can be applied to unlocking a counselor's difficulties in helping his/her relationships with others.

Change In Dynamics

Dynamic difficulties of the counselor, discovered with the aid of the supervisor, must be resolved if counselor performance is to improve. Such change is a goal shared by dynamically oriented counseling and supervision. In counseling, the dynamic change is necessary to improve the client's intrapersonal functioning (maladaptive emotion, perception, and ideation), as well as his/her interpersonal dynamics (social behavior). Changes in a counselor's dynamics as a consequence of supervision are ordinarily not as significant for the improvement of life functioning as are changes in the client as a result of counseling. This assumption is based on the fact that admittance to counselor preparation includes personal adjustment screening, so most counselor-trainees can be expected to be reasonably well adjusted people. However, problem aspects of a counselor's dynamic functions which may not be much of a difficulty in everyday life can, nonetheless, be significant hindrances to helpgiving. Latent conflicts may be activated during counseling, and others that are avoided in day-to-day living may be in the forefront of therapeutic activity. Such trouble spots in a counselor's pattern of dynamics are prime targets for change.

Therapeutic Utilization Of Dynamics

The culminating skill in psychotherapeutic supervision is therapeutic utilization of dynamics. Three kinds of dynamic utility are sought:

1. the counselor's experiencing/control of personal dynamics,

2. the counselor's planned influence on the dynamics of others, and

3. the counselor's management and utilization of dynamics in situations where no direct involvement exists.

The rationale for specifying control of personal dynamics as a factor affecting dynamic utility has been voiced by Mueller and Kell (1972, p. 5): "Learning what is therapeutic is an insufficient goal of supervision unless both parties recognize that a major part of what is therapeutic is the way in which the therapist uses himself." Counselors use themselves by "experiencing," described by Lister (1966) as a kind of intrapersonal communication which aids one to detect and modify within the immediate present subtle, moment-by moment nuances of feelings . . . . which disrupt communication with others.

When the counselor "experiences" in the manner described by Lister, he/she is controlling personal dynamics for the benefit of the other party, as well as therapeutically influencing the other's dynamics. The counselor's dynamics have a contingent relationship to the dynamics of others with whom the counselor relates, and therefore, through self-control, the counselor is simultaneously extending the influence of therapeutic control to these others.

The word "control" is not a popular one in the counseling profession. Counselors like to think of themselves as genuine people who do not exert ingenuine controls over their own honest feelings and thoughts, and, who, in the interest of preserving integrity, do not attempt to manipulate or control the behavior of others. Yet, by possessing the knowledge of how dynamics interact, the counselor has a responsibility to use this knowledge for the benefit of helpees. In this context of responsible helpfulness "dynamic control" is employed. Perhaps an illustration will clarify the point.

In the author's work as a practicum instructor he regularly observes that certain clients use sly deprecating statements to "put down" the practicum counselor. The client's passive-aggressive verbalizations normally awaken either anxiety or anger in the counselor. In the former case the counselor interpersonally reacts by trying to prove to the client that he/she is competent, and in the latter case (anger) the counselor reacts with counter aggression and "puts down" the client. Counselors who are relatively secure and have mastered the experiencing process react differently, however. They usually recognize their anxiety or anger, refuse to succumb to it, and react with an approved counseling technique--such as reflecting the client's emotion and facilitating self awareness. These "experiencing" counselors feel the same intrapersonal dynamics of anxiety or anger, but control them, and react in a therapeutically designed manner rather than in response to their own felt needs. Their dynamic "control" is certainly manipulative, in the influential sense, but the affect upon the client is therapeutic, and this is the crucial determinant in assigning value to terms such as "control" and "manipulation." Being able to overcome one's own needs in order to act in the interests of others is the height of personal and professional integrity in helpgiving. Moreover, as empirical support for the importance of therapeutic utilization continues to accumulate (Dietzel & Abeles, 1975), experiencing and personal control of dynamics become necessary components in the counselor's repertoire of competencies.

In contrast to the spontaneous experiencing technique is the counselor's influence on helpee dynamics in a planned and deliberate manner. Before encountering a helpee, the counselor can decide to behave interpersonally in such a way that helpee dynamics are affected therapeutically. To illustrate consider the case of an insecure colleague or client who continually solicits the counselor's help in negotiating avoidance of a responsibility. The counselor could assess this pattern and decide to deliberately control this person's dynamics therapeutically by encouraging and fostering responsible action.

Management and control of dynamics when the counselor is not directly involved with helpees is another application of dynamic utilization. This is accomplished as the counselor assesses dynamic evoking properties of non-counseling situations and constructively influences them for the dynamic benefit of others. Such influencing could occur in building the composition of a discussion group, consulting with a teacher who has problems with class morale, and helping to alter policies or activities of an institution.

Therapeutic utilization of dynamics is the final goal of psychotherapeutic supervision, reached through awareness, understanding, and usually some form of change in one's personal dynamics. Lister (1966) has suggested that experience and maturity are necessary for the development of dynamic utilization, but, even if this high-level skill does require a number of years to develop, it can be initiated through dynamic supervision. The dynamics-oriented supervisor facilitates birth of this skill in a counselor through the skill he or she applies during supervision. By expertly utilizing the dynamics of the supervisory relationship, the supervisor will help the counselor acquire skill in applying those dynamics in the helpgiving relationship.

METHODOLOGY

The author's experience as a counselor educator and practicing psychologist has taught him an important lesson about learning. Didactic knowledge of methodology acquired through the usual modes of reading, lecture, and discussion is, more often than not, insufficient preparation for application of that methodology. The transition from knowledge to performance is difficult and Jakubowski-Spector, Dustin, & George (1971) have cited the need for "transfer training" to facilitate it.

The methodology of psychotherapeutic supervision is quite susceptible to the barrier between knowledge and performance. Furthermore, practicing field-supervisors tend to regard the psychotherapeutic approach as being applicable only to psychotherapy in a clinic setting. In this Chapter the methodology of psychotherapeutic supervision is presented in a pragmatic and uncomplicated way, and it is related to real-life situations in supervision practice. Hopefully this presentation will encourage readers to accept the psychotherapeutic approach as a practical one.

Two basic methods exist for implementing the psychotherapeutic approach to supervision, with each comprised of numerous skills and techniques. The first method is a standardized procedure called <u>interpersonal process recall</u> (IPR), and the second is <u>unstructured and intensive therapeutic supervision</u>.

Interpersonal Process Recall (IPR)

The IPR procedure was developed initially through the work of Kagan and Krathwohl (1967) at Michigan State University. Research and further development of IPR has produced an impressive body of literature (Archer & Kagan, 1973; Dendy, 1971; Grzegorek, 1971; Kagan & Schauble, 1969; Kagan, Schauble, Resnikoff, Davish, & Krathwohl, 1969; Resnikoff, Kagan, & Schauble, 1970; Schauble, 1970; Spivack, 1970, 1972). In supervision, the IPR procedure exposes the counselor to a recorded playback of an interaction he or she had with a client. The playback can be an audio recording or video recording, although the latter is deemed more potent for eliciting intrapersonal affective material (Kagan & Krathwohl, 1967, Fuller & Manning, 1973). The playback exposure is augmented by assistance from a recall supervisor who utilizes inductive questioning to direct the counselor's attention to the intrapersonal and interpersonal dynamics of the interaction. The intent of the playback and the recall questions is to encourage counselors to identify and recall dynamics, thereby leading them to recognize some of their feelings and thoughts which interfered with effective communication in the recorded situation. The following questions are illustrative of those that a supervisor might use to lead a counselor into self-confrontation (Dendy, 1971):

1. What do you think he/she was trying to say?

2. What do you think he/she was feeling at this point?

3. Can you pick-up any clues from his/her nonverbal behavior?

4. What was running through your mind when he/she said that?

5. Can you recall some of the feelings you were having then?

6. Did anything prevent you from sharing some of your feelings and concerns about the person?

7. If you had another chance, would you like to have said something different?

8. What kind of risk would have occurred if you said what you really wanted to say?

9. As what kind of a person do you want him to see you?

10. What do you think his/her perceptions are of you?

Recall by the counselor can be supplemented with "client recall" and "Mutual recall" to form a full IPR treatment. In client (or helpee) recall the same exposure and line of questioning are employed, with the counselor observing the helpee as he/she participates in the recall session. The helpee benefits from the recall, and the counselor is offered the rare opportunity of entering into the helpee's experience in the original situation, as recalled. Recall observation helps the counselor to "become aware of and sensitive to subtle meanings underlying the /helpee's7 verbal and nonverbal behavior" (Kagan & Krathwohl, 1967, p. 93).

Mutual recall is held with the counselor and helpee following their respective individual recall sessions. In mutual recall both parties are encouraged to recall their covert experiences and to share them with one another as they observe or listen to the playback. Mutual recall illuminates the reciprocal interaction of dynamics, and the counselor becomes sensitive to the bilateral nature of human interactions.

Kagan and Krathwohl (1967, p. 96) summarized the objectives of full treatment IPR in counseling supervision as

assisting the trainee to see himself as he really is and how he looks to his counselees, to help him understand himself and to be aware of his own feelings throughout the counseling session, to enable the trainee to "check out" his personal perceptions of his client and to appropriately communicate these impressions to the client, and to open the trainee to the channels of communication both verbal and non-verbal, existing between himself and his client.

These objectives include two of the four goals that were stated previously for psychotherapeutic supervision: <u>dynamic awareness</u> and an <u>understanding of dynamic contingencies</u>. These two are prerequisites for the more advanced goals of <u>dynamic change</u> and <u>therapeutic utilization of dynamics</u>. The IPR procedures described here do not directly attend to these two advanced goals, seemingly for two reasons. An assumption in psychodynamic theory is that awareness and understanding often are sufficient for dynamic change, and guidance-to-awareness through IPR may give counselors insights sufficient to change and become more therapeutic. Another practical reason for limiting IPR's focus principally to awareness and understanding is that the procedure has been employed most frequently with beginning counselors. Video recall sessions contain some highly instructive material which is beyond the grasp of beginning counselors: the concerns of the helpees, the subtleties of their communication, the nature of the counselor's impact on them, and a host of valuable insights (Kagan & Krathwohl, 1967). Because the totality of this material is beyond the novice counselor, limiting the procedure to "attainable goals" makes sense. IPR is thus an appropriate method for initiating psychotherapeutic supervision, although it need not be restricted to use with student-counselors. Kagen and Krathwohl (1967) suggest that IPR can be used with more experienced counselors because counseling experience by itself does not guarantee that a counselor will have adequate insight into dynamics. IPR therefore is a particularly proper method for use with experienced counselors who have not been exposed to psychotherapeutic supervision.

Since the methodology of IPR requires that the supervisor have advanced skills, prospective recall-supervisors are recruited from among competent counselors who then undergo thorough training. IPR supervision training begins with the candidate learning the rationale, function and technique of recall. The supervisor-trainee then works with an experienced IPR supervisor in recorded counseling sessions to become sensitive to the specific cues which indicate that recall questions should be asked. Kagan and Krathwohl (1967, p. 15) suggested the following cues for productive IPR questions:

abrupt shifts in theme during the interview; shifts in body posture; changes in voice level, tone or pace; use of vocabulary which describes intense affect; changes in visual focus (especially glances at the counselor after the client has made a statement); instances in which either person clearly misinterpreted the other or appeared to not hear the other; possible use of metaphoric communication (e.g., "my counselor at school gets me angry"); inappropriate affect, such as a laugh following a serious comment."

These and similar cues may be indicative of heightened underlying emotionality and are potential insight points. Following training in identification of cues, taped and live IPR sessions are critiqued until the supervisor-trainee reaches a level of competence justifying the final learning experience of supervised practice.

IPR methodology has been presented as a somewhat standard procedure, but it can be altered innovatively. Gimmestad and Greenwood (1974) have employed multiple recallers (counselor trainees) in their IPR work and report that this procedure extends participation and learning to a greater number. IPR also can be applied in counseling and has been reported as effective in facilitating client progress (Kagan, Krathwohl, & Miller, 1963; Kagan & Shcauble, 1969, Kagan, Schauble, Resnikoff, Danish, & Krathwohl, 1969; Resnikoff, Kagan, & Schauble, 1970; Schauble, 1970). Dynamic insight is therapeutic for clients as well as counselor-trainees.

Still another innovative adaptation of IPR is "affect simulation." In this procedure a client is exposed to a film which encourages him/her to simulate interpersonal relations. Both the client and film are videotaped while the client views the film. Shortly after this taping, the client views the videotape of his/her reactions to the film, and a counselor trained in recall technique helps the client examine dynamics. The client's videotaped behavior becomes the focus for counseling, and the goals of dynamic supervision are criteria for success. Anticipated benefits are that the client will become more aware and understand personal dynamics, that troublesome dynamics will be changed, and that new dynamic behavior will be incorporated into the personality.

Psychotherapeutic Supervision: Unstructured Method

The unstructured implementation of psychotherapeutic supervision has been described by Altucher (1967), Arbuckle (1965, Ekstein and Wallerstein (1958), Hansen and Barker (1964), Kell and Mueller (1966), Lister (1966), Moore (1969), Mueller and Kell (1972), Patterson (1964), and Rogers (1957). The collective thinking of these authors is that the essence of counselor supervision is in the relationship and intensive interaction between supervisor and counselor as they examine

and explore together the intrapersonal and interpersonal
dynamics of the counselor's interactions with clients, consultees, colleagues, and the supervisor. The counselor brings
soemthing to the supervisor for discussion, such as an audio
or video tape of a counseling session, or a professional
problem or conflict with a colleague. If the counselor's
selected concern involves any kind of human interaction, a
potential exists for dynamic methodology to be helpful.

Unstructured Method Contrasted With IPR. An effective
way to describe the unstructured method of psychotherapeutic
supervision is to identify and contrast it with Interpersonal
Process Recall (IPR). IPR is most often used with beginning
counselors, or those who are receiving their introduction to
dynamic supervision. The unstructured approach also can be
employed with beginners at a low level of intensity, but its
full potential is reached with more experienced counselors.
In IPR the treatment is of relatively low threat, and the
relationship between the counselor and supervisor is task
oriented. The recall supervisor "leads" the counselor into
self confrontation, and resistance usually is not confronted.
Contrarily, since the unstructured approach capitalizes on the
supervisor-counselor relationship as a source of dynamics for
study and resolution, anxiety and discomfort in both parties
are more likely to be evidenced. Because of more dynamic
confrontation, resistance will probably come up and be dealt
with interpretively by the supervisor as a therapeutic
necessity.

The goals of IPR are essentially awareness and understanding of dynamics, and these are shared by unstructured
psychotherapeutic supervision; but, in addition, the unstructured approach places an emphasis on counselor and client
dynamic change at impasse points and a subsequent therapeutic
utilization of dynamics by the counselor. These two additional
goals necessitate supervisory skills which are similar but
beyond those based in IPR. Not only does the supervisor
expose the counselor to dynamics, but the supervisory process
becomes therapeutically intensive for the supervisee, since
there is examination and exploration in depth of the meaning
of dynamics, and the supervisor-counselor interaction becomes
a "working-through" emotional experience.

IPR is somewhat structured and procedural, although the
recall supervisor can be flexible in the asking of recall questions. On the other hand, unstructured psychotherapeutic supervision does not follow a set of standardized procedures
and the supervisor reacts "moment-by moment." A definite
strategy is behind the supervisor's actions, but the stimuli
offered by the counselor determine how the strategy will be
implemented.

Unstructured Therapeutic Supervision:
Relationship Conditions

The essence of unstructured psychotherapeutic supervision lies in the relationship between the supervisor and supervisee. Facilitative conditions such as empathy, genuineness, warmth, trust, and positive regard are of paramount importance. The supervisee will be examining personal dynamics and a supervisory relationship characterized by such facilitative conditions will be conducive to accomplishing this task. Pierce, Carkhuff, and Berenson (1967) and Pierce and Schauble (1970) have stressed that the counselor can grow and learn by experiencing these conditions in a therapeutic supervisory relationship.

Even though general support exists for establishing and maintaining facilitative conditions in unstructured therapeutic supervision, theoretical disagreement also exists regarding the emphasis to be placed on these conditions. Should the supervisor maintain a focus on the supervisee and concentrate mainly on providing a counseling-like interaction? Does a violation of facilitativeness occur when sometimes focusing on the dynamics of parties to whom the supervisee is relating, as a means of teaching the supervisee how to understand and relate to others?

The dynamic model of therapeutic supervision presented in this Chapter is in agreement with Lambert (1974). Lambert suggested that the supervisor need not keep a rigid and constant focus on the supervisee's dynamics, since to do so would ignore all other sources of dynamic learning. Whereas the overall level of facilitative conditions and the post-supervision self perception of the counselor are important process objectives, a flexible and personalistic supervisory style will facilitate learnings in addition to self development. In a word, psychotherapeutic supervision is more than merely the providing of facilitative conditions.

Unstructured Therapeutic Supervision
For Dynamic Awareness

The methodology for helping counselors achieve dynamic awareness via the unstructured approach is the same as for IPR. Supervisory technique consists simply of _focus_ and _response_, with the supervisor focusing on the dynamics of the interaction and making responses which lead the supervisee to give attention to these dynamics. For example, after talking over a counseling case or viewing a portion of it, the counselor might say something to the supervisor in reference to the client's responses, such as "He talked a lot about making this decision, and I wasn't sure if it was an immediate one or far in the future." Rather than follow the counselor's focus which might skirt dynamics, the supervisor would turn the focus to dynamics by asking, "Did you see any evidence of anxiety about making the decision? Can you remember how he acted when talking about it?" In this example the supervisor is helping the counselor become aware of external evidence of internal dynamics. One comment like this may not have an effect on the counselor, but repeated dynamic focusing upon strategic spots will shape the direction of the supervisory session.

The strategy behind the supervisor's technique of focus and responses is to lead the counselor without eleciting undue anxiety. Even though a certain degree of anxiety is inevitable, the first stage of unstructured psychotherapeutic supervision attempts to minimize it by beginning the focus on counselor-client interpersonal dynamics. From this beginning, a paradigm for focus and response which gradually would lead the counselor to anxiety confrontation would be the following: anxiety confrontation would be

1. interpersonal dynamics of the other party,

2. intrapersonal dynamics of the other party,

3. counselor interpersonal dynamics,

4. counselor intrapersonal dynamics, and

5. interpersonal and intrapersonal dynamics of supervision.

The supervisor depends on certain cues within these five paradigm categories that indicate where and when to focus and respond. Some of these cues were mentioned in the discussion of IPR, but many more exist. These cues are the most subtle of intrapersonal dynamics. They are not expressed intentionally, and although the counselor and helpee usually are unaware of them, they can have a dramatic effect on the behavior of both and the helping process. Lister (1966, p. 56) identified cues which show the supervisor that the counselor is experiencing discomfort, probably in reaction to the helpee or to something the helpee has said:

1. Missing an obvious "opening" for an interpretation or reflection.

2. Unusual difficulty in formulating a response to client statements; overelaborate and argumentative responses as if driving home a point.

3. Marked changes in voice tone and speech patterns.

4. Nervous motor behavior such as shifting posture, moving chair, and so forth.

In the following statement Mueller and Kell (1972, p. 52) identified cues that they interpreted as behavioral evidence of a therapeutic impasse, i.e., a state in which anxiety on the part of counselor, helpee, or both has brought helpgiving progress to a standstill:

> An abundance of seemingly irrelevant materials during sessions, an unsatisfying recycling process, repeated expressions of dissatisfaction with progress, ambivalence, gestures toward a premature termination, loss of goal directedness, confusion, and the diffuse expressions of anger and hostility are some indices of impasse. Such impasses have been stimulated by either the client or the therapist, although we are inclined to think that clients often have a major hand in their instigation.

> On the other hand, the therapist's apparent inability to bring his creative process to bear on client material, his failure to see connections, his acceptance of surface behaviors without sensitivity to underlying trends, and his seeming lack of awareness of the parallel reenactment of client problems during sessions with him often indicate that the therapist is immobilized and that it is his anxiety that is primarily responsible for the creation of impasses.

The therapeutic technique of focus and response, following a paradigm of gradual anxiety confrontation, is ordinarily an effective way of helping supervisees to discover dynamics. But with the unusually defensive supervisee, an "anxiety avoider" in Mueller and Kell's (1972) typology, or the affectively blunted individual, the goal of dynamic awareness is very difficult to achieve. These supervisees will require more than average experiential treatment, and affective simulation is an excellent beginning. Through this procedure the supervisor can control dynamically evocative stimuli and be relatively sure of the consequent dynamics experienced by the supervisee. This type of control enables the supervisor to be particularly persistent, intensive, yet non-confrontive with recall questions.

A counselor's failure to achieve dynamic awareness through a prolonged period of psychotherapeutic supervision is a fairly reliable predictor of ineffective performance on the job. While dynamic awareness does not ensure effective counselor performance, lack of it is a serious limitation. Therefore, if dynamic awareness is a stumbling block for the counselor, his/her suitability for the helping professions should be examined.

Unstructured Psychotherapeutic Supervision
For Understanding Dynamic Contingencies

The techniques selected for helping a counselor understand dynamic contingencies and see the dynamic patterns created thereby should be matched to the counselor's characteristics. Some techniques that are effective with one counselor may be useless with another. For counselors who genuinely are eager for supervision and can tolerate anxiety arising from dynamic exposure, inductive techniques which lead to understanding of dynamic contingencies and patterns are preferable.

A few random inductive techniques (reflection, restatement, clarification) may be sufficient to help the counselor see broad patterns, but the supervisor can go a step further by focusing discretely on the dynamics of a single pattern through a paradigm which parallels the sequence of the actual dynamic contingencies. For example, the supervisor could follow this line of leads:

1. How did you feel when the other person did that?

2. What's the next thing you did after you felt this way?

3. How do you think this affected the other person; what did he/she feel like; what went through his/her mind? How did he/she react?

4. Did the person act this way at any other point of the interaction? What was going on then, what were you doing?

This complete sequence of leads would not be necessary with a responsive supervisee, but it shows the path to understanding a dynamic pattern. Another inductive technique that Moore (1969) has reported is to present to the counselor an example of a dynamic pattern that is analogous to one with which the counselor is dealing. The supervisor explains the example and puts particular focus on those dynamic aspects which are analogous to those of the counselor's situation. As the counselor thinks about the example, without anxiety, its analogous properties should gradually become apparent and a more objective analysis of the counselor's dynamic pattern should result.

When inductive and analogy techniques do not produce an understanding of dynamic contingencies and patterns, and the supervisee defensively resists learning, an alternative route is required. Two strategies are recommended, the first being a set of techniques which are loaded with modeling. Sometimes these are less threatening and more penetrating than inducement and analogy. Examples are

1. reading case studies of dynamic patterns,

2. watching films of counselors who are constructively dealing with their anxiety,

3. group supervision whereby the target supervisee observes others disclosing and assessing the dynamic patterns in their helping relationships, and

4. the modeling influence of the supervisor as he/she discloses past dynamic resolutions and expresses the significance of dynamics in the present relationship with the supervisee.

Permeating all four techniques is the supervisor's implied message that dynamics and anxiety are factors to be uncovered, approached, and resolved if they are problematic, and that the supervisor will assist in this process.

A second strategy to be attempted after these other techniques have failed is to be interpretative and confrontive. Interpretation is an explanation to the supervisee of dynamic patterns in his/her helping or supervisory relationship. This is done objectively, without blame, and the first attempts may be tentative, i.e., exposing or sharing an interpretative perception. Tentative interpretations are less threatening than the firm, assured ones that can come later.

Confrontation is a presentation to the supervisee of discrepancies in his/her behavior. For example, if the supervisee disclaims having anger toward a helpee but occasionally shows this anger through a raised voice or clenched fist, the supervisor would raise this discrepancy for examination.

Unstructured Psychotherapeutic Supervision
For Counselor Dynamic Change

Supervision techniques for dynamic awareness and understanding of contingencies leads to many changes in the counselor's intrapersonal and interpersonal dynamics. This type of easily attained dynamic change is often taken for granted and is attributed to the "natural" experience of learning how to counsel. To illustrate, if the supervisor helps a beginning counselor to understand the possible relationship between his/her frowns and the helpee's feeling of disapproval, very likely the counselor will demonstrate more smiles in the next interview. Similarly, ideational changes, such as lowering exaggerated expectancies for success or eliminating anticipations of disastrous failure, also can take place merely through experience and dynamic awareness.

Those dynamic changes which occur within the counselor as a result of awareness and understanding of dynamic contingencies are of low threat to the counselor. Secure counselors, who rarely experience high degrees of threat and tend to approach and deal with anxiety-evoking situations, can make the greatest use of IPR and unstructured supervision techniques. For them, this methodology is sufficient to induce dynamic change. Whenever secure counselors are exposed to evidence of intrapersonal and interpersonal dynamics, they perform a quick reality check to verify the evidence, and, if reality verifies the evidence, they accept it and begin to change self perceptions. On the other hand, when counselors who are high in anxiety are exposed to dynamic information which is contrary to self perceptions and threatening to self esteem, this exposure evokes defenses which will block acceptance of, or identification with, the information. The high-threat counselor may superficially and intellectually exhibit awareness and understanding but will not acquire the true insight which is mandatory for dynamic change.

"Dynamic insight" is an incorporation into the self of information which previously was not known and which is probably somewhat contradictory to one's perceptions of self, others, and the world. Insight in the low-threat counselor often occurs concurrently with dynamic awareness and understanding, but fails to occur under the same conditions in the high-threat counselor. Secure counselors gain insight easily; high-threat counselors rarely do.

The experience of gaining dynamic insight can take a variety of forms, the classic one being a sudden and emotionally exhilarating acceptance of a piece of information about oneself which causes a new conceptualization to come into being. This experience may be described as "having a lightbulb turned on in a darkened room."

Insight experiences may be painful since confrontation with a feared piece of knowledge can raise one's anxiety to a very unpleasant level. Defenses are stretched to the limit, but the turning point comes when the feared dynamic information is no longer distorted or avoided. The individual then is emersed in anxiety for a brief period, only to find that the feeling quickly subsides and the dreaded information is perceived to be not so awful after all. As a result, the individual tends to feel weak and drained emotionally, but more free and whole than before.

A supervisee working with the author years ago during her graduate studies had just such an insightful experience in relation to her inability to deal with clients who were emotionally distressed. Particular difficulty occurred in situations involving clients coping with the death of loved ones. One day, after becoming upset during observation of a client who was expressing distress over the death of two family members, the counselor-supervisee again spoke of how terrible it was for people to have to face such trauma. The supervisor responded with an interpretative and confrontative lead which finally broke through the supervisee's defenses: "Whom have you lost--that it (the loss) causes you so much pain?" With that, the supervisee broke down in tears and several therapeutic sessions followed centering on unresolved grief and guilt over her father's death. Insight into her intrapersonal dynamics, and their expression and resolution, enabled her to deal more empathically, rather than sympathically, with the clients' personal problems. Since that first dynamic conflict regarding death of a loved one, the author has encountered several others and has come to realize that such a loss is one of the most traumatic events in a person's life. The successful resolution of these losses is a difficult developmental task which faces each human being.

Abrupt insights, such as the one offered in the previous paragraph make interesting reading, but insight more often occurs in undramatic ways. Insight can occur slowly as small pieces of information are gathered and integrated to form a particular understanding about one's dynamics. Supervisee resistance may accompany "slow insight," and a begrudging acceptance is not uncommon. "Post-hoc insight" may even take place following supervision, when defenses are lowered and the supervisee rethinks the supervisory experience.

To encourage acquisition of dynamic insight through unstructured psychotherapeutic supervision, the supervisor "intervenes"--focusing, exploring, and expanding supervisee dynamics through techniques such as interpretation and confrontation. When using interpretation and confrontation for insight, the objective is to help the counselor assume true ownership and responsibility for dynamics. Awareness without insight is shown when the counselor can intellectually describe problematic dynamics, but continues to experience them in help-giving situations. This situation is quite common and is an indication to the supervisor that methodology must become interventionist in nature, and thereby move the counselor toward insight.

The following excerpt, taken from an authentic supervision session, illustrates the schism that can lie between awareness and insight. The case involves a school counselor who exhibited a biased attitude toward college-bound counselees and prejudice toward vocationally-oriented students. The counselor exhibited these attitudes by

1. spending most of his time with college-bound students,

2. refusing to offer more than token guidance services to vocationally-oriented students, and

3. offending vocationally-oriented students with remarks of a condescending and prejudicial nature.

Supervisor: Tom, we've talked before about your preference to work with college-bound students, and that you seem to act less interested, even irritated sometimes, with job-oriented students. . .

Counselor: (Cutting in.) Yea, I know. . .it's one of those things you have to do. . .work with the other half. . .I realize that.

Supervisor: Do you mean that you've been trying to do more work with vocational students?

Counselor: Uh, yeah, sure. I know it has to be done.

Supervisor: Has to be?

Counselor: (Silence and a confused facial expression.)

Supervisor: Tom, you obviously don't like to work with vocationally-oriented students, and it's a chore to force yourself to do it. Am I right?

Counselor: (Silence, but an affirmative facial expression.)

Supervisor: I guess we agreed upon this point the last time we talked, but, just agreeing or intellectually realizing your preference hasn't changed it. . . and the attitude continues to affect your behavior toward vocational students.

Counselor: Well, I'm just tired of trying to relate to some of these. . .students who just don't give a damn about their future, the school. . .or anything. Why should I be expected to work with students who don't care?

In this supervisory interaction the supervisee is superficially aware of his prejudicial attitude, but does not have dynamic insight. Insight in this instance would probably be based on many of the following realizations:

1. I do have a prejudicial attitude toward vocational students. I don't like them or respect them as much as college-bound students.

2. I don't like vocational students because they don't like me as well as do college-bound students. Also, college-bound students come from my socio-economic class, their parents are my friends--the kind of people who appreciate my work.

3. My dislike for vocational students puts me on edge in their presence, and I do treat them curtly, without much warmth. It is my perception of them that precipitates my irritable emotions and behavior. I am responsible for my reactions.

4. Sometimes I exaggerate the aversiveness of vocational students. I "awfulize" about them. I also demand that they be just the kind of people I think they should be. I get carried away sometimes.

5. Regardless of whether vocational students like me or the school, they do have a right to an education, and it is my job to provide guidance services to them.

6. In spite of the resistance which I sometimes receive from vocational students, they have a need for guidance services, in many cases it is a more desperate need than college-bound students.

The supervisory techniques for promoting the counselor's acquisition of these insights include those for facilitating dynamic awareness. However, when insight has not been gained through facilitative techniques the supervisory interaction must become more "interventionist" by using the techniques of interpretation and confrontation. An interventionist interaction is offered in the following excerpt to show how such techniques could be employed by the supervisor. Note is to be made that these same techniques can be used in many different ways, depending upon the supervisor's theoretical orientation.

Counselor: Well, I'm just tired of trying to relate to some of these. . .students who just don't give a damn about their future, the school. . .or anything. Why should I be expected to work with students who don't care?

Supervisor: Tom, I'm not going to tell you what you should do, that is your decision and only you are responsible for your attitudes and behavior. But I do know this, if you continue to be at odds with the vocational students, it will be necessary for the administration to remove you from this position; and I think you can see why if you think about it,

you are getting along and providing guidance
services only to a portion of the students.

Counselor: (Silence.)

Supervisor: The real tragedy in this situation is that your
prejudice toward vocational students is not necessary and doesn't make sense!

Counselor: (Silence.)

Supervisor: (Waiting for a response from the counselor.
When it does not come:) You're just a victim of
faulty thinking and circumstances.

Counselor: What do you mean?

Supervisor: Well, I've heard you say that the vocational
students don't like you, and I know that student
approval is important. In fact, I think you are
downright angry because they don't like you.

Counselor: So what!

Supervisor: So when you come into contact with vocational
students you already have a reserve of anger
ready to dump onto them. You feel rejected and
lash back.

Counselor: Are you telling me that I don't have a right to
my feelings?!

Supervisor: No, Tom, you have a right, and I certainly understand what it's like to feel that way, but I just
think that you create this anger by demanding
that vocational students be the kind of people
you think they should be. And when they don't
live up to your demands, and on top of that when
they don't like you, then you blame them and
dump anger onto them. Do you see what I'm
getting at?

Counselor: (Nod.)

This initial supervisory intervention is just the beginning of insight for the counselor. The supervisor directively
broke through the counselor's defenses with confrontations and
interpretations of the covert attitudes and thoughts which
precipitate the counselor's anger. All the while the supervisor kept the counselor in a responsible role, never allowing
him to rationalize his unprofessional actions, yet understanding
and not condemning him for human fallacy.

The dynamic insights gained by the supervisees through such intervention is therapeutic in its effects, and its benefits generalize to the supervisees' lives outside of counseling and supervision. In the previous excerpts regarding prejudice toward vocational students, effective supervision could influence the counselor to be more accepting and tolerant of people in his private life. However, one must remember that counselor supervision is not counseling, and a distinction between the two should be maintained. Mueller and Kell (1972, p. 77) have emphasized this distinction:

> When the therapist begins to express how he felt at times of impasse, the supervisor and therapist could be inadvertently diverted into extensive excursions into the emotional life of the therapist, studying the historical development of those feelings, and their current meaning. However, we feel that the beneficial effects of such a therapeutic venture can still be experienced by the therapist and will have more meaning to him if they are directed back to his relationship with his client. Essentially, the supervisory process begins at the point of conflict that has arisen out of the therapist's relationship with the client (or other) and it should terminate in the restoration of that relationship without unnecessary derailment.

Dynamic theory posits that an individual who has gained insight can change covert and overt behavior. This is a point of conjecture though, and perhaps a more representative prevailing attitude of counselor supervisors would be to say that insight enables "some" individuals to change dynamics. Even when insight successfully promotes intrapersonal dynamic change, one is not assured that interpersonal behavior change will follow. The supervisee may still be deficient in counseling competencies and may need skill development to fill these deficits. Chapter 3 addresses this task.

Unstructured Psychotherapeutic Supervision For The Therapeutic Utilization Of Dynamics

Thus far three goals of dynamic supervision have been discussed in terms of methodology to be employed. Assuming achievement of these goals, the counselor has become aware of dynamics, understands at least some of the dynamic contingencies and patterns operative in his/her helpgiving and supervisory interactions, and has made changes in counterproductive dynamics. Now the counselor is beginning to function at a fairly sophisticated level in a dynamic sense, but the last goal of therapeutic supervision is yet to be achieved. This final goal, the therapeutic utilization of dynamics, is the counselor's skill of using and maintaining the three previously learned dynamic processes (awareness, diagnostic understanding, and change) in all forms of helping interactions.

Although the counselor's more troublesome dynamics and patterns may be resolved through psychotherapeutic supervision, a need for diligence always will exist, lest he/she become complacent. As long as the counselor engages in helping interactions, dynamics will arise to inhibit the process. The counselor may encounter aggressive persons who elicit defensiveness, sexually solicitous people who evoke attractions, dependent individuals who seek someone to carry their problems, and so on. In such cases the counselor must not react intrapersonally or interpersonally in an irresponsible manner, for such undisciplined reactions sustain problematic dynamics and are not therapeutic. The counselor must be aware of the natural tendency to be anxious, to be attracted, or to jump to the rescue; but, rather than yield to such inclinations, he/she must assess how best to act, and then act appropriately to utilize dynamics therapeutically.

Supervisors help their supervisees learn to skillfully use dynamics by employing such skills themselves within supervision, and by teaching supervisees to use the skills in counseling. During supervision the supervisor should continually disclose his/her own dynamics, encourage the counselor to do likewise, and, in general, approach the dynamics of supervision in an exploratory and problem-solving manner. A model of dynamic control is provided by the supervisor, and the counselor is encouraged to manage dynamics rather than avoid them or succumb to them unprofessionally. Kell and Mueller (1966, p. 99) suggest that the supervisor has qualities which cause others to believe that he/she can control dynamics but is willing to support others as they engage in exploration, experimentation, and learning to control their dynamics.

The counselor also is assisted during supervision to plan dynamic strategies for use in counseling and other direct interactions. With the supervisor's help, the counselor decides how to interact with the other party in a way that will be most helpful to that person. An illustrative counseling case in the author's professional background comes to mind when speaking of planned dynamic strategies. The case involved a female counselee in the eleventh grade who sought the author's attention following initial contact during routine course scheduling procedures. The student, without apparent justifications, expressed feelings of inferiority and self condemnation, and she publicly displayed anxiety attacks in the classroom and other social situations. Exploration of her problems revealed a suppressed positive self esteem which was not disclosed for fear of disapproval. Observation of her interpersonal style revealed a solicitation of peer and teacher

sympathy through the masquerade of being filled with insecurity. This masquerade behavior had succeeded in eliciting
sympathy from peers, teachers, parents, and the author!

The dynamic strategy employed in this case was for the
counselor to control sympathetic inclinations, and to socially
reinforce only the student's demonstrations of positive self-
reference and constructive, independent action. Furthermore,
after establishing rapport, the author-counselor confronted
and interpreted, in the counseling situation, the student's
interpersonal style, i.e., "act insecure and weak so that
others will approve of me."

The strategy of dynamic utilization was a success, as
indicated by cessation of anxiety attacks, and gradual increase
in expressions of self confidence and esteem. Through interaction with the author (school counselor), and later in the
larger school environment, the student learned that a positive
self-concept is more self-fulfilling and socially reinforced
than a "weeping willow act."

Planning strategies for management of dynamics in situations where the counselor is only indirectly involved is yet
another method characteristic of advanced stages of therapeutic
supervision. The supervisor helps the counselor diagnose
dynamics in these situations, and then assists in constructing
and implementing strategies to improve dynamic interaction.

A recent example of dynamic management from the author's
experience illustrates the kind of counselor activity that
the supervisor can help to plan. A group of teachers were
distressed at the difficulty they were having with "disrespectful" students. In the role of mental health consultant, the
author met with the group and utilized some of the procedures
which already have been described in this Chapter. Dynamics
that normally occur in an interaction between a disrespectful
student and a teacher were diagnosed and questions of an IPR
nature were addressed so the teachers would become aware of
their dynamic patterns.

1. What thoughts and feelings precipitate disrespectful
   behavior from a student?

2. What exactly are the disrespectful behaviors, what
   message are they intended to communicate?

3. What message is received by the teacher from the
   student's disrespectful behavior?

4. What are the teacher's intrapersonal dynamics in
   response to disrespect?

65

5. How does the teacher act (interpersonally) toward the student when experiencing such thoughts and feelings?

6. How does the teacher's action affect the student?

After dynamic patterns and their significance had been explored, strategies for interacting with disrespectful students were developed--strategies designed to be dynamically appropriate treatments. This approach to the management of dynamics through teacher consultation involved diagnosis, awareness and understanding, and reconstruction of dynamic patterns.

Summary

The methodology of psychotherapeutic supervision consists of numerous techniques which can be categorized into two basic methodological categories: IPR and the unstructured method. In supervisory practice the techniques from these two categories can be employed compatibly and integratively to achieve the goals of psychotherapeutic supervision. Figure 2.2 is an integrated listing of psychotherapeutic supervisory techniques as they relate to supervision goals and supervisee effect. The chart may be helpful to trainees and practitioners of the psychotherapeutic approach as they attempt to choose the "right" technique for their particular situation. Choice of methodology will require that the supervisor be aware of his/her goals, the intended effect on the supervisee, and the unique characteristics of the supervisee that may influence his/her receptivity to supervisory techniques.

PSYCHOTHERAPEUTIC SUPERVISION: EMPIRICAL SUPPORT

Research in counseling and psychotherapy has been plagued with methodological problems (Whiteley, 1967). Major difficulties hamper planning and employment of an experimental design that controls all intervening variables within the settings and situations of counseling. Another common problem is the difficulty in establishing a criterion which is a valid index of the dependent variable--accessibility and measurability often dictate selection of criteria. Specification, control, and measurement of independent variables--i.e. the treatment process--constitute yet another complicated set of problems (Burck, Cottingham & Reardon, 1973).

However difficult these problems seem to be for researchers in the field of counseling, they are even more troublesome for those attempting supervision research. Since supervisory treat-

Supervision Goal	Therapeutic Technique	Supervisee Effect
Dynamic Awareness	IPR proper and adaptations of IPR	Discovery and consequent awareness of one's interpersonal and intrapersonal dyanmics
	Focus and response; gradual anxiety confrontation	
	Affect simulation	
Understanding Dynamic Contingencies and Patterns	IPR proper and adaptations of IPR	A general understanding that intrapersonal dynamics precipitate interpersonal dynamics, and a personal understanding of how this contingency operates in one's own helpgiving situations
	Inductive techniques	Inductively achieved realization of dynamic patterns
	Analogy technique	Understanding one's own dynamic pattern by comparing it to an analogous pattern
	Techniques for defensive supervisors	
	Read case studies Films Group supervision Supervisor modeling	Understanding via modeling and identification with supervisor and peers
	Interpretation Confrontation	Forced exposure to threatening dynamic patterns
Dynamic Change	Facilitative techniques for dynamic insight	Self discovery of insight; low threat experience
	Interpretation and confrontation for dynamic insight	Supervisor induced insight; low threat experience
Therapeutic Utilization of Dynamics	Supervisor employing and modeling the skill of dynamic utilization within supervision	Imitative and experiential learning
	Monitoring of the counselor's dynamics during helpgiving and assistance/guidance in using dynamic-based skills	Supportive guidance and facilitation as the counselor utilizes him/herself as a therapeutic tool

Figure 2.2. Psychotherapeutic Supervision Methodology.

ment is, as yet, poorly understood, descriptive investigations and quasi-experimental studies have constituted the bulk of the research effort in this area. After a decade or so of asking, "What are we doing?", there is reason for optimism in the recent increase of experimental studies aimed at assessing the effectiveness of supervision.

A continuing problem in supervision research however is the limited number of valid dependent variables to be investigated. The independent variables of counseling, already described as difficult to specify, measure, and validate, are the dependent variables in supervision research. Thus, if one does not know that a particular counseling skill produces positive effects in clients, it is foolish to use it as a dependent variable in research on supervision. So few counseling skills have received strong empirical support that the list of dependent variables for research on supervision is quite limited.

Research in psychotherapeutic supervision is particularly susceptible to the problems mentioned, but, rather than dwell on the difficulties, a more proactive approach is to identify what has been learned. Although the limitations of past research must be recognized, one can draw some conclusions, speculate about areas where evidence is inconclusive, and plan for more and better research to broaden knowledge about counselor supervision.

In the following pages, a brief summary of research findings bearing on three aspects of psychotherapeutic supervision will be presented: counselor expectancies of supervision, effectiveness of Interpersonal Process Recall, and effectiveness of experiential supervision.

Expectations Of Supervisees

The counselor's expectations of supervision is an intrapersonable variable which fits into the psychotherapeutic approach. Knowing these expectancies will help the supervisor predict the counselor's reaction to supervision, and will enable the supervisor to make a presentation that is likely to be received favorably.

Very few investigations have dealt with the topic of expectancies for supervision, but three studies have provided descriptive information. Delaney and Moore (1966) used the Supervisor Role Analysis Form to assess the supervision expectancies of 123 pre-practicum students. A component analysis of the data yielded fifteen factors, nine of which could be related to the instructional nature of the interaction. The investigators concluded from their findings that the supervisee sample viewed the supervisor's role as dealing largely with teaching.

68

Hansen's (1965) investigation of the supervision expectancies of thirty NDEA trainees, using the Barrett-Lennard Relationship Inventory, revealed results compatible with those of Delaney and Moore. Their sample of trainees did not have high expectations for a facilitative relationship in supervision, and reported having received a more facilitative experience than had been expected.

Gysbers and Johnston (1965) administered the Supervisor Role Analysis Form to fifty-one counselor-trainees before, during, and after a practicum supervisory experience. Results showed that these counselor-trainees expressed a desire for instruction in techniques at the beginning of the practicum, but were less dependent and more autonomous toward the supervisor at the end of the experience.

Information gathered from these three inquiries must be viewed cautiously, but it tends to be consistent with the theoretical notion of Hogan (1964). He has suggested that there are four identifiable levels represented in the development of psychotherapists (counselors), and the first level fits the descriptive data on practicum counselors from the previously cited studies: the beginner is dependent, insecure, uninsightful of self and impact on others, anxious, but also motivated. The accumulated academic experience of such trainees, probably including one year of graduate-level academic study in counselor education, may incline them to expect direct instruction from, and a somewhat distant relationship with, a supervisor. Likewise, considering the supervisee's professional immaturity and lack of experience, the dependency revealed by Gysbers and Johnson (1965) is not unexpected.

If we assume that these cautious conclusions have some validity, the next question is "How will a nervous, instructionally-hungry supervisee react to dynamic supervision?" Not much research evidence to answer this question is available. An inquiry by Miller and Oetting (1966) reported responses to two open-ended questions asked of a small group of supervisees. The investigators reported that the counselors (supervisees) disliked a therapy-like supervisory approach, but they did want the supervisor to be sensitive to their feelings and ideas. An early study by Hansen (1965) supported the latter finding. This modest body of evidence suggests that even though the psychotherapeutic approach may not provide as much didactic instruction as the supervisee is accustomed to receiving, the facilitative relationship is valued.

The next logical question is whether therapeutic supervision is effective if supervisee expectancies and desires are contrary. Birk (1972) investigaed this question by permitting subjects to register preference for a supervisory approach

69

(didactic or experiential) and then treating this factor as an independent variable in her experimental design. In terms of the dependent measure of empathic response to supervisees, subjects who received their preferred type of supervision did not achieve significantly better performance than did subjects who received the non-preferred type of supervision. Findings in this one study support the probability that preference for a supervisory approach does not significantly influence results of supervision--particularly if supervision effects were perceived as positive by the supervisee.

While preference has not been shown to be a significant expectancy variable, perceived supervisor competence may be another one with potential implic ations. Hester, Weitz, Anchor, and Roback (1976) found supervisor skillfulness to be a main contributor to supervisee attraction to a supervisor, more influential than supervisor-supervisee attitude similarity.

These findings are similar to those of Beutler, Johnson, Neville, Elkins, and Jobe (1975) who concluded that a therapist's credibility is more important, when predicting outcomes of psychotherapy, than is attitude similarity between therapist and client. Perhaps future research in supervision will produce findings showing that perceived helper credibility is a most important variable in helpee expectancy for outcome.

Effectiveness Of Psychotherapeutic Supervision

The most crucial question to be answered about psychotherapeutic supervision concerns its effectiveness. Until recently, only the subjective evaluations of practitioners could be cited to support claims for effectiveness. Psychotherapeutic supervision seemed to work in practice. Recently, research on psychotherapeutic supervision has increased, and two directional trends are apparent. One is the investigation of Interpersonal Process Recall (IPR) and the other is the study of experiential supervision.

IPR effectiveness. Development and validation of IPR began with an initial research project by Kagan and Krathwohl (1967). Through an experimental design, the investigators compared a group of supervisees receiving an IPR program to a similar group receiving a more traditionally dyadic form of dynamic supervision. Criterion gain-scores on the Counselor Verbal Response Scale showed that IPR produced significantly greater gains, but that both the IPR and traditional supervision groups made significant improvement.

Numerous IPR studies have appeared since the procedure was developed. Experimental studies by Dendy (1971), Grzegorek

(1971), and Archer and Kagan (1973) illustrated IPR's efficacy in terms of criterion gains on the <u>Counselor Verbal Response Scale</u>, <u>Empathic Understanding Scale</u>, <u>Affective Sensitivity Scale</u>, <u>Personal Orientation Inventory</u>, <u>Barrett-Lennard Relationship Inventory</u>, and the <u>Wisconsin Relationship Orientation Inventory</u>. In some studies the IPR treatment was not superior to other supervisory treatments, but measurable gains were a consistent finding (Ward, Kagan, & Krathwohl, 1972). IPR has been used effectively with clients in counseling to promote growth in the direction of therapeutic goals (Kagan, Krathwohl, & Miller, 1973; Resnikoff, Kagan, & Schauble, 1970; Schauble, 1970), although a recent investigation by Van Noord and Kagan (1976) did not find stimulated recall and affect simulation to be more effective than traditional therapy.

Substantive research supports IPR as a viable supervisory procedure to improve relationship and facilitative skills of counselors. Archer and Kagan (1973) demonstrated the efficiency of IPR as they extended supervision to paraprofessionals, when preparing them to be competent IPR trainers. Although further research into the instrumental factors and long range effects of IPR remains to be done (Kingdon, 1975; Van Noord & Kagan, 1976), the IPR procedure seems to be an innovative and valuable contribution to counselor supervision.

<u>Effectiveness of Experiential Supervision</u>. As described in this Chapter, psychotherapeutic supervision is a helping process focusing on the intrapersonal and interpersonal dynamics in the counselor's relationships. The "therapeutic quality" of the process comes from insight into dynamics and from the experienced relationship with the supervisor. In respect to this latter component, a special type of psychotherapeutic supervision has arisen which places optimum importance on the supervisory relationship. <u>Experiential supervision</u> does not attempt to teach the supervisee about dynamics; instead, the experiential supervisor offers a therapeutic relationship which facilitates self growth and learning. Instrumental in the supervisory relationship is the quality of facilitative conditions (empathy, genuineness, regard, concreteness) offered by the supervisor. (See Chapter 11 for a more complete explanation of how these conditions operate in counselor supervision.)

Payne, Winter, and Bell (1972) assessed and compared the effectiveness of technique-oriented supervision, experiential supervision, and a placebo treatment in terms of the amount of skill acquired in offering empathic statements. Their results were not supportive of experiential supervision, since only the technique-oriented supervisory approach produced a significant improvement in counselors' levels of empathy. Similar results obtained by Payne and Gralinski (1968) showed that counselors receiving technique-oriented supervision and a control treatment were higher in the learning of empathy than those receiving counseling-oriented supervision. Payne, Weiss and Kappa (1972) and Birk (1972) also found didactic supervision to be superior to experiential supervision for achieving the criterion of counselor-learned empathic behavior. Ronnestad (1977) compared the three supervisory techniques of modeling, feedback, and experiential intervention in teaching counseling students to communicate empathic understanding. Post treatment ratings of counselors' empathic responding showed that the modeling method was more effective than the feedback method and the feedback method was more effective than the experiential method.

In contrast to the previously cited lack of supportive findings for the experiential approach to supervision, an experimental study by Pierce and Schauble (1970, p. 186) produced the following results:

1. Supervisees who received supervision from supervisors who themselves were functioning at high levels on the facilitative core dimensions. . .grew significantly on these dimensions;

2. Supervisees who had supervisors functioning at low levels on these dimensions did not gain; and

3. Supervisees of the high-level supervisors were functioning significantly better on the core dimensions than the supervisees of the low-level supervisors at the end of the supervision period.

A follow-up study nine months later showed that supervisees of the high-level supervisors continued to function more effectively on the core dimensions than did supervisees of the low-level supervisors, and that neither group of supervisees had changed significantly in respect to the core dimensions (Pierce & Schauble, 1971).

One is tempted to conclude from the findings of Pierce and Schauble that the supervisees of high-level supervisors actually "grew" in terms of the core dimensions as a direct consequence of the facilitative conditions received in experiential supervision, but Lambert (1974, p. 55) has aptly noted that the investigators

did not measure the level of facilitative conditions offered trainees, but assumed that it was equal to that offered clients in a counseling relationship. In fact, they gave no evidence supporting their assumption that supervisors offer identical levels of facilitative conditions in counseling and supervision.

Pierce and Schauble's (1970, 1971a) investigations do support the supervision of highly facilitative (in counseling) supervisors, but the efficacy of instrumental conditions within the supervisory treatment was not addressed.

Lambert (1974) went on to investigate the extent to which the same facilitative qualities which appear in counseling also appear in the supervisory process. Through a factorial analysis of the counseling and supervision of five experienced and facilitative (in counseling) counselors, he found that no significant differences between levels of genuineness and respect in counseling and supervision existed, but empathy and specificity were significantly higher in counseling than in supervision. On the <u>Hill Interaction Matrix</u> a significantly greater proportion of therapeutic-work statements in counseling than in supervision was reported. Lambert interpreted his findings as an indication that the assumption cannot be made that therapists function at the same levels in both supervision and counseling. The supervisory processes he studied, which were unspecified in terms of the intended approach, were more didactic than were those employed by the same subjects during counseling.

Payne and Gralinski (1968) also have investigated the effect of experiencing facilitative conditions within supervision. In their experimental design, level of empathy, as operative within experiential supervision, technique-oriented supervision, and a control treatment, did not significantly influence supervisees' post-supervision performance of empathic counseling behavior. Wedeking and Scott (1976) also found supervisee empathy in counseling to be unaffected by the supervisor's empathy in supervision.

Very little research supports a claim for the effectiveness of experiential supervision, or for the hypothesis that experiencing facilitative conditions within supervision will enable the supervisee to offer these same therapeutic ingredients to others. Precisely, empirical findings suggest that the singular treatment of experiential supervision is ineffective for the learning of facilitative counseling skills. Although Carkhuff (1969 a, p. 156) has compiled a large number of studies which associate high-functioning supervisors with supervisee gain in performing facilitative skills, the supervision and/or training they offered to supervisees included more learning principles than only those associated with phenomenal experience. Carkhuff's (1969 a, p. 153) recommendation is that

hopefully, the trainer is not only functioning at high levels on these dimensions but is also attempting to impart learnings concerning these dimensions in a systematic manner, for only then will he integrate the critical sources of learning--the didactic, the experiential, and the modeling.

A later restatement of this same notion (Carkhuff, 1972) cited the finding of a study by Vitalo (1970) which suggested that both the facilitative level of the trainer/supervisor and systematic social reinforcement were necessary to produce the verbal-conditioning effect by which trainees learn to make facilitative responses.

Conclusions drawn by Carkhuff have not been validated by subsequent research. Brady, Rowe, and Smouse (1976) replicated the Vitalo study and failed to find similar results. They interpreted their findings as supporting the contention that contingent reinforcement is the most potent aspect of effective verbal conditioning, and that the role of facilitative conditions has not been shown to be instrumental.

Indirectly in support of the instrumental role, however, is the finding by Dowling and Frantz (1975) that facilitative models generate significantly more imitative learning of ethnocentrism than do unfacilitative models. Although this study cannot be directly generalized to experiential supervision, it does suggest that, within certain subject-situation-variable paradigms, the role of facilitative behavior can be conducive to learning some classes of behavior.

The lack of support for instrumental learning effects of facilitative conditions does not mean that they do not have a place in counselor supervision, although it does raise a serious question about the viability of experiential supervision. Facilitative conditions have not been shown to be a "sufficient" treatment for the kinds of counselor learning which should take place within supervision, but it can be speculated that a facilitative supervisory relationship is a good climate for learning. The supervisor attends to the insecurities and efforts of the supervisee, relieves anxiety, and creates a working relationship within which other learnings can occur. In such a context the facilitative conditions seem appropriate and desirable.

PRACTICAL APPLICATION: ILLUSTRATIVE CASES

The practice of psychotherapeutic supervision has largely been confined to university settings, and one seldom hears of dynamic methodology being used in field supervision. In the case of IPR this is somewhat justified, since that procedure requires laboratory equipment and is geared for beginning counselors. However other kinds of dynamic methodology could just as easily be employed in field settings as in the

74

university, and there probably are adaptations of IPR that would be applicable to field work. Why hasn't psychotherapeutic supervision "caught on"? A possible reason is that field supervisors, the majority of which have not received preparation for supervision, consider psychotherapeutic supervision to be a highly sophisticated treatment, one to be expected from university professors but not from practitioners in the field. What these supervisors don't realize is that for those who have had experience in dealing with dynamics in counseling, the shift to dealing with them in supervision is not overly difficult.

The most unjustified reason for not using dynamic methodology is the argument that it is neither applicable nor useful in the "real" world of counselor practice. This argument indicates a complete lack of awareness of interpersonal and intrapersonal dynamics. The work of the counselor is constantly involved with dynamics; they are tools of the trade, utilization of which is an index of the counselor's competency and personal development.

Some synoptic cases of psychotherapeutic supervision, drawn from actual supervisory practice, are presented here to illustrate that dynamics are operative in most of the counselor's work with people, and that a wide variety of supervisory methods can be developed and applied toward meeting the goals of psychotherapeutic supervision.

Case 1: An Uptight Counselor

A guidance director was having difficulty with a counselor who recently had entered counseling after two unsuccessful years as a classroom teacher. The director noticed that the counselor was not relating well to students in her new capacity, and weekly supervisory sessions were begun on the pretext of helping the new counselor get off to a good start. The director and counselor listened to audio-tapes of several typical interviews, and the director observed that the counselor dominated her counseling sessions with cognitively oriented, closed-ended questions. She dominated supervisory sessions in a similar fashion and her tension was evident. The director gradually led her into exploring her feelings in general about counseling, and her emotional reactions to counselees in particular. The counselor discovered painfully that she was threatened by close interpersonal contact. She thought students didn't like her, and reacted with defensive authoritative behavior.

As the threat of supervision dissolved, so did her anxiety in counseling. She slowly gained confidence and found that students liked her much more when she related in a person-to-person manner. Consequently, she developed a greater degree of self esteem.

Case 2: An Insecure Beginner

The counselor in this case was enrolled in a counseling practicum course. He was a courteous and somewhat shy student whom everyone liked. In counseling with his practicum client he quickly established rapport and was off to a good start, but the supervisor noticed later that the counselor was being manipulated by the client to the detriment of counseling progress. Crucial topics were being avoided by the client, who placed responsibility for solving concerns on the counselor. Client contradictions were overlooked by the counselor, and the tone of the counseling relationship was controlled totally by the client.

The supervisor conducted Interpersonal Process Recall with the client and counselor so their thoughts and feelings during counseling could be recalled and examined. Through IPR the counselor became aware of his feelings of inadequacy, his desire to have the client like him, and how these dynamics were affecting his interpersonal counseling behavior. Client recall revealed disappointment in the counselor's lack of assertiveness, with this disappointment having been masked effectively by the client's controlling behavior--a response to his fear of "being told that I'm maladjusted."

Subsequent to IPR, the counselor's behavior was more congruent and effective. Insight into himself and the client enabled the counselor to act out of a professional intent, rather than solely from personal needs.

Case 3: A Problem With Consultation

A school counselor was having difficulty with parental consultation. The supervisor found that the counselor was satisfied with some consultation sessions and parents gave approving feedback about the helpfulness of these sessions, but other sessions were disastrous. The counselor and parents emerged from these interactions with anger toward each other, and on one occasion the parents had reported their irate dissatisfaction to the school superintendent who asked for an investigation into the counselor's conduct.

The supervisor arranged to have regular meetings with the counselor to work on the consultation problems. At first there was considerable resistance from the counselor, but the supervisor's skill at establishing a non-threatening relationship reduced anxiety and together they explored the counselor's past consultation cases. Clearly, the counselor had no trouble interacting with friendly parents, but confrontive and demanding parents evoked the counselor's anxiety and anger, and the consequential reaction was to "tell them off." The counselor felt a need to defend the school and its personnel from the implied accusations of defensive parents. Coming from a family of educators and having a strong commitment to public education, the counselor was offended personally by such parents.

A thorough exploration of intense feelings, strong attitudes, and the interpersonal behavior they spawned helped the counselor see where consultation problems began. Supervision was directed at helping the counselor learn to control intrapersonal dynamics and behave in a way that promoted progress toward consulting goals. The counselor discovered that the best way to gain public recognition for the integrity of educators was through effective professional behavior with even the most offensive consultees. The experience was rewarding when the counselor first succeeded in converting an argumentative parent into a cooperative working partner.

Case 4: A "Difficult" Colleague

A staff of counselors included one member who was arrogant and hostile toward colleagues. The behavior of this individual bordered on the unethical, but there was never conclusive evidence of professional misconduct. Yet, conflicts and continual reports of the counselor's discrediting and untruthful statements caused a serious staff morale problem.

The supervisor asked the counselor to meet for individual supervision, and at that time gave the counselor an opportunity to express perceptions of the staff and individual colleagues. One hope was that the counselor could discuss feelings and attitudes that may have prompted aggressive behavior, but the counselor was reticent and the supervisor was forced to present the problem directly in as non-threateningly a way as possible. The supervisor also suggested that they work on improving the counselor's relationship with colleagues. This choice was a forced one, and the problem would have become more severe if the counselor had refused supervision. However, the supervisee begrudgingly agreed to participate in supervision, holding fast to the attitude that the problem existed only in the minds of others.

A series of supervisory sessions followed and each one was strained. The counselor never admitted having any negative feelings or attitudes toward colleagues and treated supervision as a "requirement," but the supervisor was able to concentrate on overt conflicts that occurred within the staff. Interpersonal dynamics and their probable intrapersonal impact on others were explored. Concurrently, the supervisor consulted with other staff members concerning the handling of intrastaff conflicts.

Gradually the counselor's interactions with colleagues improved. The facilitative relationship of supervision and the examination of interactions had a positive effect on the counselor. Although the counselor had refused direct exploration of intrapersonal dynamics, arrogance and hostility faded as interactions improved.

Case 5: Applying Rational Emotive Therapy (RET) To Counseling Supervision*

The theory and practice RET (Ellis & Grieger, 1977) provides yet another point of departure for therapeutic supervision. The cornerstone of RET is the thesis that it is the individual's current, irrational ways of interpreting and evaluating life events, rather than the events themselves, that cause and maintain the individual's emotional and behavioral disturbances. In other words, individuals generally control their own destiny, particularly their emotional destiny, by the way they "personalize" their experiences. Given this premise, which has a great deal of empirical support, the major thrust of RET is three fold:

1. to help people get in touch with the basic values, beliefs and philosophies they hold that prompt them to evaluate events as they do;

2. to induce them to give up those erroneous beliefs and values that lead to emotional distress; and

3. to help them learn more adaptive and valid beliefs and values to replace those which are disturbing or maladaptive.

By way of example, take the young college student who loses his girlfriend and reacts with depression. He stays home much of the time, avoids going out with other girls or frequenting places where they used to go together, stops attending to his school work, and in general feels miserable. Most people would falsely conclude that this young man's loss caused these reactions. RET theory explains this differently. What happened to him emotionally didn't automatically follow from his loss, but from his evaluation of the loss. Specifically, to feel miserable, he had to evaluate his girlfriend's departure in the following manner: "I must have her. I can't exist without her. Life will be absolutely awful since she's gone. Since I lost her, I must be a worm whom no one can love."

---

*This supervisory case is offered by R. M. Grieger, Ph.D., an Associate Fellow and training faculty member of the Institute for Advanced Study in Rational Psychotherapy. Dr. Grieger also is an Associate Professor in the School of Education, University of Virginia.

If he had concluded something like, "I really care for her. Since I care for her, I am very sorry she doesn't care for me too, but, life goes on and I'll make it ok." he would not have felt depressed but only sad and frustrated. Thus, this young man caused his own depression by interpreting and evaluating his loss in the ways that he did.

What do these RET tenets mean for counselor education and supervision? They help the counselor-in-training develop a better understanding of ideational and emotional dynamics of clients' problems and help the counselor decide just how to intercede strategically. More germaine to this discussion, however, RET provides a focus for helping the counselor-in-training deal with his/her own emotional reactions within the counseling session.

The author's experience has been that most beginning counselors, and a good many experienced ones as well, find working with clients an emotional experience that they do not always understand and often do not know how to manage. One common emotional reaction, particularly with beginners, is anxiety. This usually results from the counselor's belief that he/she must do well with a client to gain the approval of supervisors or peers, and then perceiving himself or herself as an inadequate counselor or person because of failure to live up to that demand. A second emotional reaction common to many counselors is anger at the client. This reaction usually results when the counselor ignores the fact that disturbed people do disturbed things, and illogically demands that the client work hard, inhibit resistances, and generally make steady progress. Then, when the client does not or cannot fully cooperate, the counselor evaluates the client negatively.

In an RET perspective on psychotherapeutic supervision, the supervisor, among other things, attends to the emotional reactions of the counselor and, more importantly, to the evaluative thoughts behind these emotional reactions. The supervisor first helps the counselor get in touch with his/her feelings and thoughts, and then initiates a discussion of the validity and appropriateness of these evaluations, while helping the counselor adopt a more constructive, empathic perspective of the client.

To conclude this RET supervision case, an authentic supervisor-counselor interchange will be cited to illustrate the points made previously. George had counseled Susan for approximately two months and was getting nowhere. He had tried just about everything he knew to establish a trusting relationship and was at his wit's end. To be sure, Susan was a difficult client. She generally was suspicious, resistant and argumentative. Note in the following transcript the tact that the supervisor took in focusing on George's anger and on what lay behind that anger.

Supervisor: Let's stop the tape here, George. Now, reflect on what was taking place right then between you and Susan. What were your feelings?

George: Well, like I didn't know where to go.

Supervisor: But, I bet you were not without feeling and were stuck only in respect to techniques. What was that feeling?

George: Anger.

Supervisor: Yeah. That really came through loud and clear. Were you aware of it? (George nods yes). Well, let's talk about that some, because I've been hearing that for some time now and, at least the way you're expressing it, I'm not sure it is constructive. Do you hear the same thing?

George: OK. I guess I am angry at her.

Supervisor: Good. You're in touch with it. Now, what evaluative thinking were you doing about Susan to get yourself so mad?

George: Probably something like, "Damn it. We've been working for two months now and. . .what can I do!"

Supervisor: You've been working hard with her for two months and she. . .What?

George: Should cooperate!

Supervisor: Right. You've concluded in your head that she should be cooperating with you. That sounds like a demand on your part that she act sensibly with you. That's your premise, right? I wonder why she should do that with you. After all, she is pretty disturbed and pretty good at screwing up her life. Why is it she should act sanely with you? Are you special?

George: It does sound kind of silly of me.

Supervisor: Yeah, it does when you think about it. See how your evaluative, demanding thoughts lead to your getting yourself angry? Now, what's a better attitude to take?

George: How about something like: "She's really disturbed and, because of her disturbance, she probably will be a difficult client for me and will get in her own way of getting better. So, it's ok for her to be the way she is. But, how can I break through her resistances?" How's that?

Supervisor: Makes sense to me. But, does it make sense to you?

George: Yeah.

Supervisor: If you really take that track, you will certainly not feel angry and will probably be more effective in dealing with her. As it is, she really sucks you into her games.

George: Right.

Supervisor: Now, let's talk about ways you might respond to her argumentativeness.

In this interchange the supervisor saw that George was angry at the client, and that this anger was blocking his effective counseling performance. The supervisor helped George identify his problematic feelings (anger), and then forced him to discover the irrational self-talk with which he was precipitating the feelings. Next, the supervisor disputed this self-talk and showed it to be illogical. Lastly, the supervisor helped George to replace the illogical self-talk with a rational sentence, one that may allow for inevitable frustration and irritation over the client's lack of cooperative behavior, but would not spawn the original intense anger which inhibited counseling progress. The cognitive restructuring sequence ends as the supervisor and counselor search for appropriate counseling responses to replace the counselor's anger responses.

REFERENCES

Altucher, N. Constructive use of the supervisory relationship. Journal of Counseling Psychology, 1967, 14, 165-170.

Arbuckle, D. S. Client perception of counselor personality. Journal of Counseling Psychology, 1956, 3, 92-96.

_____. Supervision: Learning, not counseling. Journal of Counseling Psychology, 1965, 12, 90-94.

Archer, J., & Kagan, N. Teaching interpersonal relationship skills on campus: A pyramid approach. Journal of Counseling Psychology, 1973, 20, 535-540.

Bauman, W. F. Games counselor trainees play: Dealing with trainee resistance. Counselor Education and Supervision, 1972, 11, 251-256.

Beutler, L. E.; Johnson, D. T.; Neville, C. W. Jr.; Elkins, D.; & Jobe, A. M. Attitude similarity and therapist credibility as predictors of attitude change and improvement in psychotherapy. Journal of Consulting and Clinical Psychology, 1975, 43(6), 90-92.

Birk, J. M. Effects of counseling supervision method and preference on empathic understanding. Journal of Counseling Psychology, 1972, 19, 542-546.

Brady, D.; Rowe, W.; & Smouse, A. D. Facilitative level and verbal conditioning: A replication. Journal of Counseling Psychology, 1976, 23(1), 78-80.

Burck, H. D.; Cottingham, H. F.; & Reardon, R. C. Counseling and Accountability. New York: Pergamon Press, Inc., 1973.

Carkhuff, R. R. The development of systematic human resource development models. The Counseling Psychologist, 1972, 3(3), 4-11.

_____. Helping and Human Relations, Vol. I. New York: Holt, Rinehart and Winston, 1969.

Cashdan, S. *Interactional Psychotherapy*. New York: Gruen and Stratton, 1973.

Delaney, D. J., & Moore, J. C. Student expectations of the role of practicum supervisor. *Counselor Education and Supervision*, 1966, 6, 11-17.

Dendy, R. F. A model for the training of undergraduate residence hall assistants as paraprofessional counselors using videotape playback techniques and interpersonal process recall. Unpublished doctoral dissertation. Michigan State University, 1971.

Dietzel, C. S., & Abeles, N. Client-therapist complementarity and therapeutic outcome. *Journal of Counseling Psychology*, 1975, 22(4), 264-272.

Dowling, T. H., & Frantz, T. T. The influence of facilitative relationship on imitative learning. *Journal of Counseling Psychology*, 1975, 22(4), 259-263.

Ekstein, R. Supervision of psychotherapy: Is it teaching? Is it administration? Or is it therapy? *Psychotherapy: Theory, Research and Practice*, 1964, 1, 137-138.

Ekstein, R., & Wallerstein, R. S. *The Teaching and Learning of Psychotherapy*. New York: Basic Books, 1958.

Ellis, A., & Grieger, R. *Rational-Emotive Therapy: Handbook of Theory and Practice*. New York: Springer, 1977.

Fuller, F. F., & Manning, B. A. Self-confrontation reviewed: A conceptualization for video playback in teacher education. *Review of Educational Research*, 1973, 43, 469-528.

Gimmestad, M. J., & Greenwood, J. D. A new twist on IPR: Concurrent recall by supervisory group. *Counselor Education and Supervision*, 1974, 14(1), 71-73.

Grzegorek, A. E. A study of the effects of two types of emphasis in counselor training used in conjunction with simulation and videotaping. Unpublished doctoral dissertation. Michigan State University, 1971.

Guttman, M. A. J., & Haase, R. F. Generalization of microcounseling skills from training period to actual counseling setting. *Counselor Education and Supervision*, 1972, 12, 98-108.

Gysbers, N. C., & Johnston, J. A. Expectations of a practicum supervisor's role. *Counselor Education and Supervision*, 1965, 4, 68-74.

Hansen, J. C. Trainees expectations of supervision in the counseling practicum. Counselor Education and Supervision, 1965, 4, 75-80.

Hansen, J. C., & Barker, E. N. Experiencing and the supervisory relationship. Journal of Counseling Psychology, 1964, 11, 107-111.

Heller, K.; Myers, R.; & Kline, L. Interviewer behavior as a function of standardized client role. Journal of Consulting Psychology, 1963, 27, 117-122.

Hester, L. R.; Weitz, L. J.; Anchor, K. N.; & Roback, H. B. Supervisor attraction as a function of level of supervisor skillfulness and supervisees' perceived similarity. Journal of Counseling Psychology, 1976, 23(3), 254-258.

Hogan, R. A. Issues and approaches in supervision. Psychotherapy: Theory, Research and Practice, 1964, 1, 139-141.

Jakubowski-Spector, P.; Dustin, R.; & George, R. Toward developing a behavioral counselor education model. Counselor Education and Supervision, 1971, 10, 242-250.

Kagan, N., & Krathwohl, D. R. Studies in Human Interaction: Interpersonal Process Recall Stimulated by Videotape. East Lansing, Michigan: Educational Publishing Services, 1967.

Kagan, N.; Krathwohl, D. R.; & Miller, R. Stimulated recall in therapy using videotape: A case study. Journal of Counseling Psychology, 1963, 10, 237-243.

Kagan, N., & Schauble, P. D. Affect simulation in interpersonal recall. Journal of Counseling Psychology, 1969, 16, 309-313.

Kagan, N.; Schauble, P. G.; Resnikoff, A.; Danish, S. J.; & Krathwohl, D. R. Interpersonal process recall. Journal of Nervous and Mental Disease, 1969, 148, 365-374.

Kell, B. L., & Burow, J. M. Developmental Counseling and Therapy. Boston: Houghton Mifflin Co., 1970.

Kell, B. L., & Mueller, W. J. Impact and Change: A Study of Counseling Relationships. New York: Appleton-Century-Crofts, 1966.

Kingdon, M. A. A cost-benefit analysis of the interpersonal process recall technique. Journal of Counseling Psychology, 1975, 22(4), 353-357.

Lambert, M. J. Supervisory and counseling process: A comparative study. Counselor Education and Supervision, 1974, 14, 54-60.

Leary, T. Interpersonal Diagnosis of Personality. New York: Ronald Press, 1957.

Lister, J. L. Counselor experiencing: Its implications for supervision. Counselor Education and Supervision, 1966, 5, 55-60.

May, R. Power and Innocence. New York: W. W. Norton, 1972.

Miller, C. D., & Oetting, E. R. Students react to supervision. Counselor Education and Supervision, 1966, 6, 73-74.

Moore, M. The client's voice in supervision. The Art and Science of Psychotherapy, 1969, 5, 76-78.

Mueller, W. Patterns of behavior and their reciprocal impact in the family and in psychotherapy. Journal of Counseling Psychology Monograph, 1969, 16(2, Pt. 2).

Mueller, W. J., & Kell, B. L. Coping with Conflict. New York: Appleton-Century-Crofts, 1972.

Patterson, C. H. Supervising students in the counseling practicum. Journal of Counseling Psychology, 1964, 11, 47-53.

Payne, P. A., & Gralinski, D. M. Effects of supervisor style and empathy upon counselor learning. Journal of Counseling Psychology, 1968, 15, 517-521.

Payne, P. A.; Weiss, S. D.; & Kappa, R. A. Didactic, experiential, and modeling factors in the learning of empathy. Journal of Counseling Psychology, 1972, 19, 425-429.

Payne, P. A.; Winter, D. E.; & Bell, G. E. Effects of supervisor style on the learning of empathy in a supervision analogue. Counselor Education and Supervision, 1972, 11, 262-269.

Pierce, R.; Carkhuff, R. R.; & Berenson, B. G. The differential effects of high and low functioning counselors upon counselors-in-training. Journal of Clinical Psychology, 1967, 23, 212-215.

Pierce, R. M., & Schauble, P. G. Graduate training of facilitative counselors: The effects of individual supervision. Journal of Counseling Psychology, 1970, 17, 210-215.

Raush, H. L. Interaction sequences. Journal of Personality and Social Psychology, 1965, 2, 487-499.

Raush, H. L.; Dittmann, A. T.; & Taylor, T. J. The interpersonal behavior of children in residential treatment. Journal of Abnormal and Social Psychology, 1959, 58, 9-26.

Resnikoff, A.; Kagan, N.; & Schauble, P. Acceleration of psychotherapy through stimulated videotape recall. American Journal of Psychotherapy, 1970, 24, 102-111.

Rogers, C. R. Client-Centered Therapy. Boston: Houghton Mifflin, 1951.

_____. The necessary and sufficient conditions of therapeutic personality change. Journal of Consulting Psychology, 1957, 21, 95-103.

Ronnestad, M. H. The effects of modeling, feedback, and experiential methods on counselor empathy. Counselor Education and Supervision, 1977, 16(3), 194-201.

Schauble, P. G. The acceleration of client progress in counseling and psychotherapy through interpersonal process recall. Unpublished doctoral dissertation. Michigan State University, 1970.

Spivack, J. D. The use of developmental tasks for training counselors using interpersonal process recall. Unpublished doctoral dissertation. Michigan State University, 1970.

_____. Laboratory to classroom: The practical application of IRP in a master's level pre-practicum counselor education program. Counselor Education and Supervision, 1972, 12, 3-16.

Van Noord, R. W., & Kagan, N. Stimulated recall and affect simulation in counseling: Client growth reexamined. Journal of Counseling Psychology, 1976, 23(1), 28-33.

Vitalo, R. L. Effects of facilitative interpersonal functioning in a conditioning paradigm. Journal of Counseling Psychology, 1970, 17, 141-144.

Ward, G. R.; Kagan, N.; & Krathwohl, D. R. An attempt to measure and facilitate counselor effectiveness. Counselor Education and Supervision, 1972, 11, 179-186.

Wedeking, D. F., & Scott, T. B. A study of the relationship between supervisor and trainee behaviors in counseling practicum. Counselor Education and Supervision, 1976, 15(4), 259-266.

Whiteley, J. M. (Ed.) Research in Counseling. Columbus, Ohio: Charles E. Merrill, 1967.

Chapter **3**

THE

BEHAVIORAL APPROACH

TO

COUNSELOR SUPERVISION

John D. Boyd

THE BEHAVIORAL APPROACH TO COUNSELOR SUPERVISION

John D. Boyd

Counselor supervision from a behavioral approach is a direct corollary to the Behavioral Counselor Education Model proposed by Jakubowski-Spector, Dustin, and George (1971), and similar views by Delaney (1969), Hackney (1971), Hackney and Nye (1973), Krumboltz (1966a, 1966b, 1967), Levine and Tilker (1974), and many others who subscribe to the following four propositions.

1. Proficient counselor performance is more a function of learned skills than a "personality fit." Personality is actually a constellation of situation-specific behaviors, some of which may be appropriate for the counselor's role while others may not be appropriate. The purpose of counselor education is to teach appropriate counselor behaviors (skills) to trainees and to help them extinguish inappropriate behavior from their professional actions.

2. The counselor's professional role and job description is comprised of identifiable tasks, each one requiring skill behaviors. Counselor education should enable counselor-trainees to develop these skills, and supervision should assist the counselor in applying and refining the skills.

3. Counselor skills can be behaviorally defined, and these behaviors respond to the principles of psychological learning theory just as other behaviors.

4. Counselor supervision should employ the principles of psychological learning theory within its methodology.

Behavioral supervision is thus a process of helping counselors develop (if necessary), apply, and refine those skill-behaviors that comprise the counseling craft. This is done through multiple modalities based on psychological learning theory. The behavioral supervision approach is relatively new as is the behavioral approach to counseling; however, other forms of supervision, called "didactic," "technique-oriented," and "instructional" have been in practice for some time and now are being subsumed by the behavioral approach. Behavioral supervision is not totally revolutionary, but it does add more scientific rigor and psychological application to the older, directive supervision approaches.

FOCUS AND GOALS

The focus of behavioral supervision is upon the skill behaviors of the counselor. These skill behaviors are broadly conceptualized to include the counselor's thinking, feeling, and acting behaviors. Skills exist at various levels of difficulty ranging from fundamental to advanced. Some skills frequently may be used (e.g. reflection, tacting response) while other skills are to be utilized only when a particular problem or assignment arises (e.g. relaxation, thought control, and covert sensitization).

The goal of behavioral supervision is always the person-specific skill needs of the supervisee. Each supervisee should be treated as an individual with needs that are particular to him/her. Generally speaking the minimal broad goal for any supervisee would be a level of skill functioning representing the competent performance of the counselor's role and function; beyond this minimal level the goal would be a level of functioning above present performance yet within realistic expectation. The "person-specific" nature of a behavioral supervision goal is a necessary ingredient in effective methodology, and each counselor will be at a somewhat different level of skill development. Assessment of this level will be discussed later.

The ideal supervisee would be one who has gained the skills necessary for "fully functioning performance," making possible Hackney's (1971, p. 103) notion that

> the relationship between supervisor and (supervisee) should take on more of the qualities of a professional relationship characterized by consultative interactions rather than skill-acquisition relationships. The differences that exist between supervisor and (supervisee) in a consultation-professional model should be differences in experience rather than differences in counseling skills.

Hackney's suggestion that the learning of basic skills (e.g. reflective responses and open-ended leads) should occur prior to supervision would be a desirable sequence. But readers should not assume that skill development does not belong in supervision, because the development and refinement

90

of high-level skills (e.g. interpretation, confrontation, behavior-change strategies) can and should continue throughout the counselor's career--and this development can be promoted through consultative supervision and colleague interaction. Further, a realism is that some supervisees for one reason or another will enter supervision with significant skill deficiencies and inappropriate behaviors. The supervisor may encounter basic skill deficiencies such as a lack of affective listening and empathic responding, an inability to help others set goals or make decisions, and an ignorance of strategies such as assertive training, vocational exploration, and the building of study skills. Inappropriate counselor behaviors that would probably accompany deficiencies include self-referent thoughts and "mind-wandering" during helpgiving, and a profusion of advice-giving wherein offered solutions are based upon the counselor's personal experience.

The person-specific supervisory goal for a counselor having such deficiencies and inappropriate behaviors would be to help the counselor begin to perform the deficient skills and cease performing the inappropriate behaviors. If skill deficiencies and inappropriate behaviors are too serious for supervision, the supervisee must attain the goal through other routes that do not include helping duties. For a counselor-in-training the best solution may be a recycling through practicum preparation courses, or special work outside of class to acquire the needed skills and overcome inappropriate behavior. Practicing counselors with significant skill problems pose a particularly difficult problem. The supervisor may need to construct a temporary job which avoids the counselor's skill problems so that the counselor can be employed while participating in remedial training. A leave of absence for further training is another route; and termination of the counselor's duties is the last resort if all else fails. The point being made in these steps with the low-skill counselor is that the welfare of helpees is protected while the skills of the counselor are promoted through supervision and/or remedial skill-training.

METHODOLOGY

The process of behavioral supervision involves a five-step methodological sequence. First is the establishment of a relationship between the supervisor and counselor. Second is a skill analysis and assessment which will lead into the third step--setting of supervision goals. Fourth is the construction and implementation of strategies to accomplish the goal(s). Fifth supervision is finalized with a follow up evaluation and generalization of learning.

91

SUPERVISORY RELATIONSHIP

In the <u>psychotherapeutic approach</u> to supervision the relationship between the counselor and supervisor served as a source of dynamic learning. A dynamically rich supervisory relationship was established, and later the dynamics of this relationship were analyzed to discover how each party was acting and reacting. An "offshoot" of the dynamics approach, <u>experiential supervision</u>, treated the supervisory relationship as an opportunity for the counselor to receive psychologically facilitative conditions and to grow therapeutically.

<u>Behavioral supervision</u> does not consider the supervisory relationship itself to be a primary source of experiential learning or therapeutic growth, but the relationship is a very important and instrumental part of the supervisory process. In behavioral supervision, a relationship must exist between the supervisor and counselor that is conducive to learning, otherwise supervision is at a standstill. An understanding, honest, and respectful relationship in behavioral supervision is the route to this conducive learning atmosphere.

Such a "facilitative" relationship can overcome the common problem of supervisee resistance, and although a more straightforward way of handling resistance (Guttman, 1973) may exist, a psychologically comfortable relationship is the best for promoting future supervision progress. Also, a facilitative relationship offers an interaction in which formal learning activities can be conducted (e.g., role playing, modeling, reinforcement). Lastly, Jakubowski-Spector et al (1971) have made the point that behavioral supervision should attend to the counselor's covert skill-behaviors, and the only way to obtain these data is by self-report. A facilitative relationship is a necessary condition for the counselor's sharing of thoughts and feelings, thus giving the behavioral supervisor needed data for skill assessment and goal setting.

Because the supervisory relationship is so instrumentally important, Delaney (1972) has recommended taking whatever time is necessary to establish the working alliance before moving on to active methodology. Sometimes relationship building will require patience, such as when the counselor's skill deficiencies are obvious and these deficiencies temptingly await the behavioral supervisor's strategies. But rushing the supervision process is a damaging error, and the experienced supervisor knows that establishing a working alliance is the <u>top priority</u> when initiating supervision.

SKILL ANALYSIS AND ASSESSMENT

Behavioral supervision is goal directed. Two of the
methodological steps in the behavioral supervision process
are to set supervision goals (step three) and to employ
effective strategies to accomplish the goals (step four). But
in order to set goals a skill-behavior analysis and assessment
(step two) must be done. This analysis and assessment step
can be performed on a particular counselor performance, task,
or entire skill repertoire.

Using an unsuccessful consultation session as an illustrative performance target, skill analysis would proceed in
this fashion. From a consultative stance the behavioral
supervisor would work with the counselor (perhaps assisting
the counselor in self-appraisal) to behaviorally define the
discrete skills comprising the consultation performance.
Skill assessment would follow the analysis and consist of
evaluating each skill behavior in terms of the counselor's
performance capability, and then assigning the behavior to one
of the five assessment categories in Figure 3.1.

An illustration of the information that could result
from an analysis and assessment of skill behaviors in the
counselor's unsuccessful consultation performance can be seen
in Figure 3.1. In this case the counselor's performance
capability is quite low, an occurrence that is typical when
the counselor has not received training or experience in
consultation. The counselor cannot initiate consultation,
but can respond to consultee initiated contacts. Although
sometimes the counselor is at a loss for words, eye contact and
supportive statements are assets. Questions help to promote
the consultation interaction but are often peripheral to the
core of the consultee's problem. Reflections are absent but
the counselor has demonstrated this skill in counseling, so
generalization to consultation needs to be done. Perhaps the
major deficiencies in the counselor's consultation are not
knowing how to target the causal factors in the consultee's
problem and being unable to conceptualize the problem adequately. These two deficiencies make the establishment of
goals and strategies with the consultee an impossibility.
Compounding skill deficiencies is the counselor's easily
aroused anger and resentment which affronts consultees.

Analysis and assessment of counselor skills necessitate
that the behavioral supervisor have an extensive knowledge
of the skills required by the counselor's work. In the
previous example of unsuccessful consultation, the counselor
could not conduct the analysis and assessment alone because
of inexperience with the focal task--consultation. The super-

Analysis (Discrete Skill-Behaviors)	Assessment Categories (Performance Capability)
1. Expresses anger and resentment in response to consultee's hostility and other behavior.	Inappropriate counselor behaviors which interfere with task or skill performance; these should be reduced or extinguished in frequency.
2. Targeting instrumental factors. 3. Conceptualizing the consultee's problem. 4. Establishing a goal and strategy with the consultee.	Necessary skill-behaviors which are not performed and are absent from the counselor's repertoire, these should be acquired.
5. Reflecting consultee feelings. 6. Reflecting consultee's troublesome attitudes 7. Initiating consultant contact	Necessary skill-behaviors which are present in the counselor's repertoire but are not performed because the counselor cannot apply them in actual practice. The counselor must learn when and how to apply these skills.
8. Verbal responses to consultee's initiated contact. 9. Asking questions	Necessary skill-behaviors which are applied but at a low level of quality. Improvement and refinement is needed in skill application.
10. Visual attending. 11. Supportive statements.	Satisfactory frequency and quality of skill-behavior performance.

Figure 3.1. Skill Behavior Analysis and Assessment.

visor could make suggestions regarding consultation because of
familiarity with analysis and assessment skills.

The behavioral supervisor would be wise to construct a
mental model of the ideal skill repertoire of the fully
performing counselor according to function or task and,
during analysis and assessment, this model can serve as a
guide. Herr (1969) has provided a valuable contribution to
the building of such a model for school counseling by drawing
44 functions from policy statements of the American School
Counselor Association (i.e., "Statement of Policy for Secondary
School Counselors" and "Guidelines for Implementation").

1. Helps to plan and develop the guidance program in
   relation to the needs of pupils.

2. Helps to plan the curriculum in relation to the needs
   of pupils.

3. Helps each pupil, through the counseling relationship,
   to

   a. Understand himself in relation to the social and
      psychological world in which he lives

   b. Accept himself as he is

   c. Develop personal decision-making competencies

   d. Resolve special problems

4. Assumes the role of leader and consultant in the
   school's program of pupil appraisal by doing the
   following:

   a. Coordinating the accumulation and use of meaningful
      information about each pupil

   b. Interpreting information about pupils to pupils

   c. Interpreting information about pupils to teachers

   d. Interpreting information about pupils to parents

   e. Interpreting information about pupils to adminis-
      trators, curriculum committees, and other concerned
      professionals for use in educational modification

   f. Identifying pupils with special abilities or needs

5. Collects and disseminates to pupils and their parents information concerning the following:

   a. School offerings

   b. Opportunities for further education

   c. Careers and career-training opportunities

   d. Financial assistance for post-secondary education

6. Provides each pupil through systematic group guidance programs the following:

   a. Opportunity to relate his personal characteristics to educational requirements

   b. Opportunity to relate his personal characteristics to occupational requirements

7. Provides group counseling for those students unable or unready to profit from individual counseling

8. Coordinates the use of services available beyond those he can provide by doing the following:

   a. Making pupils and their parents aware of the availability of such services

   b. Making appropriate referrals

   c. Maintaining liaison and cooperative working relationships with other pupil personnel specialists

   d. Maintaining liaison and cooperative working relationships with agencies in the community where special services are available

   e. Encouraging the development and/or extension of community agencies for meeting pupil needs that are not already adequately met

9. Assists in providing placement services for pupils by doing the following:

   a. Planning with teachers and administrators for the grouping and scheduling of pupils

   b. Helping pupils make appropriate choices of school programs and develop long-range plans of study

c. Helping pupils make the transition from one school level to another, from one school to another, and from school to employment successfully

d. Coordinating his placement work with others for the most effective use of the placement services available in the school and the community

10. Helps parents by doing the following:

    a. Acting as a consultant to them regarding the growth and development of their children

    b. Providing them with information about their children (with due regard to the child's desire for confidentiality)

    c. Providing them with information about educational and occupational opportunities and requirements

    d. Providing them information about counseling programs and related guidance services available to them and their children

    e. Assisting them to develop realistic perceptions of their children's development in relation to their potentialities

11. Serves as a consultant to members of the administrative and teaching staffs in the area of guidance by doing the following:

    a. Sharing appropriate individual pupil data with them (again with due regard for the child's desire for confidentiality)

    b. Helping them to identify pupils with special needs and problems.

    c. Participating in in-service training programs

    d. Assisting teachers to secure materials and develop procedures for a variety of classroom group guidance experiences

12. Conducts or cooperates with others in conducting local research related to pupils needs and how well school services are meeting those needs by doing the following:

    a. Contacting graduates and dropouts in follow-up studies

b. Comparing scholastic aptitudes with achievement, selection of courses of study and post high school experience

c. Studying occupational trends in the community

d. Evaluating the school's counseling and guidance services

13. Carries out a program of public relations by doing the following:

a. Participating in programs of various community groups

b. Preparing and disseminating to parents graphic and narrative materials or bulletins and newsletters in order to keep parents and the community informed of guidance objectives and programs

c. Furnishing information regarding the counseling and guidance programs to local publishers, radio and TV stations

Identification of school counselor tasks can begin the supervisor's analysis procedure. Each task would then be defined in terms of discrete skill behaviors which would serve as concrete objectives.

Menne (1975) also has provided a foundation for the setting of skill objectives which comprise counseling. From the questionnaire responses of 175 counselors and therapists from throughout the United States Menne factored out twelve dimensions of counseling competency. In the order of respondents' perceived importance the dimensions were as follows:

Professional Ethics
Self Awareness
Personal Characteristics
Listening, Communicating
Testing Skills
Counseling Comprehension
Behavioral Science
Societal Awareness
Tutoring Techniques
Professional Credentials
Counselor Training
Vocational Guidance

Just as Herr's tasks were defined in behavioral terms, Menne's dimensions also could be translated into skill behaviors. General competency dimensions thus are coverted to specific targets for behavioral supervision strategies.

Another analysis and assessment procedure is to use rating scales rather than a conceptual skill-model. The scale takes the place of the model, and rating pertains to the skills listed on the scale. One such rating scale, which will serve as an illustration (see Appendix A), is a revised version of Cogan's (1977) Survey of Counselor Competencies. The Survey was originally a research tool, but as presented in Appendix A has been altered so that an analysis and assessment of ninety-nine competencies can be performed. Each competency can be analyzed in terms of importance (critical, important, non-essential) to the counselor's job duties, and then assessed in terms of the counselor's demonstrated or perceived performance capability (satisfactory, non-satisfactory).

Supervision rating instruments can be advantageous, for they increase the objectivity and ease of analysis and assessment for the supervisor lacking these skills. But disadvantages are also inherent. The analysis dimensions or categories of such instruments may not be as behaviorally definitive as traditional skill-behavior analysis, and scales sometimes present a narrow view of effective counselor performance. Assessment dimensions may also lack concrete criteria for evaluation of performance capability. Nevertheless, rating instruments do provide a gross procedure from which the supervisor can begin analysis and assessment. A short list of potential instruments for this task, taken from Zytowski and Betz's (1972) more extensive coverage, is presented in Appendix B. Readers are encouraged to read the evaluative commentary of Zytowski and Betz (1972, pp. 72-81) and to use caution in selecting any of these instruments for research purposes. An instrument which may be an effective supervision tool may not have the psychometric properties necessary for use in research.

Whatever method of analysis and assessment is employed, the translation of counseling and therapy into teachable skills is a challenge which faces supervision. This is a challenge to be tackled optimistically, for nebulous abilities such as clinical judgement are becoming susceptible to objective inquiry (Garner & Smith, 1976), and the intangibles of contemporary therapists can become tomorrow's training objectives.

Skills and Process

An error can be made in analysis and assessment if the discrete skill behaviors identified are divested of their "process dimension." When this error happens the counselor loses sight of the purpose of the focal task or function, and becomes a mechanical dispenser of skill behaviors. The sequence and flow of skills within a function must be retained, and indeed performing a set of skills in a smooth process manner is a skill in itself (see assessment categories three and four in Figure 3.1). Nowhere is the process dimension more important than in counseling. As an illustration, consider the abbreviated definitions of the following seven counseling skills:

1. Goal Setting--the verbal interaction between counselor and client during which they agree on a goal to work toward (e.g. a particular behavior change, making a decision, gaining information about a career).

2. Reflection of Feeling and Attitude--a counselor verbal response that reveals a feeling or attitude which was explicitly or implicitly expressed by the client.

3. Open-Ended Question--a questioning verbal response which allows the client maximum freedom for content and style of answer.

4. Implementing Strategies--the implementation of a plan of action by the counselor and client for the accomplishment of a counseling goal.

5. Tacting Response Lead--a counselor's verbal response which "helps the client discuss abstract concepts in more specific terms, or to associate significant behavioral events with certain environmental circumstances" (Delaney & Eisenberg, 1972, p. 82).

6. Constructing Strategies--the development of a plan of action by the counselor and client for the accomplishment of a counseling goal.

7. Conceptual Summary--a summarization of information revealed in the exploration of client concerns that creates meaningful relationships between disparate information elements.

A reading of these skill definitions probably would do little toward helping the counselor acquire, perform, and apply the skills. Even if a counselor had acquired these skill behaviors and could perform them, this learning would be less than adequate for actual practice until the purpose (effect on the client) of the skills was understood, and the process sequence of the skills was grasped. Skill-behavior analysis and assessment by the supervisor should enhance the counselor's understanding of purpose and sequence, thus adding a dimension of fidelity to skills and function as indicated in the following elaborations:

1. Open-Ended Question--a good technique for starting the counseling session and facilitating client exploration during the session. From the client talk elicited by this technique the counselor can make other good responses (reflection, etc.) and gain information about the client's concerns.

2. Reflection of Feeling and Attitude--this technique is particularly useful in the beginning of the counseling process for helping the client explore concerns from a personal frame of reference. This process is instrumental in the client's acquisition of self awareness concerning emotions and attitudes, communicates empathy and acceptance, and helps the client explore concerns at a meaningful level. Affective information from reflections is a building block for problem conceptualization.

3. Tacting Response Lead--this type of response helps the client be more specific about concerns, and explore them in detail. Precipitory antecedents and consequences can be revealed through tacting so that the client sees some of the instrumental factors in his/her problem. The concreteness generated by tacting enables the client to more objectively appraise and conceptualize the problem, leading to goal setting and resolution strategies. Tacting can occur throughout the counseling session but is particularly effective following self exploration, when the counselor and client zero-in on the tangible aspects of the problem.

4. Conceptual Summary--a summarizing statement which brings together seemingly disparate affective and cognitive information revealed in the client's exploration of concerns, and enables the client to conceptualize or create a unitary picture of concerns so that goals can be set and strategies constructed and implemented. Short conceptual summaries throughout the counseling process help the client develop a perspective and an all-inclusive one at the end of exploration prepares the client to set goals.

5. Goal Setting--From a conceptualization of concerns the counselor and client establish concrete goals which, if accomplished, will resolve or ameliorate the client's expressed concerns.

6. Constructing Strategies--After establishing goals, the counselor and client construct a plan of action which will accomplish the goals. Each party determines the amount and kind of input he/she will offer toward implementation of the strategy.

7. Implementing Strategies--The purpose of strategy implementation is to accomplish counseling goals, and to help the client acquire skills for future problem resolution and goal accomplishment. If the strategy is effective, the counselor and client subsequently review the counseling process, generalize learnings to other and future situations, and then terminate the alliance.

If a supervisor were assisting a counselor with any of these seven skill behaviors, or the whole counseling function, the elaborations of purpose and sequence would be mandatory. To reiterate, all skill behaviors have a purpose and sequence which determine the fidelity of skill performance.

SETTING SUPERVISION GOALS

After the behavioral supervisor has established a facilitative relationship with the counselor and the analysis/assessment procedure has been performed, the establishment of supervision goals is the next and third methodological step. Analysis and assessment provides the information from which supervision goals can be selected. Returning to the analysis and assessment in Figure 3.1, supervision goals will come from the discrete skill behaviors in the analysis section, and the corresponding assessment categories provide information that will help the counselor and supervisor in constructing strategies.

Setting supervision goals is a crucial aspect of the behavioral supervision process where the supervisee's cooperation and motivation can be strengthened or easily weakened by the actions of the supervisor. The counselor should have taken part in analysis and assessment, and now should have even more self directedness in choosing supervision goals. Supervision goals must be acceptable to the supervisor and counselor, but the recommendation is that the supervisor be tolerant of the counselor's choice if the goals are anywhere near realistic. The supervisor may see a skill-goal of a higher priority than the one chosen by the counselor, but to accept the counselor's choice rather than to impose the supervisor's will is often better. Any time the counselor is demonstrating self-initiated development it should be encouraged if possible. Moreover, the skill goals that the super-

Client Exploration of Self and Concerns	Conceptualization of Concern	Setting Counseling Goals	Constructing and Implementing Strategies
Open-ended questions Reflections Tacting	Conceptual Summaries	Goal Setting	Constructing Strategies Implementing Strategies

Figure 3.2. Skill-Behaviors In The Counseling Process. (States of the counseling process overlap, as well as the process positions of the skill-behaviors.)

103

visor would have chosen may be gained later, or as a result of generalization from supervision directed at the counselor's chosen goals.

Skill behavior goals can be covert and overt. Often the author has seen an inappropriate overt performance of skills, and in supervision has later learned that the counselor was impaired at the covert rather than overt level. When performing analysis, assessment, and goal setting, the supervisor should keep in mind that overt skill performance usually relies on knowledge and covert skill behaviors. In Figure 3.1 the skill-behaviors of targeting instrumental factors and conceptualizing the consultee's problem are examples at the covert (thinking) level. These covert skills are prerequisites for overt skills which occur later in the counseling process (e.g., goal setting and using strategies).

CONSTRUCTING AND IMPLEMENTING SUPERVISORY STRATEGIES

The fourth step in the methodological sequence of behavioral supervision is construction and implementation of strategies to accomplish the goal(s). Supervision strategies are the action plans that are made and implemented by the counselor and supervisor for the attainment of supervision goals. A single strategy may contain numerous learning activities, or it may be simple in structure. Supervisor offered reinforcement is an example of a simple strategy whereas microtraining involves many learning activities. Strategies are constructed rather than selected, being designed for the counselor as were supervision goals. Factors to consider when constructing a strategy are the following:

1. The counselor's preference for certain learning modes.

2. The effectiveness of the strategy for reaching the goal.

3. The feasibility of the strategy (e.g., facilities, materials, setting).

Two methodological thrusts in supervision strategies exist: a dependence on the self directedness and personal resources of the counselor, and a reliance predominantly on output from the supervisor. From the first thrust the supervisor is in the stance of a consultant to the counselor. The counselor assists in constructing the strategy and receives only consultative assistance in carrying out this process. Self monitoring and reinforcement is an example of a self-directed strategy. From the second thrust the supervisor operates as a trainer, actively participating in the strategy. Microtraining is an example of a supervisor-directed strategy.

These two thrusts are not entirely discrete and each of the supervision techniques to be addressed shortly can vary in the degree to which the supervisor acts as a consultant or active trainer. Determining which thrust to lean toward is a professional judgment to be made by the supervisor based upon the three factors mentioned previously. Consistent with the other suggestions made by this author, again the recommendation is that self development be promoted as much as possible by the supervision strategy. Where active training and the counselor's dependence upon the supervisor is necessary, the supervisor should use discretion and retain the development of counselor autonomy as a later objective.

Self-Instructional Modules

As suggested earlier the behavioral supervisor may encounter supervisees who cannot demonstrate the requisite skills for competent counseling practice. If these deficiencies are not beyond short-term remediation procedures, a number of training activities can be employed by the supervisor. Self-instructional modules are one of the most feasible such activities because they require a minimal amount of time from the supervisor.

As described by Cormier and Cormier (1976) a self-instructional module is an instructional unit that contains explicit skill-behavior objectives, evaluation procedures for assessing the extent to which the skill behaviors have been acquired and demonstrated, and the self-directed learning activities which the supervisee will follow to learn the skill behaviors. Modules can be structured packages that form the components of a classroom or laboratory course, however in counselor supervision what seems more propitious is for the supervisor to have a cache of materials and learning activities from which modules can be designed for each supervisee, with the assistance of the supervisee. Also appropriate are evaluation procedures which stress demonstration of the skill behaviors in role playing or other life-like situations.

The most common module assignment in the author's experience concerns the elementary but important skill of empathy communication and problem exploration. Many student-counselors overlook these skills and prematurely try to "solve the client's problem." But in this instance and most others, assignment to a skill module usually results in the supervisee making rapid learning progress. Supervisees who have been unable to communicate empathically, and to explore the client's concerns, have quickly acquired and demonstrated these skills.

Empirical support for self-instructional modules in supervision and counselor training is modest, mainly because the

topic has not received research attention. Supportive findings
have been reported by Cormier, Cormier, Zerega, and Wagaman
(1976) for the learning of counseling strategies. Cormier
and Cormier (1976) have cited many studies in higher education
where self-instructional modules have been used successfully.
The potential for self-directed learning in counselor training
and supervision looks promising.

Self Appraisal and Skill Monitoring

One supervision activity that obviously reflects a self-
development strategy is self appraisal and skill monitoring by
the counselor. Self appraisal has the advantage of being a
non-threatening procedure, and one that is perpetual if learned
well in supervision. Self appraisal and skill monitoring go
hand in hand. Studies in self observation have indicated that
individuals automatically evaluate the behaviors which they
observe, and attempt to influence these behaviors in a desired
direction (Cavior & Marabotto, 1976; Goldfried & Merbaum, 1973;
Mahoney & Thoresen, 1974; Thoresen & Mahoney, 1974). Hackney
and Nye (1973, p. 121) have suggested that self monitoring
(following initial appraisal) seems to interfere with unwanted
behavior by breaking the stimulus-response association and by
encouraging performance of the desired response--which then is
often reinforced by feedback of progress and a sense of
accomplishment.

Little support is found in the literature for unstructured
and subjective self appraisal. Such a procedure may be so
undisciplined as to be of dubious value. Yet, the counselor
who has a clear understanding of the elements of effective
performance can appraise and bring performance into line with
those guidelines. The key is understanding--an articulation
of effective performance (Kanfer, 1970 (a), and Cavior &
Marabotto, 1976). The author's experience has been that
counselors often have a hazy idea of what is good counselor
performance. Even those who are performing admirably may
never have articulated the skills that comprise good performance. Probably for this reason structured self appraisal has
been more popular than the unstructured variety.

Structured self appraisal and skill monitoring utilizes
some kind of structure for the counselor to follow in the
appraisal and monitoring process. The supervisor's analysis
and assessment instruments listed in Appendices A and B are
structure via instrumentation, and Herr's (1969) list of

forty-four counselor functions is another example of structure which can be used by the counselor. Any framework which helps the counselor attend to the important factors in effective performance is acceptable. A job description outlining the counselor's specific skill behaviors and behavioral criteria with which to evaluate the skills is a particularly useful document.

Modest but positive support exists for the effectiveness of counselors' self appraisal and skill monitoring. Reports by Mathewson and Rochlin (1956) and Walz and Johnston (1963) have cited observed improvement in counseling as a function of structured appraisal of audio taped interviews and unstructured observation of video recorded sessions respectively. Altekruse and Brown (1969) found that counselors appraising their counseling performance with the Counselor Self-Interaction Analysis Instrument began to use more indirective responses than counselors who used unstructured appraisal. Martin and Gazda (1970) measured significant improvement in the counselor-offered facilitative conditions of empathy, non-possessive warmth, genuineness, and intensity of interpersonal contact as a result of self appraisal employing interaction scales to assess those facilitative conditions. Austin and Altekruse (1972) unexpectedly discovered that a supervisor-absent group of practicum counselors significantly increased their understanding responses in counseling by the unstructured self appraisal of a leaderless group process. They subsequently suggested that the Counselor Verbal Response Scale (their criterion instrument) might be valuable as an appraisal tool to improve self-directed supervision.

Self appraisal and skill monitoring have their limits, they are not cure-alls and will not replace the supervisor's role. But their use can be a valuable and effective technique for the behavioral supervisor.

Peer Supervision

Peer supervision has for some time been recognized as being a valuable aid to the supervisor (Fraleigh & Buchheimer, 1969), yet this potential has never been tapped and peer supervision has received little development and research. Those few studies conducted have yielded inconsistent findings of questionable value.

Investigations by Arbuckle (1956), Stefflre, King, and Leafgren (1962), and Walton (1974) have studied the attributes which counselor-trainees value in the counselor or peer supervisors with whom they might choose to work. Confidence and strength or dominance is the one common finding in these studies, and this seems understandable. Whether the counselor is in the role of client or supervisee, an uncertainty is present which leads the individual toward sources of directive helpgiving and security.

Researchers (Bishop, 1971; Brown & Cannady, 1969; Friesen & Dunning, 1973) have illustrated that the use of peers as raters can be reliable and accurate. One can infer from these investigations that training and structure probably improve rating performance, and that an untrained rater can give destructive feedback to a fellow counselor.

By incorporating this paucity of evidence with other guidelines for behavioral supervision a number of discernible suggestions can be made for the employment of peer supervisors. The first suggestion, voiced by Fraleigh and Buchheimer (1969), is that peer supervision always should be considered supplemental to that of the behavioral supervisor--it is not a substitute.

A second suggestion is to recognize that peer supervision can be helpful or harmful, and three factors seem to be the determinants--the attitude of the peer supervisor, the format of peer supervision, and training in peer supervision. The attitude of the peer supervisor must be one of helpfulness, cooperation, and equality rather than an intent on one-upmanship (Fraleigh & Buchheimer, 1969). This attitude contributes to a recommended supervision format where feedback and sharing are the peer's primary functions with evaluation being deemphasized. Within this format the peer supervisor's task is structured yet flexible; rating scales in Appendices A and B are the basic method but a free discussion of ideas is encouraged. Dowd and Blocher (1974) have shown that awareness and reinforcement are separate variables in counselor training, but that their combined effects are stronger than either in isolation. The peer supervisor should thus promote counselor skill-awareness through ratings and shared perceptions. Positive reinforcement could be offered and more discriminative evaluation (positive and negative reinforcement) would be inherent in the rating data.

Of the three determinants in peer supervision, training is the most important because it can affect attitude and prepare the peer supervisor to follow the format. Training should include an explanation of the peer-supervision format, a modeling of peer supervision by the behavioral supervisor, and skill practice.

A third suggestion for peer-supervision is that the behavioral supervisor conduct group supervision before allowing peers to supervise each other individually. The group can be an opportunity for training and practice.

A final suggestion is that peer supervision, like self supervision, has limits. Counselors with serious skill deficiencies and those who are extremely defensive should not be candidates for peer supervision. Further, for counselors to learn where and when advanced and complex counselor skills are required may necessitate the expertise of the behavioral supervisor, and that often peer supervision is insufficient for this goal.

Modeling and Reinforcement

Two of the most powerful principles in psychological learning theory are modeling and reinforcement. Research support and the clinical application of these principles has been presented in numerous scholarly works (Bandura, 1969; Bergin & Garfield, 1971; Franks, 1969; Kanfer & Phillips, 1970b; Krumboltz, 1966a; Thoresen (Ed.), 1973), and application to counselor training and supervision has received substantial attention in the last few years. Blane (1968), Carlson (1971), Clark (1970), Davidson and Emmer (1966), and Kelly (1971) have shown that various forms of supervisor- or trainer-controlled reinforcement, offered following the performance of a desired skill behavior, can increase the frequency of that target. Canada (1973) has illustrated the importance of presenting reinforcement immediately after performance instead of a delayed presentation.

Numerous investigators have demonstrated the supervisor's or trainer's successful use of modeling for teaching focal skills to counselors. Among these individuals are Dalton, and Sundblad (1972); Dalton, Sundblad, and Hylbert (1973); Frankel (1971); Payne and Gralinski (1968); Payne, Weiss, and Kappa (1972); Payne, Winter, and Bell (1972); Perry (1975); Sodetz (1972); Rank, Thoresen, and Smith (1972); Ronnestad (1973); Silverman and Quinn (1974); and Uhlemann and Lea (1976). In some of these studies citing the efficacy of reinforcement or modeling the two learning effects are integrated, and other cognitive learning processes may have been present. Miller's (1971) findings have suggested that treatments combining both modeling and reinforcement are stronger than either effect in isolation. Instructional power also has been increased by combining modeling with instructions and rehearsal (Stone & Vance, 1976), and role play and supervisory feedback (Wallace, Horan, Baker & Hudson, 1975).

Modeling and reinforcement are not techniques or activities but psychological learning principles, and the astute behavioral supervisor does not have a cookbook of methods for utilizing them. What the supervisor does need is an understanding of how the principles can operate in supervision. A few practical suggestions will thus be offered.

1. Modeling and reinforcement can be employed within the immediate supervisor-counselor interaction, or in activities outside the supervisory dyad. Critiquing tapes and role playing are examples of activities within the dyad; viewing expert counselors on tape and self-managed reinforcement are examples of activities outside the dyad.

2. The supervisor can be a dispenser of modeling and reinforcement, or persons and activities other than the supervisor can be the media. Choosing the type of presentation for exerted learning influence is a strategy decision, and whatever source is likely to be most influential to the counselor should be chosen. For example, the supervisor's modeling of reflections may not be as potent as a film of Carl Rogers because of the higher status that trainees would probably attribute to Rogers (Mischel & Grusec, 1966; Kloba & Zimpfer, 1976). Videotaped modeling presentations are likely to have more impact than audiotaped models (Ivery, Normington, Miller, Morrill, & Haase, 1968; Stone & Stebbins, 1975; Walz & Johnston, 1963).

3. Modeling and reinforcement should be as focal and concentrated as possible. A concrete skill-behavior is the focal point, and high fidelity modeling and reinforcement should be directed there--not diffused. Modeling looses effectiveness if the viewers' attention is not directed at the focal skills (Bandura, 1969; Eskedel, 1975).

4. Learning complex counselor skills may require complex strategies which combine learning principles, involve discrimination training, and are "personalistic" (Lazarus, 1971, p. 31) to the counselor. The supervisor's confidence and ingenuity in constructing an effective strategy is paramount.

5. Modeling is often a sufficient experience for the acquisition of a skill, but sometimes the skill must be developed behaviorally through step-by-step training (employing reinforcement) in order for it to be performed (Bandura, 1969). Do not assume that viewing a skill is sufficient for subsequently performing it.

Role Playing and Simulation

Role playing and simulation exercises have been standard educational methods in counselor training (Schwebel, 1953), and their efficacy continues to be supported empirically and

110

practically (Delaney, 1969; Eisenberg & Delaney, 1970; Jakubowski-Spector et al, 1971; Mann & Mann, 1966). The impact of these procedures probably lies in the fact that numerous psychological learning principles are operative within them.

Role playing is the exercise of behaving in a contrived experience according to a prescribed role and by altering roles a number of learning situations can be presented to the counselor. In the role of helpee the counselor attempts to experience the part of the helper and act in that way. Sensitivity to helpees is promoted through this kind of role taking. The helpee role also places the counselor in a position to observe the supervisor and imitatively learn from his/her performance.

The supervisee's performance of the helpee role, whether for empathic experience or modeling of the supervisor, preferably precedes the role performance of counselor. This sequence is preferred because it gives the supervisee an opportunity to observe the skills of an effective counselor (as role played by the supervisor). Subsequent supervisee performance in the role of counselor is facilitated by this previous modeling.

Simulation, as employed in supervision, is a contrived experience which represents an experience that occurs naturally in the counselor's work. The counselor is confronted with nearly the same situational exigencies as in actual practice and is forced to react immediately with learned skills. Simulation in this manner is an effective method for facilitating skill generalization beyond the classroom or supervisory session.

A simulation technique that has received recent attention is the presentation of filmed or video taped client expressions to counselor-trainees. Kagan and Schauble (1969), Danish (1971) and Spivack (1973) reported that counselors react experientially to filmed clients as they would in a real counseling session, and that counselors can gain self understanding by discovering their responsive affect. Delaney (1969) and Danish (1971) go further than self understanding and help counselors practice responding with effective statements to the taped clients. The counselor thus can shape responding skills and receive reinforcement from the supervisor as performance improves.

Simulation and role playing are not restricted to counseling skills. Panther (1971) has successfully taught consulting skills through simulated exercises, and the list of skills that could be targeted is limitless. The supervisor should keep some guidelines in mind though, for simulation and role playing in supervision require expertise. The supervisor must be well acquainted with the situation (environment, persons, influential factors) that is to be simulated so simulation can be as real as possible. As in all behavioral methods, the focal skill must be defined and within the counselor's capability to perform. Complex skills should be divided into easily performed components. The supervisor must be able to demonstrate the skill, and the counselor may want to act the part of other parties in the situation who usually inhibit his/her performance (e.g., uncooperative parent, teacher, or client).

As Hackney (1971) has suggested, counselor supervision cannot become just another laboratory training experience, and the behavioral supervisor must not spend the majority of time in role playing and simulation exercises. But these techniques have a place in supervision as long as counselors encounter situations where they must perform skills they have not acquired or have not learned to apply.

Microtraining

The first documentation of microtraining for counselors was by Ivey et al (1968). Their microtraining program, called microcounseling, successfully trained beginning counselors in the skills of attending behavior, reflection of feeling, and summarization of feeling. Since this pioneer project, others have found various microcounseling training programs effective with the skills of attending (DiMattia & Arndt, 1974), fundamental social skills (Saltmarsh & Hubele, 1974), communication of test results (Miller, Morrill, & Uhlemann, 1970), a counseling-like verbal response set (Boyd, 1973), and multiple response techniques (Toukmanian, 1975). Guttman and Haase (1972) have supported the long-term retention of skills learned through microcounseling training, and the technique has become a particularly practical and valid procedure that personifies good counselor education (Bellucci, 1972).

Microtraining is a direct attempt to systematize training. This methodological approach follows a paradigm of training steps including intensive practice of the focal skill until it is performed satisfactorily. The basic microtraining model is as follows (Ivey, 1971):

1. The trainee attempts to perform the focal skill within a situation where it is appropriate. This attempt at performance could be a simulated, coach-client, role-played exercise.

2. The attempted performance is videotaped.

112

3. If the performance was of an interpersonal skill, the other party completes an evaluation form, and may be interviewed for additional feedback. When the focal skill does not involve another party this step can be eliminated.

4. The trainee reads a manual describing the focal skill to be learned. The supervisor is available for discussion and clarification of the focal skill.

5. Video models of an expert demonstrating the skill are shown to the trainee, and these may be positive and negative models. Discrimination training is present as the supervisor and trainee discuss the models.

6. The trainee and supervisor critique the videotaped attempt (step 1) to perform the focal skill. Discrimination is again present as the trainee identifies examples where the focal skill was performed satisfactorily, poorly, or not at all. The supervisor offers verbal reinforcement for capable skill performance.

7. The supervisor and trainee plan and prepare for another performance of the focal skill.

8. The trainee makes a second attempt to perform the focal skill, and this is videotaped.

9. Feedback and evaluation are made available to the trainee.

The construction of other microtraining programs is possible, but the nine-step model has been found most successful. Ivey (1971, pp. 8-9) offers several propositions upon which the success is based.

First, microtraining focuses on single skills. The trainee masters one skill at a time and can see him/herself improve in each one rather than being barraged with a whole set of competencies. Second, microtraining affords opportunity for self observation and confrontation. Third, video models are provided for immitative learning. Fourth, microtraining can accommodate any skill that is demonstrable and behaviorally defined. Fifth, actual performance and practice in a life-like situation make microtraining a "real" experience.

Microcounseling seems to capitalize on many of the training/learning variables that have been found instrumental in effective counselor preparation, and supervision is one of these training components that contributes feedback, reinforcement, and shaping influence on the trainee. Authier and Gustafson (1976) have recently discovered another supervisory contribution that may be unique among microcounseling components. Supervision helps the trainee reduce undesirable behavior in addition to increasing the use of focal skills. Referring to their results, they stated that

> This would seem to indicate that the supervised group more clearly discriminated the microcounseling skill from its opposite. Thus, it appears that feedback from a skilled observer, in this case the supervisor, may be necessary in learning and discrimination, especially within a very limited time span (Authier & Gustafson, 1976, p. 708).

Ivey (1971) described microtraining as an "open system"-- programs can be constructed within the limits of facilities available and for specific populations in respective settings. Where supervisors are scarce, peer supervision and self appraisal are alternatives. For some skills audio recording can substitute for videotaping. Live demonstrations can replace video models. The possibilities are many for the ingenious supervisor.

Self-Management Techniques

Throughout the behavioral supervision methodology are opportunities for using self-management techniques, and these opportunities would be especially pertinent for the supervisor following a self-development strategy thrust. Self management has been defined by Boyd and LaFleur (1974, p.2) as the ability of individuals to make personal behavioral adjustment decisions and actions based on analyses of self and the environment. A self-management technique in supervision would be a method by which the supervisee changes his/her own skill behavior with only consultative assistance from the supervisor. The behavioral supervisor helps the counselor to analyze and assess the skill behaviors required by role and function, the counselor then decides what adjustments in skill behavior are needed, and self-directed action plans are constructed to make the adjustment.

A concise explanation of self-management techniques has been presented by Boyd and LaFleur (1974) and Kahn (1976), and a more thorough discourse is provided by Hector, Elson, and Yager (1977), Mahoney and Thoresen (1974), and Thoresen and Mahoney (1974). The present coverage of self-managed techniques is limited to the following applications which the author has found to be most practical.

Overt-Stimulus Control. Mahoney and Thoresen (1974, p. 40) have defined stimulus control as those strategies involving the rearrangement of cues that have come to elicit undesired responses and/or the establishment of cues that will elicit desired responses. These cues may be divided into the overt category--observable cues in the environment, and the covert category--private events within the counselor that generate behavior. The use of overt stimulus control has had successful applicability in counseling and psychotherapy (Mahoney & Thoresen, 1974; Thoresen & Mahoney, 1974) but its utilization in supervision seems more restricted. A plethora of simuli exists to which supervisees react in a non-therapeutic manner and to attempt to rearrange these stimuli would be unrealistic. A major portion of supervision consists of helping the counselor adapt to and learn to respond therapeutically to stimuli which elicit unconstructive responses from people, the counselor included. So if a counselor is upset by strong emotion in the helpee, for example, obviously to tell the helpee to cease affect is inappropriate; rather, through supervision the counselor learns to respond to helpee emotion in a helpful way.

Some applications of overt stimulus control belong in supervision. Sometimes response inhibition or stimulus avoidance is an immediate but temporary reaction which the counselor can take when cues are overwhelming. Perhaps under certain environmental stimulus conditions the counselor performs unusually well. To capitalize on these conditions is opportunistic.

Establishment of cues to elicit desired responses is perhaps the most useful overt-stimulus control technique, and it represents a mainstay of behavioral supervision. When a counselor is responding inappropriately, or at a technique frequency level that is too low, the supervisor can (1) help the counselor learn to perform the desired skill behavior, and (2) help him/her identify those situational cues to which the skill behavior should be directed. For example, the counselor who asks closed questions learns how and when to make open-ended leads, and the counselor who uses too few leads learns of more opportunities to use them.

Covert-Stimulus Control. Whenever overt stimuli elicit undesirable responses from the counselor and the conditions are such that to control these cues would be unrealistic, then a covert-stimulus control technique may be the answer. Such techniques are one of the behavioral supervisor's means of dealing with counselor intrapersonal dynamics. Two principal techniques are modification of cognitive content and modification of cognitive process.

<u>Cognitive modification involves two dimensions--content</u>
<u>and process</u>. The <u>content dimension</u> concerns ideational content,
and the <u>process dimension</u> concerns the longitudinal-situational
pattern of focal cognitions and their antecedent and consequence contingencies. Regarding the latter, the principles
of stimulus control and operant conditioning are used to
influence certain cognitions, so that in turn the timing and
frequence of these cognitions are manipulated to produce
desirable emotion and overt behavior. The works of Albert
Ellis (1973, 1975) and Aaron Beck (1976) are representative of
the content focus in cognitive modification, and those of
Meichenbaum & Cameron (1974) and Meichenbaum (1975) are representative of a learning-theory influenced approach. The
content and process distinction is not an absolute dichotomy,
but more of a theoretical and methodological leaning.

The content emphasis to cognitive modification, as
exemplified by applications of Rational Emotive Therapy to
counselor supervision, was touched upon earlier in Chapter 2.
Changing ideational content is a technique which seems to have
more in common with the psychotherapeutic approach to supervision than the behavioral approach, and this is the reason
for its discussion in Chapter 2.

The process emphasis however is a more behaviorally-
oriented self-management technique in which the supervisee
learns to control his/her cognitive process, rather than
spending a considerable amount of time with the supervisor in
a cognitive restructuring dialogue. Self management of counselor anxiety is one promising area for <u>cognitive process</u>
control. Research has consistently linked counselor anxiety
and poor therapeutic performance (Bergin & Jasper, 1969;
Carter & Pappas, 1975; Milliken & Kirchener, 1971), and
counselor-trainees are particularly prone to experience
anticipatory anxiety and demonstrate its effects (Hagan &
Boyd, 1976; Mooney & Carlson, 1976). Self-managed anxiety
control methods, employing some form of cognitive stimulus
control, have shown efficacy for anxiety reduction in clients
(Chang-Liang & Denny, 1976; Russell, Miller, & June, 1974,
1975; Russell & Sipich, 1973; Sanchez-Craig, 1976; Spiegler,
Cooley, Marshall, Prince, & Puckett, 1976) and supervisees
(Russell & Wise, 1976). By combining the elements of these
anxiety treatments into a comprehensive method, the following
eclectic model, Cognitive Stimulus Control of Counselor
Anxiety, is suggested.

1. The <u>awareness treatment</u> of Carter and Pappas (1975),
   effective in itself, is a procedure which seems to
   change cognitive content as well as identify focal
   stimuli for later control. Awareness may act as a
   prelude for stimulus control steps. It consists of

116

helping supervisees become aware of feelings and
behaviors arising from interpersonal anxieties through
supervisor-lead group discussion. Questions by the
supervisor, outlined by Sanchez-Craig (1976), may
facilitate a cognitive reappraisal of stressful stimuli:
"Is the situation actually that bad; How can you
reinterpret the actions of that person; How can you
reinterpret your own reactions in the situation?"
(p. 8)

2. Cue-controlled relaxation training is a logical second
   step whereby the supervisee learns relaxation and
   associates the relaxed state with certain self
   generated cue words (Russell & Wise, 1976).

3. The supervisee is then instructed and encouraged to
   use the cue-controlled relaxation skill in situations
   which present anxiety evoking cues (e.g., clients,
   supervision, peer critique). An alternative self-
   managed response thus replaces the anxiety-controlled
   one (Russell & Wise, 1976; Sanchez-Craig, 1976),
   and a modification in the usual cognitive process
   takes place.

4. Practice of this self-management procedure should
   precede implementation in counseling and supervision
   situations.

Another promising application for cognitive process
control is a technique which the author has found valuable in
practicum supervision. A descriptively accurate label for
this technique is "covert planning and rehearsal." This
technique consists of a brief period of mental preparation and
imaginal rehearsal immediately before an interview. The
supervisor administers the first treatment, and thereafter the
supervisee can do it without assistance. Steps in this
technique are as follows:

1. In a regular supervision session the counselor and
   supervisor review the last helping interchange and
   plan for the next one.

2. Just before the next helping interchange the counselor
   seeks a quiet setting where he/she can think over the
   things to be performed in the upcoming session. By
   closing eyes and imagining these events taking place
   the counselor can covertly rehearse the required skills.
   The process of planning rehearsing takes up the time
   which might normally be spent in anticipating the
   fearful properties of the interchange. Further, covert
   rehearsal is an effective procedure for facilitating
   later overt performance.

117

3. The counselor is spontaneous in action and uses caution to assure that planning and rehearsal does not replace spontaneous action. If the helpee wishes to direct the interchanges away from the counselor's planned agenda it may be appropriate to follow this lead rather than force the client to follow the counselor's plan.

FOLLOW-UP AND GENERALIZATION OF LEARNING

The fifth methodological step in behavioral supervision is to evaluate the strategies and techniques employed. This follow-up should be done during the strategy and again upon completion to see if it is having the desired effect on the counselor. Adjustments must be made if the strategy and techniques are not having the desired effect.

Evaluation of strategy results is relatively easy because skill goals are behaviorally defined and observable. If the goals have been reached, the strategies are judged effective (although not necessarily efficient). When goals have not been reached an assessment of the reasons for failure should transpire. Potential reasons are as follows:

1. The supervisee does not have the prerequisite knowledge and/or acquired behavior for successful participation in the strategy or strategies. These deficiencies should be filled through remedial work.

2. The supervisee was not motivated to participate in the strategy and reach the skills goals. A discussion of the counselor's desires, attitudes, and commitment to counseling could follow to determine whether or not they are appropriate.

3. The supervisor may have offered too little assistance with the strategy, and a more thorough treatment should be started. Sometimes a self-development strategy is not as effective as one with more supervisor input.

4. During the strategy implementation the counselor and/or supervisor may not have fully understood the strategy and/or goal. By correcting this error and putting heads together the supervisor and counselor can hypothesize what strategy would be more effective and then implement that strategy.

When follow-up has shown a supervision strategy to be accountable, a final task remains before termination. The skills and learning acquired by the counselor, in the context of supervised performance, should be generalized to other performance situations that are likely to present themselves in the future. Generalization of behavior change (Kanfer & Phillips, 1970b), and transfer of training to practical settings (Jakubowski-Spector, et al, 1971) is the ultimate success criteria for behavioral supervision.

Generalization and transfer are more probable if the counselor has been personally involved in the supervision process and has been allowed, and indeed encouraged, to provide input into supervised learning. The self direction of the counselor is a crucial component in the long-term effects of behavioral supervision.

Another factor in generalization and transfer is the amount of different situations to which the counselor has been exposed--the more the better! Even discussing or simulating situations that demand unfamiliar skills can help the counselor develop "response ability."

Weinrach's (1976) model for the systematic generalization of counseling skills adds a final test even beyond the demonstration of a skill behavior. The supervisee has truly mastered a skill and can generalize it to other situations when he/she can teach it to another person. As mentioned in Chapter 1, the "fully functioning" counselor who can do this teaching for all his/her skills is ready to become a supervisor.

BEHAVIORAL SUPERVISION: EMPIRICAL SUPPORT

Behavioral supervision is an arena where the learning theory principles found effective in other circumstances should be subjected to more applied research. The assumption that learning theory will function within supervision and with supervisee behaviors as it has in other environmental situations remains to be shown. Of the many techniques suggested in this section, few have been empirically supported by actual supervision research. For techniques which have not received research attention, the author has generalized validity from counseling research and practical supervision experience.

A small but credible body of supervision research suggests that, in terms of skill-behavior change (e.g., empathic responding), behavioral supervision is somewhat superior to experiential and psychotherapeutic methods that do not systematically utilize psychological learning theory principles (Birk, 1972; Boyd, 1973; Hansen, Pound, & Petro, 1976; Payne & Gralinski, 1968; Payne, Weiss, & Kappa, 1972; Payne, Winter,

& Bell, 1972). As reviewed in this Chapter, some of the activities of behavioral supervision, notably microcounseling, reinforcement, and modeling, have received strong empirical support. Moderate support also exists for simulation exercises, self appraisal, and peer supervision. In most of these activities the exact effect of learning theory principles is unknown, and in fact we often assume that effectiveness is because of learning principles. Research is needed to unravel the tangled and interacting effects.

The direction of research in counselor supervision seems to be changing. Comparative research is losing appeal simply because it addresses a moot question; the two major approaches (psychotherapeutic and behavioral) have both been supported to some extent and measuring their degree of effectiveness is a sticky and difficult empirical task in which measurement limitations may block significant findings. A different direction is represented by situation-specific research, i.e., investigating the separate effects of techniques and principles within supervision. This research may be a more productive route to unraveling the instrumental factors in counselor supervision.

PRACTICAL APPLICATION: ILLUSTRATIVE CASES

As mentioned previously in this Chapter, the behavioral supervisor can choose to follow a counselor-directed strategy and act as a consultant to the counselor, or a supervisor-directed plan can be chosen and the supervisor will act as an active trainer. Whichever thrust is chosen, a unique strategy is constructed to meet the learning needs of the supervisee. A number of cases will be presented to illustrate the two thrusts and several different strategies.

Case 1. An Unskilled Supervisee

This case involves a practicum supervisor and a beginning practicum student. When the supervisor reviewed the student counselor's performance in role-played exercises, it was apparent that fundamental interaction skills were lacking and inappropriate behavior (social chit-chat) was profuse. The student counselor also was very nervous and defensive.

The supervisor decided that enough time remained in the practicum course for the student counselor to remedy deficiencies and attain required performance objectives, so a recycling back to pre-practicum training was not done. In a critique session the supervisor and student counselor assessed the role-played counseling performance and areas for development were identified. Rather than attempting to reduce the many inappropriate behaviors that were evidenced, the supervisor elected to focus on replacing them with appropriate skills. In this manner less criticism was directed at the defensive student counselor.

A program of simulated training exercises was developed so that the counselor could attain the skills needed in order to begin counseling with actual clients in the practicum course. For several weeks the supervisor worked with the counselor in supervisory-training sessions; the supervisor employed verbal reinforcement, role playing, and modeling to help the counselor. Heavy extra-supervision training assignments were also completed by the counselor. At the end of the remedial training program the counselor entered supervised practice in the practicum course with real clients.

Epilogue. Remedial training within supervision is certainly not the ideal--and it is hopefully the exception. But a realistic fact is that the supervisor will continually encounter supervisees who are not functioning at required skill levels. Remedial work, if the supervisor and counselor are willing, is one alternative in this situation. Termination of supervision, or referral to remedial skill training, are the other alternatives. Needless to say, the counselor's continuation in supervised practice at a less than adequate skill level is professionally unethical.

Case 2. Microcounseling For A Skill Deficiency

A supervisor and group of practicing counselors evaluated their program of services and decided that program goals could be met more efficiently through group counseling. None of the counselors had received more than a superficial reading knowledge of group counseling, and they recognized their deficiency in group counseling skills.

The supervisor helped the counselors state desired skills in behavioral terms and then designed and conducted a microcounseling training program for the development of these goals. Microcounseling took the counselors through a sequence of

1. reading literature describing and illustrating the focal skills,

2. viewing videotapes of skill demonstrations,

3. performing the skills in simulated exercises and role-playing sessions, and

4. receiving performance feedback and supervision so that the focal skills could be refined through further practice.

Following microcounseling each counselor initiated a group counseling session with clients and received more supervision as skills were used in a real situation.

Case 3. Self-Managed Improvement

Mrs. X was an uptight practicing counselor who dealt with nervousness by becoming quite verbal and asking repetitive closed-ended questions. Her counseling could be described as authoritative information gathering and advice giving. The supervisor and counselor agreed upon the goals of relaxation and improved verbal techniques as areas for improvement in counseling performance. Mrs. X completed a self-instruction program of relaxation and the supervisor helped her transfer this learning into the counseling setting. Verbal techniques were improved by listening to taped examples of open-ended questions, reflections, and other effective counselor responses, and then systematically reinforcing herself each time she used one of the techniques correctly. Approved responses replaced a large percentage of the poor ones, and coupled with relaxation, Mrs. X improved her counseling. Positive feedback from the supervisor and counselees strengthened her new skills even more.

Case 4. Professional Assertion

A guidance director in a large city school system was discouraged over the lack-luster performance of most guidance staffs in the city schools. An assessment of the problem revealed that counselors expended a large portion of their time in clerical and quasi-administrative duties that were not a part of their job description. Investigation led to the discovery that these duties were assigned to or requested of the counselors by principals and assistant principals.

Among the steps which the guidance director took to rectify the problem was the supervision of head counselors toward the goal of becoming "professionally assertive." The head counselors were not providing the leadership necessary to maintain the counselors' role and function. The counselors were inappropriately subservient to the administration.

Group supervision sessions were held to discuss the problem, and the guidance director led training sessions on the specific skills involved in being professionally assertive in response to stressful situations. The circumstances leading to subservience were simulated and head counselors role played and practiced assertive techniques. These simulations helped develop the ability to maintain the counselors' legitimate role and function.

REFERENCES

Altekruse, M. K., & Brown, D. F. Counseling behavior change
through self analysis. Counselor Education and Supervision, 1969, 8, 108-112.

Arbuckle, D. S. Client perception of counselor personality.
Journal of Counseling Psychology, 1956, 3, 93-96.

Austin, B., & Altekruse, M. K. The effects of group supervisor roles on practicum students' interview behavior.
Counselor Education and Supervision, 1972, 12, 63-68.

Authier, J., & Gustafson, K. Application of supervised and
nonsupervised microcounseling paradigms in the training of
registered and licensed practical nurses. Journal of
Consulting and Clinical Psychology, 1976, 44(5), 704-709.

Bandura, A. Principles of Behavior Modification. New York:
Holt, Rinehart and Winston, 1969.

Beck, A. T. Cognitive Therapy and the Emotional Disorders.
New York: International Universities Press, 1976.

Bellucci, J. E. Microcounseling and imitation learning: A
behavioral approach to counselor education. Counselor
Education and Supervision, 1972, 12, 88-97.

Bergin, A. E., & Garfield, S. L. (Eds.) Psychotherapy and
Behavior Change. New York: John Wiley and Sons, 1971.

Bergin, A. E., & Jasper, L. G. Correlates of empathy in psychotherapy: A replication. Journal of Abnormal Psychology,
1969, 74, 447-481.

Birk, J. M. Effects of counseling supervision method and
preference on empathic understanding. Journal of
Counseling Psychology, 1972, 19, 542-546.

Bishop, J. B. Another look at counselor, client, and supervisor ratings of counselor effectiveness. Counselor Education and Supervision, 1971, 10, 319-323.

Blane, S. M. Immediate effect of supervisory experiences on counselor candidates. Counselor Education and Supervision, 1968, 8, 39-44.

Boyd, J. D. Microcounseling for a counseling-like verbal response set: Differential effects of two micromodels and two methods of counseling supervision. Journal of Counseling Psychology, 1973, 20, 97-98.

Boyd, J. D., & LaFleur, N. K. Self management: A basic counseling goal. Focus on Guidance, 1974, 7, 1-10.

Brown, D., & Cannady, M. Counselor, counselee, and supervisor ratings of counselor effectiveness. Counselor Education and Supervision, 1969, 8, 113-118.

Canada, R. M. Immediate reinforcement versus delayed reinforcement in teaching a basic interview technique. Journal of Counseling Psychology, 1973, 20, 395-398.

Carlson, K. W. Reinforcement of empathy: An operant paradigm for the training of counselors. Unpublished doctoral dissertation. Northern Illinois University, 1971.

Carter, D. K., & Pappas, J. P. Systematic desensitization and awareness treatment for reducing counselor anxiety. Journal of Counseling Psychology, 1975, 22(2), 147-151.

Cavior, N., & Marabotto, C. M. Monitoring verbal behaviors in a dyadic interaction. Journal of Consulting and Clinical Psychology, 1976, 44(1), 68-76.

Chang-Liang, R., & Denny, D. R. Applied relaxation as training in self-control. Journal of Counseling Psychology, 1976, 23(3), 183-189.

Clark, M. D. The effects of counselor supervisor's verbal reinforcements upon counselor trainees' verbal behavior. unpublished doctoral dissertation. Arizona State University, 1970.

Cogan, D. B. Survey of counselor competencies. Unpublished manuscript. Arizona State University, February, 1977.

Cormier, L. S., & Cormier, W. H. Developing and implementing self-instructional modules for counselor training. Counselor Education and Supervision, 1976, 16(1), 37-45.

Cormier, W. H.; Cormier, L. S.; Zerega, W. D.; & Wagaman, G. L. Effects of learning modules on the acquisition of counseling strategies. Journal of Counseling Psychology, 1976, 23(2), 136-141.

Dalton, R. F., & Sundblad, L. M. Using principles of social learning for communication of empathy. Journal of Counseling Psychology, 1976, 23(5), 454-457.

Dalton, R. F.; Sundblad, L. M.; & Hylbert, K. W. An application of principles of social learning to training in communication of empathy. Journal of Counseling Psychology, 1973, 20, 378-383.

Danish, S. J. Film-simulated counselor training. Counselor Education and Supervision, 1971, 11, 29-35.

Davidson, T., & Emmer, E. Immediate effect of supportive and non-supportive supervision behavior on counselor candidates focus of concern. Counselor Education and Supervision, 1966, 5, 27-31.

Delaney, D. J. Simulation techniques in counselor education: Proposal of a unique approach. Counselor Education and Supervision, 1969, 8, 183-188.

Delaney, D. J., & Eisenberg, S. The Counseling Process. Chicago: Rand McNally and Company, 1972.

Dimattia, D. J., & Arndt, G. M. A comparison of microcounseling and reflective listening techniques. Counselor Education and Supervision, 1974, 14, 61-63.

Dowd, E. T., & Blocher, D. H. Effects of immediate reinforcement and awareness of response on beginning counselor behavior. Counselor Education and Supervision, 1974, 13, 190-197.

Eisenberg, S., & Delaney, D. J. Using video simulation of counseling for training counselors. Journal of Counseling Psychology, 1970, 17, 15-19.

Ellis, A. Humanistic Psychotherapy. New York: McGraw-Hill, 1973.

Ellis, A., & Harper, R. A. A New Guide to Rational Living. No. Hollywood, Calif.: Willshire, 1975.

Eskedel, G. A. Symbolic role modeling and cognitive learning in the training of counselors. Journal of Counseling Psychology, 1975, 22(2), 152-155.

126

Fraleigh, P. W., & Buchheimer, A. The use of peer groups in practicum supervision. Counselor Education and Supervision, 1969, 8, 284-288.

Frankel, M. Effects of videotape modeling and self-confrontation techniques on microcounseling behavior. Journal of Counseling Psychology, 1971, 18, 465-471.

Franks, C. M. Behavior Therapy: Appraisal and Status. New York: McGraw Hill Book Company, 1969.

Friesen, D. D., & Dunning, G. B. Peer evaluation and practicum supervision. Counselor Education and Supervision, 1973, 12, 229-235.

Garner, A. M., & Smith, G. M. An experimental videotape technique for evaluating trainee approaches to clinical judging. Journal of Consulting and Clinical Psychology, 1976, 44(6), 945-950.

Goldfried, M. R., & Merbaum, M. (Eds.) Behavior Change Through Self Control. New York: Holt, Rinehart, and Winston, 1973.

Guttman, M. A. J. Reduction of the defensive behavior of counselor trainees during counseling supervision. Counselor Education and Supervision, 1973, 12, 294-299.

Guttman, M. A. J., & Haase, R. F. Generalization of micro-counseling skills from training period to actual counseling setting. Counselor Education and Supervision, 1972, 12, 98-108.

Hackney, H. J. Development of a pre-practicum counseling skills model. Counselor Education and Supervision, 1971, 11, 102-109.

Hackney, H., & Nye, S. Counseling Strategies and Objectives. Englewood Cliffs, N. J.: Prentice-Hall, 1973.

Hagan, L., & Boyd, J. D. Concept-specific and verbally manifest anxiety in the initial interview. Unpublished report, University of Virginia, 1976.

Hansen, J. C.; Pound, R.; & Petro, C. Review of research on practicum supervision. Counselor Education and Supervision, 1976, 16(2), 107-116.

Hector, M. A.; Elson, S. E.; & Yager, G. G. Teaching counseling skills through self-management procedures. Counselor Education and Supervision, 1977, 17(1), 12-22.

Herr, E. L. The perceptions of state supervisors of guidance of appropriateness of counselor function, the function of counselors, and counselor preparation. Counselor Education and Supervision, 1969, 8, 241-257.

Ivey, A. E. Microcounseling. Springfield, Illinois: Charles C. Thomas, 1971.

Ivey, A. E.; Normington, C.; Miller, C.; Morrill, W.; & Haase, R. Microcounseling and attending behavior: An approach to pre-practicum counselor training. Journal of Counseling Psychology (Monograph Supplement), 1968, 15, 1-12.

Jakubowski-Spector, P.; Dustin, R.; & George, R. Toward developing a behavioral counselor education model. Counselor Education and Supervision, 1971, 10, 242-250.

Kagan, N., & Schauble, F. G. Affect simulation in interpersonal process recall. Journal of Counseling Psychology, 1969, 16, 309-313.

Kahn, W. J. Self-managment: Learning to be our own counselor. Personnel and Guidance Journal, 1976, 55(4), 176-180.

Kanfer, F. Self-monitoring: Methodological limitations and clinical applications. Journal of Consulting and Clinical Psychology, 1970, 35, 148-152. (a)

Kanfer, F. H., & Phillips, J. S. Learning Foundations of Behavior Therapy. New York: John Wiley and Sons, 1970. (b)

Kelly, J. D. Reinforcement in microcounseling. Journal of Counseling Psychology, 1971, 18, 268-272.

Kloba, J. A., & Zimpfer, D. G. Status and independence as variables in microcounseling training of adolescents. Journal of Counseling Psychology, 1976, 23(5), 458-463.

Krumboltz, J. D. Revolution in Counseling. Boston: Houghton Mifflin, 1966. (a)

_____. Stating the goals of counseling. California Personnel and Guidance Association Monograph, 1966. No. 1. (b)

_____. Changing the behavior of behavior changers. Counselor Education and Supervision, 1967, 6, 222-229.

Lazarus, A. Behavior Therapy and Beyond. New York: McGraw Hill, 1971.

Levine, F. M., & Tilker, H. A. A behavior modification approach to supervision of psychotherapy. Psychotherapy: Theory, Research and Practice, 1974, 11(2), 182-188.

Mahoney, M. J., & Thoresen, C. E. Self Control: Power to the Person. Monterey, CA.: Brooks/Cole, 1974.

Mann, J. H., & Mann, C. H. The effect of role-playing experience on role-playing ability. In B. J. Biddle and E. J. Thomas (Eds.), Role-theory: Concepts and Research. New York: John Wiley and Sons, 1966.

Martin, D. G., & Gazda, G. M. A method of self-evaluation for counselor education utilizing the measurement of facilitative conditions. Counselor Education and Supervision, 1970, 9, 87-92.

Mathewson, R. H., & Rochlin, I. Analysis of unstructured self-appraisal: A technique in counselor education. Journal of Counseling Psychology, 1956, 3, 32-36.

Meichenbaum, D. Self instructional methods. In G. H. Kanfer & A. P. Goldstein (Eds.), Helping People Change. Elmsford, N. Y.: Pergamon Press, 1975.

Meichenbaum, D., & Cameron, R. The clinical potential of modifying what clients say to themselves. In M. J. Mahoney & C. E. Thoresen, Self-Control: Power to the Person. Monterey, CA.: Brooks/Cole, 1974.

Menne, J. M. A comprehensive set of counselor competencies. Journal of Counseling Psychology, 1975, 22(6), 547-553.

Miller, N. L. The effects of videotape procedures on counselor trainees' responses. Unpublished doctoral dissertation. Arizona State University, 1971.

Miller, C. D.; Morrill, W. H.; & Uhlemann, M. R. Micro-counseling: An experimental study of pre-practicum training in communicating test results. Counselor Education and Supervision, 1970, 9, 171-177.

Milliken, R. L., & Kirchener, R. Counselor's understanding of communication as a function of the counselor's perceptual defense. Journal of Counseling Psychology, 1971, 18, 14-18.

Mischel, W., & Grusec, J. Determinants of the rehearsal and transmission of neutral and aversive behaviors. Journal of Personality and Social Psychology, 1966, 3, 197-205.

Mooney, T. F., & Carlson, W. A. Counselor trainee emotional response to initial counseling-interview stress. _Journal of Counseling Psychology_, 1976, 23(b), 557-559.

Panther, E. E. Simulated consulting experiences in counselor preparation. _Counselor Education and Supervision_, 1971, 11, 17-23.

Payne, P. A., & Gralinski, D. M. Effects of supervisor style and empathy upon counselor learning. _Journal of Counseling Psychology_, 1968, 15, 517-521.

Payne, P. A.; Weiss, S. D.; & Iappa, R. A. Didactic, experiential, and modeling factors in the learning of empathy. _Journal of Counseling Psychology_, 1972, 19, 425-429.

Payne, P. A.; Winter, D. E.; & Bell, G. E. Effects of supervisor style on the learning of empathy in supervision analogue. _Counselor Education and Supervision_, 1972, 11, 262-269.

Perry, M. A. Modeling and instructions in training for counselor empathy. _Journal of Counseling Psychology_, 1975, 22 (3), 173-179.

Rank, R. C.; Thoresen, C. E.; & Smith, R. M. Encouraging counselor trainee affective group behavior by social modeling. _Counselor Education and Supervision_, 1972, 11(4), 270-278.

Ronnestad, M. H. Effects of modeling, feedback and experiential supervision on beginning counseling students: Communication of empathic understanding. Unpublished doctoral dissertation. University of Missouri, 1973.

Russell, R. K.; Miller, D. E.; & June, L. N. Group cue-controlled relaxation in the treatment of test anxiety. _Behavior Therapy_, 1974, 5, 572-573.

Russell, R. K.; Miller, D. E.; & June, L. N. A comparison between group systematic desensitization and cue-controlled relaxation in the treatment of test anxiety. _Behavior Therapy_, 1975, 6, 172-177.

Russell, R. K., & Sipich, J. F. Cue-controlled relaxation in the treatment of test anxiety. _Journal of Behavior Therapy and Experimental Psychiatry_, 1973, 4, 47-49.

Russell, R. K., & Wise, F. Treatment of speech anxiety by cue-controlled relaxation and desensitization with professional and paraprofessional counselors. Journal of Counseling Psychology, 1976, 23(6), 583-586.

Saltmarsh, R. E., & Hubele, G. E. Basic interaction behaviors: A micro-counseling approach for introductory courses. Counselor Education and Supervision, 1974, 13, 246-249.

Sanchez-Craig, B. M. Cognitive and behavioral coping strategies in the reappraisal of stressful social situations. Journal of Counseling Psychology, 1976, 23(1), 7-12.

Schwebel, M. Role playing in counselor training. Personnel and Guidance Journal, 1953, 32, 196-201.

Silverman, M. S., & Quinn, P. F. Co-counseling supervision in practicum. Counselor Education and Supervision, 1974, 13, 256-260.

Spiegler, M. D.; Cooley, E. J.; Marshall, G. J.; Prince, H. T.; & Puckett, S. P. Journal of Counseling Psychology, 1976, 23(1), 83-86.

Spivack, J. D. Critical incidents in counseling: Simulated video experiences for training counselors. Counselor Education and Supervision, 1973, 12, 263-270.

Sodetz, A. R. The effect of videotape microtraining on counselor behavior. Unpublished doctoral dissertation. University of Missouri, 1972.

Stefflre, B.; King, P.; & Leafgren, F. Characteristics of counselors judged effective by their peers. Journal of Counseling Psychology, 1962, 9, 335-340.

Stone, G. L., & Stebbins, L. W. Effect of differential pre-training on client self-disclosure. Journal of Counseling Psychology, 1975, 22(1), 17-20.

Stone, G. L., & Vance, A. Instructions, modeling, and rehearsal: Implications for training. Journal of Counseling Psychology, 1976, 23(3), 272-279.

Thoresen, C. E. (Ed.) Behavior Modification in Education. The Seventy-second Yearbook of the National Society for the Study of Education. Chicago: University of Chicago Press, 1973.

Thoresen, C. E., & Mahoney, M. J. Behavioral Self Control. New York: Holt, Rinehart and Winston, 1974.

Toukmanian, S. G., & Rennie, D. L. Microcounseling versus human relations training: Relative effectiveness with undergraduate trainees. Journal of Counseling Psychology, 1975, 22(4), 345-352.

Uhlemann, M. R.,; Lea, G. W.; & Stone, G. L. Effect of instructions and modeling on trainees low in interpersonal-communication skills. Journal of Counseling Psychology, 1976, 23(6), 509-513.

Wallace, W. G.; Horan, J. J.; Baker, S. B.; & Hudson, G. R. Incremental effects of modeling and performance feedback in teaching decision-making counseling. Journal of Counseling Psychology, 1975, 22(6), 570-572.

Walton, J. M. Peer perceptions of counselor effectiveness: A multiple regression approach. Counselor Education and Supervision, 1974, 13, 250-255.

Walz, G. R., & Johnston, J. A. Counselors look at themselves on video tape. Journal of Counseling Psychology, 1963, 10, 232-236.

Weinrach, S. G. A model for the systematic generalization of counseling skills. Counselor Education and Supervision, 1976, 15(4), 311-314.

Zytowski, D. G., & Betz, E. L. Measurement in counseling: A review. The Counseling Psychologist, 1972, 3, 72-86.

Chapter **4**

INTEGRATIVE APPROACHES

TO

COUNSELOR SUPERVISION

John D. Boyd

INTEGRATIVE APPROACHES TO COUNSELOR SUPERVISION

John D. Boyd

An integrative approach to counselor supervision may be said to exist when methodology from one or more supervisory approaches is integrated to form a new approach. Given this liberal definition, many different kinds of integrative approaches can be formed by creating various combinations of techniques. Although this "technique-mixing" process of creating integrative approaches is a rather unscientific endeavor, it probably represents the actual practice of supervision more accurately than any other supervisory approach. Helpers are renowned for their nurturant needs and their quest for new and more techniques to improve their helping effectiveness. Supervisors are no exception.

The author contends that most supervisors subscribe to Lazarus' (1971) principle of technical eclecticism. Supervisors attempt to arm themselves with a host of techniques drawn from various approaches to counseling and supervision, and then they construct integrative methodological approaches which are comfortable for them and effective for supervisees. The supervisors' rationale for this approach is that an integrative set of techniques prepares one to be more effective across the infinite variety of supervisor situations that will be encountered than does a single approach with a narrow range of techniques. The two approaches presented in this Chapter, the Carkhuff model and psychobehavioral supervision, are based upon the integrative rationale, and each attempts to integrate methodology from the psychotherapeutic and behavioral approaches to counselor supervision.

THE CARKHUFF SUPERVISORY-TRAINING MODEL

Perhaps the most well known integrative approach to the training and supervision of counselors is that developed by

135

Robert Carkhuff and associates (Carkhuff, 1969a, b; Carkhuff & Truax, 1965; Truax, Carkhuff, & Douds, 1964). Carkhuff's model is based on his theory of the helping process and the instrumental dimensions therein (Berenson & Carkhuff, 1967; Carkhuff & Berenson, 1967; Carkhuff, 1969a). Very briefly, Carkhuff's helping process may be described as having two principal phases --a downward or inward phase of exploring one's self and concerns with consequent increased awareness, and an upward or outward phase of emergent directionality. During the downward phase the counselor offers a psychologically facilitative relationship that enables the client to explore self and problems and activate personal resources. The important counselor-offered facilitative conditions at this phase of the helping process are empathic understanding, positive regard, personally relevant concreteness, genuineness, and counselor self-disclosure. As the helpee goes deeper in self exploration and receives high levels of these facilitative conditions, the counselor promotes a transition to phase two by offering the action-oriented helping conditions of confrontation and immediacy. These action-oriented conditions encourage helpee directionality and the resolution of concerns through constructive action.

Focus and Goals

The focus of Carkhuff's integrative approach to supervisory training are the facilitative interpersonal dimensions of empathy and respect, the facilitative and action-oriented dimensions of concreteness, genuineness, and self-disclosure, and the action-oriented dimensions of immediacy and confrontation. Goals of the Carkhuff approach are

1. to enable counselors to offer effective levels of the facilitative and action-oriented conditions and

2. to equip counselors with the skills of assisting helpees to construct and implement courses of action leading to constructive resolution of difficulties.

Methodology

Two of the most important aspects of Carkhuff's (1969a) supervisory methodology are the supervisor's level of therapeutic functioning and the integration of three learning modalities:

"Perhaps the most critical variable in effective counselor training is the level at which the /supervisor/ is functioning on those dimensions related to constructive helper change (p. 152)... Hopefully, the /supervisor/ is not only functioning at high levels on these dimensions but is also attempting to impart learnings concerning these dimensions in a systematic manner, for only then will he integrate the critical sources of learning - the didatic, the experiential, and the modeling" (p. 153).

Throughout the Carkhuff model the supervisor offers psychologically facilitative conditions to supervisees (usually a group of eight to ten) while concurrently leading them through a three-stage program of integrative learning activities: discrimination training, communication training, and training in developing effective courses of action.

Discrimination Training. In discrimination training the counselor first learns to make gross discriminations between counseling which offers high levels and that offering low levels of the facilitative and action-oriented dimensions. Written exercises (choosing the best response) and listening to recorded counseling are typical gross discrimination activities. After gross discrimination has been mastered, the counselor receives training in individual discriminations. Concentrating on one dimension at a time and with supervisory assistance, the counselor learns to articulate dimensions, clarify their functions and effects, and assess their levels on a five-point rating scale through shaping exercises.

Communication Training. High levels of discrimination are a necessary but insufficient condition for high levels of communication, so communication training begins when discrimination is mastered. Focusing on each dimension singly, the counselor is supervised while responding to tape material and role playing. The goal is to reach a minimally helpful level of communication (level 3) rather than try initially for higher levels. Upon the attainment of at least minimally helpful communication levels the counselor is allowed to engage in single interviews with helpees. Although the counselor has not received training in the development of effective courses of action, the single interviews require only a facilitative interaction and do not constitute long term counseling or psychotherapy. The interviews are helpful to helpees, and extremely beneficial to counselors who can raise their levels of facilitative communication through supervised experience.

Training in Developing Effective Courses of Action. As the counselor gains single interview experience, training proceeds into the development of effective courses of action. The counselor is introduced to the skills of developing effective courses of action with the helpee, as well as receiving instruction and practice in "preferred modes of treatment" such as systematic desensitization. When these skills have been developed and demonstrated, the counselor is offered supervised experience in full-term counseling and/or psychotherapy with individuals and groups.

137

Integrated Learning Modes. The three-stage program of supervisory training activities continually integrates the experiential, didactic, and modeling learning modes. Only a brief overview of the Carkhuff Model has been presented, and Volume I of Helping and Human Relations (Carkhuff, 1969a) is the authoritative source for a full description. In Volume I plus Volume II of the same title (Carkhuff, 1969b) are presented a voluminous amount of empirical support for the Model and interesting case examples from counseling and supervision.

Forward Movement

At the heart of Carkhuff's theory of helpgiving and supervisory training are the well-known "facilitative conditions," three of which (empathy, respect, genuineness) Carkhuff has reassessed and further validated following their original presentation by Carl Rogers (1957). Because these conditions have been given such a central position in counselor preparation, that a note be offered concerning their present and future use in supervision is prudent.

A review of practicum research from 1970 through 1974, conducted by Hansen, Pound, and Petro (1976), revealed that seventeen of twenty-five studies surveyed on supervision process and training examined some aspect of facilitative communication. Based on this research the investigators concluded that several supervision approaches are effective in teaching counselors to communicate facilitatively, and that supervision research also should investigate approaches for training other counselor skills.

To complement the conclusions of Hanson, et al, the author recommends that supervisors give a careful examination to the concept of empathy before assuming competence with the concept. As research on empathy and other facilitative conditions continues, the supervisor must translate this information into practice. Four such translations are the following:

1. Some research has contrasted that of Carkhuff (1969b) and has questioned the discriminate validity of facilitative conditions and like dimensions (Avery, D'Augelli, & Danish, 1976; Boyd & Pate, 1975; D'Augelli, Deyss, Gurney, Hershenberg & Sborofsky, 1974; Muehlberg, Grasgow, & Pierce, 1969). Supervisors may want to treat these dimensions as overlapping to form a general facilitation factor. Training in general facilitative responding would be more efficient than giving separate attention and time to each dimension.

2. The influences that supervisors attribute to empathy should not overlook the possibility of accompanying

variables. Dowling and Frantz (1975) have shown that
the empathic counselor or supervisor is likely to be
exerting a potent modeling influence, while Brady,
Rowe, and Smouse (1976) and Vitalo (1970) have shown
that operant reinforcement also can exist within
facilitative communication.

Responsibility in communicating facilitatively goes
beyond the mere offering of a "minimally constructive
level;" a certain level is not unquestionably bene-
ficial--the effect depends upon how the communication
influences the receiver. Modeling and reinforcement
increase the possible effects of facilitative
conditions.

For example, empathic responses to self deprecating
helpee statements at a higher frequency than positive
self reference may conceivably reinforce negative
ideation. The counselor who models certain affective
reactions to helpee problems, even though responding
at a level 3 on facilitative conditions, may influence
the helpee to imitate this reaction. In cases such as
these an adept clinician should look beyond rated
levels and deeper into the communication process.

3. Empathy rating is a supervisory activity where research
   has provided valuable information for practice.
   Melnick (1975) found that personal-social problems
   elicit more empathy from counselors than do vocational-
   educational concerns. Counseling in response to these
   two kinds of helpee problems may not be comparable on
   the empathy dimension.

   Blass and Heck (1975) and Avery, D'Augelli, and
   Danish (1976) have produced findings which suggest
   that a considerable amount of information about the
   helpee's phenomenological perspective is needed for
   accurate and valid empathy ratings. Supervisors
   probably need more than a "spot-check" of counselor
   performance in order to rate empathy competently.
   Further, Cicchetti and Ryan (1976) have warned that a
   rater can become attuned to a particular counselor's
   style and lose the ability to discriminate among the
   varying facilitation levels of that counselor's
   responses.

4. A training guideline for facilitative communication,
   drawn from the behavioral approach to supervision, has
   been supported by Gormally (1975) and Authier and
   Gustafson (1976). From their studies these researchers

point out that effective supervision or training treatments teach counselors to discriminate among desirable and undesirable responses, and then to increase the former and decrease the latter. Three kinds of learning probably occur: learning to discriminate, learning to make new kinds of desirable responses and increasing the frequency of existing desirable responses, and unlearning undesirable response habits or decreasing the frequency of undesirable responses. Communication training may thus involve a restructuring of socially learned response patterns.

Forward movement in the supervisory treatment of core facilitative conditions demands that we improve our expertise. But supervision expertise also must be extended to other counselor skills lest counselor supervision becomes a narrow methodology.

A PSYCHOBEHAVIORAL APPROACH TO COUNSELING SUPERVISION

Another integrative approach to counselor supervision was presented at the 1974 convention of the American Personnel and Guidance Association (Boyd, Nutter, & Overcash, 1974). Called a psychobehavioral approach, it is based upon the conclusions and practical outcomes of several years of integrative supervision experience in counseling practicum courses. Portions of a paper that accompanied the program presentation are reproduced here in a brief overview of psychobehavioral supervision.

Introduction

The psychobehavioral approach to counseling and psychotherapy (Woody, 1971) represents a conceptual rationale and technical frame of reference for the integration of methodology from the two broad dichotomies (London, 1964) of <u>insight counseling</u> and action-oriented or <u>behavioral counseling</u>. Insightists typically focus on helping their clients attain self-understanding or insight into their motives for behavior, while behavioral counselors focus directly on the client's maladaptive behavior and attempt to alter it toward more adaptive modes via the judicious use of psychological learning theory. The psychobehavioral stance posits that these two approaches have the potential for a <u>reciprocally beneficial</u> integration, and that the psychobehavioral counselor should practice a "technical eclecticism."

Counseling supervision seems to be another field where the psychobehavioral approach can be implemented efficaciously. The goals and methodology of supervision and counseling are quite similar, with the two major supervision approaches (i.e., psychotherapeutic/experiential and behavioral/didactic) being a corollary to the action-insight dichotomy of counseling. A psychobehavioral approach to supervision would thus integratively employ the methodology of both the psychotherapeutic and behavioral approaches.

Propositions

I. <u>The goals of psychotherapeutic and behavioral supervision are compatible and may be reciprocally beneficial.</u>

Psychotherpeutic supervision is directed at self awareness of inter- and intrapersonal dynamics as these are experienced in the counselor's relationships with the client and supervisor. The rationale for this awareness goal is that it will facilitate the counselor's personal adjustment, a prerequisite for competent counseling performance. Behavioral supervision is directed at the skills (behaviors) of counseling; it utilizes psychological learning theory to help the counselor learn desirable counseling skills and to extinguish or reduce counselor behavior which interferes with competent counseling.

Awareness of dynamics is a goal that is compatible with behavior change. Many theoreticians assert that dynamic awareness is a desirable process goal that facilitates behavior change. Moreover, when dynamics are operationally defined as covert sensory reactions to stimuli, and when they are identified as covert antecedents for overt counseling behavior, diagnosis in psychotherapeutic supervision merges with that in the behavioral approach.

II. <u>The methodology of psychotherapeutic and behavioral supervision can be integrated.</u>

Supervision activities of the psychotherapeutic approach consist of examining and discussing the dynamics which the counselor experiences in counseling and supervision. Emphasis is on discovering dynamics, finding their antecedents, and identifying their consequences (usually counselor behavior toward the client). The personalistic meanings which the counselor attributes to the stimuli encountered in counseling are explored.

The same kind of activity is involved in the behavioral assessment that should take place as the behavioral supervisor explores the counselor's undesirable counseling behavior. "Assessing the acquired meaning of stimuli is the core of social behavior assessment..." (Mischel, 1968, p. 190). Some activities in psychotherapeutic and behavioral supervision seem

quite similar, but the intended effects of these activities
are different. In the former, insight is the goal, and in the
latter the gathering of data necessary for constructing behavioral change strategies is the goal. With only slight modification of technique, a supervision session could both impart
insight and gather behavioral data. Following the exploration
of covert dynamics a behavior change strategy could be
employed.

III. Psychobehavioral supervision is personalistic.

An important characteristic of the psychobehavioral
approach is its personalistic nature. Just as flexibility
and versatility are essential ingredients for an effective
psychotherapist (Lazarus, 1971), these also are necessary
attributes for the psychobehavioral supervisor. This supervisor must practice a technical eclecticism, employing an
integrative methodology, as well as choosing and implementing
singular techniques from the psychotherapeutic and behavioral
approaches at certain times. The characteristics of the
counselor are a factor which should dictate methodology. The
counselor should be offered a form of supervision which is
uniquely tailored to the counselor's characteristics.

For example, supervision for an emotionally independent
counselor would be different from that for a counselor with
strong nurturance and the tendency to identify with client
problems. The highly dogmatic counselor may require a different approach than the counselor who is open to experience.
Counselors who avoid affect should have supervision to assist
them with their avoidance while the affect voyeur must be
assisted with the opposite problem.

IV. During the psychobehavioral supervision process the
counselor's learning needs change, thus dictating
alterations in supervision methodology.

Those supervision techniques and strategies that are
appropriate in helping beginners face their first few counseling sessions may not be appropriate during the final stage
of a semester- or year-long supervision process. Psychobehavioral supervision should be sensitive to the developmental changes of the counselor, and indeed should focus on
such developmental tasks and stages as process goals.

V. Psychobehavioral supervision should facilitate and
utilize the counselor's self-development ability.

Two key factors in counseling supervision are instrumental, perhaps more than any other factors, in the success
or failure of supervision. The supervisor's performance is one

factor, and the manner in which the counselor reacts to supervision is the other. The supervisor is totally responsible for his or her performance, and is partially responsible for the counselor's reaction. This partial responsibility refers to the supervisor's elicitation and reinforcement of counselor self-development. Posited here is that supervision should maximally facilitate and utilize the responsible self-development (Arnold, 1962) of the counselor.

Methodology

The practice of psychobehavioral supervision, as experienced by the authors (Boyd, Nutter, Overcash, 1974), has three identifiable stages. In each stage is an effort to integrate the methodology of the psychotherapeutic and behavioral approaches to supervision in accordance with the changing needs of the supervisee. The techniques referred to in the psychobehavioral supervision process (see Figure 4.1) are explained in Chapters 2 and 3 of this text.

Initial Stage. The initial stage of psychobehavioral supervision is a time (pre-practicum and the beginning of a practicum course) when counselors are preparing for and conducting their first few interviews. During the initial stage counselors are anxious and unsure of themselves. Advantageous methods from the psychotherapeutic approach are a self-development interview with the supervisor for an exploration of anxieties and expectations, interpersonal process recall focused on interpersonal dynamics, and experiential supervision focusing on intrapersonal dynamics. From the behavioral approach come self-appraisal techniques, global discrimination, much operant reinforcement from the supervisor, and the extra-supervisional use of modeling and structured exercises (microcounseling) for the improvement of skills. The purpose of this initial stage is to reduce anxiety, establish a cooperative working relationship with the supervisee, and begin self-directed skill improvement.

Intermediate Stage. This stage encompasses the learning that a neophyte counselor would gain during supervised practice (practicum course or in the field). Awareness of interpersonal dynamics has been acquired and initial anxieties have been overcome. The counselor may already have made skill improvements during the initial stage, and may feel secure enough so that a more confrontive supervision treatment is possible. Techniques from the psychotherapeutic approach appropriate at this stage are interpersonal process recall focusing on intrapersonal and interpersonal dynamics, the examination of dynamic patterns in counseling, therapeutic feedback from the supervisor regarding the dynamics of the supervisory sessions, and referral to counseling if the supervisee needs therapeutic assistance with problematic intra-

143

PSYCHOTHERAPEUTIC METHODOLOGY	BEHAVIORAL METHODOLOGY

Initial Stage

Self-development interview before counseling practice begins: focus on relationship between supervisee's personality and the counselor's role, anxieties, expectancies, and so forth	Self appraisal of competencies before practice begins
	Self appraisal of skill-behaviors in first few counseling sessions
Interpersonal Process Recall-- focus on interpersonal dynamics	Global discrimination: showing the counselor effective vs. inappropriate skill behaviors
Within a counseling-like interaction assist the counselor to explore those intrapersonal dynamics of his/her first attempts at counseling	Extensive use of operant reinforcement, support, and encouragement
	Refer supervisee to modeling tapes, structured exercises, and so forth, for self improvement of skills

Intermediate Stage

Interpersonal Process Recall-- focus on interpersonal and intrapersonal dynamics	Supervisor helps the counselor become more discriminative in self appraisal
Within unstructured supervision sessions: examination of the dynamic patterns in counseling	Identification of skill deficiencies, set goals, construct strategies, begin a self-management plan, reinforce self-directedness
Therapeutic feedback from the supervisor regarding the dynamics in supervision	Active training within supervision sessions via role playing, modeling, shaping exercises, and so forth
Referral to counseling if appropriate	

Terminal Stage

Assistance in using your experiencing as a therapeutic tool	Refinement of skills
Development of counselor's own style, less dependent on following guidelines	Emphasis on professional judgement: selecting and employing strategies
	Successful completion of self management projects

Figure 4.1. Psychobehavioral Supervision Process.

144

personal dynamics. Behavioral methodology includes a more discriminative evaluation of the counselor's performance, the identification of skill areas that need improvement, the initiation of self-managed behavioral strategies, and active training within supervision sessions via role playing, modeling, shaping, and so forth.

Terminal stage. This psychobehavioral stage is reached when the counselor is functioning at a capable level and supervisory-training activities are not needed. The supervisor can be a consultant without ever leaving that stance for active training. The counselor is assisted in the psychotherapeutic technique of using experiencing as a therapeutic tool. The counselor's most comfortable style of counseling emerges and a perspective on future development is gained. Behaviorally, the supervisor assists the counselor in refining skill-behaviors, making professional judgments concerning diagnosis and strategies, and in completing self-managed behavioral adjustments.

Summary

The psychobehavioral approach to counselor supervision is more of a conceptual rationale and technical frame of reference than a verified approach. The propositions and guidelines of the approach have arisen from practitioners' inquiry and have not been researched formally. If research were to be directed at the psychobehavioral notion, it would target specific supervision situations rather than the entire approach. This is the crux of the psychobehavioral notion--that supervision must discover what methodology is most effective in what situations, and that the practitioner must practice a technical eclecticism in order to match the best technique with situations encountered.

PRACTICAL APPLICATION: ILLUSTRATIVE CASES

Two case examples for integrative supervision are presented, the first of which applies an integrative approach to the supervision of group counseling. Case 1 is presented not only to demonstrate an integrative approach but also to illustrate that supervision methods can be adapted and applied to whatever skill-activity the counselor is attempting to practice, in this instance group counseling. The second case example is a lengthy session of counseling supervision which had a dramatically beneficial influence on a supervisee. The case demonstrates a variety of supervisory techniques employed within a rather intensive supervisory interaction.

Case 1*: An Integrative Approach To The Supervision Of Group
          Counseling

Sally is a counselor in a high school of three thousand students located on the outskirts of a city of a quarter million people. She was employed as an English teacher when the school first opened and eight years later became a counselor, a position she has held for the past six years. Sally is in her mid-thirties and lives by herself in what she describes as a well-ordered life. She further describes herself as a happy person and one who thoroughly enjoys working with adolescents.

Sally is a dedicated professional counselor, active in the state guidance organization and a perpetual student, always taking courses and attending workshops to upgrade her counseling skills. She is recognized by her colleagues as an aggressive and innovative counselor.

Sally does a lot of group counseling with a variety of themes and goals like career decision making, living with parents, weight watchers and self awareness. Sally describes her success with groups as good but lacking.

I do best when giving out information and am showing people how to run things, but I've never been able to get a group to, you know, really get together. Everything seems to go well when I talk and suggest different activities, but when I stop the group seems to stop.

By direct observation and listening to audio tape recordings of various groups the supervisor determined that Sally was attempting to facilitate groups predominently with a potpourri of techniques, exercises, and games without really having an understanding of timing and levels of group functioning. The resulting effect of Sally's leadership was to create an atmosphere of superficial acceptance and trust, one which lacked genuine cohesiveness, sharing and risk taking. Meaningful growth within the group membership was very low.

Further exploration with Sally revealed that, in actuality, Sally was using "technique" in an effort to form more humanized relationships. Sally had difficulty in assessing her own perceptions of what was occurring within herself and the group. This factor limited Sally's potential for establishing relationships with the members of the group and created an

_____

*This case was submitted by Dr. Richard Lear, Charlottesville, Virginia.

atmosphere of "doing to" rather than "exploring, experiencing, and sharing excitement, joy and a sense of caring."

Sally and her supervisor mutually determined that Sally needed to learn how to share the feelings and perceptions within herself and to understand that when these feelings are communicated, we fulfill ourselves and in turn give the members of a group the opportunity to fulfill themselves. Group supervision involved Sally's participation as a member of an unstructured group experience while concurrently cofacilitating a group with an experienced supervisor. Tape (video and audio) critique sessions were held immediately following the group sessions and in these the supervisor encouraged Sally through interpersonal process recall questions to explore her own feelings at various points of the group session. Emphasis also was placed on how she could better share her own feelings and perceptions with the members of the group.

As Sally developed more spontaneity within the group, her "experience" as a group member became rewarding and exciting. She became a group member in the affective sense, and progressed through the stages and crises which characterize group involvement. Following Sally's group membership experience she co-led a group with her supervisor who helped her develop the leadership skills necessary to facilitate the kind of group process she had experienced.

The results of supervision were gratifying. Sally learned to allow more time for the group to develop a working relationship by staying with the members at their various developmental stages and sharing her own feelings and perceptions as these were experienced. When Sally was adept in eliciting more self-exploratory behavior from group members, she was then supervised in the use of intervention strategies and techniques which helped the group members to do more in-depth exploration, try new behaviors, and develop a positive self perception.

Case 2: A psychobehavioral Supervision Session

The following five excerpts were transcribed from an audio-recording of the fourth supervision session with a counseling-practicum student who was enrolled in a master's degree program in guidance and counseling. Collectively the five excerpts illustrate the psychobehavioral approach to counselor supervision as the supervisor utilizes techniques from interpersonal process recall and experiential supervision, shifts to rational-emotive techniques for dealing with some of the counselor's ideational dynamics, and then closes the session with a behaviorally oriented role-playing exercise which combines modeling, skill practice, and social reward. The purpose of this integrative set of techniques is to help the counselor become aware of those dynamics which inhibited counseling progress, learn to control these dynamics, and replace inappropriate interview behavior with appropriate counseling skills.

At the time of this supervision session the counseling practicum was in mid-semester and the counselor (Bob) had conducted several interviews with other clients. In previous interviews Bob had demonstrated a congenial social manner, but this was accompanied by dominating verbal behavior, anxiety over counseling performance, and a lack of empathic communication. Within interviews Bob was so busy worrying about the "right thing to say" that he failed to listen attentively to the client.

Bob had a tendency to emotionally identify with clients, to experience sympathetic feelings for them, and to become frustrated when a solution to their concerns could not be found; all of these were causing him difficulty. Bob's frustration often changed to depression as he would blame himself for not being competent enough to solve client concerns.

In the interview which serves as the central topic for this supervision session, Bob encountered a client (Gail) whose sister had been killed five months earlier in an automobile accident. Coincidentally, Bob had also suffered the death of a loved one, his mother, six months before this interview. As Gail expressed grief over her sister's death, this stimulus evoked overwhelming feelings of grief within Bob. These feelings of grief, in addition to the previously mentioned dynamics of sympathy, frustration and depression, rendered Bob somewhat helpless in terms of proactive counseling performance.

First Excerpt

Supervisor (S):   I'd like to do a certain kind of supervision with you today. . . .and. . .the intent of the approach is to help you recall as much of the session as you can. The purpose of recalling is to help you examine some of your reactions, for example, as you mentioned to me earlier today, the reaction of identifying with the client.

Counselor (C): (laughing) That's really unhealthy, isn't it?

S: No, I'm not saying that, in fact, I hope we can examine your thoughts and feelings without judging.

C: O.K. What do you want to do?

S: Well, let's just discuss some things in general, and then look at portions of the videotape.

C: O.K.

S: How do you feel you got along with Gail (the client)?

C: I thought it was really easy for her to talk . . .just because I've gone through some of that, I thought I said some things that were . . .said things for her, which she was experiencing. Like the dreams.

S: And it was easy to bring up stuff like that because of what you've gone through?

C: Yea, we've shared the same things, at least I thought we had and that she was feeling those things.

S: Un, huh (nodding)

C: The only thing I guess I really didn't like about it was. . .when I was thinking in those sessions. . .I felt that I had added too much of my own personal experience and therefore taken away some opportunities that she might have had to keep on talking.

S: Un, huh. . .felt like you got into talking about your experience.

C: Yes. . .more than I wanted to. . .not that mine was different, it's just that I felt like she would have talked more.

Interpretation of the First Excerpt

The first excerpt demonstrates that the counselor had a superficial awareness of a troublesome dynamic pattern before supervision began. The counselor knew he had "identi-

149

fied" with the client, and gives a hint of self condemnation ("That's really unhealthy, isn't it?"). Given this state of awareness, the supervisor merely facilitated it with inter-personal process-recall questions, reflective responses, and directed supervision toward the goal of helping the counselor to more fully understand the counselor-client dynamic pattern.

Second Excerpt

S: Let's take a look at this tape, and by the way, I'll handle the on-off button, but please signal me any time you feel something significant is happening between you and the client. Either something that was going on with her. . .or. . .a feeling, thought, or experience which you had that you felt was significant. . .O.K.?

C: O.K.

A videotape excerpt was played in which the counselor began the counseling session by giving a five-minute monologue of personal information about himself.

S: Did she ask you about. . .

C: (Interrupting) No, I did that purposely because Frank (another supervisor) observed last week's interview and said that I should be more self disclosing, so that's why I did it. . .I was uncomfortable doing it that way . . .except that I thought. . .well, here it is, five minutes of me. But I really with-drew from that other client.

S: How do you think this beginning affected the client?

C: I don't know. . .what her reaction was.

S: Let's see it.

Interpretation of Second Excerpt

Video playback revealed to the counselor and supervisor that the personal monologue had not damaged the interview, but to speculate exactly how the client interpreted it was difficult. From the monologue incident both the counselor and the supervisor understood the fact that the counselor had been affected dramatically by the other supervisor's advice of the

150

previous week, and had held a very definite objective (to disclose) in his mind that influenced his counseling behavior. This interpretation was made later in the session.

> S: You look as though you had this objective to disclose in your head and wanted so much to do it. . .because it was a way to improve your counseling. . .that you just blurted it out in the very beginning.

> C: Yea, I guess so. (downcast facial expression)

> S: No harm done! In fact, maybe this behavior is a good way to learn something about yourself. . .that when your needs are strong, in this case to improve performance by disclosing, they can propel you into acting in certain ways.

Third Excerpt

The third excerpt occurred shortly after the second one, and the supervisor's goal continued to be dynamic understanding. However, the focal dynamics of this portion of the session became the counselor's perfectionistic demands, his performance mistakes, and a subsequent condemnation of himself. After viewing a videotaped segment of the interview in which the counselor had ignored the client's feelings and had launched into a treatise on his own grief reactions to parental loss, the tape was stopped at the insistence of the counselor, and the following dialogue ensued.

> C: That's. . .that's really bad. That's just really bad. . .That's just really bad! (Voice escalates in loudness) (Laugh) Turn it back on, oh, let's hope it gets better.

> S: What are you reacting to?

> C: I'm talking too much! That has nothing to do with. . .I don't want to do that!

> S: Well, how did you get into it? What ticked off a reaction in you so that you started talking about your mother?

> C: Probably thinking. . .that unless I explained a little bit more she wouldn't understand that I understood. But I went so far into my own thing. One week I withdraw and don't say

151

anything about myself and the next week that's
all I talk about. I just want to tell myself
to shut up!

S: I think what you're looking for is a middle
ground. . .where you're making disclosures
and being genuine. . .enough to let the
client know that you've had those same
experiences and are really with it.

C: Yea, that's it. . .I know.

S: But keep the focus on him. . .if we can say
there's a "boo boo" here it's that. . .where
you maintain too much focus on yourself and
not on her.

C: Can we stop looking at it (the videotape)
. . .(nervous laugh). . .I don't want to see
the rest. Turn it off! That probably sums
up the whole thing!

S: Bob, are you "awfulizing"* this thing now?

C: No, no. . .yes, I am. It is awful to me, I
don't want to be like that!

S: O.K. That's why we want to look at it.
Because if you can get in touch with some of
the things which went through you emotionally,
cognitively. . .during this counseling
session. Those are variables which precip-
itated your keeping a focus on yourself.

C: O.K. (very subdued tone, obviously upset)

S: And it's not awful. . .(noticing the counselor's emotion). . .hmm??

C: Turn it on. . .(the counselor is teary eyed)

(fifteen second silence)

S: What's going on now? (in a soft and warm
tone)

---

*Awfulizing is a term which is frequently used in the liter-
ature on rational-emotive therapy. It means a tendency to
exaggerate the aversiveness of something or someone.

C: I see that as awful (voice trembling). . .
it's not the way I want to be at all (soft
crying).

S: The way you are is not the way you want to be.

C: The way I am in that tape is not the way I
want to be in a counseling session. (continued voice tremor) (long silence) It's
frustrating being at one end or the other.
Not. . .not reaching the middle, not. . .One's
as bad as the other. Two weeks ago it was
that I wasn't involved and this one is bad
on the other aspect. Why do I do that?

S: Sounds as though you're really frustrated
because you go one way or the other.

C: Yea, I can't. . .I am!

S: I guess I can't agree with you that this is
awful. . .let me tell you what I mean.
Whenever you talk to someone about an
emotional experience they're having, it
sometimes taps the emotional things that you
are working on--that are alive in your life.
There's a great drawing out of your personal
material, and it's very hard to deal with
that. You know what I mean?

C: Uh, huh.

S: Ah. . .so that if somebody had said to me
before your interview, hey, this client is
going to talk to Bob about the death of her
brother, I would have said, the chances are
very great. . .that Bob is going to have a
tough time dealing with that emotionally,
because it's going to remind him of the pain
he's gone through and is going through. . .
(counselor nods). . .and I wouldn't have
said, Bob is really going to do a lousy job
with this client because he's such a lousy
counselor and it's going to be awful! Because
. . .if it had been me in there talking to a
client who had a problem similar to mine, I
would have found it difficult to deal with
that. . .and I probably would have done some
things which under other circumstances I
wouldn't have done. I would have made
boo-boos!

C: <u>You</u> wouldn't have. . .cause I don't see you that way at all.

S: You see me as perfect?

C: Almost. . .yea. You really have it under control I think.

S: Well, that's a nice compliment except that it's unrealistic (laughing and smiling).

C: I don't know that side of you, I just see you as extremely competent, that's all!

S: I think I am competent. . .but what I'm saying to you is that having emotional experiences like you had in this session. . .does not . . .it doesn't mean that you're not competent!

C: But not as effective as I could have been.

S: Probably not, yea. And that's not bad. . . that's realistic. . .whenever a client presents a problem that hooks your emotions one of the first things you must ask yourself is "can I handle it."

(The supervisor continued by exposing Bob to several examples of counselors identifying with client problems and thereby losing their effectiveness.)

C: Yea, I see what you mean.

S: But another thing that is happening to you today, in addition to this identification, is what I think you've been doing all semester. You find something you're doing which is not desirable, which you wish you had not done, and then you start awfulizing and putting yourself down. . .for not being perfect.

C: (Crying). . .but I want to be perfect.

S: Why. . .do you want to be perfect? I'm serious, that's a good question, why do you want to be perfect? What will you have when you're perfect that you don't have now?

C: More self respect. . .(long silence).

154

S: Maybe you should look at ways of getting more self respect, in ways other than being perfect. . .because that's a delusion. . . cause you're never going to be perfect.

C: No, so I won't be a counselor (still teary eyed). I'll be perfect in something else!

S: Is it difficult for you to have self respect and acceptance, as long as you're making boo-boos. . .in counseling or anything else?

C: Yes; counselors can't make mistakes because they are dealing with people's lives. They shouldn't leave people worse off after counseling.

S: You think that your client is now worse off?

C: No, but I don't want her to have all that information and feelings about me. If I lay out all that garbage she probably will. I won't be able to help her as much, she won't respect me. Does that make sense?

S: I think you are imposing your standards of perfection upon her. (counselor laughs) I think you're saying "she's not going to like or respect me because I wasn't a perfect counselor."

C: She probably won't know that I'm not a perfect counselor!

S: That's right, good! (counselor and supervisor laughing softly)

C: She probably won't know but I know. . .she won't know she got a raw deal.

S: Hold it! I thought we established about five minutes ago that she (the client) didn't have any bad reactions to this counseling session--that you really didn't leave her worse off than before and give her a raw deal.

C: I know.

S: O.K. so that's not an excuse to disturb yourself, right?

C: Yea, I guess.

S: Do you see how you just used it to upset yourself? But it's not a logical reason, so let's wipe it out!

C: (Laughing at himself) All right, I guess.

S: You really hate to give it up, don't you. Even though you know it's an irrational notion, not based on fact, you keep telling yourself you are a lousy counselor and person. In fact you try to make up reasons to support the nutty notion.

C: (Laughing) I guess I know she had a pretty good session.

S: So what's left to disturb yourself with. . .

C: Those little tiny imperfections.

S: Right, some boo-boos like focusing too much on yourself. And the reasons you did that were probably some encouragement last week from Frank, to disclose, and the fact that this client's problem tapped a problem which you are dealing with yourself.

C: But I would like to have more control than that!

S: That's why we're here in supervision. . .to help you work out this thing. . .but we can't do that until you stop awfulizing your mistakes and demanding a perfect performance.

C: O.K., O.K., turn it on.

S: Bob, before we look at more, can you tell me why this tape is not awful? I'm serious now, it's important for you to know why it's not awful, so give it a try.

C: It's not awful because I can be expected to be somewhat emotionally involved since I am still going through that myself. It's not awful because the whole session turned out well, and that she liked me and I think respected me when she was finished. And it was helpful to her.

Interpretation of the Third Excerpt

A great deal of rational emotive intervention was employed in this third segment because Bob began to engage in a self defeating pattern of intrapersonal ideational dynamics which he had exhibited in previous supervision sessions. Bob had made some performance mistakes (i.e., identified with the client and dominated the interview with self reference), then proceeded to unrealistically exaggerate their consequences and implications, and completed the sequence by depressing himself with self condemnatory ideation. Breaking up this intrapersonal dynamic pattern was necessary so that the counselor could regain "free attention," learn from mistakes, and develop appropriate skills.

For those unfamiliar with rational emotive technique the supervisor's behavior may seem quite forceful, but such confrontation is often necessary if an individual is to break out of an illogical ideational set. The supervisor identified Bob's irrational ideas, vigorously disputed them, and then forced Bob to dispute them. Bob's ability to dispute his awfulizing was a positive sign indicating that he had gained an insight into his irrational thinking habit, and that he could overcome it. The sign proved to be valid as Bob immediately calmed down and ceased the awfulizing ideation.

Various psychotherapeutic techniques could have been used by the supervisor in response to Bob's emotional upset over his performance mistakes. The rational emotive technique was preferred because the supervisor had used it effectively in therapy, and because prior reflections and encouragement had not been sufficient to discourage Bob from his self disturbing dynamics.

Fourth Excerpt

Following the rational-emotive confrontation supervision returned to an examination of the dynamics which comprised the counselor's identification with the client's problem. As this fourth excerpt progresses the supervisor's techniques change. Initially, open leads and reflective responses were used to help the counselor understand the dynamics which constituted his emotional identification, then the supervisor slowly begins to focus on the counselor's skill-behavior and to encourage the counselor to explore alternative ways of responding to the client which would have been more appropriate. The supervisory approach gradually shifts from the psychotherapeutic model to the behavioral model.

S: What feelings did you have there (referring to an incident on the videotape)?

C: I was thinking that's just how it is, it feels that way, like it will never go away. People say your pain will pass but it doesn't.

S: What Gail said about her grief reminded you of yours? (Counselor nods) and you really got into your grief, felt it again? (Counselor nods)

S: (Silence). . .where was Gail while you were feeling your grief. . .what do you think was going on in her?

C: (Silence). . .I don't know. . .I guess she was listening to me talk about it.

S: Un hum. . .

(Videotape segment was viewed.)

S: What's going on here?

C: Just another of those places where. . .she mentioned fears about losing more loved ones . . .and I could recall doing exactly that . . .

S: How did you respond to her. . .I mean. . .as you thought about your having done that. . . what then did you say to Gail?

C: Well, there it is, you can see it!

S: What do you see?

C: I see myself talking about me everytime she pushes my button.

S: What would you rather have done?

C: Talked about her.

S: O.K., let's look at some places where your emotional button was pushed, and you focused on yourself, and let's find some better ways to have responded. O.K.? (Counselor nods)

(Videotape segment was viewed.)

158

S: Here's a good place. Was your button pushed here?

C: I guess.

S: You're recalling how little time you feel you spent with your mother, responding to what Gail said about not spending enough time with her sister. (Counselor nods)

S: What would have been a better response?

C: Oh. . .(silence). . .I don't know! What could I say?

S: To answer that, maybe we should identify what it is you should be trying to do in an initial interview. . .and then find a response which does those things.

C: I'm trying just to help her talk about her problem. . .I guess! (Frustration evident in the counselor's voice)

S: And let me add something to that. . .you are trying to communicate understanding while helping the client explore her thoughts and feelings. . .does that sound right?

C: Yes, but how do you do all that. . .there's so much you're supposed to be doing!

S: It sounds like a lot, doesn't it? (Counselor nods) But it's far easier than you think, Bob. Let's take a simple verbal technique that we've talked about in seminar--the reflective response. If you had used one right here it would have communicated empathy and encouraged the client to further explore her concerns. That one little response would have done all that!

C: (The counselor is silent, attentive, yet with an exasperated facial expression. The supervisor interpreted it as indicative of the counselor's feelings of helplessness and incompetence.)

S: (Smiling). . .looks easier than it is I guess. . .can you think of a reflective response that would have fit here?

159

C: . . .ah. . .You're wishing you had spent more
    time with her.

S: Great. . .see how easy that was. (Both the
    supervisor and counselor are now laughing,
    at themselves and the struggle to solicit
    one reflective response from the counselor.)
    This is not the only one, we could make up
    lots of reflective responses, the crucial
    thing is just to communicate the deep
    perceptions, feelings, and attitudes you
    hear from the client.

C: Yes. . .and I really do understand what she's
    going through!

S: Right, you have a reservoir of empathic
    sensitivity that. . .well I'm sure few others
    have. . .because of your common experience.
    Let's look at some other points where you
    could use this strength by being empathic.

    The counselor and supervisor examined several more
segments where a reflective response and/or open-ended lead
was constructed to replace inappropriate counselor responses.
Appropriate counselor disclosures were also practiced. The
counselor seemed to be gaining confidence and skill when
suddenly he encountered a segment on the videotape which
stymied him--his emotional button was pushed again! The client
was discussing dreams about her deceased sister, dreams which
were filled with hostility toward survivors of the car wreck
which claimed her sister's life. Dynamics in the client
exactly paralleled those in the counselor, and the supervisor
sensed an emotional impasse but didn't understand it. As a
method of better understanding the counselor's dynamics, helping
the counselor to understand himself, and demonstrating effective
counselor responding, the supervisor entered role playing with
the counselor.

Fifth Excerpt

S: Bob, why don't you play the role of the
    client, and I'll be the counselor, O.K.?
    And we'll see what turns up, and at least you
    can see one way of dealing with dreams.

C: O.K. I'm the client. . .ah. . .I sometimes
    have a dream about the wreck, and the guy
    who was driving the car is standing there. . .

160

S: He wasn't harmed?

C: No, and he's standing there. . .and I just want to scream at him. . .

S: What would you like to say to him. . .

C: (Interrupting) that he shouldn't be here, that it isn't fair. . .I just almost want to hit him.

S: It seems so unjust that he wasn't hurt. . . that you lost your sister and there he stands; it's like he's responsible for her death and. . .

C: (Obvious tension in the counselor, fists clenched, jaw muscles prominent from clenched teeth) Yes, I want to hurt him but know it won't do any good.

S: Nothing you could do to him would bring her back, or even take away your pain.

C: (The counselor's head is drooped, hands hanging loosely)

Interpretation. The role-playing exercise has thus far helped Bob gain a personal insight about his own anger. Vicariously, he has been therapeutically affected. While this is certainly desirable because it promotes a needed dynamic change in Bob (i.e., to resolve attitudes and feelings about his mother's death), it does not teach the counseling skills which Bob must acquire for an improved performance. In the next few minutes of this excerpt the supervisor attempts to bring closure to the therapeutic experience and move on to skill building, showing Bob that effective counseling skills promote the kind of insight he has just experienced.

S: (Supervisor leaves role playing and reenters his own role) Bob, how do you feel about the way I've responded?

C: I think you're right, that it doesn't do any good to be angry.

S: You've found this out for yourself. . .when your mother died?

C: Yes, and today it fell into place.

S: How did it fall into place?

161

C: Cause of what you said. I was. . .almost hated my father because he had not treated mother well. . .but there's no use. . .

S: Bob, let me take you away from. . .your own feeling. . .look at all I've said to you. . . just a few reflections. . .but they helped you look at yourself and learn something.

C: Yea. . .

S: I didn't do much work at all. . .just listened to what was going on in you and put it into words. . .and if we had gone further I probably would have used some leads, and even some RET things if there were some irrational ideas uncovered.

C: O.K.

S: Let's switch roles, I'm the client and you are the counselor. O.K., slow and easy. . . O.K. . .(Supervisor now enters the client's role for the role-play exercise). I have these dreams about the driver of the car in which my sister was killed and they're really upsetting.

C: What are the dreams like?

S: Oh. . . I see the wrecked car and the driver is standing there looking at it. . .and I just want to walk up and start beating on him.

C: What are some of the things you'd like to say to him?

S: You shouldn't be here, it's not fair that you're here. . .Look what you did to my sister. . .I just want to destroy him. . . hurt him. . .

C: Dr. Boyd, I. . .I don't know how to explain this. . .(The counselor is stumped and leaves the role playing to seek help from the supervisor.)

S: What could you say just reflectively. . . you're trying to help me (the client) understand what's going on inside. . .

C: Ah. . .O.K. . .(Reentry to role playing)
. . .You really resent the fact that he's
alive. . .that your sister died and it
doesn't seem fair to you. . .

S: (Back in the client role) Yea, yea, I guess
that's what it is. . .I really feel like I
want to destroy him. . .but. . .but even if
I did that it doesn't seem like it would
help. . .

C: (Leaving role playing, Bob again seeks
guidance) I guess my next rambling thought
is what would your brother want you to do.

S: O.K., that's a thought-provoking question,
but let's not try to give the client an
answer, Bob, just reflect, O.K., just help
the client explore. . .try reflecting what
I just said. . .I'll say it again (Reentry
to client role) I just feel like really
destroying him, punishing him in the worst
way. . .but it wouldn't make things any
better.

C: It wouldn't do you any good. . .it's futile
. . .to seek revenge.

S: (Leaving role playing to reward the counselor)
See!? All you have to do is reflect that
stuff because when I heard you say it's
futile to seek revenge that sums it up
perfectly. Inside I'm saying yes, that's
just the way it is.

C: Yea. . .I see. . .it's just hard for me to
only reflect and not jump in with a solution.

S: There's much more you can do than just
reflect, you can offer leads, share your
perceptions, and open up alternatives--
but you can do all of this in a manner which
does not remove responsibility from the
client. You can do this without offering
solutions. Let's try it. . .I'm the client
and you respond flexibly with leads and
responses.

S: (As client) I've got all this anger toward
the driver, and I want to hurt him but even
if I did. . .vengence would be pointless. . .

and I'm just stuck here with all these lousy feelings, there isn't anything I can do.

C: So, you're really confused and wondering what to do with the feelings you have.

S: Yes, there's nothing I can do. . .

C: Maybe you should allow yourself some time to be confused.

S: What do you mean?

C: (Laughing, because the supervisor as client is pressing for an answer) Maybe it's all right to be angry and hurt, natural.

S: Yea, but how can I be sure of that and how long will it take?

C: (Silence, then the supervisor prompts the counselor to reflect). . .seems like forever getting over some things.

S: Bob, that's great, you're really with me!!

C: (In an exuberant tone) Yea, Oh I just never think of these things!! I think of solutions.

S: What you did here that was so good was to give me several reflections, accurate ones, and then when you thought I was demanding that my grief go away, you offered a thought about allowing myself to have it. Then when I pushed you for answers you couldn't give, that no one could give, you went back to reflecting my frustration. That was good counseling, quite appropriate for a first interview.

C: Yea, I can't believe it.

S: It really helped me. All you did was really listen and reflect, you weren't responsible for coming up with quick solutions. You did share a constructive thought, but not a solution.

C: I don't like the responsibility of finding solutions. . .this is so much easier. . .and better.

164

Epilogue

This particular supervision session was the turning point in the laboratory practicum for Bob. Before this session he had been plagued with an excessive amount of performance anxiety, a lack of confidence, and an inability to use basic counseling skills such as empathic responding, open-ended leads, and genuine sharing responses. After this fourth supervision session Bob's performance improved remarkably as he continued to counsel with Gail in a second interview. He was much more empathic than in any previous interviews, his verbosity was significantly reduced, and appropriate reflections and leads were numerous. Gail's exploration of her grief and fears about death was enhanced and reached a depth of self disclosure which is normally not present in a second interview. She continued counseling with Bob for a total of four interviews.

Bob went on to complete the laboratory practicum course in a satisfactory manner, making rapid skill improvements during the last half of the semester. Counseling became an enjoyable activity for him, one that brought him a sense of competence. Personally, Bob made great strides in reestablishing a relationship with his father which had deteriorated since his mother's death.

The psychobehavioral approach to supervision was probably a more efficacious treatment for Bob than either a strictly psychotherapeutic or behavioral approach. Psychotherapeutic supervisory techniques were successful in helping Bob break up the blockade of intrapersonal dynamics which prohibited his skill improvement, but the therapeutic treatment was obviously insufficient to produce effective counseling skill-behavior as evidenced by Bob's initial struggle within the role-playing exercises to perform fundamental listening and responding skills. Yet, through the learning paradigm of role playing (and in the absence of his usual prohibitive dynamics) Bob began to replace inappropriate social behaviors with approved counseling skills, and this transformation continued throughout the semester.

REFERENCES

Arnold, D. L. Counselor education as responsible self development. Counselor Education and Supervision, 1962, 1,
185-192.

Authier, J., & Gustafson, K. Application of supervised and
nonsupervised microcounseling paradigms in the training of
registered and licensed practical nurses. Journal of
Consulting and Clinical Psychology, 1976, 12, 63-68.

Avery, A. W.; D'Augelli, A. R.; & Danish, S. J. An empirical
investigation of the construct validity of empathic understanding ratings. Counselor Education and Supervision,
1976, 15(3), 177-183.

Berenson, B. G., & Carkhuff, R. R. Sources of Gain in Counseling and Psychotherapy. New York: Holt, Rinehart and
Winston, 1967.

Blass, C. D., & Heck, E. J. Accuracy of accurate empathy
ratings. Journal of Counseling Psychology, 1975, 22(3),
243-246.

Boyd, J. D.; Nutter, J.; & Overcash, S. A psychobehavioral
approach to counseling supervision. Program and paper
presented at the American Personnel and Guidance Association Convention, New Orleans, Louisiana, 1974.

Boyd, J. D., & Pate, R. H. An analysis of counselor verbal
response scale scores. JSAS: Catalogue of Selected
Documents in Psychology, 1975, 5, 198.

Brady, D.; Rowe, W.; & Smouse, A. D. Facilitative level and
verbal conditioning: A replication. Journal of Counseling
Psychology, 1976, 23(1), 78-80.

Carkhuff, R. R. Helping and Human Relations, Volume I. New
York: Holt, Rinehart and Winston, 1969. (a)

_____. Helping and Human Relations, Volume II. New York: Holt, Rinehart and Winston, 1969. (b)

Carkhuff, R. R., and Berenson, B. G. Beyond Counseling and Psychotherapy. New York: Holt, Rinehart and Winston, 1967.

Carkhuff, R. R., & Truax, C. B. Training in counseling and psychotherapy: An evaluation of an integrated didactic and experimental approach. Journal of Consulting Psychology, 1965, 29, 333-336.

Cicchetti, D. V., & Ryan, E. R. A reply to Beutler et. al.'s study: Some sources of variance in accurate empathy ratings. Journal of Consulting and Clinical Psychology, 1976, 44(5), 858-861.

D'Augelli, A. R., Deyss, C. S.; Guerney, B. G., Jr.; Hershenberg, B.; & Sborofsky, S. L. Interpersonal skill training for dating couples: An evaluation of an educational mental health service. Journal of Counseling Psychology, 1974, 21(5), 385-389.

Dowling, T. H., & Frantz, T. T. The influence of facilitative relationship on imitative learning. Journal of Counseling Psychology, 1975, 22(4), 259-263.

Gormally, J. A behavioral analysis of structured skills training. Journal of Counseling Psychology, 1975, 22(5), 458-460.

Hansen, J. C.; Pound, R.; & Petro, C. Review of research on practicum supervision. Counselor Education and Supervision, 1976, 16(2), 107-116.

Lazarus, A. Behavior Therapy and Beyond. New York: McGraw Hill, 1971.

London, P. The Modes and Morals of Psychotherapy. New York: Holt, Rinehart and Winston, 1964.

Melnick, R. R. Counseling responses as a function of method of problem presentation and type of problem. Journal of Counseling Psychology, 1975, 22(2), 108-112.

Mischel, W. Personality and Assessment. New York: John Wiley and Sons, 1968.

Muehlberg, N.; Drasgow, T.; & Pierce, R. A factor analysis of therapeutically facilitative conditions. Journal of Clinical Psychology, 1969, 25(1), 93-95.

Rogers, C. R. The necessary and sufficient conditions of therapeutic personality change. Journal of Consulting Psychology, 1957, 21, 95-103.

Truax, C. B.; Carkhuff, R. R.; and Dowds, J. Toward an integration of the didactic and experiential approaches in counseling and psychotherapy. Journal of Counseling Psychology, 1964, 11, 240-247.

Vitalo, R. L. Effects of facilitative interpersonal functioning in a conditioning paradigm. Journal of Counseling Psychology, 1970, 17, 141-144.

Woody, R. H. Psychobehavioral Counseling and Therapy, New York: Appleton-Century-Crofts, 1971.

Chapter **5**

THE

SYSTEMS APPROACH

TO

COUNSELOR SUPERVISION

John D. Boyd

THE SYSTEMS APPROACH TO COUNSELOR SUPERVISION

John D. Boyd

Systems technology has had an auspicious debut in counseling and guidance during the last decade. The systems approach has been proposed as an accountable one for counselor education (Berenstein & LeComte, 1976; Canada & Lynch, 1975; Horan, 1972; Saylor, 1976; Thoresen, 1969; Winborn, Hinds, & Stewart, 1971) and the programatic delivery of helping services (Blocher, Dustin, & Dugan, 1971; Hosford & Ryan, 1970; Ryan & Zeran, 1972; Schmuck & Miles, 1971; Shaw, 1973). The ACES Committee On Counselor Effectiveness (ACES, 1969) has recommended that supervisors be trained in systems techniques.

The systems approach to counselor supervision is defined here as the application of systems technology to the supervisory function. The skills involved are in the form of thought processes, and the approach itself is a thinking mode: "a way of organizing and conceptualizing a phenomenon that will lead to the realization of specified goals" (Blocker, Dustin, & Dugan, 1971, p. 28). The systems approach is

> a disciplined way of analyzing as precisely as possible an existing situation by determining the nature of the elements which combine and relate to make the situation what it is, establishing the interrelationships among the elements, and synthesizing a new whole to provide means of optimizing system outcomes" (Ryan & Zeran, 1972, p. 13).

In no way is the suggestion made that any of the approaches presented in this book are sufficient individually for the supervisory function, and this is true for the systems approach. However in one place the systems approach particularly is applicable and valuable, and this is in the planning and management of a program of services. The supervisor can use systems techniques in the operation of a supervision program and when supervising the planning and management of a helping-services program.

171

FOCUS AND GOALS

In the psychotherapeutic, behavioral and integrative approaches to supervision the focus is directly on the counselor and the counselor's performance. A distinguishing feature of the systems approach is that the counselor and his/her performance are only a part of a larger and more encompassing conceptualization termed a system. Supervision focus is on the system which is defined as:

> . . .an integrated and related set of components (subsystems) organized for the purpose of obtaining a specific objective (Horan, 1972, pp. 162-163).

> . . .the orderly organization of parts to make a whole in such a manner that each part is related to every other part, so a change in one part of the whole affects every other part, with each part and the totality of all parts functioning to produce specified outcomes (Ryan & Zeran, 1972, p. 13).

The system of primary focus in counselor supervision is the program of helping services which the counselor is responsible for delivering. However, the supervisor must recognize that helping service programs are not isolated systems, they are usually subsystems (components) of larger systems. The school guidance program is a clear example; it is a component of the school's educational program, which itself is a subsystem of the supporting society. Guidance goals reflect and contribute to school system goals which reflect and contribute to society's objectives. The systems approach places all contingent systems in perspective.

By focusing on the "big picture," the systems approach sets a direction for the accomplishment of goals which are desperately needed for the accountability of helping-service programs. Demonstrated effectiveness is one of these goals. The counselor and supervisor must be able to demonstrate the effectiveness of their programs in attaining specified objectives. Efficiency is another goal of the systems approach, gained by the harmonious coordination of program components, and the utilization of team members based on a realistic division of labor and their special competencies.

A third goal of the systems approach, as applied through counselor supervision, is to elicit the creative, innovative, and problem-solving potentials of the counselor and supervisor. The systems approach enables an individual to understand and deal with complex problems. A "systems thinker" is challenged by difficult situations and responds with professional assertiveness.

As summarized by Blocher, Dustin, and Dugan (1971), a systems approach

> Offers us a way of focusing on the larger picture—the total environment that impinges upon any single individual or group. It enables us to identify the key variables and factors at work within a total process. In doing this, it enables us to specify the outputs or outcomes that we expect or desire from a given process and to conceptualize the needed inputs or interventions that will be needed to produce those ends (p. 3).

METHODOLOGY

Consistent with the supervisor role model presented in Chapter 1, the assumption is made that the supervisor will be in a consultative stance when implementing systems methodology. In this stance the supervisor is not the administrator or director for a program of helping services, but instead is a consulting supervisor to counselors, head counselors, and perhaps program directors and administrators. From the consultative stance the supervisor will collaborate with counselors and supervise the use of systems methodology as counselors develop, manage, and evaluate programs, and as they serve as system consultants to other system personnel. Also, the supervisor will employ systems techniques when planning and managing the supervision program. The skills and techniques of system analysis, synthesis, flowchart modeling, writing performance objectives, simulation, and systems technology information are basic to the systems approach.

System Analysis

The skill of system analysis is a conceptual one. It is the skill of identifying and visualizing systems and the components and operations of the system. The system analyst can pinpoint problems, and the macro-conceptualization of a system enables him/her to see the environment in which the problem exists and the elements in that environment which have a relationship to and influence on the problem. System analysis is thus a diagnostic breakdown skill.

A supervisor employs system analysis on a daily basis. If problems arise within the helping-service program (system), the supervisor can track them down with system analysis. Maintenance of the program should include a routine system analysis—an evaluative look at the entire operation. Additionally, the supervisor will continually be called upon to use the system analysis skill when assisting counselors to manage their own activities and the specific system components (e.g., testing program, college counseling) for which they are responsible.

When a supervisor performs a system analysis on a program of helping services, many separate analysis tasks are performed, each having underlying evaluative questions that are answered by the information gained through investigation. For illustration a number of these basic analysis tasks are offered. illustration.

Basic System Analysis Tasks

Task 1: Identify the target system (helping-service program) to be analyzed, and any larger systems of which it is a part.

This task provides the supervisor-analyst with a picture of the target system and its environmental context. After only one analysis task the analyst begins to identify some of the environmental forces which impinge upon the target system.

Task 2: Identify the needs of the population served, and the needs of any larger systems which the target system serves.

A helping-service program always directs its efforts toward client-population needs as well as needs of parent systems (e.g., school system, society, district or state).

Task 3: Identify the goals of the target system.

Goals of a target system ordinarily reflect the needs of the population or larger system(s) which it serves.

Task 4: Analyze the congruency between goals of the target system, and the needs of the population and larger system(s) served.

Sources of discrepancy, which necessitate a change in target system goals, are as follows:

A. Goals of the target system may not reflect the needs of the population and larger systems served.

B. Goals of the target system may be deficient, not encompassing some important population and/or larger system needs.

C. Goals of the target system may not be realistic, encompassing too many population and/or larger system needs.

Task 5: Identify the helping services and functions which are performed by the target system.

    A. Are services and functions absent from the program that could be effectively employed to reach system goals?

    B. Is the program capable of performing existing services and functions--does it have the necessary personnel, skills, time, materials, and so forth?

    C. Are the existing services and functions of the system the most effective and efficient methods for accomplishing system goals?

Task 6: Identify and assess the degree of coordination among the system's components (services or functions) and personnel.

    A. Does overlap and inefficiency occur.

    B. Does sufficient communication exist among system personnel so that each is aware of how his/her efforts relate to those of other personnel and to program goals?

Task 7: Identify the evaluative methods by which the target system determines if it is reaching its goals.

    A. Are these evaluations valid?

    B. Do these evaluations cover all system goals?

Task 8: Identify the methods by which the target system remains "open", (i.e., receptive to and solicitous of a continuing stream of information from the population and larger system(s) served).

    A. Are the existing methods actually used?

    B. Are so few methods present that the target system is somewhat closed?

    C. Do too many methods exist; or, does the system fail to discriminate among incoming data, becoming hypersensitive to it?

Task 9: Identify the processes by which the target system changes as a result of making use of incoming information from the population and larger system(s) served, and from system evaluations.

An open and effective system is sensitive to its
environment, and adapts to changing conditions therein.
A closed system of helping services which does not
adapt will quickly become outdated and will be seeking
to meet needs and accomplish goals which are irrelevant.

Synthesis

Contrasting the breakdown skill of analysis is the
"putting-together" skill of synthesis. Synthesis is the
establishment of relationships between previously unrelated
parts, and the combining of these parts into a new whole. Ryan
and Zeran (1972, p. 14) have equated synthesis with innovation.

Analysis and synthesis are back-to-back skills, and
they represent an orderly process for creating a new system or
improving an existing system, as opposed to a trial-and-error
or intuitive approach (Hosford & Ryan, 1970). Information
gained from the nine analysis tasks mentioned earlier could
lead to the following synthesis actions:

1. Reorganization and/or establishment of a comprehensive
   and realistic set of system goals which are congruent
   with and a reflection of the needs of the population
   and larger system(s) served.

2. Reorganization and/or establishment of a comprehensive
   and realistic set of helping services which would effectively and efficiently reach system goals, and the
   establishment of functional communication channels
   among personnel and system components so that interchange leads to moment-by-moment coordination and
   system unity.

3. Reorganization and/or establishment of evaluation
   methods by which the system can assess the effectiveness of its helping services by determining if goals are
   being accomplished.

4. Reorganization and/or establishment of a "change
   function" within the system. This function would consist of methods for receiving and processing information
   from the environment and from system evaluations (see
   item 3), and then changing the system where needed
   in order to keep it effective and in congruence with
   environmental conditions.

Flowchart Modeling

Analysis and synthesis is aided by the drawing of
graphic models to depict systems, system components, and the

relationship among components. A graphic form makes information and abstract concepts more understandable, and the process
flow is analoguous to a roadmap--prescribing a systematic rout-
ing toward system goals (Hosford & Ryan, 1970). Figure 5.1
is a flowchart model constructed by Hosford and Ryan (1970,
p. 226) for the development of counseling and guidance programs.

In Figure 5.1 numbers 1.0 to 10.0 are identifiers referring
to sub-systems within the total model, and smaller numbers
indicate the functions within each subsystem. The symbol
($\longrightarrow$) is a signal path between functions indicating the flow
of action, information, and objects. Each function element can
produce feedback(F), output that feeds back to another function
and has an effect on it.

The construction of a model requires extensive effort,
usually the product of a supervised team effort. Persons
unfamiliar with models may be confused by such figures and a
narrative description should accompany them. A description of
Figure 5.1 is presented later in the practical application
section of this Chapter.

Writing Performance Objectives

The writing of performance objectives is a system-approach
skill which is crucial to the accountability of any helping-
services program (Horan, 1972; Thoresen, 1969). A performance
objective is a system objective stated in terms of the desired
behavior of the target population (school students, clientele,
counselor-trainees). Three criteria to meet when writing
performance objectives are the following (Hosford & Ryan, 1970):

1. the objective should state the outcome in terms of
   behavior that the target individual will demonstrate;

2. the conditions are described under which the behavior
   will occur;

3. an acceptable level (extent or degree) of performance
   should be specified.

Well written performance objectives are pertinent to broader
program goals; they are realistically attainable and are
measurable. These quality criteria are evident in the following
performance objective from a school guidance program. The
objective is the type for which a guidance program could assume
responsibility and be held accountable.

School Guidance Program Broad Goal: Informed and realistic
career decisions by school students.

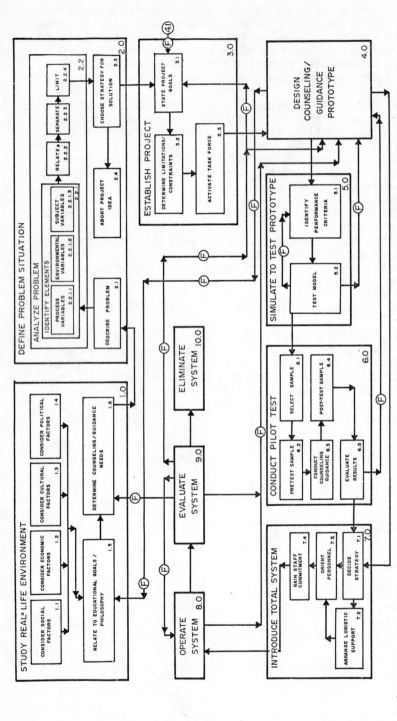

Figure 5.1. Counseling And Guidance Program Development System Model (Hosford & Ryan, 1970, p. 226). Reprinted With Permission From American Personnel And Guidance Association, Copyright 1970.

Performance objective: Following the administration of an interest and aptitude test, and participation in three group counseling sessions where the test results are interpreted and discussed, each ninth grade student will choose three career areas for later study in career education class.

The system-skill of writing performance objectives is needed by supervisors when they assist counselors and program directors with program development and change. If counselors do not themselves have the skill, an in-service training workshop may be required, with follow-up supervision of skill implementation. Numerous pitfalls which the author has encountered can occur in such training and supervision, the foremost being that writing objectives becomes an obsessional end in itself and is carried to extremes. A classic example of this pitfall is the teacher who sought the author's praise for a list of one hundred and fifty behavioral objectives that were established for an elementary grade curriculum. Such a large number of objectives rarely serves a useful function; actual evaluation of them is not feasible nor can one do justice to that many, therefore accountability for their accomplishment would be impossible. Exhaustive lists are usually an attempt to state every suspected behavioral influence of the professional upon the target population.

A different approach to writing behavioral objectives is to view them as useful tools to serve the helping service program. Instead of writing grandiose objectives, supervisors can stick to basics which are realistic for their particular helping-service programs. As a program gains maturity and basic objectives are met, the old objectives can be replaced with more sophisticated ones. This pragmatic view is reflected in the following illustrative list of Supervision Goals and Objectives which comprises the core of a year-long supervision program. The objectives relate to a supervisory program serving a number of small helping-service programs, each one staffed by three or four counselors and a program director.

Illustration of
Supervision Goals and Objectives

Broad Supervision Goal: An Accountable Helping-Service Program

Performance Objective: The counselor, in colloboration with the counselor staff, program director, and supervisor, and through group meetings and individual assisgnments, will plan the helping service program each year. The plan will reflect the past year's evaluation results and other evalutive data offered by the staff regarding program relevance and accountability.

Performance Objective: With supervisory assistance, the counselor will be responsible for monitoring a particular function, service, or designated area of the helping-service program and will report on its operation to the program director and counselor staff in several regularly scheduled program management meetings.

Performance Objective: The counselor will utilize the supervisor's assistance in conducting a yearly evaluation of that function, service, or designated area of the helping service for which he/she has monitoring responsibility, and will present an evaluative report to the program director and to the counselor staff within program evaluation meetings.

Performance Objective: The program director will meet with the supervisor at regularly scheduled times for consultative assistance regarding program administration, management, and evaluation.

Broad Supervision Goal: Accountable Counselor Services and Activities

Performance Objective: Following the yearly establishment of the helping-service program by the staff, the counselor, in consultation with the supervisor, will prepare a personal plan of activities for that year which coincides with the program and contributes to it.

Performance Objective: The counselor will consult with the program director and supervisor during the year when professional problems block the satisfactory implementation of his/her planned activities, and will meet with the supervisor twice yearly to review progress on the activity plan.

Performance Objective: The counselor will prepare an evaluation of his/her activity program at year's end, review it with the supervisor, and based upon the evaluation will make recommendations for next year's activity program.

180

<u>Broad Supervision Goal</u>:   Self-Directed Competency Development

>   <u>Performance Objective</u>:   In consultation with the
>   supervisor, and using the supervisor's assistance
>   to a mutually agreed upon degree, the counselor will
>   each year select and engage in a series of competency
>   development activities and summarize these learning
>   experiences in a report to the supervisor and program
>   director.

>   <u>Performance Objective</u>:   As part of the counselor's
>   competency development program he/she will select
>   and engage in at least one skill-training experience
>   each year (outside the in-service program), and will
>   share the experience with colleagues during a
>   regularly scheduled staff supervision session.

>   <u>Performance Objective</u>:   Each year the counselor will
>   demonstrate to the supervisor, through an approved
>   pre-post assessment procedure, the acquisition or
>   improvement of one skill-behavior or skill-activity.

>   <u>Performance Objective</u>:   As a part of the counselor's
>   competency development program, he/she will partici-
>   pate with the staff, program director, and supervisor
>   in planning an in-service training program, and with
>   supervisory assistance will prepare and conduct at
>   least one in-service training session during the
>   year.

<u>Broad Supervision Goal</u>:   Counselor Personal Adjustment

>   <u>Performance Objective</u>:   The counselor will utilize
>   the supervisor for confidential discussions of
>   personal life concerns and issues which may influence
>   the counselor's performance of his/her professional
>   duties.

>   <u>Performance Objective</u>:   The counselor will confiden-
>   tially discuss professional problems with the super-
>   visor which arise from inter-personal conflict with
>   staff members or clientele.

<u>Broad Supervision Goal</u>:   Professional Orientation and
Development

>   <u>Performance Objective</u>:   Counselors in their first
>   year of practice will meet frequently and regularly
>   with the supervisor during the first month in their

position, and monthly thereafter during the year, for supervisory assistance in adjusting to a new position, preparing an activity plan, and establishing a professional identity and role.

Performance Objective: Newly employed but experienced counselors will frequently and regularly meet with the supervisor during the first week in their position, and bi-monthly thereafter during the year, for supervisory assistance in adjusting to a new position and preparing and implementing an activity plan.

Performance Objective: Within regularly scheduled staff meetings the counselor will be informed of and encouraged to participate in professional development activities (e.g. professional organizations, conferences, legislative lobbying, and so forth).

Worth noting is that the performance objectives in the foregoing list are immediate objectives, i.e., performance behaviors that are demonstrated in the present. The supervisor has considerable control over the elicitation of these behaviors and therefore can be held accountable for them.

Another type of objective which is important, but for which the supervisor cannot accept total responsibility because he/she does not have the necessary controls, is the ultimate performance objective. An ultimate performance objective is that ideal which hopefully will be produced by immediate performance objectives. For example, one immediate performance objective under the broad goal of self-directed competency development is: "each year, the counselor will demonstrate to the supervisor, through an approved pre-post assessment procedure, the acquisition or improvement of one skill-behavior or skill-activity." This immediate performance objective hopefully will lead to the ultimate objective of a master counselor who consistently functions at facilitative levels of empathy, respect, and honesty, and who demonstrates mastery in consultation skills, counseling skills, and program management. Obviously this ultimate objective is highly desirable and it produces a strong motivational striving, but the supervisor does not have the omnipotent powers to guarantee its attainment. Therefore, the recommendation is that the supervisor base his/her accountability only upon those objectives which can be realistically produced, and that the supervisor relegate ultimate objectives to the realm of covert ideals. Whereas the supervisor needs ideals for which to strive, basing accountability upon them would be self-defeating.

182

Another characteristic of the foregoing illustrative list of Supervision Goals and Objectives is that it may deceive the reader into thinking that the accomplishment of such fundamental things does not require a full-time professional who has been specially trained in supervision methodology, and that the objectives could probably be accomplished without a supervisory function. The supervisor, who translates complex systems and their operations into understandable concepts via system techniques such as performance objectives and flow-charting, must be prepared to correct deceptions and oversight. The supervisory program chart presented in the summary for Section Two, immediately following Chapter 5, depicts the amount of supervisory activity required to accomplish the foregoing list of performance objectives. An examination of this chart should make it obvious that competent supervision requires extensive time and skill.

Simulation

The technique of simulation is employed to test a newly created system and can be used also when analyzing an existing system to determine weaknesses. Simulation consists of the verbal and mental exercise of applying the system to a host of expected situations and running a variety of inputs through the system to check on practicality and to check whether or not operations would be smooth and results predictable.

Simulation is one of several system techniques which would be employed by the supervisor to accomplish performance objectives regarding the planning of a helping-services program or to prepare an activity plan for an individual counselor. In the former case the supervisor would meet with a staff of counselors and together they would apply the newly developed or revised program to situations that were likely to occur in the future. Each component and operation of the system would be exercised and evaluated.

A similar simulation meeting with an individual counselor would check out his/her activity plan to be sure it was realistic and likely to reach intended goals and objectives. An enjoyable method for conducting such a simulation conference is to create a game-like atmosphere in which the supervisor offers difficult situations for the counselor to simulate through the activity plan. The counselor is challenged to create the most effective plan possible, one that could accountably process any input situation, and then to "problem solve" and adapt system operations to unusual input situations offered by the supervisor.

Systems Technology Information

Systems technology is foreign territory for most counselor supervisors, but a solid foundation of knowledge about systems is a prerequisite for the supervisor who becomes a "consultant-expert" when working with counselors on a systems project. References throughout this presentation on the systems approach are excellent informational sources, and they give a more thorough treatment to systems information than is possible in this Chapter. Several additional sources by systems authorities are recommended:

Burns, D.P. Behavioral objectives: A selected bibliography. Education Technology, 1969, 9, 57-58.

Kennedy, D.A. Some impressions of competency-based training programs. Counselor Education and Supervision, 1976, 15 (4), 244-250.

Krumboltz, J.D. Stating the goals of counseling. California Personnel and Guidance Association Monograph, 1966, No. 1.

Personnel and Guidance Journal (special issue). Technology in Guidance, 1970, 28 (3).

Ryan, T.A. Systems techniques for programs of counseling and counselor education. Educational Technology, 1969, 9, 7-17.

Silvern, L.C. Systems approach - What is it? Educational Technology, 1968, 8, 5-6.

Silvern, L.C. Systems engineering of education I: Evolution of systems thinking in education. Los Angeles: Education and Training Consultants Co., 1968.

THE SYSTEMS APPROACH: EMPIRICAL SUPPORT

The systems approach is an empirical method (Thoresen, 1969) and each application provides evidence of effectiveness. Evaluation is a definitive element of a system. Objectives are stated in behavioral terms so that the success of the system is actually observable, and ongoing system evaluation is conducted through the cybernetic concept of feedback (see Figure 5.1). Feedback is the information flow by which the components of a system influence and are influenced by each other. "The critical feature of feedback is information flow that alters (controls) the component receiving it. Information flow that does not have the capability of producing change is not feedback" (Thoresen, 1969, p. 8).

The effectiveness of a system thus is known to its creators; ineffectiveness is antithetical to the systems approach. A more difficult empirical question is comparative effectiveness--is the systems approach better than other methods of doing things?

This may be a moot question, because systems methodology is not an all-or-none entity. Any program or methodological approach will implement something akin to systems techniques; an effort without any systemization is erratic behavior. A more realistic issue for counselors and supervisors is whether a deliberately concerted application of systems methodology can improve existing programs.

Studies of organizational development in industry and school systems, reviewed by Schmuck and Miles (1971), provide considerable support for the improvement of existing organizations through the infusion of systems technology (including the training of personnel). Complementing research evidence are objective reports of successful applications of systems technology in guidance programs (Personnel & Guidance Journal, 1970, 28, pp. 31-34) and counselor education (Horan, 1972). Thus, available evidence suggests that the systems approach to program planning and management leads to accountable results. The systems approach is not a panacea, but its principles and methodology bring about efficient and effective programatic efforts.

SYSTEMS APPLICATION IN COUNSELOR SUPERVISION

A supervisor will find that the application of "systems thinking" permeates daily acitivites. One major application would be the systems design of a supervision program. The structure of such a systematic program is presented in Section Two, following Chapter 5. Another application is in the development, management, and evaluation of a program of helping services. Hosford and Ryan (1970) have applied the systems approach to the development of counseling and guidance programs and have constructed a systems model (See Figure 5.1) for program development which is applicable to the development of any helping-services program. The model's components represent the steps that a supervisor and team of counselors would follow; the narrative description by Hosford and Ryan is reprinted in the next section of this Chapter as a guide to supervisors who want to lead a group of counselors in the systematic development of a helping-service program. Figure 5.1 should be consulted as the description of the ten functions are read. The ten functions are as follows:

Study real-life environment (1.0)
Define problem situation (2.0)

Establish project (3.0)
Design counseling/guidance program prototype (4.0)
Simulate to test program prototype (5.0)
Pilot-test model (6.0)
Introduce system (7.0)
Operate system (8.0)
Evaluate system (9.0)
Eliminate system (10.0)

SYSTEMATIC DEVELOPMENT OF A HELPING-SERVICE PROGRAM

Study Real-Life Environment (1.0)

A counseling and guidance system cannot function effectively apart from the real-life environment of which it is a
part. In 1.0 the focus is on this real-life environment. In
1.1, 1.2, 1.3, and 1.4 some of the dynamic conditions which combine to make up the real-life environment are considered.
Inclusion of these social, cultural, economic, and political
factors as dynamic conditions in the environment carries an
implicit mandate (1.5) for awareness of the value structure
and the immediate and long-range goals of the total educational
enterprise in which the counseling and guidance program is to
function. In considering these real-life environment factors,
assessment of need for counseling and guidance is explicated
(1.6). In this subsystem the relevance of counseling and
guidance to the changing conditions of the real world is
achieved.

Define Problem Situation (2.0)

This function serves the purpose of elucidating the need
for counseling and guidance identified in 1.6. The general
description of the problem situation (2.1) is followed by
analysis of the problem (2.2). Analysis involves identification
of elements (2.2.1) including process variables, environmental
variables, and subject variables; determining relationships
among these elements (2.2.2); separating the elements (2.2.3);
and limiting elements (2.2.4). Analysis of the problem
should result in a decision (2.3) as to whether or not the
situation is one that calls for developing a counseling and
guidance program (3.0) or would be better left to some other
avenue of endeavor, in which case the program idea is aborted
(2.4).

Establish Project (3.0)

Assuming the decision is reached that a counseling and
guidance program is in order, the parameters of the program
must be defined. This calls for stating the mission goal (3.1),

186

determining limitations and contraints (3.2), and activating
a task force to develop the program (3.3). Clarity in stating
the mission goals is of paramount importance. The need for
launching an all-out counseling and guidance program will be
non-existent particularly if the program purpose is vaguely
defined. If at the outset the outcomes are not clearly
intended, the chance of determining if or when the program
goals have been realized is impossible.

Design Counseling and Guidance Program Prototype (4.0)

Figure 5.2 is an expansion of Design Counseling/Guidance
Program Prototype (4.0) subsystem in Figure 5.1. In this
function three tasks are implemented at the outset: assess
resources (4.1), study student population (4.2), and process
data from the environment (4.3).

Assessing resources involves identifying available personnel, time, finances, and facilities. The assessment of
resources, study of student population, and data from the
environment lead to definition of alternative strategies and
determination of priorities (4.4). Once resources have been
determined, goals may need to be redefined. This is shown in
Figure 5.2 through the use of a feedback loop from assess
resources (4.1) to state project goals (3.1).

Broadly stated, program outcomes set up in 3.0 must be
defined in terms of immediate and ultimate subject behaviors;
this is accomplished through role-analysis (4.5). "Role" is
simply that behavior necessary for effective functioning
within a social group. In the counseling and guidance context,
for example, we assume that a person should be able to demonstrate self-actualizing behaviors, achieve economic efficiency,
perform civic responsibilities, and be socially productive in
the community, as well as demonstrating facilitating behavior
in the counseling and guidance situation. The role description
achieved in 4.6 as a result of synthesizing those behaviors
identified in role analysis should result in a definition of
the behavioral objectives (4.6.2) of the counseling and guidance program. These behaviors should be stated in terms of
knowledge, skills, and attitudes required for fully functioning
in the community. In addition, the behaviors should elaborate
intended levels of achievement and describe exact conditions
under which client behaviors will be demonstrated. The signal
path from role analysis (4.5) back to study of real-life
environment (1.0) indicates that the definition of role takes
place in relation to the real-life environment from which the
person has come and to which he/she will return.

Processing of data (4.3) involves continuing data
collection, analysis, and interpretation to keep role-analysis

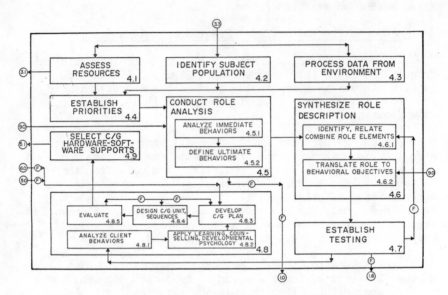

Figure 5.2.   Design Counseling/Guidance Program Prototype.   A
Detail Design Of Space 4.0 With Same Title In
Figure 5.1 (Hosford & Ryan, 1970, p. 227).   Re-
printed With Permission From American Personnel
And Guidance Association, Copyright 1970.

in tune with the real world. This serves the purpose of keeping the system dynamic and makes possible the maintenance of harmony between the system and the environment.

Testing (4.7) of the subject group identified in 4.2 will determine extent to which the target population--in this case the students--possesses the immediate and ultimate behaviors described in role definition (4.5); and on the basis of this information we can make any necessary redefinition of the counseling and guidance program needs (1.6). An important activity is to use criterion-based tests to measure subject behaviors against program objectives. The program which is expected to produce the client behavioral outcomes is put together in 4.8. In this subsystem analysis of client behaviors (4.8.1) and the relation of this information to experience and knowledge from learning psychology, counseling psychology, and developmental psychology (4.8.2) is necessary. Objects, information, and actions which mediate interaction between individuals in the subject group and the counseling and guidance process variables must be identified and synthesized in a counseling and guidance plan (4.8.3). This plan serves the purpose of guiding and directing construction of specific counseling and guidance experiences and environments and development of counseling and guidance units and sequences (4.8.4). The plan is checked against the real-life environment to insure optimum transfer from the counseling setting to the real world. The plan developed (4.8.3) results in development of specific counseling and guidance units and sequences will be supported by hardware and software (4.9) which are identified, evaluated, selected, and combined to make for effective and efficient counseling and guidance.

In making the counseling/guidance units, the human counselor is included as one of the media elements, together with other machine, audio, and video adjuncts. Creation of the counseling/guidance units involves comparing alternative strategies in terms of costs and benefits. The counseling and guidance units and sequences make up the program. Each sequence and unit, as well as the total program, must be evaluated (4.8.5) and then revised as needed. This continuing evaluation and revision is shown by the signal paths between 4.8.3, 4.8.4, and 4.8.5.

Simulate To Test Program Prototype (5.0)

Before the counseling and guidance program is implemented, simulation to test the program should be carried out either with the computer or by verbal walk-through so that necessary repairs can be made before the program is launched. As the model is simulated one could find that costs could make initiation of a full-blown program in the real-world impractical,

189

without changes in the design. Possibly a comparison of alternatives will point up particular combinations to maximize the counseling and guidance program operation in terms of goal achievement.

Pilot Test The Model (6.0)

An initial try-out of the newly designed counseling and guidance program units and sequences should be made on a trial-run basis involving only a limited number from the subject population. If results from a pilot test of sequences and units indicate these guidance elements to be effective, then the total program should be subjected to a field test. This will be followed by further refining and modification before total implementation. The field test serves the important function of permitting collection and analysis of performance data and comparison of these data against program objectives. Evaluation carried out as part of field testing should determine the extent to which the system satisfies criteria of effectiveness.

Introduce The System (7.0)

The results of evaluation during field testing of the counseling and guidance program determine when, how, and for whom the total system will be established. Specification for staffing, facilities, equipment and community involvement to implement the plan designed (4.8.3) can be drawn up. Such specifications must be subjected to check and possible modification on basis of data gathered through simulation and field testing. Checking and revising are indicated by the feedback signals from 5.0 and 6.0 to 4.8.3 (Figure 5.1).

Many systems fail because of ill-conceived or inadequate plans for initiation of the model. To specify staff, facilities, equipment, and community resource requirement is not enough. Some provision must be made to decide on a strategy for launching the system (7.1). This is accomplished by arranging logistic support (7.2) to the new program. Personnel should be thoroughly trained not only in the use of the new media, methods, techniques, and materials utilized in the sequences and units of counseling and guidance but also in the behaviors required for implementing new roles which they may fulfill. A concerted effort must be made to see that counseling and guidance system operators are committed to the new program (7.4) before the system becomes operational (8.0).

System Operation (8.0), Evaluation (9.0), and Elimination (10.0)

This discussion has been concerned primarily with development of a counseling and guidance system. Therefore, evaluate

190

system (9.0) and eliminate system (10.0) (Figure 5.1) will be discussed only in relation to program development.

The results of the subsystem, introduce system (7.0), lead directly to system operation (8.0). Here is where the model is put into operation, with a full complement of logistical support, inclusion of client population of counseling and guidance units and sequences. System evaluation (9.0) has the effect of looking at ways in which the target group is able to perform in the real-life world. The focus in 9.0 is on the behaviors of the clients after their return to the larger community. Are they adjusting to demands of society? Are they achieving economic efficiency, civic responsibility, self-actualization?

Our society changes rapidly, with conditions undergoing constant change. Only by feedback from client performance in the real world to system goals, design, and operation can the system be validated. An essential is for continuous evaluation to be built into the total system model. This is shown as a feedback signal from evaluation (9.0) to determining needs (1.6), which has the effect of checking the program against real-life world demands.

In evaluation, the system products are tested against criteria formulated in 4.6 when behavioral objectives of counseling and guidance were defined. This appears as feedback in the signal path from 9.0 (evaluation) to 4.6 (developing behavioral objectives).

Effectiveness of a counseling and guidance system should never be taken for granted. A constant checking operation should be maintained (9.0), and whenever an indication occurs that any unit or sequence is not serving the purpose for which it was intended, re-examination of the item should be made. As a general rule, piecemeal patching-up of weak or malfunctioning systems is not desirable; better to analyze the total system.

In presenting this generalized model, the intent has been to provide a means for producing a model for counseling and guidance program development. The use of this generalized model for designing and evaluating counseling and guidance programs can lead to several benefits to those with vested interest in achieving effective, efficient programs.

Communication within the profession and between the profession and others involved in counseling and guidance can be facilitated. The obligation for accountability can be satisfied. Weaknesses, gaps, missing links in a system working against wholeness, strong interrelationships, compatibility,

191

and optimization can be emphasized. Increased creativity and innovation can be achieved. Improvements in the total system, strengthening of functions, and tightening of interrelationships among functions can be realized through the provision for continuing evaluation in light of previously defined behavioral objectives.

SUMMARY

The systems approach to counselor supervision has been defined as the application of systems technology to the supervision function via a conceptualizing/problem-solving process which leads to the attainment of specified goals. Operationally, systems thinking takes the form of techniques such as analysis, synthesis, flowcharting, etc. which are employed by supervisors as they establish their own supervision programs, and as they teach these techniques to supervisees and oversee subsequent implementation.

Counselors and supervisors are known for their work with people, and indeed nearly all helping services depend upon the practitioner's interpersonal competence. But the goals and objectives toward which these interpersonal competencies are directed cannot be reached through uncoordinated helping efforts. The work of professional helpers must be systematically planned, managed, and evaluated in order to be accountable, and the systems approach can lead supervisors and counselors toward this accountability.

REFERENCES

Association for Counselor Education and Supervision, Committee on Counselor Effectiveness. Commitment to Action in Supervision: Report of a National Survey of Counselor Supervision, 1969.

Bernstein, B. L., & De Comte, C. An integrative competence-based counselor education model. Counselor Education and Supervision, 1976, 16(1), 26-36.

Blocher, D. H.; Dustin, E. R.; & Dugan, W. E. Guidance Systems. New York: Ronald Press, 1971.

Burns, D. P. Behavioral objectives: A selected bibliography. Educational Technology, 1969, 9, 57-58.

Canada, R. M., & Lynch, M. L. Systems techniques applied to teaching listening skills. Counselor Education and Supervision, 1975, 15(1), 40-47.

Horan, J. J. Behavioral goals in systematic counselor education. Counselor Education and Supervision, 1972, 11, 162-170.

Hosford, R. E., & Ryan, T. A. Systems design in the development of counseling and guidance programs. Personnel and Guidance Journal, 1970, 49, 221-230.

Kennedy, D. A. Some impressions of competency-based training programs. Counselor Education and Supervision, 1976, 15 (4), 224-250.

Krumboltz, J. D. Stating the goals of counseling. California Personnel and Guidance Association Monograph, 1966, No. 1.

Personnel and Guidance Journal (special issue). Technology in guidance, 1970, 28(3).

Ryan, T. A. Systems techniques for programs of counseling and counselor education. Educational Technology, 1969, 9, 7-17.

Ryan, T. A., & Zeran, F. R. Organization and Administration of Guidance Services. Danville, Ill.: Interstate Printer and Publishers, 1972.

Saylor, R. H. Managing competency-based preparation of school counselors. Counselor Education and Supervision, 1976, 15(3), 195-199.

Schmuck, R. A., & Miles, M. B. Organizational Development in Schools. Palo Alto, California: National Press, 1971.

Shaw, M. D. School Guidance Systems. Boston: Houghton Mifflin Company, 1973.

Silvern, L. C. Systems approach - what is it? Educational Technology, 1968, 8, 5-6.

_____. Systems Engineering of Education I: Evolution of Systems Thinking in Education. Los Angeles: Education and Training Consultants Company, 1968.

Thoresen, C. E. The systems approach and counselor education: Basic features and implications. Counselor Education and Supervision, 1969, 9, 3-18.

Winborn, B. B.; Hinds, W. C.; & Stewart, N. Instructional objectives for the professional preparation of counselors. Counselor Education and Supervision, 1971, 10(2), 133-137.

Chapter **6**

SUMMARY AND SYNTHESIS

OF

SECTION TWO

John D. Boyd

SUMMARY AND SYNTHESIS OF SECTION TWO

John D. Boyd

A great amount of material about counselor supervision has been covered in Sections One and Two. The author's treatment of this material has constituted a system analysis of the counselor supervision topic, leading to the present juncture where those system elements explicated through analysis (e.g. supervisory concepts, approaches, and techniques) must be "synthesized" into a new whole if an improved supervision system is to be built. Furthermore, synthesis is needed if readers are to translate rhetoric into practice. For these reasons a brief review and synthesis of the foregoing five chapters are offered.

In Section One an analysis of counselor supervision yielded a definitive conceptualization in which supervision was a purposeful function comprised of four main activities. In order to accomplish the supervisory purposes of facilitating counselors' personal and professional development, promoting counselor competencies, and promoting accountability, the supervisor employed the four activities of consultation, training and instruction, counseling, and evaluation. The supervisor's proposed role was to use the consultation activity as a homebase and stance, from which to enter the other three supervisory activities as exigencies dictate. The recommendation was that a "self-directional thrust" be followed throughout the supervisor's duties: counselors would be encouraged to utilize fully their talents, to continue their self development as people and professionals, and to direct cooperatively the helping service program.

Section Two extended the supervisor's methodology beyond activities by proposing four methodological approaches to supervision practice: psychotherapeutic, behavioral, systems, and integrative. Three of these approaches are ideologically pure while the integrative approach is formed by integrating techniques from the psychotherapeutic and behavioral approaches. Having explained activities and approaches, the author now proposes in this concluding portion of Section Two that the most efficacious practice of counselor supervision is produced by

197

synthesizing activities and approaches. From this perspective, supervision approaches offer a vast array of techniques and concepts with which to exercise supervision activities. By making all possible integrations between and among approaches and activities, a synthesized methodological framework emerges which serves as a utilitarian model for supervisory practice (See Figure 6.1).

Activities		Approaches
1. Consultation		
2. Counseling	Synthesized	1. Psychotherapeutic
3. Training and ──►Methodological◄── 2. Behavioral		
Instruction	Framework	3. Systems
4. Evaluation		

Figure 6.1. A Model For Supervision Practice.

Competent performance of the synthesized methodology requires a technically eclectic repertoire of supervision skills and the ability to integratively employ them in response to novel situations. The "complete" supervisor is thus prepared to meet situational exigencies with whatever activity and eclectic set of techniques is most efficacious. He/she can react to emergencies with aplomb and can plan and execute a supervision program which fully exercises a synthesized methodology. Such a supervision program, founded upon the synthesis framework, might resemble the one displayed in Figure 6.2.

The setting for this supervision program, for illustrative purposes, has only general characteristics. It consists of a helping service program, staffed by several counselors and a program director. An administrative superior has authority over the program, and the program director is responsible to him/her. These setting characteristics would apply to most helping service programs in schools, agencies, universities, and other localities.

A cursory examination of the program chart reveals several characteristics which merit attention before a narrative description is offered. One important characteristic is that program goals and performance objectives reflect the purposes of counselor supervision that were mentioned in Chapter 1. Also evident in the performance objectives is a "self-direction emphasis" whereby counselors plan, manage, and evaluate the helping service program, and direct their own personal, professional, and competency development.

	PROGRAM DIRECTION		SYNTHESIZED METHODOLOGY	
Supervision Goals	Performance Objectives	Activities	Approaches	Practical Application Strategies
Accountable Helping Service Program	Counselors plan the helping service program.	Consultation	Psychotherapeutic Systems Behavioral	Group planning meeting(s) with the counselor staff, including the program director.
	Each counselor monitors the operation of a program element throughout the year, and participates in the staff's ongoing program management.	Consultation Training & Instruction	Systems Behavioral	Supervision sessions with individual counselors to assist with the monitoring and ongoing management of program elements. Training in system skills if necessary. Group meeting(s) with the counselor staff for program management.
	Counselors conduct a yearly evaluation of the helping service program and each of its elements (one of which is the supervision program).	Consultation Evaluation Training & Instruction	Systems Behavioral	Supervision session(s) with individual counselors to assist with the evaluation of program elements. Training in evaluation skills if necessary. Group meeting(s) with the counselor staff for program evaluation.
	Program director utilizes individual consultation sessions.	Consultation Training & Instruction Evaluation	Systems Behavioral Psychotherapeutic	Consultation sessions with the program director for assistance with issues and problems of administration, management, and evaluation.

Figure 6.2. A Comprehensive Supervision Program.

	PROGRAM DIRECTION		SYNTHESIZED METHODOLOGY		
Supervision Goals	Performance Objectives	Activities	Approaches	Practical Application Strategies
Accountable Counselor Services and Activities	Counselors prepare personal activity plans for the year.	Consultation Training & Instruction	Systems Behavioral	Supervision sessions with individual counselors to assist with the preparation of activity plans that contribute to program goals.
	Counselors consult with the supervisor and program director regarding problems which block their work.	Consultation Training & Instruction Counseling	Systems Behavioral Psychotherapeutic	Problem solving supervisory sessions, requested by the counselor.
	Counselors evaluate their activities and make recommendations at year's end.	Consultation	Systems Behavioral	Supervision sessions with individual counselors or in a group.
Counselor Personal Adjustment	Counselors utilize the supervisor for discussion of personal life issues which influence professional performance.	Counseling Consultation	Psychotherapeutic	Brief counseling or consultation, sought by the counselor or initiated by the supervisor, to resolve personal problems and/or minimize their effect upon professional performance.
	Counselors confidentially discuss with the supervisor their professional, interpersonal conflicts.	Counseling Consultation	Psychotherapeutic	Brief counseling or consultation, sought by the counselor or initiated by the supervisor, to resolve professional, interpersonal conflicts.

Figure 6.2. Continued.

PROGRAM DIRECTION		SYNTHESIZED METHODOLOGY		
Supervision Goals	Performance Objectives	Activities	Approaches	Practical Application Strategies
Self-Directed Competency Development	Each year counselors select and engage in a plan of competency development activities.	Consultation	Systems Behavioral Psychotherapeutic	Individual or group supervision sessions to help counselors assess their competencies and prepare a plan for competency development.
	Counselors participate in in-service training activities, and each counselor conducts one in-service training session.	Consultation Training & Instruction	Behavioral Psychotherapeutic	Supervisor offered inservice training and collaboration with counselors as they conduct in-service sessions.
	Counselors select and participate in a skill training experience and share it with the staff.	Consultation Training & Instruction	Behavioral Psychotherapeutic Systems	Supervisor support for counselor's outside training experiences, and regular training sessions for counselors who want it.
	Counselors demonstrate the acquisition or improvement of one skill-behavior or skill-activity.	Consultation Evaluation	Behavioral Psychotherapeutic	Assessment of recorded performance. Observation of live performance. Documentation from course instructor. Completion of a written project.

Figure 6.2. Continued.

| | PROGRAM DIRECTION | SYNTHESIZED METHODOLOGY | | |
Supervision Goals	Performance Objectives	Activities	Approaches	Practical Application Strategies
Professional Orientation and Development	First-year counselors participate in monthly supervision sessions.	Counseling Consultation Training & Instruction	Psychotherapeutic Behavioral Systems	Monthly supervision sessions to facilitate adjustment to a new position and the establishment of a professional identity and role, and to assist in the preparation and implementation of an activity plan.
	Newly employed, experienced counselors participate in bi-monthly supervision sessions.	Counseling Consultation Training & Instruction	Psychotherapeutic Behavioral Systems	Bi-monthly supervision sessions to facilitate adjustment to a new position, and to assist in the preparation and implementation of an activity plan.
	Counselors receive information about professional development activities, and are encouraged to participate.	Consultation	Psychotherapeutic Behavioral	Information offered about professional activities. Discussions of professional issues. Participation in and support of professional service.
	Counselors receive encouragement and skill training in professional assertion.	Consultation Training & Instruction	Psychotherapeutic Behavioral Systems	Promotion of a professionally assertive attitude, and special training in the skills of professional assertion.

Figure 6.2. Continued.

The most distinguishing program characteristics to notice, however, are that (1) the three supervisory approaches having ideological purity (psychotherapeutic, behavioral, and systems) are used integratively in various combinations to conduct supervisory activities and practical application strategies, and that (2) the supervisor operates from a flexible activity-role wherein he/she continually moves from the home-base activity of consultation to the other three supervisory activities (counseling, training and instruction, evaluation) in order to make practical applications of supervision methodology. These two program characteristics are an explicit demonstration of the author's concept of synthesized methodology and the following narrative will further elucidate this concept as each of the five goal-based segments of the program chart are described in order.

A COMPREHENSIVE SUPERVISION PROGRAM

NARRATIVE DESCRIPTION

Five related dimensions to this supervision program, each having a column on Figure 6.2, are as follows: Goals, Performance Objectives, Supervisory Activities, Supervisory Approaches and Techniques, and Practical Application Strategies. By reading the chart horizontally, across columns from left to right, the relationship among entries should be apparent. Goals are translated into performance objectives, and these are matched with the activities, approaches/techniques, and practical application strategies with which they can be accomplished.

An Accountable Helping Service Program

The first goal-based segment of the comprehensive supervision program is directed toward program accountability. Accountability is translated into four performance objectives of the helping service program

1. counselor planning of the helping service program,

2. monitoring of a program element,

3. counselor evaluation of the program, and

4. program director utilizing supervisory assistance.

The supervisor accomplishes the first performance objective --counselor planning of the helping-service program--through consultative assistance offered to counselors in planning meetings. Although the supervisor and program director may provide leadership in the meetings, program planning is the shared responsibility of the staff of counselors. Methodology used by the supervisor within the planning meetings is drawn from the psychotherapeutic, behavioral, and systems approaches. Skills from the psychotherapeutic approach are used to understand and supervise the group dynamics of the planning meeting; program planning can break down if the group does not function smoothly. Another utilization of dynamic skill is in supervising counselors to be sensitive to client dynamics when planning the helping service program. Counselors, thereby, can direct the program at important developmental tasks and stages which evade the awareness of dynamically insensitive observers.

Concepts and techniques from the systems approach are used by the supervisor to help the counselors create a helping service program which has the characteristics of an accountable system. A "skill analysis and assessment" (from the behavioral approach) might be done to make sure that planned services do not surpass the staff's performance capability.

The second performance objective in segment one of the chart is the monitoring of a program element (e.g., a particular service or function) and participation in the staff's program management. This objective spreads program management among staff members, and they are given consultation from the supervisor who lends his/her "systems thinking" to the management process, and may train the counselor(s) in system skills which are needed for program management.

Program evaluation constitutes the third performance objective, approached through the activities of consultation and evaluation, and also training if counselors lack evaluation skills. Each year a program evaluation is conducted by the staff, and through individual and group consultative meetings the supervisor, perhaps in tandem with the program director, coordinates and facilitates program evaluation efforts. Counselors having had monitoring and management responsibilities for a service or function throughout the year are particularly well prepared to evaluate that target.

The last objective in segment one of the program (Figure 6.2) is the program director's use of supervisory assistance. While the director of a helping service program is the undisputed administrative leader and the supervisor does not contend for any administrative responsibilities, in many ways the supervisor can assist the program director and be an ally. The supervisor's objective perspective on a difficult issue or decision is often invaluable, and his/her systems skills can contribute to sound judgements on matters of program administration, management, and evaluation. In certain instances the supervisor can instructionally pass along a systems skill not held by the director. An additional asset for the director is that the supervisor is often in a strategic position and has the necessary skills to assess the dynamics of the counselor staff and to provide intervention. Interpersonal rifts among staff members, staff morale, the director-staff relationship, and counselors with personal adjustment problems are examples of areas in which the supervisor's therapeutic expertise can be of significant assistance to the program director.

Accountable Counselor Services and Activities

An accountable program or system depends upon the accountability of each of its components. Thus, the first goal of this supervision program--an accountable helping service program--is inextricably related to the second goal--accountable counselor performance of services and activities.

Counselor accountability begins with the performance objective of planning activities for the year. Through individual consultation sessions and the use of systems technology the supervisor helps counselors to prepare activity plans which have the characteristics of an accountable system. The supervisor and counselor view the helping service program as a system to which counselor efforts will contribute. Ideally, everything the counselor does in the performance of his/her duties should contribute efficiently and effectively to the goals of the helping service program. When all staff members understand this relationship and attempt to prepare activity plans with this in mind, the congruency among program parts is increased greatly and the program becomes a more accountable system.

Another system characteristic of a counselor's activity plan is effectiveness. The supervisor will encourage the counselor to write performance objectives and identify other means for evaluating his/her activities and services. One must plan ahead for evaluation, although the actual evaluation will be done later.

During the consultation process the supervisor may discover that counselors do not have sufficient planning skills to prepare an accountable set of services and activities. In this case the behavioral supervision approach can be invoked and instruction/training done to fill skill deficiencies.

A second performance objective under the goal of accountable counselor services and activities concerns consultation for the resolution of "practical problems" (i.e., unexpected difficulties which inevitably and normally arise for every counselor in the daily exercise of his/her duties). The supervisory strategy for dealing with these difficulties is for the supervisor, alone or in tandem with the program director, to consult with counselors and to help them engage in systematic problem solving. Together the supervisor and counselors systematically analyze problems, explore possible solutions, and execute solutions. Such problem-solving conferences will sometimes reveal a skill-need in the counselor, and training can be used to give the counselor the expertise needed to better handle the practical problem. In other instances a dynamic difficulty in the counselor or another staff member is uncovered and counseling may ensue. Still a third possibility is that the practical problem can be alleviated or solved by certain administrative actions taken by the program director. Depending on the cause of the counselor's problem, the supervisor may use the systems, behavioral, or psychotherapeutic approaches, or more likely, a synthesized methodology.

The last performance objective under the goal of accountable counselor services and activities is evaluation by counselors of their planned activities. This would be accomplished by counselors continually evaluating their activities as these are executed throughout the year, and at year's end summarizing the results and making recommendations for improvement to the program director. Supervisory assistance through individual and group consultation sessions would be offered; instruction in evaluation procedures could be given to counselors not having these skills.

Self-Directed Competency Development

The third goal of this supervision program is to set in motion a self-directed process of competency development within each counselor, thereby overcoming and preventing the complacency which eventually can lead to incompetence. To begin the self-directed process the counselor would assess his/her competencies, identify strengths and weaknesses, and prepare a plan of competency development activities. Supervisory consultation concerning these tasks involves a few system concepts and techniques to help the counselor write a competency development plan; skill analysis and assessment can identify skill-objectives for the plan, and psychotherapeutic techniques would help the counselor find dynamic targets for competency development. Strategies for the development of these chosen competency-goals should be mutually agreeable to the counselor and supervisor, and should follow the guidelines for effective learning/training modalities espoused by the behavioral supervision approach (see Chapter 3).

At the heart of counselors' competency development plans is an inservice training program (see second performance objective) led by the supervisor but carried out by the counselors. The supervisor conducts some of the program's inservice sessions and focuses on skills chosen by the counselors. Multiple strategies from the behavioral supervision approach, and experiential/dynamic strategies from the psychotherapeutic approach, are used to teach the focal skills. Participation in inservice training sessions is expected of counselors, each taking the responsibility of leading one session (with assistance from the supervisor if desired).

The third performance objective under the competency development goal asks that counselors go outside the inservice training program to participate in one skill-training experience. This experience can be acquired from the supervisor or any reputable source (e.g., course, workshop, internship with another counselor), and it should conform to guidelines of effective instruction which have been described in Chapter 3 (behavioral supervision approach). Supervisor-offered instruction would probably implement a behavioral, psychotherapeutic, or integrative strategy for the teaching of skill-objectives chosen by the counselor and agreed upon by the supervisor.

Performance objective four focuses on an evaluative criterion of the competency development process--demonstrable skill-gain. Through inservice training, supervisor-offered training, or other learning experiences, the counselor is expected each year to demonstrate the acquisition or improvement of one skill-behavior or skill-activity. While this observable criterion is probably not the only learning evidence that could be offered by counselors subsequent to a year-long competency development program, the acquisition or improvement of one skill-behavior or skill-activity is an accountable one. The rationale behind performance objectives three and four is that a great amount of knowledge acquisition and other intangible gains can take place through competency development activities, but while these gains are valuable they represent only the means to the ultimate goal of improved counselor performance. Therefore, observable performance behavior is the most accountable index of the competency development process.

Counselor Personal Adjustment

The omission of counselor personal adjustment from the goals of a supervision program would be an oversight, but an understandable omission nonetheless because of the reluctance of supervisors to intrude upon the personal domain of supervisees. The personal adjustment goal and objectives in this program follow a principle advocated in Chapter 1: that the supervisor facilitates and promotes counselors' personal adjustment, intervenes at their request for short-term counseling, and intrudes only when counselor performance is affected

deleteriously by personal stress. Practical application of
the principle takes the form of brief counseling sessions or
psychotherapeutic supervision sessions, initiated by the supervisor or counselor. These sessions are for the purposes of
(1) resolving personal adjustment problems or referring the
counselor to appropriate helping services, (2) temporarily
altering the counselor's duties to take account of his/her
stress, and (3) resolving interpersonal conflicts between
staff members.

The key to successfully accomplishing those performance
objectives under the personal adjustment goal is not just
competent performance of counseling or consultation. The
supervisor must have established an atmosphere of trust,
respect, and honesty before counselors will cooperate with
supervisory intrusions. Furthermore, counselors and the supervisor must sincerely believe that we all encounter difficult
developmental stages, and that seeking a helper to accompany
us at these times is an act of maturity and strength. Helpers
enable us to assault problems with our full complement of
resources.

Professional Orientation and Development

As mentioned in Chapter 1, counselors have struggled to
create a "professional status" for themselves, but their
profession has not received nearly as much recognition as they
would like. One reason for this state of affairs is that
counselors seem to have a weakness in professional self image
and the commitment to a specific role and function. Considering
this inner fraility the fact that counseling is an overlooked
professional is not surprising because recognition from outside
a profession never precedes a display of professional strength
from within the profession.

The last goal in this model supervision program is to
increase the professional strength of counselors by giving
them a professional orientation and by promoting their professional development. "Professional orientation" is defined as
an orientation to the profession and/or a new position for
incoming members, while "professional development" refers to
the establishment and maintenance of a clear professional
identity and role and function.

Professional orientation is approached through the first
two performance objectives by giving consultative assistance
to counselors who are entering new positions. The supervisor
introduces them to all aspects of the position, is regularly
available to anwer questions and to help solve problems, and
offers guidance and technical assistance in the preparation
and initial implementation of an activity plan. Because newly-

employed counselors are unfamiliar with the helping service
program they particularly need assistance with their activity
plans.

The orientation process can demand supervisory skills
from all three pure approaches. Doubts, insecurities, and
stresses of beginning a new position and the interpersonal
frictions created as a new member enters the counselor staff,
can be dealt with from the psychotherapeutic approach or
outright counseling. During consultation sessions the behavioral and systems approaches can be utilized as the supervisor
instructs the counselor in skills of the position where the
counselor is not satisfactorily prepared. Job demands will
not be threatening if the counselor is offered supportive
supervision and remedial training.

Professional development is facilitated through the professional model set by the supervisor's behavior, through his/her
treatment of counseling as an important profession, and through
treatment of the counselor as a skilled professional. Through
this modality of "personal influence" the supervisor can instill
the counselor with pride in his/her profession and professional
self.

Specific supervisory activities to promote professional
development include staff discussions of professional issues,
provision of information to counselors about professional
development activities (e.g., meetings of professional organizations, conferences, pertinent legislative lobbying), and
participation in and/or support for counselors' professional
service (e.g., holding office, convention presentations,
publications). The gist of these activities is that action is
taken by counselors to strengthen the profession.

Professional assertion is another form of counselor
action that strengthens the profession, and it is the last
performance objective of the supervision program. Professional
assertion has been defined as the expression and exercise of
the counselor's professional role and function by overcoming
institutional constraints, interpersonal conflicts, and
miscellaneous problems which inhibit or prohibit professional
practice. A state of professional nonassertion exists when
counselors silently repress their counseling function because
the institution housing the helping-service program restricts
professional practice. For example, a school which prohibits
personal-adjustment counseling greatly restricts the counselor's
role and function. A state of nonassertion also exists when
counselors cannot show accountability to critical and powerful
lay people or administrators who force the helping-service
program into cutting staff and services because helping services
are alleged ineffective. Additionally, nonassertion is

present when counselors offer a mediocre helping-service program because they cannot overcome practical problems such as reticent clientele, lack of local funding, or shortage of personnel.

Supervisors can combat nonassertive behavior with psychotherapeutic and instructional techniques which promote a professionally assertive belief system. Counselors can be made aware of their professional role and function, that they have been prepared to exercise this role and function, and that they have a right as professionals to implement their role and function. Assertive beliefs are the bedrock upon which assertive skills are laid, but beliefs do not automatically produce assertive behavior. Most nonassertive counselors will need supervisory training in institutional and socio-political influence strategies so they can deal effectively with the institutions and governing bodies of society. They can profit from the acquisition of interpersonally assertive techniques which enable them to stand up for their professional rights in the face of criticism and oppression. Finally, counselors can increase their professional assertiveness by learning systematic problem-solving skills with which to analyze, form strategies, and persistently attack the practical problems which hamper professional practice.

ACTIVATING THE SUPERVISION FUNCTION

Supervision programs having a comprehensive set of goals and a synthesized methodology can significantly strengthen a helping-service program. However, such programs are not established easily, and where the supervision function does not exist the initiation of a program may seem impossible. Multiple roadblocks (i.e., absence of trained personnel, no funding for a supervisory position, and resistance from threatened counselors) are usually present to discourage supervision advocates. These prohibitive factors can be overcome through the conceptualization of supervision presented in Sections One and Two and the following steps:

Step 1--Laying the Groundwork

In helping service programs where the supervision function is nonexistent, a source of advocacy for the function must be identified or created. Advocacy can initially come from counselors and/or administrative superiors, but eventually it must be held by both parties if supervision is to have adequate support. The author's experience has been that the supervision function springs from the interest and commitment of counselors and program directors. Administrative superiors (non-counselors) must be educated about supervision and

210

persuaded to allow and support it. Therefore, the first
recommended step for beginning a full or partial supervision
program is to garner support and commitment from counselors,
who then educate and persuade administrative superiors.

Step 2--Identifying Supervisors

Once approval has been given by counselors and administrators for development of the supervision function, the next
step is to identify supervisors. If within the local situation
an experienced counselor in the helping-service program is
present who has gained supervisory training and possesses
the qualifications mentioned in Chapter 1, this person might
be a prime candidate for a supervisory position. If the program
does not have a candidate, the alternatives are to seek and
employ a full-time or part-time supervisor, or prepare a
staff member as a supervisor. The preparation alternative can
be accomplished by identifying the counselor(s) with the best
qualifications and then preparing that person through in-
service training or university coursework.

Step 3--Establishing Supervision Parameters

The comprehensive supervision program depicted earlier in
Figure 6.2 is fairly broad in scope and is not one to be
developed and implemented quickly. Supervision programs
usually have modest beginnings and are developed over time
as the supervisor and staff become accustomed to the function
and learn to use it to their advantage. Therefore, readers
are encouraged to take selectively from this text those aspects
of supervision which will be valuable and practical in their
respective settings and situations. However, a few parameters
are essential to a worthwhile supervision program and these
cannot be overlooked or compromised.

A written supervision program is mandatory for survival
of the supervisory function. Such a program is a tangible
roadmap to which the supervisor can refer when supervisory
responsibilities seem ambiguous, and it serves as a contract
binding the supervisor, counselors, and administrative superiors. All three parties should help to construct and then
approve the supervision program.

Discreteness of the supervision function is another
parameter. When supervision is performed by a professional
have a valid supervisory role, the purity of the function
is not sorely jeopardized. But when supervision is one of
several functions performed via an administrative position, it
can become contaminated with other functions and lose the
properties which make it worthwhile. Worse yet, it can slowly
disappear as the administrator opts for the most comfortable

211

duties. If the only possible implementation of supervision is through a multi-functional role, then supervision should be given a discrete part of that role.

The final parameter is time allotment--for the supervisor(s) and counselors. Within their respective job descriptions time must be allotted to perform supervisory activities and participate in them. A common mistake is to make broad plans requiring more time than is available or agreeable with administrative superiors.

THE FUTURE

Many more parameters and steps could be suggested for the development of a supervision program, but the author believes that the future of supervision depends more on the professional self respect of counselors and their desire for competence than on the step-wise following of advice. Human resources within the counseling profession far surpass the overt display of talent, because many counselors have never realized their potential or had the encouragement to develop it. But when insecurities, apathy, and complacency give way to professional self respect, counselors do seek actively the kind of supervision which will release their tremendous potential. Perhaps those counselors who have already passed through this personal/professional growth stage, probably without the assistance of supervision, are the advocates with whom lies the future of counselor supervision.

SECTION THREE

Preparation

SECTION THREE

PREPARATION IN COUNSELOR SUPERVISION

A PERSONAL ACCOUNT

OVERVIEW

An objective and erudite account of preparation in
counselor supervision requires the support of referent literature and impirical evidence, neither of which exist in enough
quantity to base a chapter on supervision preparation. This
situation is a dilemma for those who wish to acquire knowledge
about the preparation of supervisors, for very few published
sources of information exist from which to learn, and the
situation particularly problematic for the author because
he wants to transmit information about supervision preparation,
but finds such information relatively nonexistent. The
author is left with only one alternative--to draw upon the
learning experiences that he and colleagues have had while
engaging in the preparation of counselor supervisors. A
principal origin of knowledge about any endeavor resides in
the acquired learnings of practitioners, and logic suggests
that this also should be true for supervisory preparation.
As long as readers recognize that knowledge acquired in this
manner is subjectively perceived and only minimally verified,
a personal account can provide a valuable information base
from which to launch discourse and research.

From this rationale the author has written the following
Chapter as a "personal account" of learnings and ideas gathered
through experiences as supervisee, supervisor, and instructor
of supervisors. The Chapter begins with a brief overview of
supervision preparation, offers suggestions on how to focus
preparation on consumers' needs, and then presents six learning
targets and respecive instructional modalities for the preparation of supervisors.

Chapter **7**

PREPARATION IN

COUNSELOR SUPERVISION

A PERSONAL ACCOUNT

John D. Boyd

PREPARATION IN COUNSELOR SUPERVISION: A PERSONAL ACCOUNT

John D. Boyd

Need for preparation in counselor supervision was documented in Chapter 1, and this material will not be reiterated. Stated succinctly, the rationale behind preparation in counselor supervision is that it is worthwhile; the supervisor who has undergone formal preparation in supervisory methodology will be much more effective than an unprepared supervisor. This rationale is in the minds of those who enter supervision preparation--supervisor-candidates who wish to develop the knowledge, skills, and performance proficiency necessary for quality supervisor practice.

Supervisor-candidates are a diverse group of professionals who share a desire to supervise their professional peers (counselors). The author has encountered some of the following candidate groups:

1. Experienced counselors from agency settings who want to offer supervisory services and coordinate in-service training.

2. Head counselors, guidance directors, and pupil personnel administrators from school settings.

3. Clinical and counseling psychologists who supervise staff counselors, social workers, and paraprofessionals in counseling centers, mental health clinics, and psychiatric hospitals.

4. School counselors who want to learn how to supervise high school students as peer counselors.

5. Nursing supervisors who work with psychiatric nurses.

Preparation of these supervisor-candidates is ordinarily done in two settings, those being universities and field settings where supervision is practiced. In universities the most commonplace method of supervisory preparation is a course which includes supervision among its topics of study, or a course devoted entirely to supervision. Preparation done at field settings is frequently called "in-service training," and is presented in a workshop format.

Both university courses and in-service workshops consist of two basic preparation components--classroom learning experiences and supervised practice. Classroom learning can be accomplished through a host of instructional methods, and there is virtually no limit to the ingenuity an instructor can employ. Typical classroom instructional methods are lectures, discussion, video and audio modeling tapes, skill-training exercises, and experiential exercises.

Supervised practice, the second basic preparation component, consists of the instructor being exposed to the candidate's supervision performance with actual supervisees, and later meeting for supervision sessions which focus on the performance. The instructor can be exposed to candidate performance through the following modes (in order of preference): observation of the live performance or co-supervision; observation of a video recording of the performance; hearing an audio recording of the performance; and exposure to the supervisor-candidate's retrospective description of the performance. "In vivo" observations generally produce much more material for supervision than do observational techniques more removed from the live performance.

The two preparation components of classroom learning and supervised practice can be present in a university course by integrating supervised practice into classroom activities, or by placing supervised practice in a separate course or a post-classroom practicum. In-service training workshops cannot separate classroom learning from actual practice; the consumers of in-service training (usually practicing supervisors) want their classroom learnings to be translated into skills and techniques of practical value, and they seek supervision of their attempts to perform immediately this methodology. Credible in-service workshops integrate classroom preparation and supervised practice.

FOCUSING SUPERVISION PREPARATION

Preparation in counselor supervision, whether done in a university course or an in-service workshop, poses a question of focus for the instructor. Should the instructor present a standardized preparation program, or try to prepare each candidate in the specific supervisory duties of his/her prospective practice setting? To answer this question the author will offer two suggestions, one regarding supervision courses and the other, in-service workshops.

Supervisor-candidates in a university course have differing goals for practice; following preparation they will disperse themselves among numerous employment settings such as public schools, clinics, agencies, and universities. Preparation for this group of candidates must be standardized somewhat, for it is virtually impossible to focus on all of their practice goals. A line of demarcation exists however which can provide a slight focus to the supervision course: this concerns whether candidates want preparation for the type of supervision done by university-based counselor educators, or supervision as performed by field-based supervisors in service delivery settings.

Counselor supervision from professional counselor educators is limited predominantly to supervision done in didactic or practicum courses, or from supervisory consultants to school systems and agencies (Boyd, 1977). Supervision of counseling probably consumes the majority of time, with the supervision of classroom exercises and field practicums taking up the remainder. Preparation for these supervision duties should put an emphasis on understanding the level of supervisor-candidates' personal and professional development, the supervision of their neophytic attempts at counseling, the construction of classroom learning exercises, and the supervision of students' field practicum experiences.

Field-based supervisors in schools and agencies oversee a broader range of counselor duties than does the counselor educator. Essentially, supervisors in the field oversee all of a counselor's work, which would include such things as consultation with parents, teachers, and other helping professionals; individual counseling; group counseling; group guidance and psychological education; testing; planning and management of the helping-service program and individual activity plans; report writing; and evaluating. Although counselor educators may touch some of these supervision duties in classroom exercises and field practicums, the field-based supervisor deals with these activities daily, and to a more extensive and intensive degree. Preparation of field-based supervisors therefore must equip them with the knowledge and skills to oversee a broad range of helping services and duties.

A course in counselor supervision can be focused on the counselor educator's supervisory duties, or it can be aimed at field-based supervision. In either case, a common core of knowledge and skills will characterize supervision preparation regardless of audience. To this core can be added simulation exercises and the study of applied strategies and programs more directly focused on supervisory situations in the field or in a counselor education program.

Supervision preparation for in-service training is more easily accomplished within a workshop setting than in a course, and the consumers for in-service preparation often request a specialized program. A demand for specialization is generated when the principles, approaches, and methods of counselor supervision are adaptively applied in a somewhat unique way and in a distinctive setting. For example, the supervision of paraprofessional "hot-line" counselors would differ from the supervision of certified rehabilitation counselors because of differences in the type of clientele and counseling per-formed, the skill-level of the supervisees, demands of the professional setting, and numerous other variables. In such cases the supervision instructor must do some "tailoring" of the in-service preparation program to meet candidates' special needs and situations.

Supervision instructors frequently are called upon to design specialized in-service preparation for field-based supervisors; the author has found the following series of overlapping steps to be an effective model for the shaping and designing process.

1. <u>Psychological Understanding of the Supervisor-Trainee</u>. The first step in custom designing a preparation pro-gram is to understand the supervisor-trainees. Psychological variables to assess are attitudes, beliefs, expectations, learning styles and preferences, and anything else about the trainees which may influ-ence how they will react to preparation and super-vision practice. Assessment is most feasible through informal discussions with individuals and small groups. A T-group experience in the beginning of training is another effective method for easing trainee tension, facilitating group cohesion, and gathering data to aid the instructor's understanding.

2. Situational Analysis. Another type of understanding that will aid the instructor in designing a preparation program is situational understanding. The instructor seeks to understand the overall professional setting in which trainees are or will be practicing supervision, and the tasks and activities which comprise the supervisory role. Situational analysis is aimed at discovering the environmental variables and job demands which impinge upon the supervisors and influence their behavior. Analysis methods are informal; interviews and the study of written job descriptions are the most practical methods. A site visit for observation is more time consuming but yields valuable information.

3. Skill Analysis and Assessment. When the instructor is investigating the supervisors' role and job demands in step 2, the process of skill analysis is started. Skills required to perform the supervisory role and job description are identified, and later, either before or at the beginning of training, the instructor assesses the skill repertoire of candidates comparing their proficiency level to job demands. Trainee and employer assessments of trainees' past job performances are gathered also.

4. Synthesis. Data gathered in steps 1, 2, and 3 are synthesized before the instructor attempts to design a preparation program. From an understanding of the trainees, their situation, skills, and past performance, the instructor can determine "if" and "how" in-service preparation can improve supervision. If preparation is warranted, its goals are established.

5. Preparation Design. Step 5 is relatively easy when the previous four have targeted the goals for training. This last step consists of choosing preparation methodology which will accomplish preparation goals.

Illustrative Case

An organization of helping-service agencies in a metropolitan area asked a supervision instructor to offer a workshop which would improve the performance of counselor supervisors. To prepare for the workshop, the instructor visited a cross section of the participating agencies and interviewed counselors and supervisors. At a later date counselors in all agencies received a mailed questionnaire from the instructor requesting an evaluation of the supervision they had received in the past, and soliciting their input about supervision needs and the type of supervision they desired. Supervisors in the agencies received self-assessment forms for the rating of their skills and were asked for input regarding their preferences for supervisory training.

From the information gathered through interviews and questionnaires, the instructor identified three important characteristics about the supervisors:

1. they were defensive about counselor evaluations of their supervisory efforts;

2. a few supervisors had received considerably more preparation than the others and were relatively advanced in skill-level; and

3. several different theoretical orientations and professional ideologies were represented in the group.

Also identified through the study were four areas for profitable training:

1. supervision of case conferences;

2. construction and conduction of in-service training programs;

3. individual supervision of difficult counseling cases; and

4. supervision to improve organizational efforts of counselor staffs.

Based upon these supervisor characteristics and training areas, the intructor designed an in-service training workshop. A T-group experience was planned as an appropriate beginning for the workshop; such an experience would allow supervisors to ventilate and resolve their apprehension and defensiveness about counselor evaluations, and allow the instructor to explain the workshop's purpose and how supervisor input had been used to tailor the training. Learning exercises were developed so that the highly skilled supervisors were mixed among those at lower skill levels, and thereby could offer leadership and peer assistance.

Workshop content was designed to be theoretically and ideologically eclectic so that supervisors from different disciplines and backgrounds would not encounter conflict. Techniques and methods from the psychotherapeutic, behavioral, and systems approaches to supervision were applied to the tasks of supervising groups and individuals, conducting in-service training, and promoting organizational effectiveness.

This fictional case is just one illustration of how a supervision instructor could design an in-service workshop for a specific trainee group and setting. The design process is simply one of identifying supervisory skill needs and meeting these needs with appropriate preparation. In the remainder of this Chapter the supervision instructor is offered learning targets and instructional modalities which could be used to meet the preparation needs of practicing supervisors through in-service workshop training, or the preparation needs of supervisor-candidates in a university course.

LEARNING TARGETS: INSTRUCTIONAL GOALS AND MODALITIES IN SUPERVISION PREPARATION

Preparation in counselor supervision is a challenging task for the instructor, one which poses two questions that must be answered before preparation can begin: "What should a counselor learn in order to become a competent supervisor?" "How does a supervisor-candidate learn these things?" In the remainder of this Chapter the author has offered an answer to these questions via six learning targets. As used herein, a learning target is a module having instructional goals--i.e., specific learnings which the supervisor-candidate should gain, and the instructional modalities by which the instructor can ensure that candidates acquire these learnings. The six learning targets are listed in Figure 7.1 in order of presentation within a course or workshop.

Instructional Goals

Preparation in counselor supervision can involve a range of learnings surpassed by few, if any other, preparation areas. In the course of preparation the supervisor-candidate may memorize factual information, acquire and/or alter patterns of thought and attitude, practice unfamiliar cognitive operations (analysis, synthesis), develop new conceptual frameworks, and learn to perform behavioral skills. These different kinds of learnings form four categories which can serve as broad instructional goals for supervision preparation: factual and conceptual information, experiential learnings, performance skills, and the tasks and duties which form an applied methodology. As these four goals are discussed within each of the author's six learning targets, readers will recognize that they are sequentially dependent. Facts, concepts, and experiential learnings tend to facilitate the development of skills, and applied practice depends upon the performance of skills.

225

LEARNING TARGETS	INSTRUCTIONAL GOALS	INSTRUCTIONAL MODALITIES
Introductory Perspective	Factual and Conceptual Information	Didactic Modality
Psychotherapeutic Approach	Experiential Learnings	Modeling Modality
Behavioral Approach	Performance Skills	Simulation Exercise
Effective Personal Supervisory Style	Applied Methodology	Supervised Practice
Systems Approach		
Supervised Practice		

Figure 7.1. Supervision Preparation--Sequentially Presented
For Learning Targets, Instructional Goals, And
Instructional Modalities.

Instructional Modalities

Instructional goals within each learning target are accomplished through multiple instructional modalities. As proposed by Lazarus (1976), numerous modalities exist through which people learn and by which people are taught. This proposition is supported by counselor educators such as Hackney and Nye (1973), Jakubowski-Spector (1971), and Krumboltz (1967) who advocate multiple learning routes in counselor preparation, and the research reviewed in Chapter 3 tends to be particularly supportive of supervisory training methods which invoke several kinds of learning principles and instructional modalities. Generally speaking, evidence and opinion is growing within counselor education and supervision in favor of using multiple instructional modalities so that multiple learning modalities can be influenced in the learner.

Many instructional modalities can be used to prepare supervisors, but this Chapter will not attempt to exhaust them. Rather, the author chooses to present four modalities which have, over the years, proven particularly reliable and effective (see Figure 7.1). Through these modalities the instructor can assault the instructional goals of supervision preparation.

Didactive Modality. The didactic instructional modality is probably the most familiar, consisting of the three traditional pedagogical methods of reading, lecture, discussion, and structured didactic exercise. Considerable criticism of educators who rely solely on didactic teaching methods exists, but this should not discourage the supervision instructor from using them. The mistake made by pure didacticians is that of excluding other potent instructional modalities. Through didactic instruction supervisor-candidates gain factual and conceptual information, and may develop new cognitive operations, all of which facilitate and enhance their capacity to learn from other instructional modalities.

Modeling Modality. A second instructional modality, which is often most effective following the didactic one, is imitative learning or modeling. The skills of supervision are novel to most candidates, and reading, hearing, and talking about methodology does not guarantee its performance. Didactic learning may give supervisor-candidates the ability to understand the activities, skills, and tasks of supervision, but without modeling the performance of methodology is very difficult to achieve. The absence of observational learning forces the supervisor-candidate to discover, through trial-and-error performance attempts, the behavioral form and appearance of supervisory skills. Much of this drudgery can be avoided simply by presenting models which show the candidate how to perform skills. Following a modeling presentation most learners can approximate focal skills much more accurately than before.

227

The supervision instructor is the most impactful model for supervisor-candidates. While the skills of videotaped experts may look smoother than the instructor's often impromptu attempts, there is no substitute for the live demonstration of a difficult skill, particularly when such a demonstration is requested by learners who are having difficulty with the acquisition of that skill. Furthermore, the author is a staunch believer in the maxim: "If you can't do it, don't try to teach it!" Supervisor-candidates want an instructor who is a supervisor, one who can demonstrate methodology, thereby achieving instant credibility even when demonstrations are imperfect in style.

Other types of modeling for supervision preparation are audio and video tapes, films, role played vignettes by supervisor-candidates, and written transcripts of supervision sessions. sessions. Whatever modeling procedure is employed, it is suggested that the instructor present the model as "one way" to perform methodology, learning the student freedom to develop a competent

Simulation Exercise. A simulation exercise is one which approximates reality, and within supervision preparation these exercises are designed to approximate as closely as possible the reality of actual supervision practice. There is a stage in the preparation of supervisors when they are not proficient enough to supervise authentic supervisees, yet they need simulated supervision practice so that methodology studied through the didactic and modeling modalities can be rehearsed. Moreover, through simulation one can gain the dynamic learnings which ordinarily only occur through the experience of supervising a counselor. Simulation is an indispensable instructional modality for a fundamental reason which is stated in this old Chinese proverb: "I hear and I forget, I see and I remember, I do and I understand."

Supervised Practice. This fourth modality for supervision preparation is perhaps the oldest and most important. From ancient times to the present day supervised practice has been the principal method for teaching crafts and professions. The value of supervised practice to counselors, before and after formal preparation, has been the central message of this entire text, and now the author proposes that supervised practice is just as valuable a learning modality for supervisor-candidates.

Supervising the practice of supervision places the instructor in the position of being a "supervisor of supervisors," a position particularly analogous to that of supervising counselors. The instructor is usually supervising a neophyte or less-experienced supervisor, the relationship between the instructor and supervisor-candidate has the dynamics of the

228

typical supervision interaction, and the methodology for
supervising counselors applies equally well to the supervision
of supervisors. Supervised practice has given the author some
of his most rewarding experiences in the preparation of supervisors, and supervisor-candidates have consistently rated this
modality as the most important one in their preparation.

As used in this Chapter, supervised practice of counselor
supervision is treated as both a learning target and an
instructional modality. It is a module containing a wealth of
learnings in applied practice, and it is a mode for acquiring
these learnings.

LEARNING TARGET ONE
AN INTRODUCTORY PERSPECTIVE TO COUNSELOR SUPERVISION

Supervision preparation must begin somewhere among the
vast range of learning alluded to earlier in this Chapter - but
where should that starting point be? Some instructors might
think that one starting point is as good as another, but the
author decidedly disagrees. His experience in the preparation
of supervisors and counselors, as well as with clients in
counseling and psychotherapy, has been that people learn most
readily when lessons are preluded by an introduction which
overviews the material to be covered. Such an introduction
reduces the ambiguity which can inhibit learning progress, and
gives the learner an awareness of the relationship among
disparate parts of the lesson. After such introductions supervisor-candidates have frequently exclaimed to the author:
"Now I know where we're (the class) going, and how it all
(course material) fits together!"

Based on the foregoing rationale, an appropriate starting
point for preparation in counselor supervision is an overview
of the material to be taught. This overview consists of facts,
concepts, and understandings which provide students with an
introductory perspective of the supervision field. Such an
introductory perspective would include the following items.

1. A concrete and operational definition of counselor
   supervision. The vague ideas and nebulous definitions
   which characterize unprepared supervision aspirants
   should be replaced with a specific and functional
   definition. Throughout supervision preparation
   students return again and again to the definition of
   counselor supervision; gradually the definition is
   changed from an initial memorization to a meaningful
   conceptualization.

2. An understanding of the purposes of counselor supervision. Grasping and adopting these purposes (see Chapter

229

1) is the root of professional identity. It is an oversight for the instructor to prepare supervisor-candidates in methodology without helping them recognize the purposes of this work. Supervisors who do not have a professional purpose are prone to disillusionment, loss of motivation, and career dissatisfaction.

3. <u>An awareness of supervision methodology</u>. The methodology of counselor supervision includes four activities (consultation, counseling, training and instruction, evaluation); four major approaches (psychotherapeutic, behavioral, integrative, systems); and a host of tasks and duties which are unique to the supervisor's setting and job description. In subsequent learning sessions the supervisor-candidate receives training in this methodology, but in the beginning it is sufficient that instructors merely promote an awareness. A general understanding of how the skills and techniques from approaches and activities are synthesized and applied in actual practice should accompany this awareness.

4. <u>A knowledge of supervision settings and practices</u>. An introductory perspective to counselor supervision would be incomplete without exposure to the various supervision settings and practices. Supervisor-candidates do not ordinarily realize that practices can vary greatly from one type of setting to another. By grasping this knowledge candidates take the first step toward developing the versatility needed to adapt supervision practice to novel settings and situations. Subsequent learning sessions continue the development of versatility.

5. <u>An understanding of the nature of the supervisory relationship</u>. As explained in Chapter 11, the relationship between supervisor and supervisee is a constant variable in all supervisory methodology. Though theorists may disagree on the relative importance of the relationship, it is an accepted fact that competent supervision necessitates successful interpersonal relations with supervisees. Supervisor-candidates cannot begin too early to understand the dynamics of the supervisory relationship, particularly those candidates who will be engaging concurrently in supervised practice and classroom preparation. They need to explore the anxieties and expectations within supervisees and themselves and to devise strategies for establishing the supervisory relationship.

6. <u>A conceptualization of the longitudinal supervision process</u>. The "longitudinal process" refers to those changes taking place in the supervisee and the nature

of supervision across time. If supervisor-candidates
are preparing to supervise practicum students in a
university setting they should understand what happens
to these students as they participate in a practicum
course. A field-based supervisor should be aware of
the career development and personal adjustment changes
which occur during a counselor's tenure, and how these
will affect the counselor's need for and reaction to
supervision.

Supervision instructors may want to add more facts, concepts, and understandings to this list, for an introductory
perspective can be anything the instructor desires. But
regardless of content, the principle behind the introductory
perspective is that a clear and inclusive view of the supervision field will enhance and promote learning.

Instructional Modalities

The author's first learning target in supervision preparation, an introductory perspective, is primarily a goal of
factual and conceptual information which is accomplished through
the didactic modality of instruction. In other words, a
perspective on counselor supervision gradually crystallizes in
the minds of supervision-candidates as they read about supervision, listen to lectures from the instructor, and discuss
thought-provoking questions and issues. Candidates can read
in Chapter 1 about most of the facts and concepts mentioned
in the previous itemized list, but that Chapter does bot include
information about supervisory approaches, dynamics of the
supervisory relationship, and the longitudinal process of supervision. This content must be provided through supplementary
readings (which can be drawn from reference lists) and the
instructor's lectures.

Group discussions can be a very effective method for
promoting the introductory perspective, although the efficacy
of this method depends upon the group's constellation and
dynamics, and the instructor's group leadership skills. The
author has encountered some groups where discussion was minimal
in quantity and quality, and his leadership skills seemed
inconsequential. Other groups have provided a tremendous
learning experience to participants, requiring only facilitative
efforts from the instructor. Throughout his experiences,
some common verbal leads and discussion questions have been
consistently productive.

VERBAL LEADS AND DISCUSSION QUESTIONS

1. If a person told you that he or she was a supervisor of counselors, what questions would you ask in order to determine if this person is truly supervising? What criteria or guidelines would prompt your questions?

2. Can a professional do an effective job of supervising counselors if supervision is one of several functions in his/her position?

3. What are some of the pseudo-supervision activities that are performed under the guise of counselor supervision?

4. Can the helping professions profit from supervision in counselor preparation and practice settings; if so, how?

5. Give a fictional but realistic example of how counselor supervision could achieve one of its purposes with a counselor.

6. Why is there more than one approach to counselor supervision?

7. Explain how a supervisor, from each of the four major approaches to counselor supervision, would perform the four activities of supervision (consultation, counseling, training and instruction, evaluation).

8. Explain what is meant by the term "synthesized methodology," and give examples.

9. Name some of the different settings in which counselor supervision is performed, and compare and contrast supervision practice in these settings.

10. What are some of the positive and negative experiences you have had as a supervisee?

11. If you were a supervisee, what kind of relationship would you like to have with your supervisor?

12. As a supervisor, what kind of relationship do you want with your supervisees?

13. What are some of the attitudes, expectancies, and emotions that you would expect to see in a supervisee who had never before received supervision, and how would these intrapersonal dynamics affect the supervisory relationship?

232

14. What steps should a supervisor take to establish a relationship with a supervisee? Role play these steps with a member of the discussion group.

15. Looking back over your experiences as a counselor, where and how did you gain significant learnings that improved your performance, and what were these learnings?

16. How would you expect a student-counselor to change during a one-semester practicum course? What changes would you expect in a practicing counselor who receives supervision during a two-year period?

These examples are intended to elicit inductive and deductive reasoning from supervisor-candidates, leading to self-generated learnings and learnings gained from listening to other group participants. A few of the questions have an experiential dimension to them and instructors may wish to emphasize this dimension within group discussions. Questions which ask participants to reflect on their past experiences as counselor and supervisee are intended to foster self awareness, and through self awareness of participants' own experiences a better understanding of their supervisees should accrue. Imagery exercises which ask participants, in their "mind's eye," to become the supervisee and experience instructor-induced situations is another technique which can add variety to group discussions and tap the experiential realm. Covert rehearsal and role playing of relationship-building skills can also be done in the group setting. In short, many innovative techniques from other instructional modalities can be infused into group discussions. Most of these techniques are employed more frequently for other learning targets and will be discussed in those sections of the Chapter.

LEARNING TARGET TWO
THE PSYCHOTHERAPEUTIC APPROACH

When supervisor-candidates have developed an introductory perspective of the counselor supervision field it is time for the second learning target in the preparation sequence--the psychotherapeutic approach. Candidates enter study of this approach with a familiarity acquired in learning target one; they know that the psychotherapeutic approach is one of four major approaches to counselor supervision, and that methodology from these approaches can be synthesized. They realize that there are four supervision activities, as well as numerous tasks and duties, where techniques from the psychotherapeutic approach can be applied. Candidates have also been introduced

to the concept of intrapersonal and interpersonal dynamics
when they studied the supervisory relationship.

As instructors enter the second learning target they must
determine the instructional objectives for preparation in the
psychotherapeutic approach, and they must select instructional
modalities with which to reach these objectives. "What should
supervisor-candidates learn, and how should they learn it?"

Factual and Conceptual Information

Within all four of the major approaches to counselor
supervision, a considerable amount of factual and conceptual
information must be learned if one is to develop proficiency
with the psychotherapeutic approach. The author has attempted
to condense this information and present it in Chapter 2,
but recently published articles and the instructor's own input
should supplement chapter material. Key points of factual and
conceptual information which the supervisor-candidate should
learn about the psychotherapeutic approach are as follows:

1. A concrete definition of intrapersonal and interpersonal
   dyanmics. This definition gives candidates a standardized base from which to learn the psychotherapeutic
   approach, and the preparation needed to identify
   dynamics.

2. The "dynamics theory" of counselor supervision. Only
   a summary of this theory was offered in Chapter 2, so
   the instructor should consult appropriate references
   and provide the theoretical rationale through lecture.
   Candidates need a reason for learning and employing
   psychotherapeutic supervisory methods.

3. A knowledge of the six dynamic sources in a supervision
   triad. This knowledge is very important because it
   directs the candidates attention toward dynamic sources.
   The candidate learns where to look for dynamics.
   Further learning of the psychotherapeutic approach
   depends on this attentional skill.

4. An understanding of dynamic contingencies. The
   candidate must learn that intrapersonal dynamics
   influence and are reflected in interpersonal actions;
   that interpersonal actions stimulate intrapersonal
   dynamics in other people; and that inner dynamics are
   thereupon expressed interpersonally. Once candidates
   understand this "contingency chain" they can begin to
   unravel dynamic patterns.

5. An understanding of dynamic patterns. If a candidate
   successfully learns the first four items of this list an

understanding of dynamic patterns will emerge. The
instructor can promote this understanding by exposing
the candidate to common patterns and through exercises
testing the candidate's ability to diagnose and explain
patterns.

6. <u>A knowledge and understanding of the goals of psychotherapeutic supervision.</u> Having gained a knowledge of
   dynamics and dynamic theory, and before studying
   methodology, the candidate can profit from an understanding of the goals of psychotherapeutic supervision.
   These goals will give a purpose to methodology.

7. <u>A knowledge of Interpersonal Process Recall (IPR).</u>
   The information candidates receive about IPR, before
   skill training, should concern its goals, techniques,
   and practices.

8. <u>A knowledge of the unstructured method of psychotherapeutic supervision.</u> As with IPR and the unstructured
   method, candidates should learn that supervisee anxiety
   and defensive behavior serve as guidelines for the
   supervisor's application of methodology. Psychotherapeutic supervision is responsive to supervisee dynamics,
   and methodology is adapted to meet each supervisee's
   dynamic make-up.

In addition to reading Chapter 2 and related journal articles, the use of instructors' lectures and group discussions has
been found to be of particular importance in teaching factual
and conceptual information about the psychotherapeutic approach.
During lectures material that has been read is clarified and
translated into performance terms through anecdote and
illustration. For example, supervisor-candidates understand the
"dynamics" concept more readily if a clearcut supervision case
example is presented, preferably one taken from the instructor's
supervision experience.

Another didactic technique for promoting an understanding
of the psychotherapeutic approach is group discussion which
relates didactic material to the life experiences of supervisor-
candidates. To implement this technique the instructor asks
candidates to recall a memorable helping interaction from their
past, an interaction in which the candidate was affectively
influenced by the helpee. The candidate then is requested to
analyze the interaction in terms of dynamics and share the case
with the group. Through discussion of these "real life" cases
the concept of dynamics and dynamic patterns comes alive.
Candidates discover that dynamics have been present in their
helpgiving interactions, and they become comfortable with the
disclosure and discussion of dynamics. During discussion the

instructor can offer assistance with dynamic analysis, and later, in order that candidates begin to think as supervisors, the discussion can be influenced through instructor leads such as the following:

> What influence would the dynamics in this case be likely to have upon the course of the helpgiving interaction?

> Can you identify any dynamics in the counselor that, if changed, would improve the helpgiving interaction?

> How would this counselor be likely to react to psychotherapeutic supervision?

> Can you think of some IPR questions that would evoke dynamic awareness and understanding in the counselor and/or helpee?

> What are the techniques from the unstructured method of psychotherapeutic supervision that you would use if you were supervising this counselor?

Experiential Learnings

Experiential learnings consist of lessons about intrapersonal and interpersonal dynamics which are most significantly learned through dynamic experiences. A dynamic lesson is a learning about one's own dynamics as these transpire in a helping relationship with another person. Having learned a dynamic lesson, the learner (supervisor or counselor) is better prepared to deal in the future with the dynamics and situation of the lesson. Some of the dynamic lessons which contribute to competence in the psychotherapeutic supervision approach will be described, followed by a discussion of how such lessons can be learned through simulation exercise and supervised practice.

Experiential Lessons

Performance Anxiety. Supervisor-candidates are often fearful of a "bad" supervision performance. They expect the worst and exaggerate the awfulness of a less than perfect performance. It is important for the candidate to accept nervousness as a part of his/her first attempts at supervisory performance, but not to exacerbate nervousness into intense anxiety. The candidate must learn to strive for a realistic level of performance, to accept the fact that everyone gets stumped sometimes and performs poorly, and to use a self management process for managing performance anxiety.

Interpersonal Threat. Much of the anxiety which counselors and supervisors experience is rooted in the interpersonal interactions they have with helpees. Under certain inter-personal conditions a dynamic pattern emerges with helper anxiety being the prominent emotion. (Space limitations do not permit a full treatment of such anxiety patterns, as there are many.) Experiential lessons in these cases result in an unlearning or resolution of the helper's anxiety so that more appropriate professional behavior can replace anxiety responses.

Attraction and Approval. Two related experiential learnings concern the supervisor's attraction to the helpee, and/or the supervisor's need for approval from the helpee. Supervisor-candidates should become aware of and control those attractions they have toward supervisees so these dynamics will not influence their objective judgement and supervision behavior. Likewise, if supervisors have a strong "need" for supervisee approval they will seek praise rather than concentrate on effective supervision--which may not bring them approval! They must overcome the quest for approval in order to become a competent supervisor.

Aversion and Anger. Somehow counselors get the idea that they should like everyone, and this attitude is the counterpart of the "need" for approval (everyone should like and approve of me!). When counselors become supervisors they therefore conclude: "I must like all supervisees, it is wrong for me to be averse to any of them." Similarly they sometimes think that it is wrong and unprofessional of them to be angry at supervisees. The dynamic lesson to be learned about aversion and anger is that these are inevitable human emotions which, if not exaggerated, do not necessarily ruin one's supervision behavior. Rather than repress these impulses the supervision-candidate should become aware of and manage them.

Responsibility. Counselor supervision is a cooperative venture between the supervisor and counselor. The supervisor is responsible for his/her supervision behavior--the choosing and performance of effective methodology. The counselor is responsible for his/her learning behavior--sincere attempts to improve performance through supervision and self-directed activities outside of supervision (e.g., taping, critiquing, reading, exercises). In most cases, but certainly not all, if these two areas of responsibility are met the result will be an improvement in counselor performance.

Supervision-candidates are prone to overstep the boundaries of their responsibility and accept the supervisee's responsibility, especially when supervisees place their responsibilities on the supervisor. The result is a supervisor who becomes emotionally upset over supervisees' failure to learn, and consequently condemns him/herself for inadequacy. Supervisors can avoid this problem if they learn to stay within their own areas of responsibility, and not to punish themselves for the irresponsibility of supervisees.

Dynamic lessons such as these five are acquired by supervisor-candidates through experiential learning, the same kind of experiential learning through which counselors go in psychotherapeutic supervision. Instructors set in motion this experiential learning by employing the techniques of psychotherapeutic supervision in simulation exercises and during supervised practice. Simulation exercises for experiential learning are conducted in the classroom, and supervised practice is conducted in field settings and university laboratories.

Simulation Exercise

Within a classroom or workshop facility, how can a supervision instructor help candidates to experientially become aware of dynamics, understand contingencies and patterns, and learn how to change dynamics and therapeutically use them? Many instructors decide to abbreviate classroom instruction and go straight to supervised practice in an effort to answer this question. They rationalize the decision by saying "there's really only one way to learn supervision and that's through doing it!" The author has been guilty of this rationalization on more than one occasion.

Supervised practice is one of the best ways (not the only way) to experientially learn the dynamic curriculum of supervision preparation; it also has a serious drawback. The instructor cannot induce or plan for the experiential lessons of supervision practice; he/she must wait for them (if they occur) and facilitate their process when they occur. This is a haphazard experiential learning program at best.

A more deliberate and efficient plan for experiential learning can be conducted through simulation exercise. The instructor can plan to induce, through simulation, those dynamics which naturally take place in supervision practice. As candidates experience these dynamics the supervisor can promote the learning of dynamic lessons by applying techniques drawn from Interpersonal Process Recall (IPR) and the unstructured method of psychotherapeutic supervision. Three simulation exercises which the author has used for experiential learning are the affect simulation exercise, the coached supervisee exercise, and the peer supervisee exercise.

Affect Simulation Exercise

Affect simulation as described by Kagan and Schauble (1969) is a valuable classroom exercise for teaching dynamic lessons. As adapted to supervision preparation, affect simulation

238

consists of the instructor presenting a video tape of provocative supervisee vignettes to a group of supervisor-candidates, encouraging disclosure of their affective reactions (intrapersonal dynamics) to the supervisees, and then helping candidates gain awareness and understanding of these reactions through IPR questions. The instructor's IPR leads and other facilitatory responses should create and communicate the dynamic lesson that intrapersonal dynamics are a human function which need not be supressed and hidden from others or oneself; that, to the contrary, supervisors must be aware of their dynamics.

The affect simulation exercise can be extended by having a group discussion subsequent to affective disclosures. Timing of this activity is just right for supervision candidates to consider how their intrapersonal dynamics influence their interpersonal behavior, and to realize the significance of dynamic contingencies for the supervisory relationship.

Coached Supervisee Exercise

The coached supervisee exercise offers more experiential learning than is possible with affect simulation. In this exercise the instructor prepares confederate supervisees to theatrically play roles or personality types which are difficult to handle in supervision. Supervisor-candidates are instructed to conduct a brief supervision session with these confederates, even though they have not yet been trained in the methodology of psychotherapeutic supervision, or any other approach. Candidates are assured that they are not expected to demonstrate high levels of skill proficiency, and that the exercise is one in which they can try their wings at supervision without being responsible for helping an actual supervisee. They are informed that the supervisees are role playing, but they are not told the content of these roles nor that the exercise is for experiential purposes.

Experiential learning is present to a great extent in the coached supervisee exercise, for supervision candidates encounter dynamics such as performance anxiety, various kinds of interpersonal threats from the supervisees, and assorted attractions, aversions, anger states, and feelings of responsibility for supervisee progress. Instructors can design supervisee roles for the simulation of any dynamics they think are important to encounter, and these plans usually have a fair success rate. But instructors are advised that the prediction of human dynamics is rather unreliable, and they must be prepared to deal with the unexpected. Supervisee roles which have provided provocative stimuli in the authors' exercises are as follows:

239

A defensive supervisee who is aggressive toward the supervisor and makes sly derogatory remarks.

A defensive and anxious supervisee who is reticent and does not actively participate in the supervision process.

A supervisee who is insecure and self effacing. He/she shows dependency on the supervisor, is profuse with compliments toward the supervisor, and simultaneously acts helpless about performing adequately as a counselor.

A flirtatious supervisee of the opposite sex.

A supervisee who is arrogant, "knows it all," and doesn't see any reason to be in supervision.

A supervisee with aversive values or personal characteristics: selfish, manipulative, hostile toward society, cynical, and so forth.

Immediately following candidates' sessions with the confederates they enter a group or individual supervision session with the instructor. Because encounter with coached supervisees generates more dynamic activity in supervisor-candidates than does affect simulation, supervision following the encounters is more demanding on the instructor. The group supervision process begins with the establishment of a non-threatening atmosphere and open discussion by the participants. Gradually the instructor begins to use IPR leads and other psychotherapeutic supervisory techniques. The instructor's goals are to help candidates (1) explore the dynamics they experienced, (2) understand their dynamic patterns, (3) provide insight and self-management strategies for changing their problematic dynamics, and (4) devise plans for therapeutically utilizing dynamics with their supervisees. These are the goals of psychotherapeutic supervision.

Peer Supervision Exercise

The last simulation exercise to be mentioned under experiential learning is also a skill-practice exercise, and it will be discussed later in the Chapter in that capacity. Presently the "peer supervision exercise" is offered as a way for participants to learn dynamic lessons. As employed with a group of supervisor-candidates the instructor completes the following steps:

1. Participants conduct and record (audio or video) a counseling or consultation session with an actual helpee. This recording will later be used for supervision (see step 3).

2. The group is organized into supervisor-supervisee dyads; half of the participants are assigned the role of supervisor and the other half serve as supervisees.

3. Participants who are assigned as supervisors conduct and record a psychotherapeutic supervision session with their assigned supervisees. This session focuses on the recorded helping interaction from step 1.

4. Upon finishing the supervision sessions supervisees either write a retrospective review of their supervision experience or have a group session with the instructor to share their experiences. The write-up or review is aimed at helping the supervisees become aware of their dynamic learnings, and at critiquing the supervisory methods they received.

5. Participants who served as supervisors can also recall dynamics and evaluate their recorded supervision performance individually with the instructor or in a group. They can profit from experiential learning and the skill practice inherent in the supervisor's role.

The peer supervision exercise must be conducted twice if participants are to have the opportunity to experience both the supervisor and supervisee roles. There are advantages to a third and fourth trial also--participants (as supervisees) are exposed by the additional experience to another supervisor who may practice the psychotherapeutic approach in a different manner; when they portray supervisors, participants are given a second chance to practice skills with a new supervisee.

Supervised Practice. When a supervisor-candidate gains the necessary competence to work with authentic counselors he/she can enter supervised practice and open up another opportunity for the learning of dynamic lessons. The candidate practices supervision independently or engages in co-supervision with the instructor, the instructor observes the candidate's performance, and later they meet for a supervision session; i.e. the instructor supervises the candidate's supervision performance. The instructor fosters the learning of dynamic lessons by using psychotherapeutic supervision techniques to help the candidate identify and become aware of dynamics, change dynamics, and therapeutically use dynamics. In essence, the candidate's experiential learning process during supervised practice is one of participating in the psychotherapeutic supervision offered by the instructor.

An illustration would be the supervisor-candidate who encounters an arrogant counselor during supervised practice and engages in a power struggle with the candidate. The instructor

241

would use psychotherapeutic supervision to help the candidate
become aware of his/her feeling of threat, anger, and desire to
subdue the candidate. Then the candidate would be assisted
in resolving these feelings, and in developing appropriate
supervisory strategies for dealing with the counselor.

Skills and Applied Methodology of the Psychotherapeutic Approach

Preparation in the psychotherapeutic approach to counselor
supervision begins with the instructor attempting to teach and
facilitate the acquisition of factual and conceptual information, continues with instructional attention given to experiential learnings, and concludes with classroom preparation,
with instruction in skills and applied methodology. Following
skill preparation the supervisor-candidate is ready for
supervised practice.

The skills of psychotherapeutic supervision are contained
in Interpersonal Process Recall (IPR) and the unstructured
method, both of which were described in Chapter 2. Once the
supervisor-candidate learns to perform these two methods their
composite skills can be applied in other supervisory tasks and
duties. The remainder of this section on the psychotherapeutic
approach is devoted to an outline and description of skills as
they appear in IPR and the unstructured method, along with
suggested modalities for teaching the skills.

Interpersonal Process Recall. The IPR method of psychotherapeutic supervision accomplishes the goals of dynamic
awareness and an understanding of dynamic contingencies via
four techniques, which are as follows:

1. Recognizing Dynamics. By observing a helping interaction the IPR supervisor should be able to spot
   observable cues of intrapersonal dynamics in the helper
   and helpee, and to identify the kinds of interpersonal
   dynamics demonstrated by the two parties.

2. Formulating Recall Questions. Upon recognizing dynamics
   the supervisor must quickly formulate a question which
   would elicit dynamic recall in the helper or helpee.

3. Asking Recall Questions. There is a considerable
   amount of expertise required in the asking of recall
   questions. Timing, voice inflection, and nonverbal
   behavior must be shaped into a manner that is non-
   threatening, yet evocative.

4. Counselor, Client, and Mutual Recall. IPR questioning
   is adapted to recall with counselors, clients, and both
   parties. Another adaptation is using the IPR technique
   in affect simulation exercises.

To reduce the IPR method to four simplistic sounding techniques seems sacrilegious, for there is so much expertise present when IPR is practiced by an authority. But these fundamental skill behaviors must be mastered if the supervisor-candidate wants to develop a beginner's competence in IPR.

Unstructured Psychotherapeutic Supervision. There are more identifiable skills in the unstructured method of psychotherapeutic supervision than in IPR, and the supervisor-candidate is allowed more latitude in style. Skills from IPR provide a foundation for learning the unstructured method, and some of these skills are extended beyond the IPR structure to form new skills.

1. Supervisor Experiencing. A monitoring of one's intrapersonal dynamics and interpersonal expression is called an "experiencing skill." This is perhaps the most basic skill of the unstructured method, for without it supervisor's see only others' dynamics, and they cannot model the therapeutic utilization of dynamics for their supervisees.

2. Focus and Response. This technique is an adaptation and extension of IPR recall leads. The focus of supervisor leads is extended beyond the counselor-helpee relationship to include the supervisor-counselor interaction. If supervisees deny awareness of obvious dynamics the supervisor may intermingle confrontive responses with IPR leads. Analogies may also be offered to implant awareness in affectively blunted supervisees. The focus and response skill is more threatening for the supervisee than IPR, but it is potentially more valuable in terms of awareness and dynamic insight.

3. Inductive Techniques. The goal of inductive techniques is an understanding of dynamic contingencies and patterns. This is done with a sequence of leads that will stimulate inductive reasoning in the supervisee. The inductive leads are infused with other verbal techniques that highlight the supervisee's insights and dynamic learnings (e.g., reflection, clarification, summary).

4. Dynamic Insight. Creating dynamic insight within psychotherapeutic supervision calls for the same skill that creates insight in counseling and psychotherapy. The client or supervisee is taught or helped to construct a new percept which is subsequently employed to place meaning on environmental events and other aspects of reality. Interpretive skills, drawn from the supervisor's therapeutic orientation (client-centered, RET, Gestalt), are the principal method.

243

5. Therapeutic Utilization of Dynamics. A series of
   skills comprise the therapeutic utilization of dynamics.
   The series begins with the diagnostic skill of identifying dynamic patterns within the supervisor-coun-
   selor-helpee triad. Problematic dynamics or patterns
   are targeted for change, and the supervisor determines
   how he/she can have a dynamically constructive influence
   on the counselor. This plan for dynamically influencing the counselor is then conducted.

Instructional Modalities. Supervisor-candidates develop
the skills of psychotherapeutic supervision through the
instructional modalities of modeling, simulation exercise, and
supervised practice. The factual and conceptual information
previously learned through the didactic modality, plus experiential learnings, is a necessary prelude but an insufficient
preparation for the performance of psychotherapeutic methodology. Skill training through modeling and simulated exercise
is therefore necessary to develop skill performance.

The author does not presume that there is only one way to
train supervisor-candidates in the psychotherapeutic approach,
and a classic training model will not be imposed on readers.
But the author does assume that constructing effective skill-
instruction procedures is a difficult task, and that instructors
may get some new and helpful ideas through exposure to his
procedures.

The author's training efforts are directed first at IPR,
and when this method is mastered training moves on to the
unstructured method of psychotherapeutic supervision. The
training procedure for IPR begins by providing supervisor-
candidates with video-taped demonstrations of IPR which can be
made by the instructor or ordered pre-prepared. Candidates
are given an uninterrupted observation of the model, and then
it is played a second time with a narrative description from
the instructor. During this second observation the tape is
periodically stopped to point out discrete skills, and each
skill may be played several times to ensure an observational
learning effect.

Shortly after the modeling presentation, preferably on the
same day, candidates are asked to perform IPR skills in a
simulated response exercise. A video-taped counseling session
is played, and candidates are instructed to look for dynamics.
Immediately following the observation, and without discussion
of the counseling session, the tape is played again in 2-3
minute intervals. Between intervals the candidates are given a
few minutes to write IPR questions which they would ask the
counselor and client if they were conducting IPR with them.
Upon completion of the tape candidates form small discussion

244

groups to share and critique IPR questions, or form a large group in which the instructor teaches the proper IPR techniques and assists candidates in critiquing their IPR responses.

The skill practice which candidates are afforded in the simulated response exercise prepares them to participate in the peer supervision exercise, previously discussed as a technique for experiential learning. When the peer supervision exercise is directed at skill practice candidates are asked to conduct and record a thirty-minute IPR session with a peer. Each candidate conducts IPR (skill practice), and also serves as a supervisee for a fellow peer (experiential learning). Candidates' IPR performances are later supervised by the instructor in small groups.

Both of these simulation exercises are extremely valuable learning methods, and participants enjoy them. Another advantage is that the exercises expose participants' IPR skills so the instructor can evaluate and determine when a supervisor-candidate is ready for supervised practice with actual supervisees.

Training for the skills of unstructured psychotherapeutic counseling is similar to IPR training. Candidates receive a video-taped demonstration of a supervision session, attentionally isolate the discrete skills, and then practice the skills in a triadic simulation exercise adapted from Spice and Spice (1976).

Candidates form triads and adopt the roles of supervisor, counselor, and client. These roles are rotated among the three participants, and the exercise is conducted three times so that each participant can get the skill practice inherent in the supervisor's role. The exercise begins as the counselor and client role play a brief counseling or consultation session according to a script which puts some interesting dynamics into the case. Counselor and client portray this script while the supervisor observes the session. An unstructured psychotherapeutic supervision session between supervisor and counselor follows, and the client role becomes an observer role as this participant critiques the supervisor's performance. The entire exercise can be audio or video taped if the instructor wants to supervise participant performance.

Satisfactory skill performance of IPR and the unstructured supervision method in simulation exercises is the author's criterion for allowing supervisor-candidates into supervised practice. When they finally earn entry to this last preparation stage, the instructor uses his/her supervisory contact with the candidate for continued dynamic lessons and further shaping and refinement of skills.

Applied Methodology. Psychotherapeutic supervision skills can be applied in tasks and duties other than IPR and the unstructured method. Wherever the supervisor is called upon to deal with dynamics, an opportunity exists for psychotherapeutic methodology to be applied. Skill training in the psychotherapeutic approach should be followed by preparation in applied methodology. Modeling, simulation exercise, and perhaps supervised field work assignments can assist supervisor-candidates to apply psychotherapeutic skills to novel situations, such as in the following list:

1. Paraprofessional counselors in your agency have been expressing anger toward clients who disagree with their values. How can you help them come to grips with their anger so they can counsel with such clients?

2. Two staff counselors are involved in a personal dispute which is hampering their professional work. Within a supervision session could you use techniques from the psychotherapeutic approach to help each counselor resolve his/her bitterness?

3. A group of teachers have anxieties and resistant attitudes about parent conferences, and their department head asks you to offer a supervisory group experience to help them resolve these intrapersonal dynamics.

4. School counselors ask you, the supervisor, to help them improve their unsuccessful relationship with a school principal.

5. Your task is to present an inservice workshop to a group of counselors on the topic of improving relations with culturally different clients. Apply techniques from the psychotherapeutic approach in the workshop.

6. The counselors under your supervision are planning to conduct group guidance sessions with parents of school-age children. Within the group they want to foster parents' awareness and understanding of the dynamic interactions they are having with their children. Supervise these counselors with the psychotherapeutic approach.

Summary

The psychotherapeutic approach to counselor supervision is a preparation target consisting of information, experiential learnings, skills, and applied methodology. Instructional/learning modalities for preparing supervisor-candidates in these areas are didactic instruction, modeling, simulation exercise, and supervised practice. If preparation in the psychotherapeutic approach is effective, candidates will be able to perform interpersonal process recall, unstructure psychotherapeutic supervision, and apply psychotherapeutic supervisory techniques to novel situations where human dynamics are present.

LEARNING TARGET THREE
THE BEHAVIORAL APPROACH

Learning target three in supervision preparation is the behavioral approach; in terms of focus, goals, and methodology, it stands in stark contrast to the psychotherapeutic approach. The contrast does not usually bother supervisor-candidates, however, for instead of being affronted by this new and different learning target they tend to embrace it as though it were a long awaited solution to a frustrating problem. An examination of the preparation program for learning target two, the psychotherapeutic approach, explains this receptivity.

Supervisor-candidates enter learning target two having no formally-developed skills, and upon being introduced to the psychotherapeutic approach they apply their energies toward learning its methodology. In simulation exercises they intently try to develop the skills of IPR and the unstructured method, unaware of other supervisory skills which could be employed in these same situations. At this point in training, during simulated practice of psychotherapeutic supervision skills, a frustrating phenomena arises. In classic terms the phenomena is this: the supervisor-candidate (through psychotherapeutic techniques) leads the counselor to a thorough and accurate understanding of the dynamics in a helping case, and the candidate assists the counselor in determining how he/she should interpersonally act toward the helpee in order to implement a constructive dynamic plan. However, the counselor does not know how to perform the necessary interpersonal behaviors (counseling techniques), and the candidate does not know how to help the counselor develop these behaviors. Both the candidate and counselor become frustrated.

The author believes that such frustration situations are inevitable in supervision preparation regardless of which methodological approach is taught first. Any single supervision method will have limitations, and by practicing the method in simulated or actual supervisory situations the practitioner will encounter the experience of skill inadequacy. Since the experience is unavoidable, instructors may as well use it to their advantage, and the best time to capitalize is at the beginning of learning target three. A suggested procedure is included in this Chapter.

Factual and Conceptual Information

The author begins preparation in the behavioral approach by eliciting introspection and recall of the experiences supervisor-candidates had during simulated practice of the psychotherapeutic approach. Discussion of these shared experiences, clarified by the instructor, gradually leads to the conclusion that there must be supervisory techniques outside the psychotherapeutic approach which can also be of value in demanding situations. As candidates' receptivity of and desire for other methods reaches a peak, the instructor leads them into a didactic study of the behavioral approach. Reading, lecture, and discussion is aimed at the factual and conceptual information in these items.

1. A concrete definition of behavioral supervision, and any understanding of the propositions underlying the behavioral approach.

2. Knowledge of the focus and goals of behavioral supervision.

3. An understanding of the behavioral supervision process and how its five skill-steps contribute to the process.

4. A conceptualization of the counseling process, an identification and behavioral description of the counselor skills and techniques within the process, and an understanding of the influence each skill and technique has upon the client.

5. A conceptualization of the skill repertoire for a fully-functioning counselor.

6. Knowledge of the typical kinds of goals which are set in behavioral supervision.

7. Knowledge of the typical strategies in behavioral supervision and an understanding of the learning principles upon which the strategies are based.

8. An understanding of how supervisee skill learnings from behavioral supervision can be generalized.

Didactic preparation in the behavioral approach is rather taxing for supervisor-candidates who have not previously studied and practiced the behavioral approach to counseling. They must grasp a new way of thinking about human behavior—a learning theory conceptualization.

Of particular challenge to all candidates are informational items 4-7, and the instructor should put a didactic emphasis there. The author has found the following discussion exercises and homework assignments to be helpful:

Item 4. A written homework assignment is required for this learning, and it has the proportion of a major paper. Candidates are asked to describe their conceptualization of the counseling process as clearly and concretely as possible, including a behavioral description of skills/ techniques and their influence upon the client. The purposes of this assignment are to facilitate candidates' awareness of their counseling orientations, to make them question the effects of their techniques, and to think of their counseling model in terms of skills.

Item 5. Supervisor-candidates must be aware of the skills which comprise the counselor's work if they are to supervise the development and refinement of these skills. A conceptualization of this total skill repertoire can be developed by inspecting various counselor job descriptions, role and function statements, and so forth, then translating them into skill terms.

Item 6. Reading supervision case studies and listening to those presented by the instructor familiarizes candidates with skill goals that may arise in behavioral supervision.

Item 7. Chapter 3 presents a number of behavioral supervision strategies, and each one should receive in-depth study. A "take-home" quiz which carries candidates into reference sources is unparalleled as a self-instructional tool. The instructor must devise such instructional techniques so that candidates can engage in independent study between classes, because there is never enough classroom time to learn the numerous strategies.

Behavioral Supervision Skills

The skills of behavioral supervision have been explained in Chapter 3, and only a brief description will be offered before launching into the instructor's modalities for teaching/ training them. Although the skills are discussed as though they are discrete, and they can be implemented this way, supervisor-candidates should be reminded that skills ordinarily flow together in a supervisory process.

Establishing A Relationship. In behavioral supervision the relationship goal is to establish an interaction conducive to learning. This skill can be given a minimal amount of instructional time if it was treated more extensively in learning target two.

Skill Analysis and Assessment. This skill is defined as analyzing a performance in terms of skill-behaviors, and assessing the counselor's performance capability for the skill-behaviors.

Setting Supervision Goals. Behavioral supervision is directed at skill goals which are established by the supervisee and supervisor. Goals fall into the categories of undesirable behaviors that should be changed and desirable skill-behaviors that should be developed or improved.

Constructing and Implementing Strategies. The behavioral supervisor, cooperatively with the supervisee, is responsible for constructing and implementing supervisory strategies for goal attainment.

Follow-up and Generalization of Learning. The behavioral supervisor is responsible for evaluating supervisory strategies, ensuring that goals were attained, and generalizing learned skills beyond the original learning situation.

Instructional Modalities For Skill Instruction

Most of the skill-instruction modalities employed in learning target two (the psychotherapeutic approach) also are used for preparation in behavioral supervision skills. The modality which begins the author's skill preparation is modeling - the presentation of live and video-taped demonstrations of behavioral supervision. Repeated presentation of modeling segments showing the five skills of behavioral supervision, along with the instructor's input about each skill, tends to enhance observational learning.

Simulation. Following the presentation of models, training becomes a simulation learning experience in the skills of analysis and assessment, goal setting, strategy construction, and skill generalization. Audio-or video-taped counselor performances (counseling, consultation, or any work activity) are played for supervisor-candidates, and they are asked to

1. list the counselor skills which are demonstrated,

2. rate the counselor's demonstrated performance capability for these skills,

3. recommend skill-goals for the counselor to seek in behavioral supervision,

4. recommend a supervisory strategy for each goal, and

250

5. suggest other counselor situations to which the supervisory skill-goals could be generalized.

As candidates participate in this exercise and share their recommended goals, strategies, etc. they simulate through the behavioral supervision process and learn from each others' performances.

The triadic supervision exercise, explained in learning target two, is another simulation exercise for practicing the skills of behavioral supervision. It is particularly useful for classroom practice of discrete skills following observational learning.

Peer supervision is perhaps the simulation method of greatest fidelity for instructing candidates in the skills of behavioral supervision. In learning target two the "peer supervision exercise" casts candidates in the roles of supervisor and supervisee; they practice psychotherapeutic supervision (supervisor role) with their peers and received psychotherapeutic supervision (supervisee role) from their peers. Supervision is focused on a recorded counseling session which each candidate made at the beginning of training. Exactly the same procedure is followed in learning target three; the same recorded counseling sessions are employed as candidates practice and receive behavioral supervision. At the completion of this exercise they will have had the rare experience of practicing both the psychotherapeutic and behavioral approaches, and receiving both approaches as supervisees.

Although the peer supervision exercise is the most valuable simulation exercise in learning target three, it does have limitations. One limitation is that peer supervisees are likely to be at a high skill level and candidates will therefore get an atypical practice experience. Instructors should make candidates aware of this fact, and prepare them for the reality of low-skilled supervisees.

Perhaps another limitation, characterizing all skill instruction in learning target three is a lack of opportunity for candidates to practice numerous behavioral strategies. The triadic supervision exercise and peer supervision exercise afford candidates the opportunity to implement only two or three strategies at best, and this number is far from enough. If skill instruction is nearing an end and some important behavioral strategies have not been implemented by the trainee group it is prudent of the instructor to develop a short simulation exercise which involves candidates in the intellectual or imaginal application of these overlooked methods.

Supervised Practice. The supervised practice of behavioral supervision is conducted after supervisor-candidates have acquired skills through modeling and simulation exercise, and are capable of actual practice. Instructors supervise the actual practice of behavioral supervision skills by observing candidates' performances and/or reviewing recordings of these performances in supervisory sessions with the candidate. The instructor may find it helpful to use the skill steps of behavioral supervision in these sessions, starting with an analysis and assessment of the candidate's skill performance. Instructor and candidate then agree upon skill goals to work on, and they either perfect these skills within their sessions, develop skill-learning homework assignments, or both. The instructor's strategies (role playing, self-instruction module, microtraining) for helping the candidate reach skill goals are drawn from the behavioral supervision approach.

As supervised practice progresses the instructor will find that candidates have difficulty in deciding how much responsibility and direction to put into behavioral supervision. Some candidates are timid and practice a "counselor-directed" brand of supervision which is really an avoidance style. They want to leave the supervisee to his/her own resources, and enact a laissez-faire policy rather than performing the types of strategies which facilitate the supervisee's self direction: self-instructional modules, self appraisal and skill monitoring, and self management. Candidates and instructors alike must realize that strategies which foster counselors' self-direction require effort and experise--probably more expertise than possessed by the supervisor-candidate. Candidates therefore need the instructor's assistance.

The "supervisor-directed" thrust, whereby the supervisor assumes major responsibility for setting the course of supervision and employing interventionist techniques (e.g., role playing, micro-training, co-counseling), is just as demanding as the counselor-directed thrust. Candidates need the instructor's technical assistance in planning and performing interventions with low-skill counselors, and they particularly need encouragement during difficult and slow supervision cases. Instructors must be wary, on the other hand, of candidates who revel in a directive supervisory style, for if their techniques are "control-oriented" they can be a destructive influence on supervisees. If supervision preparation cannot change a candidate's style of interpersonal domination the instructor is ethically obligated to terminate that candidate's preparation.

Another matter of special concern for instructors during supervised practice of behavioral supervision is candidates' evaluations of supervisee skill performance when these evaluations are used as criteria for grade assignments (e.g., in a

practicum course) or employer evaluations. The author's
experiences in this matter have taught him to allow candidates
to make evaluations in such cases, for this is an important
learning experience, but also to make his own independent
evaluation. If a discrepancy is found between the two evaluations a conference is held to investigate the differences,
and if agreement on a common evaluative report is not reached,
the instructor's evaluation is reported.

Experiential Learnings

Supervision instructors who are more devoted to experiential instruction than is the author, can probably conjure up
many classroom exercises for experiential preparation in
behavioral supervision, and they are encouraged to do so. But
for this Chapter to remain an honest personal account the
author must admit that he has attended to experiential learnings
for preparation in behavioral supervision only during simulation
exercises and supervised practice. Those experiential learnings mentioned herein are from these two sources.

Supervisee Skill Levels. The foremost experiential
lesson discovered by supervisor-candidates during supervised
practice in behavioral supervision is that supervisees evidence
a vast range of skill levels and learning abilities, and that
these different levels have consequences for the practice of
behavioral supervision. Candidates are pleasantly surprised to
find that some counselors enter supervision at a high level of
skill functioning and can easily develop new skills. Behavioral
supervision for these counselors is an enjoyable process of
skill shaping and refinement, and a pleasant exposure to
advanced skills.

Candidates also learn that some counselors enter supervision without the ability to perform fundamental skills, and
that these counselors do not easily profit (learn) from supervision. Great patience is demanded from the candidate, for
behavioral supervision becomes a skill-by-skill compensatory
training process. Further, if the candidate is responsible for
an evaluation of the counselor's performance, and if this evaluation has implications for an academic grade or job security,
then supervision presents a question of professional and ethical
judgement--"Should the candidate give an honest evaluation which
will have detrimental consequences for the supervisee?"

Dynamics Versus Skills. Another experiential lesson which
occurs during simulation exercises and the supervised practice
of behavioral supervision deals with an issue of dynamics
versus skills. The issue is both sematic and practical.
Semantically, supervisor-candidates learn that dynamic theorists
and learning theorists talk about virtually the same constructs

but with different language. Imprecisely, through a process of semantic pragmatism, they learn that covert behavior is synonomous with intrapersonal dynamics, and that overt interpersonal behavior is synonomous with interpersonal dynamics.

Practically, candidates begin to examine the psychological relationship between intrapersonal dynamics (a slighted realm in behavioral supervision) and skills (overt skill behaviors). This investigation is the beginning of methodological integration which will later occur and be fostered in learning target four. The candidate begins to learn what Mahoney (1977) has suggested that the instrumental variables in human behavior may influentially interact. Translated into supervisory jargon intrapersonal dynamics influence each other, and as a singular collective construct, they influence interpersonal dynamics; likewise, interpersonal behavior, whether performed or received from another person, affects one's intrapersonal dynamics.

There are two experiential lessons in particular which clarify the dynamics versus skills issue. First, there are counselors for whom dynamic strategies are impossible until they learn the interpersonal skill behaviors needed to act toward the client in a dynamically constructive manner. Dynamic strategies require behavioral skills!

Second, there are counselors who have developed adequate skills but are incapable of performing them satisfactorily because of intrapersonal dynamics such as anxiety, self condemnation, and grief. The competent performance of counselor skills requires stable, healthy intrapersonal dynamics!

Resolution of the dynamics versus skills issue can begin during simulation exercises in the behavioral approach, but resolution is not accomplished until supervisor-candidates can discover for themselves how to marry (in a technical sense) the psychotherapeutic and behavioral approaches. An opportunity to make this discovery is offered in learning target four.

Situational Skill Performance. Another experiential learning from supervised practice concerns the "situational nature" of skill performance. Supervisor-candidates learn that a counselor's skill repertoire is never independent of the situations in which it is performed. The counselor who performed proficiently last week with helpee X may perform poorly this week with helpee Y.

Basically there are two reasons for this situational influence. Counselors need time and assistance to generalize skill learnings to new and different situations; psychological learning theory tells us that generalization is not automatic, but rather is a difficult learning process. Another reason is

that the stimuli in a new situation may elicit intrapersonal
dynamics in the counselor which sabatoge skill performance.
When a counselor's skill performance suddenly drops in quality
the behavioral supervisor should assess these two possible
reasons for situation influence and take appropriate behavioral
or dynamic steps to help the counselor master the situation.

Applied Methodology

An interesting instructional activity to close learning
target three is a discussion, and perhaps some intellectual
simulation, regarding the applicability of behavioral supervision skills and methods. The behavioral approach is most
applicable through the supervisor's training and evaluation
activities, and there are many situations in which the supervisor must train counselors and evaluate their performance.
The following typical situations challenge candidates to apply
their behavioral supervision skills:

1. You are responsible for hiring the school counselors
   for a new school system. What counselor skills would
   you use as employment criteria, and how would you
   assess them?

2. As the instructor of a practicum course, what would
   be your skill criteria for grade assignments, and how
   would you evaluate practicum students?

3. Your newly-appointed position is director of guidance
   in a small school system. The superintendent of the
   school system gives you a charge: "Can you do something about counselors X and Y? We thought they would
   be excellent counselors because they were straight A
   students in graduate school, but they can't seem to
   plan their activities or get a program started. Also,
   they don't consult with teachers. Is there any hope
   that they can learn how to do these things?" How
   would you tackle this assignment?

4. A counselor seeks your consultation because he/she is
   fearful of starting group counseling. The counselor
   knows it is needed, but has not been prepared to
   counsel with groups. What are the supervisor's
   options?

5. Assume that you are the supervisor for a large group
   of agency counselors. How would you choose the skill
   goals for their in-service training? What type of
   supervisory-training strategies would you use, and how
   would you evaluate training success?

6. You are a counselor educator who is teaching a pre-
   practicum course on counseling techniques. What are
   your skill objectives for the course--what skills
   should student-counselors have before entering the
   practicum? How would you prepare students in these
   skills?

Summary

The knowledge and skills required to practice the behavioral approach to counselor supervision comprise learning target three. Didactic instruction is used to teach the factual
and conceptual information of behavioral supervision; skills
are trained through modeling, simulation exercise, and supervised practice; and experiential learnings are produced in both
the skill training and supervised practice phases of preparation. As candidates develop the ability to practice behavioral
supervision, and assuming they have been previously trained
in the psychotherapeutic approach, they become aware of the
efficacy of skill and technique integration and the possibility
of discriminatively employing methodology from both approaches.

LEARNING TARGET FOUR
AN EFFECTIVE AND PERSONAL SUPERVISORY STYLE

Classroom preparation in learning targets two and three
does not allow supervisor-candidates the opportunity to develop
their own personal styles of supervision, and by the time
learning target three is finished candidates are motivationally
eager to do so. They want the freedom to experiement with
psychotherapeutic and behavioral methodology and to discriminatively apply techniques. Supervisor-candidates also want
to discover their characteristic manner of supervisory
performance. Learning target four gives them the opportunity
to begin developing a personal and effective style, and this
developing process will continue throughout the remainder of
preparation as other supervisory techniques are learned and
adopted.

Instructors should not assume that each supervisor-
candidate must develop a distinctive and unique way of implementing supervision, nor that there is some kind of "mystique"
in one's personal style. A supervision style is something
that develops naturally and is not a "contrived" goal which
the candidate seeks. The rationale behind style development
is that candidates are more likely to become effective supervisors if they find and utilize the natural abilities and
performance manner which they brought with them to preparation,
and if they develop and practice a technically eclectic
methodology.

As candidates begin the fourth preparation target they do not have a precise idea of their preferred or most effective supervisory style, nor does the instructor. Style is particularly unpredictable for candidates with a relatively small amount of counseling experience or a lack of exposure to personality theories and counseling approaches. The supervision styles of such candidates will change commensurate with exposure to new help-giving techniques. Candidates who have explored many approaches to counseling and have developed a stable help-giving approach will reflect this stability and orientation in their supervisory style.

A supervisory style is developed by practicing supervision and discovering whether one prefers to emphasize the psychotherapeutic or behavioral approach, and by incorporating techniques from one's counseling approach into supervision. The result is a supervision style which is somewhat unique to the individual supervisor. For example, by examining the author's transcript of psychobehavioral supervision at the end of Chapter 4, readers can begin to describe his supervisory style. One supervision case is not a reliable index but it tells us the following in this instance:

1. The supervisor employed reflective techniques and showed the capacity to offer "counselor-directed" supervision.

2. The supervisor demonstrated a directive employment of techniques when intervening in the supervisee's problem dynamics.

3. The supervisor engaged the supervisee in role playing to train her in deficient skills--the later part of the supervision session relfected a behavioral approach.

If these characteristics were observed in numerous cases, we could say that the supervisor is a proponent of the psychobehavioral approach to counseling supervision, and that he maintains a balance between psychotherapeutic and behavioral techniques. Furthermore, he uses a rational emotive orientation to psychotherapeutic supervision when providing insight and working for dynamic change.

Facilitating Development

A supervisory style is not taught, it must be developed through opportune learning experiences. The preparation strategy for learning target four is to avail supervisor-candidates of learning opportunities through which they can develop their supervisory styles. Four kinds of learning opportunities comprise the author's method for facilitating

effective personal styles: experiential learnings, didactic
exposure to integrative supervision approaches, unstructured
simulated practice, and supervised practice.

Experiential Learnings. Supervisor candidates go through
many experiential learnings during classroom preparation for
the psychotherapeutic and behavioral approaches, and some of
these experiences have relevance for the development of a personal and effective style of supervision. Learning target four
can begin by soliciting these experiential learnings, and a
suggested procedure is to practice the experiential recall
technique. In a group setting candidates are asked to recall
their simulated practice of psychotherapeutic and behavioral
methodology from learning targets two and three, and to share
instances of wanting to break out of the approach they were
using and to employ alternative techniques. Recall would
include the following:

1. Experiencing aversion to the methodology they were
   practicing.

2. Using a technique against their better judgement.

3. Receiving an aversive reaction from the supervisee
   in response to a technique.

4. Encountering a situation where one supervision approach
   or technique would clearly be better than others.

5. Failing to succeed in using a certain supervision
   method.

6. Desiring to switch from one approach to the other.

7. Sensing an impulse to do something creative, but then
   suppressing it because it would look foolish.

8. Imagining, after finishing the simulation exercise,
   how your performance should have been done.

By encouraging the uninhibited expression and exploration
of these incidents the candidates will discover that some of
their ideas and impulses were based on sound judgement while
others were not of high quality. The instructor can help
candidates sift out their valid and creative ideas, and as
group members gain confidence in their judgements they may form
some conclusions about how to discriminatively and integratively
practice supervisory methodology.

Didactic Exposure. When the group has reached the peak of
its experiential productivity the instructor can didactically
expose candidates to some factual and conceptual information

about integrative approaches to supervision. Chapter 5 reviews two integrative approaches, the Carkhuff (1969) supervisory training model and a psychobehavioral approach. Exposure to this material further reinforces candidates' search for a personal style whereby a comprehensive repertoire of methods is employed.

The author has found Carkhuff's model for interpersonal skill training to be a valuable one for supervisor-candidates to learn per se, and several hours are usually spent familiarizing them with the model's training process, its training exercises (e.g., discrimination exercises, communication exercise), and the rating scales used to assess facilitative conditions. Study of the Carkhuff model focuses on learning how to conduct it, and on ferreting out the integrative principles and methods in the model. Exposure to the psychobehavioral approach offers more principles by which candidates can guide their technically integrative efforts.

Unstructured Simulated Practice. The experiential recall exercise and didactic study of integrative supervision approaches usually evoke candidates' ideas about how to integrate the methodologies of psychotherapeutic and behavioral supervision. Since they have already developed basic skills from these two approaches (via learning targets two and three), candidates eagerly await the opportunity to put integrative ideas into practice. Unstructured simulated practice is a learning exercise where ideas can be converted into performed skills.

In learning targets two and three simulated exercises were structured; candidates were instructed to practice a particular supervision approach or method, and they were not given the freedom and responsibility to choose methodology. In learning target four the restrictions of structured exercise are lifted and candidates enter the simulated practice of supervision without instructions regarding methodology. They are free to practice whatever approach and techniques they choose, provided that the methodology is appropriate and competently performed.

All of the simulated practice exercises in learning targets two and three can be employed in an unstructured manner so that candidates have the freedom to integrate methodology and form personal styles. However, the peer supervision exercise is the author's favorite because of its efficiency. As a homework assignment it can be performed between classes or workshop sessions, and candidates already know its procedures from their skill-training experiences in learning targets two and three. To employ the peer supervision exercise as an unstructured training experience, the instructor simply arranges new dyads and tells candidates to conduct a supervision session with whatever methodology they consider most effective and comfortable to perform. Candidates are encouraged to "responsibly experiment" by implementing their ideas on the discriminative and integrative use of supervision methodology.

During the exercise some candidates may boldly attempt new methodology, while others are more cautious and stick to traditional practice. Some candidates employ a behavioral format and attempt to integrate dynamic techniques, and some may follow a predominantly psychotherapeutic approach with behavioral skills interjected. The route which candidates take to search out a comfortable and effective style is not important if it is done with seriousness and due regard for the supervisee's welfare.

Upon completion of the exercise candidates should receive the instructor's supervisory assistance in reviewing and evaluating their performance. They must discriminate between effective and ineffective aspects of the performance, make adjustments in technique and style, and prepare for another simulated practice session. Through this practice and critique process, across several repetitions of the peer supervision exercise, candidates develop the beginnings of an effective and personal style of supervisory practice.

Supervised Practice. When classroom preparation is completed and candidates enter supervised practice (see learning target six), they have an unlimited opportunity to further develop and refine the personal supervisory style which was begun in the classroom. As explained in learning target six, the instructor's assistance is needed during supervised practice to help the candidate correctly choose methodology and employ it at the opportune time. The candidate will move back and forth between the psychotherapeutic and behavioral approaches, and at times may integrate techniques to form a psychobehavioral method.

The completion of one's personal style of supervision is probably never accomplished during preparation, and perhaps it is a life-long process. A realistic instructional purpose is thus to help supervisor-candidates get to know themselves, their preferences, and their special talents, etc. and to encourage their continued learning and responsible experimentation toward a more effective supervisory style.

Summary

Learning target four offers supervisor-candidates the opportunity to responsibly experiment with supervision methods and begin the development of an effective and personal supervisory style. The seeds which are sown in this fourth

instructional module continue to grow throughout preparation
and blossom during supervised practice (learning target six).
At that time candidates will have developed an individualistic
manner of performing a comprehensive set of supervision skills,
approaches, and activities.

LEARNING TARGET FIVE
THE SYSTEMS APPROACH

Supervisor-candidates who receive preparation in the
psychotherapeutic, behavioral, and integrative approaches
may think they have conquered supervisory methodology in its
entirety, and to a certain extent their assumption is valid.
They have been exposed to the major approaches for "interpersonal supervision." But what they don't realize is that
counselor supervision is not totally interpersonal in nature;
the supervision function consists of more than interpersonal
dealings--there is an "impersonal" dimension.

Many supervisors would argue that the impersonal side of
counselor supervision is administration, for it is common to
see administrative duties performed by those who hold supervisory positions. However as explained in Chapter 1, a strong
case can be made for the separation of administration and
supervision as discrete functions, and the author is a firm
advocate of this separation. Instead of administration, the
impersonal dimension of supervision suggested by the author is
program development, maintenance, and evaluation.

Counselor supervisors are responsible for programs of
training and supervision, and for overseeing helping-service
programs. In both of these responsibilities the systems
approach offers supervisory methods of first-order applicability, and learning target five proposes to teach supervisor-
candidates how to make the applications. Candidates are shown
that systems skills complement the psychotherapeutic and
behavioral techniques they have already acquired, and at least
three instances of complementarity exist:

1. Supervisors use systems skills to plan, manage, and
   evaluate inservice training programs, but they also
   rely on the techniques of behavioral supervision to
   set skill goals and construct viable training
   strategies.

2. Systems skills can help the supervisor develop an
   accountable program of supervisory services, but as
   demonstrated by the comprehensive supervision program
   presented in Chapter 5, the skills from four supervisory activities and three supervisory approaches are
   needed to implement the program.

261

3. The systems approach has been extensively applied to the development, management, and evaluation of helping-service programs, but the supervisor is dependent on the psychotherapeutic and behavioral approaches for the supervision of counselors who staff the program.

Candidates thus learn that supervisors can be effective with interpersonal supervision, but they lack the ability to establish accountability in a program of services if their systems skills are deficient. Inversely, one can be a skilled systems technologist but be unable to implement supervisory services if skills from the psychotherapeutic and behavioral approaches are missing. If the instructor's introduction to the systems approach carries forth this message, and demonstrates the functionality of systems skills, supervisor-candidates will enthusiastically enter the didactic study of the systems approach. Items of factual and conceptual information, such as included in this list, should be learned through readings (such as Chapter 5 and selected references), lecture, and discussion.

Factual and Conceptual Information

1. An appreciation of the focus and goals of the systems approach, and the relationship of systems skills to other supervisory methodology. As described in the beginning of this section, candidates should be given an introduction to the systems approach which places it in proper perspective.

2. An understanding of the "system" concept. Supervisor-candidates should be able to define a system, and conceptualize a system. Conceptualization means that the candidate is cognizant of the boundaries of a system, system components and the relationship among components, system goals, and the relationship between a system and environmental variables (e.g., parent systems, human populations, other systems).

3. Awareness and understanding of helping service systems. Candidates should be made aware of the various helping-service systems in their respective localities, and should develop an understanding of how these systems operate. Speakers from social service agencies, clinics, private organizations, and so forth, can offer insights regarding their systems, and literature describing helping-service systems can also be studied.

4. Knowledge of systems skills. Before candidates receive skill training they should have a reading knowledge of systems skills.

262

5. An awareness of practical applications. The supervision instructor can familiarize candidates with the supervisory application of systems skills. They should see how systems skills are used to develop, manage, and evaluate programs of counselor training, supervision, and helping services.

Didactic instruction in these items of factual and conceptual information is the first phase of preparation in the systems approach to counselor supervision. The second phase suggested by the author is to teach three methods of applying systems skills in supervisory situations. These three areas of applied supervisory practice are systematic skill-based training, program functioning, and systematic problem solving.

Systematic Skill-Based Training

Preparation in the supervisory application of systems skills begins with candidates learning how to develop and conduct systematic skill-based training programs. Readers will recall that training and instruction is one of the four generic activities of counselor supervision (see Chapter 1), and that in-service training is an important facet of a comprehensive supervision program (see Chapter 5). Systematic skill-based training is therefore a prominent part of the supervision function.

By the time candidates reach learning target five they have been primed with knowledge and skills from the behavioral approach that can be utilized in the development and conduction of systematic training programs. They can identify the skill-needs of individual supervisees, match these with training strategies, and conduct strategies in a dyadic supervisory relationship. They have not, however, been prepared to develop or conduct training programs for groups of counselors, and this task requires systems skills. To illustrate, the development of an in-service training workshop for the staff counselors of a helping-service program would include these system skills:

1. System analysis would be done to determine those counselor skills that are deficient or which need improvement within a helping-service program.

2. Synthesis and the writing of performance objectives would be used for setting training goals.

3. Flowchart modeling could be used to map out the components of the training program.

4. Simulation of the training program should be done before using it with actual trainees.

263

Candidates' ability to develop and conduct training programs comes about as they learn systems skills, integrate these with skills from behavioral supervision, and practice the integrated set of skills by actually developing and conducting skill-based training programs. These kinds of learning experiences can be offered to candidates through participation in a supervised instructional project. For example, supervisor-candidates can be given a fictional population and set of circumstances, and asked to develop a training program which provides the population with valuable counseling skills. The instructor can monitor the group's work progress and guide its efforts through the appropriate systems skills; or, a set of explicit instructions can be followed. If a population of counselors is available the project can actually be performed. The author has supervised several such projects where supervisor-candidates have developed and implemented systematic skill-based training projects with groups of guidance students, dorm counselors, and school psychology trainees. Candidates have reported that the projects are demanding of their energy and talents, but rewarding in terms of learning experience. Samples of actual or simulated projects, which would be supplemented with additional demographic and situational information if used in preparation, are as follows:

1. Prepare and conduct an inservice training program for a group of twenty school counselors in their first year of practice.

2. A group of counselors in a university counseling center asks you to recommend an inservice training program to upgrade their skills; how would you proceed on this project?

3. Paraprofessionals have been employed by a mental health center to assist patients, recently released from a psychiatric hospital, to adjust to everyday life. You are to prepare and conduct a twenty-hour training program which will equip the paraprofessionals with interpersonal skills needed in their work. Given generous funding for your inservice project and the authority to employ other trainers, how would you proceed?

4. You are teaching a pre-practicum course to graduate students in guidance and counseling. Develop and conduct a twenty-five-hour training program in basic counseling skills which would prepare the students, as much as possible, to conduct educational and career counseling with adolescents.

5. The student council in your high school wants to begin a peer counseling program. Develop and conduct a program for the selection and training of peer counselors.

Systems Skills In Program Functioning

Another area for the supervisory application of systems
skills is the development, management, and evaluation of
helping-service programs. Instructional projects can be used
to teach this application of systems skills just as they were
employed to teach skill-based training. To begin such a project
supervisor-candidates as a group are asked to develop a
helping-service program for an institution or setting of their
choice, or for a situation offered by the instructor. Examples
of institutions and settings, in abbreviated form, are the
following:

A public school (elementary, middle, senior high) with a
well-defined population

An agency which dispenses a certain type of helping-
service (drug rehabilitation, family counseling, career
guidance)

A university counseling center with a well-defined student
population

The candidate group is requested to develop the program
according to a set of systematic steps such as outlined by
Hosford and Ryan (1970) and presented in Chapter 5. Through
these steps they are expected to utilize the systems skills of
analysis and synthesis, writing performance objectives, flow-
charting, and program simulation. The instructor should guide
and facilitate the group's work efforts, thereby modeling
appropriate supervisory behavior. By participating in the
project candidates learn to systematically develop a program,
and by observing the instructor they learn how to lead counselors in a program development project.

Program Management. When the helping-service program has
been developed and candidates have gained experience in applying systems skills for that purpose, the instructor can turn
instruction toward another application of the systems approach
--management of a helping-services program. Systems skills
as applied to program management can be taught through Hollis'
(1975) LORS (Learning Oriented Reality Structured) technique:
a simulated meeting of counselors and their supervisor for the
purpose of program management.

The meeting is conducted by five or six candidates who
play counselor roles according to scripts written by the
instructor; the instructor assumes and supervisor's role, and
the program to be managed is the one previously developed by
the candidates. Because only five or six candidates can play
roles, remaining candidates become a participating audience

265

which keenly observes the simulated meeting process, takes notes, and makes comments and recommendations at periodic pauses in the exercise determined by the instructor.

The program management meeting proceeds as the supervisor (instructor) leads the group of counselors in a thorough analysis of program functions and outcomes as these have transpired in the operation of the program. If faulty program components are identified the counselors make plans to correct them. Changes in the needs of the client population and the program's environment are analyzed and program adjustments are made if necessary. While these system analysis steps sound abstract, they take tangible form in the dramatization. Candidates learn through the role-played scripts and simulated meeting process that faulty program components can be things such as a poorly planned group guidance service, a lack of clearly defined performance objectives, or a skill-deficiency in counselors which prevents them from adequately performing an activity. They discover that those changes in clients and the environment which influence program management are commonplace events such as an influx of new residents into a community, the sudden appearance of a drug problem in the client population, or relocation of the helping-service program in a new building. Through dramatization the management of a helping service program becomes a reality, and systems skills are vividly demonstrated by the instructor.

Program Evaluation. The LORS technique can likewise be employed to teach the application of systems skills for program evaluation. Simulated meetings for program evaluation are dramatized through a new set of scripts, different candidates play the counselor roles, and the meeting is focused on evaluating the helping service program which was developed and managed in previous exercises. The supervisory group process which evolves in the dramatized meetings can show how it is possible for counselors to share program evaluation duties, that various evaluation techniques can be employed, that performance objectives are easier to evaluate than vague goals, that supervisory systems skills are valuable, and so forth. Evaluation results are translated (via system analysis and synthesis) by the group into programmatic changes. The existing flowchart model of the program is altered to depict the changes, some new performance objectives are written, and the revised program is simulated.

Supervision instructors may wish to expedite preparation in program development, management, and evaluation by using only didactic instruction, and in some instances time may not allow dramatization. But shortcuts in preparation are to be avoided whenever possible, and for those who can afford the time to be thorough the author refers them to LORS:

<u>Experiential Technique For Program and Staff Development</u>
(Hollis, 1975) where extensive instructions are given for the
instructional use of dramatizations.

Systematic Problem Solving

The third and last application of systems skills in learning target five is through systematic problem solving.
Supervisors need problem-solving skills because they are
continually sought out by counselors who are encountering
professional difficulties. Because they do not have a storehouse of answers supervisors often respond in an unhelpful
manner. One such response is the supervisor's suggestion that
nothing can be done about the problem and that the counselor
must endure it. This kind of response leads counselors to
frustration and depression--a feeling of powerlessness.
Another typical response which is only occassionally appropriate
is the supervisor's acceptance of total problem-solving
responsibility, and an attempt to remove counselors' problems.
This response spawns counselor dependency.

A third response which is superior to the first two is the
supervisor's application of systematic problem-solving skills.
In this approach the supervisor involves counselors in a
cooperative strategy whereby they follow a set of problem-
solving steps leading to constructive action on the problem.
As counselors are led through these steps they learn how to
independently solve problems and thereby gain a valuable skill.

The systematic problem-solving strategy which the author
teaches to supervisor-candidates consists of six steps which
are adapted from Carkhuff (1973) and the problem-solving
model in Tom Gordon's effectiveness training programs. Each
step, within the strategy, as conducted with a group of
counselors, will be discussed.

Systematic Problem-Solving Strategy

Problem Exploration
Problem Definition
Identify Courses of Action
Plan a Course of Action
Implement Action Plan
Follow-Up Evaluation

<u>Problem Exploration</u>. Systematic problem solving usually
begins when the supervisor is meeting with a group of supervisees. The supervisor notices some cues that indicate the
counselors have a problem (grumbling, frustration, anger),
or the counselors may openly announce that they are experiencing
a difficulty. Whatever the indicator the supervisor helps the

267

counselors freely explore the problem; of particular importance is exploration of counselors' affect, as well as factual information. The supervisor uses reflective and tacting responses to facilitate counselors' awareness of the problem, and to solicit diagnostic information.

Problem Definition. Information gained through problem exploration leads the supervisor and counselors to a definitive understanding of the problem. Generally, problems can be defined as technical, emotional, or mixed (technical/emotional). Technical problems are objective difficulties such as a case-load that is too large, insufficient facilities, or a counselor skill deficiency. Emotional problems are troublesome affective states such as frustration, anger, or depression. Mixed problems are those where counselors are encountering technical difficulties and emotional upset.

The supervisor's greatest potential mistake during problem exploration and definition is to overlook counselors' affective dynamics and treat all professional problems as though they are technical. Systematic problem solving requires that the supervisor be sensitive to the intrapersonal and interpersonal dynamics in professional problems.

Identify Courses Of Action. When the problem has been understood and defined, the supervisor encourages counselors to explore constructive courses of action. This encouragement often elicits some counselor dynamics which are part of the problem--most notably an external locus of control and low frustration tolerance. Counselors often express helplessness to solve problems, particularly when there is a past history of futile attempts. Another dynamic roadblock to constructive action is counselors' impatient demands that problems be resolved immediately without long-term effort. Supervisors must react to these dynamics with skills from psychotherapeutic supervision; the dynamics are exposed, understood, and restructured before going further with the problem solving process. Proper motivation for systematic problem solving rests on the two beliefs that counselors have the capacity to exert constructive action, and that professional problems can be constructively influenced by counselors although persistent and arduous effort may be required. Counselors must have these two beliefs before problem solving is possible.

Given proper motivation in counselors the supervisor leads them in a "brainstorming" exploration of constructive action strategies. After compiling a list of ideas the counselors evaluate and choose the best ones. The course of action with the greatest probability of success is chosen.

Plan A Course Of Action. Following the choice of an action strategy to constructively influence a problem, the counselors' next step is to develop an action plan. Counselors are assisted by the supervisor in determining how they will actually implement the action strategy they have chosen. The work required to implement the strategy is divided among the counselors, capitalizing upon individuals' abilities, work efforts are coordinated. The supervisor's system skills of analysis, synthesis, and flowcharting are utilized in the planning process, and the completed plan is simulated before implementation.

Implement Action Plan. Counselors' implementation of an action plan represents a concerted and coordinated assault on a professional problem. Implementation is monitored by the supervisor, and his/her consultative assistance is available to each counselor. Additionally the supervisor may have a special part to play in the plan. The author has discovered that supervisors are often in the most strategic position to implement certain portions of the action plan, and in so doing they truly become "partners" with the counselors.

Follow-Up Evaluation. The last step in systematic problem solving is to evaluate the results of action taken toward a professional problem. If implementation of an action plan is of short duration a follow-up meeting can be held after the plan is completed; long-term plans should include periodic evaluation meetings during implementation. Evaluation is done by reviewing the results of the action plan, and if the problem has not been resolved to a satisfactory degree the original plan is revised and continued, or a replacement plan is designed and implemented.

Preparation In Systematic Problem Solving

The LORS dramatization technique and supervised practice are the author's two instructional modalities for preparing supervisor-candidates in systematic problem solving. By participating in a dramatized problem-solving meeting, or observing such a dramatization, candidates experience a close approximation of systematic problem solving as it occurs in actual practice. They can also observe the instructor's skills and he/she leads a group through the problem-solving steps. Several professional problems are offered as examples of situations that could be dramatized through a problem-solving meeting.

Counselor Problems For Dramatization

1. A group of school counselors meet to discuss conflicts they are having among themselves over the use of limited facilities. An unhealthy competition has arisen

among the counselors in their quest to get access to typewriters, tape recorders, and a group counseling room.

2. The counselors in a community agency raise the problem of an increased level of drug addiction seen in their clientele, and the counselors' lack of preparation for this type of case.

3. In a monthly staffing meeting the counselors in a university counseling center bring up a problem they are having with a student services director. The counselors have requested the director's permission to conduct counseling groups in dormitories and the director has curtly denied permission without discussion or explanation. Because group counseling in the dormitories has been such a success in the past the counselors want to pursue the matter and gain permission.

4. The supervisor in a public-funded agency, having a staff of six counselors, notices that the counselors are becoming resentful and somewhat depressed about a private counseling agency that has recently been established in the community. Within a staff meeting some of the counselors openly express anger toward the new agency, its fee schedule, and its highly touted services. They resolve to be uncooperative toward the agency if it requests information or assistance with a case, and they also voice disillusionment over the lack of community appreciation and funding for their work. As the supervisor listens to the counselors he/she realizes that a serious morale problem has arisen.

5. A staff of school counselors in a rural middle school has voiced the need for additional facilities and guidance materials to the school principal, but for the last two years the school budget has not allocated any funds for this purpose. The counselors bring the problem to the supervisor.

6. Several new counselors have been employed in a university counseling center, and as they begin to function it is discovered that their activity plans for the year duplicate many of the activities performed by other staff counselors. The experienced staff members defend their activities and the new employees are intimidated and stymied. Quick resolution of the conflict is needed before it escalates.

Classroom instruction in problem solving should later be followed by actual practice under the instructor's supervision. In a field setting (school, agency, university) the supervisor-candidate would lead a group of counselors in a problem-solving activity, and the instructor would either observe the performance or co-lead the group. The instructor's role is to facilitate the candidate's efforts and offer direct help only if the candidate is somehow blocked or thrown off course in the problem-solving process. Successful completion of a problem-solving group process marks the end of supervisory preparation in this area.

Summary

Learning target five can be defined as the supervisory application of systems skills in the areas of systematic training, program functioning, and problem solving. Didactic instruction is employed by the instructor to give supervisor-candidates a foundation of factual and conceptual knowledge about the systems approach, and is followed by instructional experiences in which candidates participate in the application of systems skills.

Instruction should prepare candidates to develop and conduct a skill-based training program, to supervise the development, management, and evaluation of a helping-service program, and to lead counselor groups in a systematic problem-solving process.

LEARNING TARGET SIX
SUPERVISED PRACTICE

Target six is the capstone of supervision preparation; through this module supervisor-candidates become capably functioning supervisors. As candidates enter this last learning target they possess an impressive amount of supervisory knowledge and skill gained through prior learning targets, and most of these competencies have been practiced in simulation exercises. Classroom instruction can be terminated or at least reduced to periodic seminars, and supervisor-candidates are placed in settings where counselor supervision is being practiced. There they attempt to perform the supervision function while the instructor or a site-based supervisor oversees their performance.

Two basic types of supervised practice experiences exist in which candidates can implement the supervision function: practicums in counseling supervision and practicums in counselor supervision. Practicums in counseling supervision consist of candidates supervising the counseling performance of

271

supervisees, and this type of practicum is usually done in a university where candidates have access to student-counselors who are making their first attempts at counseling. Practicums in counselor supervision consist of candidates supervising all facets of counselor practice, and these practicums are conducted at the site of a helping-service program.

Supervised Practice In Counseling Supervision

The author proposes that if supervisor-candidates receive exposure to more than one supervisory approach or activity they will inevitably attempt to integrate the methods to some extent. Thus, instructors can expect to see candidates struggle with the integration process during supervised practice, and instructors are responsible for helping candidates resolve the struggle. Successful resolution results in an effective and personalistic style of supervision comprised of a synthesized methodology.

In counseling supervision the possibilities for methodological synthesis are more limited than in counselor supervision. The supervisor's duties and tasks are not as varied as in counselor supervision and the four generic activities of supervision are more narrowly employed. Another limitation to synthesis is that the systems approach is not as applicable as the psychotherapeutic and behavioral approaches. Candidates therefore develop supervisory styles by synthesizing only psychotherapeutic and behavioral methodology, and these styles may collectively be termed a psychobehavioral approach to counseling supervision (see Chapter 4).

Instructors of practicums in counseling supervision play an instrumental role in helping supervisor-candidates develop and practice effective psychobehavioral supervision. Their assistance is particularly crucial in four areas: (1) preparing for a psychobehavioral supervision session, (2) learning the steps and procedures of the session, (3) synthesizing methodology, and (4) managing the longitudinal process of psychobehavioral supervision.

Preparing For A Psychobehavioral Session

Although the author does not advocate the imposition of an instructor's supervision style upon a supervision-candidate, there are instances where candidates seek and can profit from directive instructional output. Preparing for a psychobehavioral supervision session is one of these instances; candidates need suggestions on preliminary procedures. They should not be expected to perform a lengthy sequence of minute behavioral acts, but general suggestions are in order.

A good way to begin psychobehavioral supervision is to have a "get acquainted" meeting during which the supervisor and counselor can become comfortable with each other. In this meeting the counselor can discover that supervision will not be as threatening as expected, and the supervisor gains an understanding of the counselor by acquiring information about preferred counseling approaches, self perceptions of skill-strengths and weaknesses, professional aspirations, etc. The supervisor can also offer support and encouragement as the counselor nears the first counseling session.

Anytime following the initial meeting the counselor can begin to counsel, and these sessions are audiorecorded. The supervisor observes the counseling session, takes notes, and makes an appointment with the counselor for a supervision meeting. This meeting is counseling supervision proper, a concentrated supervisory focus on the counselor and the counselor's audiorecorded performance. To prepare for the meeting the counselor should review the audiotape, write a self assessment of his/her counseling performance, and also a summary of the counseling session. The self assessment is simply an appraisal of the counselor's dynamics and skills, and the counseling summary is a concise record of information and observations gathered by the counselor during the counseling session. (Doctoral-level psychologist trainees would supplement these forms with a psychological assessment of the client.) Both the self assessment and counseling summary forms can be constructed by the instructor or adapted from sources such as Practicum Manual for Counseling and Psychotherapy by Dimick and Krause (1975), and Psychological Report Writing by Hollis and Donn (1973). Example forms are displayed in Appendix C.

A Psychobehavioral Supervision Session

The steps and procedures of a psychobehavioral supervision session are not dogmatically sequenced, for the supervisor relies on cues from the counselor to determine what methodology should be employed. But there are some definite guidelines which the supervisor can follow to give continuity to the session. These guidelines concern how to open the session, the performance of a proper methodological process during the session, homework assignments, and an appropriate closing.

Opening the Psychobehavioral Session. The opening of a psychobehavioral supervision session is most efficient when the counselor brings self assessment and counseling summary reports to the supervisor. Writing these reports requires the counselor to view his/her performance, the client, and the interview with depth and objectivity. Furthermore, the supervisor can quickly appraise the counselor's perspective by reading the

273

reports during the first five minutes of the session, perhaps while the counselor sets up a tape recorder and prepares to play the recorded interview. Then, the supervisor and counselor can briefly negotiate where to begin the supervision session and how to spend the hour.

Process of the Session. An appropriate opening to a psychobehavioral session correctly places the supervisor in a consultant stance and encourages self direction in the counselor. The process of the session flows smoothly from this beginning. Supervisor and counselor can discuss the dynamics of the interview and the strengths and weaknesses of the counselor's skill performance. They should listen to the recorded interview in segments (skipping unimportant sections) and the supervisor alternately or simultaneously employs dynamic and behavioral techniques. For example, after listening to a particular segment of the interview where the counselor is dissatisfied with his/her performance, the supervisor might ask several dynamic recall questions to help the counselor understand the counselor-client interaction. This would aid the counselor's understanding of his/her performance and the behavior of the client. The counselor's intrapersonal dynamics could be explored and more constructive dynamics simulated. Given this restructured dynamic foundation the supervisor could then use behavioral supervision to help the counselor develop and/or practice desirable counseling skills (interpersonal dynamics) to substitute for previously undesirable performance.

Homework Assignments. As the recorded interview is examined the supervisor and counselor may uncover areas of unsatisfactory dynamic or skill performance that require more practice than can be accomplished in the supervision session. Assuming these areas do not preclude the counselor's continuation of supervised practice, the supervisor may assign homework assignments so the counselor can practice deficient areas. Assignments should produce a product (short paper or taped exercise) which can be turned in to the supervisor as evidence of assignment completion. Illustrative assignments are a skill-practice exercise, an affective sensitivity exercise, writing a short paper on a particular counseling strategy, reading a counseling case and analyzing the dynamics, or listening to an instructional tape and taking a self-scoring quiz.

Closing the Psychobehavioral Session. Supervision is a complex experience for counselors, who will leave the session with only fleeting awarenesses and fragmented intentions if the supervisor does not draw things together. Therefore, the final few minutes of a psychobehavioral supervision session should be spent summarizing the session, reviewing homework assignments, and simulating the counselor's plan for the next counseling interview. Such a conclusion will solidify the dynamic lessons and skill-based learnings of supervision so they can be permanently recorded and retrieved for later practice.

Synthesizing Psychotherapeutic and Behavioral Methodology

The distinguishing characteristic of a psychobehavioral supervision session, and a skill which is difficult to teach and learn, is the technical integration of methodology from the psychotherapeutic and behavioral approaches. Throughout the psychobehavioral session a supervisor may move back and forth between approaches and/or simultaneously employ methods from both approaches. A continuous process of choosing and changing methodology is being employed, and this decision-making process is the core skill behind technical integration and psychobehavioral supervision. Several guidelines for technical integration have emerged in the author's work, mainly in response to the questions of candidates in supervised practice.

Methodology for Opening the Session. One guideline for technical integration concerns the question of how to open the supervision session; for example, "Should I use the psychotherapeutic or behavioral approach?" Supervisor-candidates sometimes panic before their first session because they don't know where to start. The guidelines recommended in this situation is to let the supervisee decide. On the supervisee's self-assessment report there is usually a clear indication of the type of supervisory assistance desired, and if not, the supervisor can simply ask the supervisee what kind of assistance she/he wants. If the request involves skill performance, the behavioral approach is appropriate; skill analysis and assessment would be the technique with which to begin. Requests for assistance with the counselor-client interaction, or other dynamic matters, should cue the supervisor to begin with techniques for dynamic awareness from the psychotherapeutic approach.

The opening methodology of a supervision session can be changed at the supervisor's disgression, and thus it is not disastrous if the supervisee initially leads the psychobehavioral supervisor in an unproductive direction. Regardless of where the supervision session begins, the skill of the supervisor can later seek out deficit areas of the counselor's performance requiring supervisory attention.

Continuous IPR. A second guideline for psychobehavioral methodology is to employ a continuous flow of intrapersonal-dynamic recall leads throughout the supervision session. The purpose of this guideline is to provide an awareness and understanding of these dynamics to the supervisee from all parts of the supervision performance, thereby teaching counselors to utilize their "experiencing" process. Furthermore, the continuing dynamic focus is likely to uncover subtle areas of dynamic difficulty which warrant more entensive psychotherapeutic methodology. In this way dynamic leads are scanning for dynamic trouble spots.

Continuous Skill Scan. The psychobehavioral supervisor maintains a constant attentional scan on interpersonal skill performance, just as dynamic leads maintain a focus on intrapersonal dynamics. Through observational responses the supervisor enhances supervisee awareness of what skills were performed, the intended purpose, and the apparent effect on the client. When the supervisor's skill scan identifies unsatisfactory areas of skill performance a more concentrated use of behavioral methodology is utilized (i.e., goal setting and strategies).

Integration Points. The integration of psychotherapeutic and behavioral methodology occurs at "points of integration" in the psychobehavioral supervision process where the supervisor shifts from one approach to the other, or simultaneously uses techniques from both. One such point of psychobehavioral integration is the weaving together of supervisory responses toward intrapersonal dynamics and interpersonal skills so that awareness of each and their contingency is facilitated. This integrative response pattern is a foundational skill of the psychobehavioral approach.

Another integration point arises when the psychobehavioral supervision process has temporarily settled into a psychobehavioral nich so that an area of troublesome intrapersonal dynamics can be treated. The supervisor employs psychotherapeutic techniques, induces a change in the supervisees intrapersonal dynamics, and then shifts to behavioral supervision in order to help the supervisee translate the dynamic change into an improved interpersonal skill performance. For example, if the supervisee overcomes a fear of confronting the client through psychotherapeutic methods, the skill of confrontation should then be practiced and refined to complete the psychobehavioral treatment.

Integration should also occur when the psychobehavioral supervision process is entering a temporary period of behavioral methodology for the improvement of a skill performance area. Before launching into the behavioral treatment, the psychobehavioral supervisor first explores the supervisee's intrapersonal dynamics within the performance area. If problematic dynamic difficulty which warrant more extensive psychotherapeutic methodology. In this way dynamic leads act as a scanner for dynamic trouble spots.

Abrupt Shifts When Blocked. The psychobehavioral supervision process usually involves many transitions from one approach to the other, and supervisor-candidates are taught to carefully and smoothly make these transitions. One exception, however, are abrupt shifts in method when supervision progress is blocked. Occassionally, if supervisors find their supervisory methods to be devoid of effect, it is advisable to abruptly shift one's techniques to the alternative supervisory approach. To illustrate, the author recalls numerous supervisees who were unresponsive to psychotherapeutic techniques but responded nicely to behavioral supervision.

Whenever an abrupt shift in methodology has been made, and the alternative method is successful, the supervisor should then return to the unsuccessful supervisory approach. The supervisee may be able to profit from the formerly unsuccessful approach.

Longitudinal Supervision Process

A final area of the counseling supervision practicum where supervisor-candidates are particularly dependent on the instructor's assistance is in the development of awareness and understanding of the longitudinal supervision process. Candidates can easily become so involved in the performance of counselor supervision that they lose sight of the process, i.e., the longitudinal sequence of their methods and the supervisee's changing needs. Process awareness is important to supervisors because it enables them to recognize the supervisee's past needs and learnings, and from these to predict and plan for future needs and learnings that are likely to occur. Without process awareness supervisors constantly struggle to remain cognizant of supervisee changes, and they often find themselves reacting with hindsight.

Process awareness is especially instrumental in psychobehavioral supervision because supervisors must be able to forsee, or at least sense immediately, those points in the supervision process where methodology should be changed. As noted earlier in this section the psychobehavioral supervisor makes frequent changes in methodology, moving back and forth between the psychotherapeutic and behavioral approach, as well as simultaneously using techniques from both approaches.

Instructors can help candidates develop process awareness by continually commenting upon and reflecting the ongoing supervision process. The candidate should also be forced through open-ended leads, to think about the supervisee's past skills and dynamics, to see the changes taking place, and then to predict and plan for future happenings.

Another technique for building process awareness is to ask candidates to review thoroughly their supervision cases and prepare case study reports. To complete this assignment candidates must engage in introspection and articulate the supervision process which they experienced. Three case reports from supervisor-candidates, illustrating several different formats, are presented in Appendix D. These reports will also demonstrate to readers how the four generic activities of supervision can be infused into the counseling supervision process.

Supervised Practice In Counselor Supervision

A practicum in counselor supervision offers candidates a wealth of learnings most accurately described as lessons in applied practice. A lesson occurs each time the supervisor-candidate learns how to practically implement a supervision activity or approach which was studied in the classroom. The value of a practicum in counselor supervision is determined by the opportunity it offers for lessons in applied practice; the ideal supervised experience is one in which candidates can participate in a comprehensive supervision program. Such an ideal experience would offer candidates the opportunity to do the following:

1. Perform supervisory duties which reflect the three purposes of counselor supervision.

2. Perform the four generic activities of counselor supervision.

3. Perform methods and techniques from the psychotherapeutic, behavioral, and systems approaches to counselor supervision.

4. Practice a synthesized supervision methodology.

5. Develop a comprehensive supervision program.

Ideal experiences in supervised practice are not mythical, and instructors can construct them if they know the proper composition. To construct an ideal practicum in counselor supervision the instructor needs, first, a placement setting which offers the opportunity to accomplish the five items listed above. Second, the instructor must have a compendium of supervisory performance assignments by which supervisor-candidates can systematically engage in a comprehensive supervision practice. Performance assignments are simply the practical application activities of a comprehensive supervision program, such as the following list drawn from the model program in Chapter 6.

PERFORMANCE ASSIGNMENTS FOR A PRACTICUM
IN COUNSELOR SUPERVISION

1. Conduct program planning meetings with a group of counselors

2. Conduct individual and group supervision sessions for program management purposes

3. Conduct individual and group supervision sessions for evaluation of the helping-service program

4. Consult with the director of the helping service program regarding administrative problems

5. Consult with the counselor staff as they prepare yearly activity plans

6. Consult with the counselor staff as they evaluate completed activity plans

7. Conduct problem-solving conferences with individuals and groups of counselors

8. Conduct individual or group supervision sessions to assist counselors in the assessment of their competencies and the preparation of a plan for competency development

9. Collaborate with counselors in developing and conducting an in-service training program directed at counselors' skill deficiencies

10. Offer individual and group supervision sessions focusing on competency areas where the supervisor has expertise

11. Conduct individual supervision sessions for collaborative evaluation of counselors' competency plans and their demonstration of competency improvement

12. Perform consultative/counseling sessions with counselors regarding personal problems, or professional problems of an affective nature

13. Conduct periodic meetings to assist newly-employed counselors in becoming oriented to their positions and starting an activity plan

14. Inform counselors of professional development activities and encourage their participation

15. Evaluate the supervision program in which you have participated and evaluate your performance in the program

16. Last Performance Assignment: Write an accountable and comprehensive supervision program for the setting where you expect to practice supervision in the future.

The learning opportunities and performance assignments of supervised practice can be condensed into a single performance objective which guides the candidate and instructor. If candidates accomplish this objective they have proven themselves competent for the independent practice of counselor supervision. In the remainder of learning target six is discussed the following performance objective:

> During supervised practice of counselor supervision the candidate will demonstrate the development of an accountable and comprehensive program of counselor supervision, and the performance of a synthesized supervision methodology sufficient to implement the program.

Development Of A Supervision Program

The first part of the performance objective for a practicum in counselor supervision, to develop a supervision program, is a fundamental competency; its inclusion in a preparation program for counselor supervision is unquestioned. A question remains however about when to ask supervisor-candidates to complete the objective. Learning target five (the systems approach), which precedes supervised practice, is the module in which candidates receive classroom instruction in systems skills and the program development competency. This module seems to be the logical place for candidates to develop a supervision program, and indeed the author usually presents didactic coverage of the topic such as included in Chapter 6. But candidates are not expected to actually develop a supervision program during learning target five because they lack practical experience. If candidates attempt to develop a supervision program before having the experience of supervised practice their products tend to be unrealistic and abstract. Candidates need the learnings which come from participating in a supervision program and acquiring an "inside view" of program operations. For these reasons the development of a supervision program is positioned as the last performance assignment in the counselor supervision practicum.

Assuming that candidates demonstrate satisfactory performance in the practicum and reach the last performance assignment, they then call upon numerous resources to complete the assignment. Program planning skills are employed from the systems approach, and practical learnings from supervised practice prove invaluable. Candidates may consult model programs and descriptions of supervision practice such as presented in Chapters 8 through 11, and they are provided assistance in program development from the instructor. The program is satisfactorily constructed when it meets these guidelines.

GUIDELINES FOR DEVELOPMENT AND EVALUATION OF SUPERVISION PROGRAMS

1. Program goals are stated concretely, are directed at the three purposes of counselor supervision, and reflect the needs of the supervisee population.

2. Program objectives are stated behaviorally and are congruent with program goals.

3. Supervision methodology encompasses the four activities and three approaches of counselor supervision, and is directed strategically at program objectives.

4. The program facilitates counselors' self development, and cooperatively involves them in the conduction of the program.

5. The program can be implemented realistically by the supervisor within the limitations of its setting (facilities, funding, staff, etc.).

Synthesized Supervision Methodology

The second part of the performance objective for a counselor supervision practicum is to perform a synthesized supervision methodology which is sufficient to implement a comprehensive program of counselor supervision. Candidates are expected to utilize the four generic activities and the three major approaches of supervision in such a manner that supervision practice becomes a synthesis of activities and approaches. The resultant synthesized methodology should encompass a range of performance assignments representative of a comprehensive supervision program.

An "apprenticeship" form of supervised learning is recommended to instructors as a feasible and effective way of helping supervisor-candidates learn to perform a synthesized methodology via completion of performance assignments. The candidate is placed in a supervision program as an intern or apprentice, and is assigned to a senior supervisor in the program. By following the senior supervisor (also called a "site-supervisor") in his/her professional duties, and

281

participating in these duties, the candidate will have an opportunity to complete the performance assignments of the practicum.

At the beginning of the practicum candidates may be given only a small amount of responsibility while they acclimate themselves to the supervision program and engage in observational learning. As the practicum progresses they can be offered more responsibility and can work in tandem with the senior supervisor. Co-supervision becomes the learning modality. By the end of the practicum candidates should be practicing independently as the senior supervisor occupies the role of silent observer.

Senior supervisors play a vital role in the supervision practicum by ensuring that candidates complete a comprehensive list of performance assignments, and that candidates practice a synthesized methodology. The senior supervisor's role is carried out by cooperatively planning the candidate's performance agenda, gradually increasing responsibilities and independence, and steadily accomplishing performance assignments through co-supervision practice. The candidate continually is shown how to recognize the "points of integration" which exist in the practice of counselor supervision, and how to synthesize methodology.

Summary of Learning Target Six

Supervised practice in counseling supervision and counselor supervision is the sixth learning target in the author's program of supervision preparation. This module is the final preparatory stage where classroom learning is translated into actual supervision practice. Supervisor-candidates attempt to practice an effective psychobehavioral style of counseling supervision, and to formulate and put into practice an accountable and comprehensive program of counselor supervision through a synthesis of supervisory activities and approaches.

SECTION THREE: EPILOGUE

The preparation program outlined in Section Three is presented as a stimulus and guide for supervision instructions, and they are encouraged to selectively choose and adapt material for their specific preparation circumstances. Although the program is designed to facilitate a synthesis of supervision methodology, the author wishes to emphasize that supervisor-candidates are not coerced into synthesis. Rather, the instructor and candidate mutually engage in a search for the most effective supervisory practice; whatever form this practice assumes is acceptable if it is accountable. Perhaps the same principle can guide instructors in the selection of preparation methods on the basis of accountable results.

REFERENCES

Boyd, J. D. Supervision and the counselor educator. *Virginia Personnel and Guidance Journal*, Spring, 1977.

Carkhuff, R. R. *Helping and Human Relations, Volume I.* New York: Holt, Rinehart and Winston, 1969.

_____. *The Art of Problem Solving.* Amherst, Mass.: Human Resource Development Press, 1973.

Dimick, K. M., & Krause, F. H. *Practicum Manual for Counseling and Psychotherapy.* Muncie, IN.: Accelerated Development, 1975.

Gordon, T. Effectiveness Training, Inc., 532 Stevens Avenue, Solana Beach, California, 92075.

Hackney, H., & Nye, S. *Counseling Strategies and Objectives.* Englewood Cliffs, N. J.: Prentice-Hall, 1973.

Hollis, J. W. *LORS: Experiential Technique for Program and Staff Development.* Muncie, IN.: Accelerated Development, 1975.

Hollis, J. W., & Donn, P. A. *Psychological Report Writing: Theory and Practice.* Muncie, IN.: Accelerated Development, 1973.

Hosford, R. E., & Ryan, T. A. Systems design in the development of counseling and guidance programs. *Personnel and Guidance Journal*, 1970, *49*, 221-230.

Jakubowski-Spector, P.; Dustin, R.; & George, R. Toward developing a behavioral counselor education model. *Counselor Education and Supervision*, 1971, *10*, 242-250.

Kagan, N., & Schauble, P. G. Affect simulation in interpersonal process recall. *Journal of Counseling Psychology*, 1969, *16*, 309-313.

Krumboltz, J. D. Changing the behavior of behavior changers.
    Counselor Education and Supervision, 1967, 6, 222-229.

Lazarus, A. A. Multimodal Behavior Therapy. New York:
    Springer, 1976.

Mahoney, M. J. Reflections on the cognitive-learning trend in
    psycho-therapy. American Psychologist, 1977, 32(1), 5-13.

Spice, C. G. Jr., & Spice, W. H. A triadic method of super-
    vision in the training of counselors and counseling
    supervisors. Counselor Education and Supervision, 1976,
    15(4), 251-258.

SECTION
FOUR

Supervision
In
Action

SECTION FOUR

SUPERVISION IN ACTION

OVERVIEW

In the first three sections of this text have been presented an analysis and synthesization of the supervision literature. Also proposed were a crystallized rationale and a methodological framework for use as guides for the study and practice of counselor supervision and the preparation of supervisors. Section Four will give the reader an opportunity to further clarify and expand the proposed supervisory rationale and practice model by relating it to the contemporary views and practices of supervision leaders from four different settings. These leaders have been chosen to contribute to Section Four because of their experience and distinguished supervisory accomplishments in respective settings.

Chapters 8 through 10 have been written from authors' individual frames of reference and not for the sake of agreement with the editor's formulations. Consequently, presentations will coincide with and constructively extend the editor's supervisory rationale and practice model, as well as raise technical and conceptual differences. Editor's notes for each chapter will highlight these points of congruence and difference. The composite of Section Four is a realistic picture of how supervision can be envisioned and practiced in various settings and by different supervisors.

Chapter **8**

SUPERVISION OF COUNSELORS

IN

ELEMENTARY AND SECONDARY

SCHOOLS

Roger Aubrey
Associate Professor of Psychology and Education
George Peabody College for Teachers
Nashville, Tennessee

SUPERVISION OF COUNSELORS IN ELEMENTARY AND SECONDARY SCHOOLS

Editor's Notes

Counselors in elementary and secondary schools typically do not receive supervision, but they do comprise a professional group which could significantly profit from supervisory assistance. In Chapter 8 Dr. Roger Aubrey discusses why supervision of school counselors has not flourished. He then prescribes a supervisory function--more narrow in scope but similar to the conceptualization in Chapter 1--which would best suit the school counseling profession. Aubrey's formulation is that supervision is an activity directed toward the ultimate goal of accountability in guidance and counseling programs, and that training and evaluation are companion activities. Other supervision activities which fall under accountability include developing and managing guidance and counseling programs; assessing the impact of guidance and counseling services on students; and monitoring and improving individual staff performance.

A particularly strong point in this Chapter is the mandate for accountable guidance and counseling programs rather than the mere dissemination of helping services. The principal responsibility of the supervisor is to put this distinction into practice; system skills as described in Chapters 5 and 10 are invaluable methods for developing, maintaining, and evaluating programs. Dr. Aubrey also emphasizes that the efficacy of a guidance and counseling program is dependent upon the competencies of its staff. The supervisor is responsible for assuring, through evaluation and preparation, that counselors are competent to perform the activities and functions of the program. Behavioral supervision seems to be the most appropriate approach for work with counselor competencies. Dr. Aubrey provides some very useful tools that fit into that framework. He presents competency analysis tables that will aid in the supervisor's evaluation and preparation activities. The importance Dr. Aubrey places on staff competency development is further demonstrated in his model supervision program.

Roger F. Aubrey

Roger Aubrey (Ed.D.) has been supervising elementary and
secondary school counselors for over thirteen years. His first
experience as a supervisor was as Director of Guidance and
Counseling for the University of Chicago Laboratory Schools.
He later served eight years as Director of Guidance and Health
for the Brookline, Massachusetts, Public Schools.

Dr. Aubrey has also prepared counselors at the university
level, including Wisconsin State University, University of
Maine, Fairfield University, Northeastern University and
Boston University.

Dr. Aubrey's first published article appeared in the
Counselor Education and Supervision journal and was concerned
with the practicum experiences of elementary school counselors.
Since that time, he has published over forty articles and
authored or co-authored five books, many of them dealing with
supervision. He also served as President of the ACES in
1973-74.

Currently, Dr. Aubrey is Associate Professor of Psychology
and Education at George Peabody College for Teachers in Nashville, Tennessee. He is also the Coordinator of Human Development Counseling Programs for that institution.

SUPERVISION OF COUNSELORS IN ELEMENTARY AND SECONDARY SCHOOLS

Roger F. Aubrey

Supervision of practicing elementary and secondary school counselors is largely an unrecorded event. In fact, a review by this writer of issues of the Journal of Counselor Education and Supervision from 1966-1976, indicated only seven articles exclusively devoted to this topic (Appleton & Hansen, 1968; Krumboltz, 1967; Lister, 1966; O'Hara, 1968; Pinson, 1974; Schultz, 1969; Shoemaker & Splitter, 1976). A similar search of issues of The School Counselor from 1968-1976, revealed only three articles remotely connected with the area of supervision of school counselors (Boyd & Walter, 1975; Noble, 1968; Trotzer, 1971). Finally, a study of the contents of the Personnel and Guidance Journal from 1967-1976, reveals but two articles dealing solely with the supervision of practicing school counselors (Dunlop, 1968; Lindberg, 1972).

Not only is the supervision of practicing school counselors unrecorded, it is essentially devoid of research and any empirically derived body of knowledge. Much of what passes for literature in this area is in reality a series of suggestions for improving the position of the guidance supervisor (Biggers & Mangusso, 1972; Donigian & Wellington, 1971); or a description of the efforts of university-based counselor educators to upgrade the skills of practicing counselors (Cramer, 1970; Doverspike, 1972; Pietrofesa & Van Hoose, 1971; Pulvino & Perrone, 1973; Schwartz & Sherman, 1975); or some infrequent studies of counselor effectiveness and/or job satisfaction (Boy & Pine, 1968; Dietz, 1972; Joseph & Drury, 1971; Wicas & Mahan, 1966). Simply stated no evidence exists that public school supervisory personnel play any role in the systematic and continuous supervision of school counselors.

WHO SUPERVISES COUNSELORS AND DOES IT MATTER?

Lack of data on counseling supervisory practices in elementary and secondary schools is similar to a great extent to findings on supervisory practices in the teaching profession. In both cases practically no research exists "in which a carefully-developed, comprehensive method of supervision based on theory is applied experimentally and its effects at least partially assessed" (Mosher & Purpel, 1972, p. 60). Further, careful studies in the field of teaching indicate little or no change in teacher effectiveness even when these individuals did receive supervision (Biddle, 1964; Lucio & McNeil, 1962).

Lack of data regarding supervisory practices in school settings creates problems which are compounded and confused by the additional concern of determining the identity of counselor supervisors. The range of potential supervisors extends from county and/or state officials to directors of guidance or head counselors to building principals. Nonetheless, in actual practice supervision of counselors is largely the responsibility of either the building principal or the guidance director (Filbeck, 1965; Humes & Lavitt, 1971; Kemp, 1962). However, this narrowing of supervisory personnel to two possible sources is not so simple as might appear.

Determination of supervisory responsibilities for both programs of guidance and individual counselor performance has never been adequately addressed. As a consequence, supervision remains as one of the most pressing problems in the counseling profession today (Kehas, 1965). Much of the difficulty in deciding who supervises counselors stems from the authority conflict between building principals and directors of guidance. Traditionally assumption is that principals have a direct line relationship to all school personnel within their building. In turn, guidance supervisors usually have operated on a staff relationship with school counselors. This relationship clearly places most counselor supervisors in a subordinate role when dealing with school principals. The result of these two administrative patterns of supervision has led investigators to note that "in many systems the director of guidance has no one to direct except the office staff" (Biggers & Mangusso, 1972, p. 136).

The supervisory conflict between designated directors of guidance and building principals has received a fair amount of attention in guidance and counseling literature but the impact on actual practice has been very little. (Brown, 1967; Calia, 1965; Humes, 1970; Hummel & Bonham, 1968; Kehas, 1965). Building principals have been quite reluctant to relinquish authority and autonomy to any person functioning in a staff relationship and this action has hindered both counselor program development and supervisory practice (Aubrey, 1973; Kehas, 1968). As a consequence, this issue remains a major stumbling block in refining supervisory practice, upgrading counselor competencies, and extending guidance program development.

ARE UNIVERSITY SUPERVISORY MODELS

APPROPRIATE FOR SCHOOL SETTINGS?

The nature of the supervision of counselors in school settings differs in many ways from the supervision as practiced in university preparation programs. This distinction seems necessary in discussing school supervision in order to avoid the unquestioned acceptance by school supervisors of models inappropriate or unadaptable to their setting (Aubrey, 1969). Further, little doubt exists that supervision at the university level is conducted by individuals with a higher degree of supervisory competence than in schools (Ryan, et al. 1969). This fact too must be taken into account in creating and/or modifying school models of counselor supervision.

Supervisory programs utilized in the graduate preparation of school counselors are distinguished from programs and procedures used in school settings by the following characteristics:

1. University programs usually are designed for neophytes and beginning counselors. They do not account for sizeable differences in preparation and experience and many of these preparation programs were specifically created for practicum students (Delaney, 1972; Hansen & Warner, 1971).

2. University programs predominately are oriented to the process and skill of individual counseling whereas school supervisory procedures recognize multiple counselor competencies (e.g. writing, consulting, diagnosis, testing, coordination, group work) and their impact on diverse students.

3. University programs assume a high level of supervisory competence while school programs must take into account a wider range of supervisory skills or in some cases perhaps none at all.

4. University programs set aside a significant amount of time for supervision whereas school supervision is often an ephemeral and hurried process (Biggers & Mangusso, 1972).

5. University programs often stress the individual counselor's effectiveness in achieving objectives with individual counselees; school procedures assess the effectiveness of a number of counselors in producing change for an entire class, grade level or student body.

6. University programs use assessment devices, equipment and techniques researchable and exportable to other settings; school procedures utilize "homemade" and idiosyncratic assessment devices and rating instruments.

7. University programs influence the growth and development of the counselor by blending preparation and supervision; school programs more sharply differentiate the process of supervision from that of preparation and often equate supervision with evaluation.

8. University programs reflect the theoretical and assumptive structures of particular schools of counseling and psychology; school procedures are eclectic, atheoretical and in some cases structureless.

9. University supervision has a relatively wide and extensive literature to draw upon; school models are barren.

The differences between university and school models of supervision do not necessarily indicate a gross incompatibility. In fact, many features of university supervisory programs lend themselves quite readily to school settings. An excellent example is the use of videotapes in simulated counseling incidents (Eisenberg & Delaney, 1970; Kagan, 1970; Spivack, 1973). This technique, plus numerous others, could enhance public school supervisory practices immeasurably. However, for this influence to occur, public school supervisors would first have to understand clearly the nature of supervision. In addition, they would have to prize this function as an integral part of their current roles.

University and school practitioners of supervision frequently employ three concepts in discussing the practice of supervision. The three concepts are evaluation, preparation and supervision. Often these concepts are used interchangeably, while at other times they demarcate distinct and discrete functions. A working definition of each term at this point seems necessary to clarify supervision as a unique and separate activity.

WHAT DO SUPERVISORS MEAN BY THE TERMS
EVALUATION, PREPARATION, AND SUPERVISION?

One revealing note is that the term evaluation infrequently is used by both supervisors and counselors. Indeed, the words supervision and/or preparation are much more widely quoted in the literature. Nonetheless, evaluation is utilized by all supervisors and to construct a working definition of this term and how it complements and differs from supervision seems important.

A simple working description of evaluation is to define it as a procedure or method used by a supervisor to examine and judge the performance of a counselor or guidance program in attaining a desired outcome. This definition clearly acknowledges the judgmental role of the evaluator (supervisor) and sets evaluation apart from supervision and preparation in that the evaluator, at the moment of evaluation, is neither preparing nor supervising the counselor. Instead, the evaluator is interested primarily in assessing the effectiveness of the counselor in achieving a clearly stated goal due to actions or behaviors initiated by the counselor.

If supervision is a "reluctant profession" (Mosher & Purpel, 1972), then evaluation is a resistent calling. However, obviously one cannot supervise adequately the performance of others without on occasion evaluating those performances. Evaluation therefore enters the practice of supervision as an adjunct activity to ensure objectivity, to protect the interests of students, to determine the competency level of a given counselor with a specific method or technique, to gather data as an aid in directionality, and to record accurately the influence of a given behavior or program on a desired outcome. Without evaluation, supervision is at best impressionistic and subjective; at worst, it is prejudicial and unjust.

Evaluation is concerned primarily with examining and judging the performance of a counselor or guidance program in attaining a desired outcome. Therefore, evaluation must confront the underlying problem of what constitutes effective counseling and what elements produce effective programs of guidance. Preparation complements and balances evaluation in that preparation is an enabling function to make sure the counselor or guidance program is successful. Preparation is therefore a specific aspect of supervision concerned with increasing the counselor's conceptual and skill repertoire. It is an activity designed specifically to prepare someone in a skill or proficiency leading to success in practice.

One counselor educator (Carkhuff, 1971, 1972) appears to totally equate supervision and preparation. Carkhuff (1972) in particular feels that "the most efficient and effective means for improving the quantity and quality of responses in the helpee's repertoire is training" (p. 15). Further, Carkhuff views supervision as a form of consulting in which the relationship between supervisor and counselor "is defined by the greater quantity and quality of responses which the helper has in his response repertoire as compared to the helpee" (p. 24).

Although Carkhuff's point of view is well taken, a distinction between the functions of preparation and supervision seems necessary. One key difference between preparation and supervision would appear to lie in the area of desired outcomes. An exclusive preparation focus would view the counselor's failure to achieve a given objective as a skill deficiency to be ameliorated by additional preparation. The process of supervision, on the other hand, cannot be so generous in assessing the situation. This is so because of the supervisor's responsibility, not only to the counselor, but also to the well-being of the client(s) of the counselor.

Supervision in its simplest and most direct connotation is an activity designed to guarantee that certain guidance and counseling goals and outcomes are accomplished. In this sense, supervision uses evaluation and preparation as means and methods of achieving desired outcomes. Doubtfully schools have conceived of the supervisory role as purely evaluation and/or preparation. Evaluation is simply too narrow a framework and does not contain sufficient elements to ensure that desired outcomes are attained. Preparation also is limited in that preparation focuses primarily on the counselor and not the counselee and/or the system it serves.

In an ideal sense, supervision serves both the counselor and the intended audience of the counselor. Supervision directed solely for the benefit of the counselor does an injustice to the students and programs served by the counselor. On the other hand, supervision aimed only at broad objectives and outcomes is the worst form of accountability which relegates the counselor to a mechanical and automaton existence. As a consequence, enlightened supervision should focus on both the improvement and enhancement of the counselor and the accomplishment of objectives benefiting students.

THE DOUBLE-PRONGED NATURE OF SCHOOL SUPERVISION

If supervision is to monitor and improve the proficiencies of the counselor, while at the same time assuring maximum benefit to students, a necessary starting point in supervision is the question of the goals and outcomes of guidance and counseling. It would be illogical and unproductive to conceive of the supervision of counselors in a framework commencing with skill acquisition until such time as one knows which outcomes demand what skills and competencies. Similarly, a given skill or technique should not dictate or prematurely limit the potential contribution of counselors to the welfare of students. The suggestion therefore is that those learning experiences identified and determined as legitimate counselor objectives should serve primarily as the key starting point in counselor supervision.

Unfortunately, the practice of school counseling has often restricted the potential contribution of counselors to students by overemphasizing a specific technique such as individual counseling (Cantrell, Aubrey, & Graff, 1974; Carlson, 1973; Eckerson, 1972; Gelatt, 1971; Kehas, 1970; Mathewson, 1962; Tiedeman, 1967). This exclusive emphasis on one method, such as individual counseling, has tended to unduly restrict the scope and purview of guidance and counseling and has limited the counselor to an armament of only one major technique (Aubrey, 1972). Individual counseling in this instance might therefore appear to be the functional sine qua non of most school counselors, while at the same time being recognized as "no longer the only function of a guidance program" (Gelatt, 1969, p. 145). A goal of supervision therefore might well be to ascertain if a given counselor was spending too much time in using solely a technique of individual counseling and not spending enough time in group work, diagnosis, coordination, consulting, management and so on. Obviously, this goal would be equally true if the method under study were testing or any such other technique.

Whether a counselor is spending too much time, or not enough, in the use of a specific counseling technique is actually a matter of means and ends. Counseling and all other competencies and functions included under the umbrella of guidance are means available for the attainment of guidance and counseling ends. One real and apparent danger of any profession erected on a service model is the intermingling of the methods and techniques of the profession with the end goals the profession seeks to attain. The real problem presents itself when the techniques and methods acquire implicit goals that tend to override the explicit goals they were created to serve.

CLARIFYING PROFESSIONAL TERMINOLOGY

Individuals designated by schools as supervisors of guidance and counseling serve in many capacities. In addition to monitoring and improving individual staff performance, supervisors bear a heavy responsibility in developing and determining the effectiveness of guidance and counseling programs through periodic assessments of their impact on students. This responsibility carries with it the assumption that supervisors actually are accountable for the development and management of clearly articulated programs of guidance and counseling.

Programs of guidance and counseling are viewed by the author as quite distinct from what is often referred to as a service or ad hoc set of services. In addition, the terms guidance and counseling are viewed as separate and discrete. Therefore, to define these terms at this point seems essential. The point will become clear later that supervision of individual counselors is impossible without equal "supervision" of the programs and functions they perform.

For the purposes of this Chapter, a distinction will be made between the terms guidance and counseling. "Counseling" will be used to refer to a method or technique, applied to individuals or groups, to enhance their personal development and psychological competencies. Further, counseling is a process incorporated primarily under the administrative rubric of guidance and is viewed as one of many essential functions and services under the overall framework of services to students.

"Guidance" will be used to refer to a comprehensive system of functions, services and programs in schools designed to affect the personal development and psychological competencies of students. As an educational concept, guidance is the sum total of those planned experiences for students designed to achieve such developmental or educational outcomes. As an educational service guidance, like teaching, consists of a number of functions and operations to be utilized by students in attaining developmental and educational objectives. Finally, guidance, as a practice, is descriptive of the work of the school counselor (Kehas, 1968, p. 22), and other supportive personnel when engaged in guidance activities.

GUIDANCE AS THE PROVISION OF SERVICES: "GUIDANCE AND COUNSELING SERVICES"

Two terms frequently are used quite loosely to operationally describe guidance and counseling. These terms are "guidance and counseling services" and "guidance and counseling functions." The suggestion is that these terms do much more than simply describe organizational components or practices in the field. These terms also imply a perspective and outlook on how the guidance and counseling program is to be organized, supervised, and practiced. In short, these terms reveal basic orientations by guidance personnel as to how, when, where, and why interventions in the lives of children, adolescents, and adults are to occur.

300

"Guidance and counseling services" are discrete skills performed by guidance personnel and available to students by need or on demand. The term "skills" in this context refers to individual competencies of guidance personnel used in achieving guidance outcomes. Examples of skills would include individual and group counseling, student appraisal and diagnosis, achievement and intelligence testing, and so on. In practice, these skills would meet Carkhuff's (1972) definition of "behaviors that are operational, repeatable, and predictable within a delimited range of effects" (p. 21).

"Guidance and counseling functions" by contrast are activities engaged in by guidance personnel to achieve overall objectives such as student advancement in decision making, problem solving, career planning, and ego development. These functions require the use of one or more specific competencies, and in some instances, an extensive knowledge base in such areas as the psychology of careers, colleges, and vocations. The functions of guidance and counseling traditionally have included such activities as the orientation of new students to school, testing, the placement of students for work and continuing education, the evaluation of pupil growth, student record keeping, group and career guidance, and appraisal of troubled students for referral or treatment. Collectively, the skills of counselors and the functions they perform are the services of guidance and counseling.

Guidance and counseling defined as a set of services has been recognized as a serious weakness by many guidance writers. Mathewson (1962) was one of the first to note this problem and commented that "it is the widely prevailing image of guidance as a service at problem or decision points which tends to delay the perception of the process as one that is cumulative, continuous and developmental" (p. 106). At a later point, Sprinthall (1971) echoed these sentiments by noting that "the service concept has so dominated guidance and counseling that more basic and significant questions are not being acknowledged, let alone answered" (p. 20).

A final weakness in the service orientation to guidance and counseling is the stress and priority given to skills and techniques at the expense of programs and theory. Sprinthall (1971) has addressed this problem and noted that "equating guidance with educational service (rather than just with education) promotes the current overemphasis on the technique of guidance rather than a concern with the purpose of the intervention" (p. 21). A service orientation therefore has tended to make guidance and counseling respond like a parasite on the host body of education. Although at times this symbiotic relationship may have appeared advantageous to each, the current dearth of substantial guidance and counseling theory and research may have been the eventual price of this relationship.

301

GUIDANCE AS PROGRAM: "GUIDANCE AND COUNSELING PROGRAMS"

"Guidance and counseling programs" are by contrast an alternative to the services of guidance and counseling. A guidance and counseling program contains the essential ingredients of a service orientation, namely skills and functions, but does not view these as randomly dispensable commodities. Instead of focusing on problems or crises in individuals or the school, guidance and counseling programs organize functions and skills according to predetermined short- and long-range objectives. In turn, these goals are based on principles that counselors can defend psychologically and educationally.

Programs of guidance and counseling differ from services of guidance and counseling in that they have something tangible to impart that can only be implemented through a carefully planned series of experiences. As a consequence, programs also differ from services in viewing school time as flexible, controllable, and modifiable according to objective, audience and method.

Programs of guidance and counseling must have a sound educational and psychological rationale for inclusion in the structure and organization of the school. In contrast, a service approach can justify inclusion solely on grounds of providing supportive skills and functions. For example, individual counseling on matters pertaining to career or college choice is unchallenged as a reason for inclusion of such services in the school system. This service has unquestioned legitimacy for school personnel. However, if a semester credit course on decision making, taught by school counselors, (relative to college or jobs among other decisions, for example), were made available to all high school students as a substitute to individual counseling on careers and colleges, the existing system would be seriously questioned. Further, unlike a service approach which accommodates its purposes to the existing scheme of things, a programmatic approach seeks institutional changes and adjustments because of the need for time and space allocations for programs.

Non-Curricular Programs

Programs of guidance and counseling take two forms. One form consists of an organized constellation of counselor skills and guidance functions requiring periods of time and access to students. (Non-Curricular Programs) The second form includes subject matter and content organized and arranged in a formal scope and sequence. (Curricular Programs) The first form of guidance program however does not contain a formal curriculum of learnings similar to traditional academic disciplines.

302

As an example of the first form of a guidance and counseling program, consider an urban school recently ordered to integrate black students by busing. The counselor staff in this school decided to plan a series of student group meetings involving blacks and whites in anticipation of difficulties. Those staff members participating bring with them skills in individual and group counseling. In addition, the guidance function of orientation is brought into play as a legitimate reason for this program. The combination of counselor skills and a legitimate guidance function results in a program of guidance and counseling necessitating time, space, organizational accommodations and administrative approval. However, the initial objectives evolved into a program because guidance and counseling skills and function were viewed as capable of initiating a series of meaningful learning experiences for students that would prevent a potentially damaging situation.

Curricular Programs

The second form exhibited by guidance and counseling programs is quite similar to curricula in the various school disciplines. This form includes subject matter and content organized and arranged in a formal scope and sequence. Content-centered programs of guidance and counseling first appeared in the early years of the vocational guidance movement. These programs later were submerged by the new emphasis in the 1950's on counseling psychology (Super, 1955). However, in submerging, vocational guidance did not disappear as a course offering in the public schools. Instead, the lack of interest by guidance personnel in many instances led business teachers, industrial arts personnel, homemaking instructors and others to pursue this area (Hoppock & Stevens, 1954; Lowenstein & Hoppock, 1953; Mezzano, 1969; Sinick, Gorman, & Hoppock, 1966).

Today, an awakened interest exists in content programs of guidance. This interest is evidenced both in the tremendous increase in commercially produced programs and curricula (Alschuler, 1973; Bessell, 1969-1972; Boocok, 1967; Dinkmeyer, 1970-1973; Gelatt, Varenhorst, & Carey, 1972; Gelatt et al. 1973; Limbacker, 1969,) as well as in university developed content and curricular programs (Dowell, 1971; Erickson, 1973; Griffin, 1972; Hansen, 1970; Mackie, 1974; Mosher & Sullivan, 1974; Sprinthall & Erickson, 1974; Winefordner, 1974).

Content and subject-matter programs of guidance and counseling, as well as programs revolving around a constellation of skills and functions to be implemented, require discrete time segments and students. Such programs also are organized and formulated essentially with a view toward either the prevention of anticipated student problems or the strengthening and enhancement of normal development. Also, the majority of guidance and counseling programs are organized with a group or classroom focus. Finally, both types of guidance and counseling programs eschew the notion that time is their master. Instead, time within the context of schooling is viewed as flexible, negotiable and existent for the provision of legitimate programs for students.

A comparison of a service and program approach to guidance and counseling may appear much like a portrayal of the "good and bad guys." Obviously more virtues lie in careful planning, clear articulation, wise use of available time, educational justification, sound organization, and flexibility than in the converse. However, what little evidence now exists certainly points to the serious lack of effective programs of guidance and counseling in this country (Armor, 1969; Carkhuff, 1972; Ginzberg, 1971; Kaufman & Lewis, 1968; Kohlberg, LaCrosse, & Ricks, 1970; Tamminen & Miller, 1968).

In summary, the essential difference between programs and services of guidance and counseling lies in the dynamic and initiatory nature of the former. Programs require outreach and examination, and therefore, avoid the passivity and complacency of a service approach. Programs also concentrate more on student need systems and developmental objectives whereas service approaches are more limited to counselor skills and role. Finally, a service approach addresses staff time usage in a static manner based on past and present demands whereas a programmatic model views time as flexible and modifiable according to objective and methodology.

RELATIONSHIP BETWEEN COUNSELOR SKILLS AND PROGRAM DEVELOPMENT

Development of effective programs of guidance and counseling obviously is tied to the skills of counselors. This means that counselors must not only exhibit mastery and proficiency in all the facets of individual counseling, but also must develop a high degree of skill in complementary functions such as consulting, diagnosis, group work, coordination, testing, and so on. Without these additional competencies, programs of guidance and counseling suffer a procrustean fate of having to adjust the needs of students to the limited skill repertoire of counselors. Further, the role and function of the counselor should not be defined or limited by existing skills and techniques. This is not fair to either student or counselor and obviously limits the growth potential of each.

Supervisors of public school counselors often may be forced to delay program development until such time as their staff members master existing skills and acquire new competencies. For example, suppose a counselor supervisor should wish to initiate a comprehensive program whereby all new elementary school children and their parents are to be interviewed by a trained counselor prior to actual school experience. For this situation to occur, a number of counselor competencies must first be present. Among these skills are interviewing, assessment and diagnosis, and counsulting. The lack of these skills could impede the goals of early identification of children with special needs, placement with the appropriate teacher and peer group, referral to specialists when called for, and so on. As a consequence, the supervisor must first assess the staff's current mastery of those skills that would be required for the total program to be implemented. If these skills are inadequate or totally lacking, the supervisor must scrap the program until such time as training allows for minimal competencies in all areas.

Although well-developed programs based on attainable objectives should dictate counselor role and function, the profession of school guidance and counseling is faced today with numerous problems in this respect. Currently, the work of many school counselors is defined, not by clearly stated objectives based on student outcomes (Sullivan & O'Hare, 1971), but by a small repertoire of skills, e.g., individual counseling, placement, and scheduling, a practice which limits the contribution of the counselor to students. The counselor is further hampered by a lack of organizational and managerial expertise which frequently surfaces when counselors attempt to elicit responsiveness from building principals and others within the power structure of the school (Cook, 1971). Finally, many counselors lack a conceptual framework differentiating and harmonizing their role as a counselor of students and their role as an integral agent of short- and long-term guidance programs.

The development of powerful and effective programs of guidance and counseling is primarily the responsibility of guidance and counseling supervisors. However, participation in program development is an obligation of all school counselors. Together, supervisors and staff through program development may discover some deficiencies in delivery systems centering on skills and techniques. These competencies, then, must become the focal point for the supervisor before programs can be developed and implemented successfully.

SKILL MODEL FOR ASSESSING COUNSELOR COMPETENCIES

In determining the skill adequacy of school counselors in specific competency areas, few guidelines exist. One logical starting point could be an analysis of the traditional functions of guidance and counseling (testing, placement, career guidance, orientation, pupil evaluation) and the skills needed to implement these functions. Another manner of determining what skills or competencies a school counselor should possess is to look at university preparation programs and what skills they purport to offer to successful graduates. Similarly, state departments of education require certain certification standards and these too can be examined for specific skills and competencies. Also, professional organizations frequently prepare literature on this matter. However university preparation and school certification requirements rarely list specific competencies as such. Instead, they typically list courses taken and minimum and maximum hours allocated for this purpose. Professional organizations are even more vague when addressing this issue.

A simple means of identifying the existing and desired skills of counselors is the construction of a list of competencies now utilized by counselors in school settings. This list would cover skills required for the implementation of current functions and programs engaged in by both elementary and secondary school counselors. The list also would include competencies necessary for the successful development and implementation of future programs of guidance and counseling. For purposes of clarification, the terms skills and competencies will be used interchangeably and Carkhuff's (1972) definition of skills will be employed. As mentioned previously, Carkhuff defined skills as "behaviors that are operational, repeatable and predictable within a delimited range of effects" (p. 21).

In Figure 8.1 that follows is listed a number of distinct counselor skills using Carkhuff's criteria. The skills are not listed in order of importance and no attempt will be made to establish a hierarchy of counselor skills. In fact, conditions related to setting, audience and program make it highly unlikely that any hierarchial series of counselor competencies could be constructed even though individual counseling would be viewed as the foundation for all additional competencies. Further, this figure does not take into account the quantity nor quality of a given counselor's knowledge or information base concerning guidance and counseling functions such as careers, colleges, employment opportunities, standardized tests, and so on. Obviously, this information is an extremely important consideration because the successful implementation of many guidance functions rests on a suitable integration between the skills and knowledge possessed by the counselor.

PURPOSES OF FIGURE 8.1

Figure 8.1 is a listing of counselor competencies in accord with Carkhuff's definition of a skill. Each competency listed

306

COMPETENCY	UNIVERSITY ACQUIRED	WHERE ACQUIRED (check or list)		
		SCHOOL EXPERIENCES (List)	IN-SERVICE TRAINING PROGRAM	OTHER EXPERIENCES (List)
1. Individual Counseling				
2. Group Counseling				
3. Teaching (large group)				
4. Consulting				
5. Testing				
6. Diagnosing				
7. Researching and Evaluating				
8. Writing				
9. Curriculum Developing and Appraising				
10. Organizing and Managing				
11. Coordinating School and Community Resources				
12. Orally Expressing				
13. Referring and/or Placing				

Figure 8.1 Needs Assessment Of School Counselor Competencies and Potential Preparation Areas.

in this figure lends itself to direct observation and is repeatable. Also, all of these skills are operational and trainable. Further, each competency represents a documented skill currently employed by a large number of elementary or secondary school counselors in work settings. Finally, these competencies, singularly or in concert, represent the gamut of known skill ingredients in implementing and developing existing programs of guidance and counseling.

Figure 8.1 is organized and arranged for three purposes. First, this figure could be used by guidance supervisors in screening candidates for possible counselor positions. This could be accomplished by the supervisor using the figure in a checklist fashion to note a candidate's existing skills during a formal interview. The counselor candidate also could simply write in next to each competency the manner or procedure in which the competency was acquired. Obviously, the use of the figure in this manner does not establish the degree of proficiency in a given skill, but rather, the presence or absence of a given competency.

The second purpose of Figure 8.1 relates to a periodic assessment by guidance supervisors of current staff skills. This assessment could be utilized in conjunction with yearly staff evaluations or might be necessary before considering new programs. In either instance, the supervisor would review with each staff member the separate competencies and determine the current functioning level of the counselor. Some skills might have to be viewed directly or observed by video or audiotape in order to establish their identity. Others, such as writing and curriculum development, could be appraised by the products themselves. A guidance supervisor at the conclusion of this assessment would then have individual profiles of existing strengths and deficiencies of all staff members.

The third purpose of Figure 8.1 is a staff needs assessment for in-service training purposes. By compiling a skill profile on each staff member, the guidance supervisor can easily organize a composite of the entire staff. In turn, this composite would identify areas of staff strength, weakness and in-service training needs and also would serve as a guide in the development of new programs by pinpointing individual staff strengths and total staff potential for specific program implementation.

The skills listed in Figure 8.1 require some education and substantiation. Many of these skills are part and parcel of most university counselor education programs. However, some of these skills are acquired and/or perfected primarily in the context of the school. A few of these skills, i.e., curriculum development, are relatively new competencies and require exploration and justification. As a consequence, each skill will be briefly examined and a rationale given for its inclusion and necessity as a school counselor competency.

Individual Counseling

Competency in individual counseling has been recognized as a necessity for school counselors since the emergence of vocational guidance as a profession some seventy years ago (Shertzer & Stone, 1968; Super, 1955). The skill of individual counseling is critical to the work of school counselors for at least three reasons. First, competency in individual counseling is an essential technique in assisting students with developmental concerns, personal problems and educational demands. Second, competency in individual counseling carries with it the ability to form quick and productive relationships with a variety of individuals. This ability is essential for counselors in their advocacy role for students, in work with parents and teachers, and as potential resource obtainers for students with special needs (Dustin, 1974; Dworkin & Dworkin, 1971). Finally, competency in individual counseling is important because learning to counsel can help individual counselors become more effective human beings. Carkhuff & Berenson (1967) noted that counseling preparation is "another instance of living effectively, including especially the involvement in inter-personal learning processes which are facilitative of the development and growth of all of the persons involved" (p. 213).

Group Counseling

Group counseling has increasingly become an essential skill for practicing school counselors for a number of reasons. First, group counseling has proven its effectiveness with both children (Hansen, Niland, & Zani, 1969; Howard & Zimpfer, 1972; Ohlsen, 1973; Rose, 1972) and adolescents (Gazda, 1971; Mahler, 1969; Ohlsen, 1970) in school settings. Second, group counseling is obviously much more economical and efficient than individual counseling in reaching large numbers of students. Third, group counseling has been documented as the most effective mode of counselor intervention with some students, instead of individual counseling or other complementary skills (Mahler, 1969). Fourth, group counseling competencies increase the counselor's ability to function effectively as both a member and a leader in adult groups dealing with school concerns (Jacobs & Spradlin, 1974; Sugar, 1975). Fifth, group counseling skills and experience aid the counselor in a consultation role with teachers by enabling the counselor to pass along techniques and useful advice (Vriend & Dyer, 1973). Finally, group counseling skills enable a counselor to become an effective group leader which will add to the counselor's proficiency in dealing with large group and/or in teaching responsibilities.

Teaching (Large Group)

Although many states require certification as a teacher as a prerequisite for counselor certification, this requirement is not true in all states, and even where it does exist it does not imply a high degree of skill. Nevertheless, the question of the desirability of teaching experience for school counselors has yet to be decided, even though considerable attention has been given to this area (Cohen, 1961; Hudson, 1961; Kehas & Morse, 1970; Peterson & Brown, 1968; White & Parsons, 1974). Unfortunately most studies related to this issue have sought to prove that counseling effectiveness and/or employability are not related to prior teaching experience. As valid as this claim may be, it obscures another key consideration: namely, the desirability of the skill of teaching in effectively imparting knowledge directly related to guidance and counseling objectives to large groups of students and/or other audiences, i.e., parents and teachers. This skill is especially critical in view of recent developments in the fields of career guidance (Borrow, 1973; Crites, 1974; Herr, 1974; Hoyt, 1975; Marland, 1974) and psychological education (Mosher & Sprinthall, 1971; Sprinthall & Erickson, 1974). Without the necessary competency to deal effectively with large groups of students, apparently counselors will either decline this opportunity or be unable to deal successfully with the experience of large groups of students. This refusal also could lead to counselors neglecting the growing area of parent education and the in-service training of their teaching colleagues. Conceivable, the skill of teaching could be acquired by counselors without the additional course work demanded for typical teacher certification. However, without this important skill a number of critical and significant contacts with students, teachers and parents will not occur. In addition, a number of potentially powerful programs of guidance and counseling will not be developed and/or implemented by counselors.

Consulting

Until recent years, the skill of consulting was used much more frequently by school social workers and psychologists than by counselors. In addition, skill in consulting was viewed typically as a competency to be used with an individual, a family or a small group. However, in the past decade references to consulting as a distinct counselor skill has increased considerably and counselors more and more have consulted, especially at the elementary school level (Carson, 1972; Dinkmeyer & Carlson, 1975; Faust, 1968). In addition, a dramatic shift has occurred in the intended audience of consulting. Today, consulting is not aimed only at individuals and small groups, it also is seen as a viable tool in bringing about change in a given social system or institution (Blocker &

Rapoza, 1972; Dinkmeyer & Carlson, 1973; Fullmer & Bernard, 1972; Sprinthall, 1971). In fact, Fullmer and Bernard (1972) defined the chief task of consulting as "the improvement of learning environments" (p. 81). As a consequence, competency in consulting seems a must for all school counselors because of the inescapable fact that counselors are thrust daily into numerous situations demanding consulting skills. However, of greater importance is the fact that counselors can do little to change debilitating environmental conditions for students without this competency. This was noted and challenged by Lortie (1965) almost ten years ago when he questioned

> whether American schools can make good on their affirmations of individualism in the years ahead unless specific arrangements are made to defend the individual student against powerful bureaucratizing forces. Will counselors be the ones to seize this responsibility as their core task? (p. 138).

The answer to Lortie at this point certainly would have to be a qualified "no" if based on current counselor education programs, certification standards, and feedback from counselor practitioners (Ruben, 1974; Stiller, 1974). These three sources indicate little in the way of university preparation and/or in-service training to prepare counselors for this function. This fact is indeed disturbing because consulting is listed as a necessary and desired competency in the American School Counselor Association role statements for both elementary (1966) and secondary (1974) school counselors.

Testing

The use of individual and group tests by counselors has a long history and needs little review (Linden & Linden, 1968). Shertzer and Stone (1971) listed the following reasons for counselor competency in this area:

1. To secure accurate and reliable information about each student's abilities, aptitudes, interests, and personal characteristics.

2. To provide an improved basis for prediction regarding the likelihood of success in those activities in which prospective performance can be measured.

3. To help students arrive at decisions basic to planning their educational and vocational futures.

4. To diagnose student problems.

5. To help evaluate the outcomes of guidance or counseling (pp. 235-236).

Diagnosing

Although many similarities exist between testing and diagnosing, Tyler (1964) noted one major difference. The

> most distinctive feature of counseling (guidance) as compared with other varieties of psychological appraisal is that it is appraisal with the client rather than of him. It is his own awareness, not the counselor's, that is important . . . The task of the counselor is to facilitate the client's self-appraisal rather than to make an objective diagnosis (pp. 78-79).

Tyler's analysis may hold if we view testing and/or diagnosing as an individual or one-on-one relationship. However, the use of diagnosis as one prime skill of the counselor extends beyond that of simply working with an individual student for self-appraisal, as worthy as this goal may be. Instead, diagnosing frequently reaches beyond the individual in assessing the impact of a social system (classroom) or institution (school) on multiple individuals (Aubrey & McKenzie, 1977). Diagnosis also is a competency utilized in objectively attempting to observe the patterns of interaction among many individuals at the same moment in time. Diagnosing, therefore, is a skill encompassing many techniques that allow counselors to appraise individual and group phenomenon, social systems, and institutions. Although diagnosis is practiced daily by school counselors, it is highly doubtful if this skill is more than impressionistic guesswork in many instances (Sprinthall, 1971). However, the inevitability of its daily use necessitates proficiency in this area for all working school counselors.

Researching and Evaluating

In an exhaustive study of research on students and the school counselor role, Kehas(1972) concluded that "the questions and issues on which research is founded have been and are being established by persons other than counselors or other school people" (p. 2). Although this conclusion is not a surprising one to university personnel or experienced researchers, it does point to a serious deficiency in counselor preparation and practice. The matter is serious because, as a special ACES Committee noted some years ago (1967), "the school counselor has a continuing professional responsibility to define his goals, evaluate the effectiveness of his program in attaining these goals, and study methods and procedures for increasing his effectiveness" (p. xii). In addition, researching and evaluating can no longer be avoided by counselors and supervisory staff because of the growing public demand for accountability (Katz, 1973; Krumboltz, 1974).

Research need not connote to counselors an odious task replete with complex designs and advanced statistics. For counselors, research can be an objective study of the effectiveness of guidance and counseling programs and practices. As Kehas (1972) also has observed, researching and evaluating are simply processes of inquiry whereby we attempt to test out our experiences and generalizations in order to expand our knowledge of guidance and counseling. Kehas felt so strongly about the potential contribution of working counselors that he concluded that "studies by counselors could prove more sensitive to the important questions and the dynamics of their work than what is presently in the literature and could contribute powerfully to the development of knowledge about counselor role" (p. 8).

Writing

Many counselors admit that their writing skills are poor. On the other hand, just as many assert that they are overburdened with paper and clerical responsibilities (Armor, 1969). Somehow, the connection between competency in writing and functions related to clerical duties is never made. Skill in writing is essential to counselors because of the many writing tasks associated with case study reports, college work, career and vocational placement, research and evaluation, communications to parents and faculty, releases to the media and various agencies, and so on. Neglect of this skill may well be one reason that counselors continually bemoan the numerous clerical responsibilities assigned to their function (Stintzi & Hutcheon, 1972). Increased competency in writing and related communication skills may be one way to improve the current plight of the secretarial counselor. Suggestions and examples of reports can be found in Psychological Report Writing: Theory and Practice by Hollis and Donn. It may even be a means of shifting part of this responsibility to other parties. However, all counselor tasks associated with writing should not be disparaged or discarded. Proficiency in this area can assist students in numerous ways. One specific instance where counselors can significantly influence student outcomes through writing is in the area of curriculum development, and represents one of the largest untapped reservoirs of guidance.

Curriculum Development and Appraisal

Skill in curriculum development for counselors was probably first conceived by Jesse Davis (1914) some seventy years ago. Davis felt strongly that a need existed for a weekly period in schools devoted to vocational and moral guidance. For Davis, guidance was "of most value when it is in some way applied to the actual thinking and acting of the pupil. In this connection, guidance means the pupil's better understanding of his own

character, it means an awakening of the moral consciousness"
(p. 17). This belief was later followed by the work of Brewer
(1935) who felt guidance could assist students by "a direct
attack, with a curriculum of activities and guidance, designed
to give children the opportunity to learn living in the laboratory of life" (p. 3). Unfortunately, the formal school curriculum has been a seldom-used vehicle by counselors in helping
students. Commenting on this factor, Munson (1971) noted that
"We have tended to isolate guidance, particularly the counseling function. In the process we have created a wall between
the classroom teacher and the school counselor" (p. 335).
This wall is slowly giving way as illustrated by a dramatic
increase in recent years in commercially produced guidance
curricula (Alschuler, 1973; Bessell, 1969-1972; Dinkmeyer,
1970-1973; Gelatt, Varenhorst & Carey, 1972; Gelatt et al 1973;
Limbacher, 1969), as well as curricula stimulated by university
personnel (Dowell, 1971; Erickson, 1973; Griffin, 1972; Mackie,
1974; Mosher & Sullivan, 1974; Sprinthall & Erickson, 1974).

The combination of these two sources of curriculum programs
and materials makes it imperative that the school counselors
develop curricular competencies for two reasons. First, the
plethora of emerging programs and materials requires analytical
skill plus an ability to synthesize elements from discrete
curricula into combined wholes. Second, and most important,
curriculum programs offer a powerful method of attaining
guidance objectives for large numbers of students in an effective and efficient manner. As a consequence, skill in constructing, implementing and evaluating these approaches is
critical. Mosher and Sprinthall (1971) have defined this type
of curriculum as "a comprehensive set of educational experiences
designed to affect personal, ethical, aesthetic and philoso-
phical development" (p. 9). The ability to design and/or
synthesize elements from other curricula differentiates this
competency from teaching and large group skills although each
obviously complements the other.

Organizing and Managing

In a classic study on the role and personality of the
school principal, Hemphill, Griffiths, and Frederiksen (1962)
distinguished between two contrasting approaches in assessing
a record of administrative performance. They noted that "one
has to do with the content of the performance, or what is done,
and the other with the style of the performance, or how it is
done" (p. 86). They further felt that both approaches were
necessary in evaluating administrative performance. The usefulness of these approaches in analyzing the work of school counselors seems obvious. First, school counselors require competencies in organizing and managing because of the definition of
their role and the realities of school structure. Unlike
teachers, counselors are held accountable for multiple tasks

requiring the coordination and continuity of large numbers of pupils. Second, if counselors are to assume responsibilities for functions requiring organizing and managing skills, then these skills must be identifiable and trainable. Third, a distinction between the content and style of performance clarifies both preparation and assessment issues by an equal focus on both process and outcome factors. Finally, if counselors wish to extricate themselves from the morass of administrative functions they now assume, it will occur through an acquisition of better, not lesser, organizational and managerial competencies.

Coordinating School and Community Resources

Sources of help for students exist both within and outside the context of the school. Frequently, these sources of aid are unknown to students and their parents. Additionally, the sources themselves often have no knowledge of the individuals most in need of help. Counselors typically assume some responsibility for the coordination of these human resources. This coordination involves securing, screening, and delivering appropriate resources to needy students with dispatch. Coordinating also entails an ongoing process of monitoring and orchestrating multiple resources within and outside the school. Competency in this area demands some managerial and organization skills, but in addition, the ability to articulate a multiplicity of resources over an extended period of time. Finally, the skill of coordinating demands competency in diagnosing and blending what students need with sources of help and gain.

Orally Expressing

The vision of a counselor seated across from a student in a small office may conjure up one kind of communication skill utilized by counselors. On the other hand, a counselor addressing a faculty meeting or a large gathering of students or parents is utilizing another type of communication skill. In both instances the counselor must be able to relate clearly, concisely, and effectively to other people. However, skill in individual counseling does not necessarily prepare the counselor to relate to large groups of individuals any more than does skill in this latter area correspond to individual counseling effectiveness. Oral expression skills are necessary for counselors in both human and public relations. Incompetency in this area leads to misunderstanding, avoidance, and a diminution of outreach and communication.

Referring and/or Placing

The functions of referring and/or placing necessitate a combination of competencies and a large knowledge base.

Counselors engaged in these two activities must acquire considerable information and data before they are able to help students. However, in the process of acquiring data and information about referral agencies, colleges, armed services, job opportunities, careers, private physicians and psychiatrists, tutors, and the like, counselors also must develop competencies in analyzing and evaluating these resources. Further, the process of referring and/or placing requires some diagnostic skill on the part of the counselor in determing what resource(s) is appropriate for a given student or family of the student. As students' ages advance, the counselor may be prone to place increasingly the responsibility for decision making on the student. However, for a needy or abused child of six, the counselor may have little choice but to select directly the most helpful and appropriate course of action. Finally, the counselor must develop or possess a degree of initiative and resourcefulness in seeking out sources of aid for students. The fact that some counselors are rich in referral and placement resources whereas others are consistently barren and dry is simply no accident. When counselors are meagre and destitute, they enfeeble their counselees as well.

TOWARD A TAXONOMIC REPRESENTATION OF COUNSELOR COMPETENCIES

To this point, each counselor competency listed in Figure 8.1 has been considered and evidence presented for its inclusion as a necessary counselor skill. Previously the statement was made that the main purpose in constructing Figure 8.1 was not to develop a detailed level of specificity for each competency. Rather, Figure 8.1 was seen as useful in fulfilling three purposes in supervision. First, Figure 8.1 could be used as a broad screening device in interviewing prospective counselor candidates for school positions. Second, Figure 8.1 could be utilized by a supervisor in periodically assessing individual staff members' current skills and training needs. This could be accomplished by either having the staff member fill in the form indicating areas in need of in-service training, or, the supervisor could simply ask the counselor directly and take notes. Finally, supervisors could integrate the individual profiles of staff members acquired by using Figure 8.1 and construct and composite for the entire staff. This process would give the supervisor sufficient cumulative data to formulate program and in-service training needs.

One weakness and limitation of Figure 8.1 relates to the problem of specificity. Another weakness is the absence of limitation of existing measurement and assessment devices for these competencies. The presence of absence of specific skills was listed simply in Figure 8.1 without showing the degree or level of proficiency of a given skill. As a consequence, Figure

8.2 was constructed to overcome this weakness by delineating sub-categories under each skill heading.

Figure 8.2 is a crude taxonomic representation of how supervisors might graphically and conceptually deal with the multiple concerns of counselor evaluation, supervision and in-service training. The scope of this Chapter does not permit developing a complete and comprehensive taxonomy for all thirteen competency areas. However, Figure 8.2 can be used as an eclectic paradigm in depicting how a breakdown of skills might proceed.

In Figure 8.2 the first competency listed is individual counseling. This skill has been divided into three sub-categories by using some basic principles advanced by Ivey (1971). Further, the three sub-categories are then operationalized by adding behavioral criteria to each following the work of Guttman and Haase (1972). A more refined and sophisticated treatment of each category would necessitate a behavioral description of each major competency, the creation and definition of additional sub-categories, a number of observable and repeatable counselor behaviors under each sub-category, and, available designs or instruments for assessing separate and observable behaviors.

The second competency listed in Figure 8.2 is group counseling. This skill also is divided into a number of sub-categories following the micro-analysis of group leadership functions suggested by Bates and Johnson (1972, pp. 61-76). A number of counselor behaviors are listed under each sub-category and could be checked by the supervisor in the appropriate right-hand columns.

The third competency listed in Figure 8.2 is teaching and/or large group skills. This skill has been sub-divided into three categories. The first sub-category borrows from the work of Flanders (1964) some verbal behaviors of teachers found related to student outcomes. The remaining two sub-categories are based on findings of Hill (1969) in relating teacher behavior to effective discussion skills or group members.

The remaining ten competencies are not sub-divided as fully as the first three. Instead, a number of suggested sub-categories are listed under each competency without listing behaviors usually required for each. Supervisors could list under each of these sub-categories appropriate counselor behaviors in relation to the topical heading. They also could add additional sub-categories or delete the ones suggested by this writer. Finally, supervisors also could add competency headings omitted by this writer.

COMPETENCY	RATING (Check One)		
	SATIS-FACTORY	MINIMAL PROFI-CIENCY	IN NEED OF TRAINING
1.0 Individual Counseling			
1.1 Attending Behavior			
1.11 Maintaining adequate eye contact			
1.12 Relaxed and natural physical posture			
1.13 Accurately follows verbal behavior of client			
1.2 Reflection of Feeling			
1.21 Discriminates between client affect and content			
1.22 Reflects to client affective elements of verbal message			
1.3 Summarization of Feelings			
1.31 Recalls sum of clients affective statements			
1.32 Restates sum of clients affective statements			
2.0 Group Counseling			
2.1 Traffic Directing			
2.11 Blocking distracting statements without rejecting members			
2.12 Blocking invasion of privacy of members			
2.13 Facilitating inter-action among members instead of participating with group leader			
2.2 Modeling			
2.21 Attends to all members equally and follows verbal behaviors			
2.22 Confronts members with genuineness, empathy and concreteness			
2.23 Gives feedback that is current, useful and helpful			

Figure 8.2. Paradigm And Needs Assessment of School Counselor Competencies and Training Needs.

318

	RATING (Check One)		
COMPETENCY	SATIS-FACTORY	MINIMAL PROFI-CIENCY	IN NEED OF TRAINING
2.3 Interaction Catalyst			
2.31 Initiates group process forward movement			
2.32 Involves members in productive experiences			
2.33 Confrontation of members is effective and helpful			
2.34 Values of members are explored			
2.4 Communication Facilitation			
2.41 Reflects content of members clearly and accurately			
2.42 Links one member's comments to other			
2.43 Reflects feelings of members accurately and sensitively			
3.0 Teaching (large group)			
3.1 Verbal Behavior			
3.11 Accepts student feelings			
3.12 Gives praise and encouragement			
3.13 Accepts and makes use of student ideas			
3.14 Gives directionality when needed			
3.15 Gives constructive criticism			
3.2 Social Tasks			
3.21 Expedites interaction and participation			
3.22 Uses time segments for maximum effectiveness			
3.23 Relieves group tension when necessary			
3.24 Confronts and tests reality			
3.25 Clarifies and summarizes individual and group responses			

Figure 8.2. Continued.

319

COMPETENCY	RATING (Check One)		
	SATIS-FACTORY	MINIMAL PROFI-CIENCY	IN NEED OF TRAINING
3.3 Content Matter			
3.31 Selects appropriate materials and experiences			
3.32 Devises logical sequence of learning experiences			
3.33 Can assess impact of educational experiences on individual and group			
4.0 Consulting			
4.1 Establishing Relationships			
4.2 Interviewing			
4.3 Advice-giving			
4.4 Follow-up			
5.0 Testing			
5.1 Instrument Selection			
5.2 Group Testing			
5.3 Individual Testing			
5.4 Evaluation of Data			
5.5 Use of Data			
6.0 Diagnosing			
6.1 Problem Analysis			
6.2 Individual Appraisal			
6.3 System Appraisal			
6.4 Institutional Appraisal			
6.5 Summarization and Conclusions			
6.6 Applicability of Results			
7.0 Researching and Evaluating			
7.1 Problem Analysis			
7.2 Instrument Selection			
7.3 Design and Statistics			
7.4 Application			
7.5 Analysis			
7.6 Application of Data			
8.0 Writing			
8.1 Format			
8.2 Style			
8.3 Effectiveness			

Figure 8.2. Continued.

	RATING (Check One)		
COMPETENCY	SATIS-FACTORY	MINIMAL PROFI-CIENCY	IN NEED OF TRAINING
9.0 Curriculum Developing and Appraising			
9.1 Appraisal of Commercial Programs			
9.2 Synthesis of Discrete Programs			
9.3 Construction of Programs			
9.4 Evaluation of Programs			
10.0 Organizing and Managing			
10.1 Performance Content			
10.2 Performance Style			
11.0 Coordinating School and Community Resources			
11.1 Screening			
11.2 Securing			
11.3 Delivery			
11.4 Follow-up			
12.0 Orally Expressing			
12.1 Style and Form			
12.2 With Individuals			
12.3 With Groups			
13.0 Referring and/or Placing			
13.1 Initiative and Resource-fulness			
13.2 Appropriateness of Resource			
13.3 Accommodating Student and Resource			
13.4 Follow-up			

Figure 8.2.   Continued.

RESOLVING INTER-STAFF CONFLICT AND
INCREASING STUDENT DELIVERY SYSTEM

A final variation of Figure 8.1 is illustrated in Figure 8.3. This figure is an attempt to clarify for supervisors areas of potential and actual conflict between members of pupil personnel staffs. The suggestion is that one possible manner of tracing sources of staff conflict is by examining the competencies of various pupil personnel workers. In so doing, a supervisor may discover that areas of actual conflict revolve around skill areas common to all. For example, conflict between counselors, psychologists, and social workers may center around areas associated with diagnosing and consulting. Conceivably, all three specialists feel competent with these skills and a battle for territorial rights might occur whenever one of the skills is required.

On the other hand, conflict among pupil service specialists may arise due to a lack of competency on the part of specialists. For example, group work may be the preferred way of helping a group of students. However, because of a lack of staff skills in this area, all three specialists may act on this problem separately with entirely different intervention postures. The counselor in this instance may prefer individual counseling, the social worker consulting and the psychologist testing. The problem arises in allowing specialists to define problems and intervention measures by a narrow band of competencies limiting the potential benefits to students.

A final source of conflict between counselors, social workers, and psychologists may occur because people avoid the use of certain skills. By utilizing Figure 8.3, a supervisor may discover a skill area mastered by two or more specialists. However, the competency may not be employed in a given instance because of reluctance of the specialists to engage in the function. For example, counselors and psychologists may have skills in researching and evaluating. A situation may arise where this competency seems necessary but is not being employed. The supervisor by checking a table of staff competencies can quickly ascertain whether or not the skill exists among staff members and question, where appropriate, its lack of use.

A final use of Figure 8.3 is related to the creation of a more effective pupil personnel department. The suggestions is that a wider distribution of these thirteen competencies among pupil personnel workers would reduce friction and increase staff effectiveness with students. This distribution would change the focus of determining what intervention posture is desirable from a speciality orientation to one of competency orientation. The wide distribution of competencies would blur

322

COMPETENCY	COUNSELOR*	PSYCHOLOGIST*	SOCIAL WORKER*
1. Individual Counseling			
2. Group Counseling			
3. Teaching (large group)			
4. Consulting			
5. Testing			
6. Diagnosing			
7. Researching and Evaluating			
8. Writing			
9. Curriculum Developing and Appraising			
10. Organising and Managing			
11. Coordinating School and Community Resources			
12. Orally Expressing			
13. Referring and/or Placing			

*CODE: In rating the competencies, place next
         to each the following weightings for
         summarization and analysis purposes:

    0 = Skill non-existent
    1 = Minimal proficiency level
    2 = Satisfactory proficiency level
    3 = Able to train other staff members

Figure 8.3. Pupil Personnel Competency Assessment Of
             Counselors, Psychologists And Social Workers.

lines of demarcation among and between pupil personnel specialists and concentrate more on a prescription for student development than on a description of specialist treatment. In so
doing, it would increase greatly the probability that a programmatic approach would replace a strictly service function in
all areas of pupil personnel work.

DEVELOPING A MODEL SUPERVISORY PROGRAM

A model supervisory program to be utilized with elementary
and secondary school counselors is difficult to conceptualize.
This difficulty stems in part from the tremendous differences
in school settings and intended audiences. Another compounding
factor is the availability and expertise of school supervisors
to implement the model. Finally, few if any exemplary supervisory programs now exist and this lack of a comparative base
limits initial expansion in this area.

Figure 8.4 is a broadly sketched model supervision program
for elementary and secondary schools. Reflected are many of
the views presented in this Chapter. The program begins by
listing six comprehensive objectives under the column labeled
GOALS. These objectives are the starting points for various
key aspects of a comprehensive supervisory program. They are
listed in a logical and preferred sequence of activities and
the suggestion is that they be implemented as such.

Column two in Figure 8.4 is labeled ACTIVITIES. This
column describes the work activities in which supervisors and/or
staff must engage to realize the six objectives listed under
GOALS. These work activities also are described in a suggested
sequence that best allows successful attainment. The experiences suggested under ACTIVITIES may vary by locale, but the
emphasis on the conjoint work of both supervisor and staff in
formulating policy will not.

The third and final column in Figure 8.4 is labeled OUT-
COMES. This column makes explicit the objectives listed under
GOALS and the experiences engaged in under ACTIVITIES. As a
consequence, OUTCOMES can be used throughout the creation of a
model supervision program as a bench mark for how well day-to-
day practices approximate long-range expectations.

A reading of Figure 8.4 reveals a strong bias in favor of
supervisor and staff cooperation in the development of any
supervision program. This sharing of responsibility seems
essential if supervisors expect staff members to exhibit some
ownership and respect for the final product. In addition,
many of the desired OUTCOMES are predicated on the collaborative
efforts of supervisor and staff.

GOALS	ACTIVITIES	OUTCOMES
I. Establish supervisor and staff written guidelines for staff and program development.	Staff/supervisor meeting for guideline clarification. Staff preparation of written guidelines. Supervisor preparation of written guidelines. Staff/supervisor meeting(s) for guideline synthesis/resolution.	Written document of staff/supervisor agreed upon priorities for staff and program development (including procedures for supervision, in-service training and evaluation).
II. Survey of all staff to determine current level of functioning and areas in need of training/improvement.	Individual conference between each staff member and supervisor to rate counselor competencies. Visitation schedule of supervisor/counselor arranged for observation of selected competencies in field setting. Staff member collection of data and evidence to substantiate competencies and outcomes non-attainable by observation. Supervisor/staff member conference to evaluate visits and data and to establish time line for improvement.	A competency profile for each staff member devised by supervisor but discussed and arrived at conjointly. This profile would describe staff members current level of functioning and contain a prescriptive section for future work and improvement.

Figure 8.4. Model Supervision Program.

325

GOALS	ACTIVITIES	OUTCOMES
III. Integration and synthesis by supervisor of all staff member competency profiles in order to organize and implement selected training programs for individuals and groups.	Supervisor tabulates all staff member competency profiles. Supervisor determines competency areas most in need of upgrading for individuals and/or groups. Supervisor organizes individual and group training programs utilizing own staff as trainers whenever possible. Supervisor follows up training programs by evaluation and visits to staff in field settings.	Upgrading of selected skill deficiencies by individuals and groups, expansion of staff members able to train others.
IV. Establish written guidelines and procedures for recruitment of new staff.	Staff/supervisor meeting to discuss charge, i.e. written guidelines designating desired competencies of new staff, means of determining competencies, interviewing procedures by staff and supervisor, criteria for final selection of candidate(s).	Written document of staff/supervisor with mutually agreed upon guidelines and procedures for recruitment of new staff.

Figure 8.4. Continued

GOALS	ACTIVITIES	OUTCOMES
V. Establish written guidelines and procedures for elimination of inadequate staff.	Supervisor presents to the staff, procedures and criteria to be used in phasing out staff not amenable to training and supervision. Staff responds to supervisor procedures and criteria and suggests changes/improvements. Supervisor finalizes procedures and criteria and implements in the field.	Written document initiated by supervisor revised vis a vis staff suggestions and put into practice.
VI. Broadening of competency base of pupil service workers beyond counselors (social workers, psychologists, special education, and so forth).	Supervisor of counselors involves supervisors of related areas in planning conference. Conference focuses on sharing and expansion of competencies of all pupil service personnel. Competency areas to be strengthened, identified and workshops/training set up. Competency areas of overlap or possible role conflict pinpointed and clarified. A common task orientation to replace one centered on role or competency.	Reduction of friction and territoriality among various pupil service specialities by a broader competency base in a number of specific skills resulting in a task orientation to work instead of role or assigned function.

Figure 8.4. Continued.

In Figure 8.4 also is stressed the creation of certain written polities and procedures as a starting point in building a model supervision program. These documents are seen as minimal and necessary in the attainment of long-range purposes. In addition, they are critical in bringing a degree of fairness and consistency to the entire practice of counselor supervision.

SUMMARY

Supervision of practicing school counselors is largely unrecorded and lacking in documentation. No substantive body of knowledge exists in this critical area and probably no major impetus will change this situation in the near future. This is partly because of a lack of interest by university personnel; but even more so, this lack also is the result of the neglect of school personnel and professional associations to seek and promote counselor supervision.

A clarification of the terms supervision, preparation and evaluation seemed necessary in covering the global area of supervision. A further distinction was drawn between viewing guidance and counseling as providing ad hoc services in contrast to programmatic functioning. The latter view expanded the nature of supervision to include sequential and planned programs of guidance and counseling as well as distinct skills related to counselor functioning.

Supervision was conceived as possessing a double-pronged nature focusing on both the improvement and enhancement of individual counselors as well as the accomplishment of objectives benefiting students. A relationship was established between the improvement of counselor competencies and the concomitant development of powerful programs of guidance and counseling. To this end, a skill model was introduced for purposes of assessing existing counselor competencies.

Finally, the suggestion was that school supervision of counselors be moved into a model containing a taxonomic representation of desirable counselor competencies. A paradigm was introduced as a suggested working model toward this end. An elaboration of this model also was suggested as a potential means of resolving role conflict among school counselors, psychologists and social workers.

REFERENCES

Alschuler, A. Developing Achievement Motivation in Adolescents:
Education for Human Growth. Englewood Cliffs, New Jersey:
Educational Technology Publications, 1973.

Appleton, G. M., & Hansen, J. C. Continuing supervision in the
schools. Counselor Education and Supervision, 1968, 7,
273-281.

Armor, D. J. The American School Counselor. New York: Russell
Sage Foundation, 1969.

Aubrey, R. F. And never the twain shall meet: Counselor training and school realities. The School Counselor, 1972, 20,
16-24.

_____. Misapplication of therapy models to school
counseling. Personnel and Guidance Journal, 1969, 48,
273-278.

_____. The organizational victimization of school
counselors. The School Counselor, 1973, 20, 346-354.

Aubrey, R. F., & McKenzie, F. W. The school counselor as environmental researcher. Chapter in L. Goldman's (Ed.),
Research and the Counselor. New York: John Wiley, 1977.

Bates, M. M., & Johnson, C. D. Group Leadership: A Manual for
Group Counseling Leaders. Denver: Love Publishing Company,
1972.

Bessell, H. Human Development Program: Activity Guides -
Levels B, I, II, III, IV. El Cajon, California: Human
Development Training Institute, 1969-1972.

Biddle, B. J. The integration of teacher effectiveness research.
In Contemporary Research on Teacher Effectiveness. B. J.
Biddle and W. J. Ellena (Eds.). New York: Holt, Rinehart
and Winston, 1964, 1-40.

329

Biggers, J. L., & Mangusso, D. J. The work of the guidance administrator. Counselor Education and Supervision, 1972, 12, 130-136.

Blocher, D. H., & Rapoza, R. S. A systematic eclectic model for counseling-consulting. Elementary School Guidance and Counseling, 1972, 7, 106-112.

Boocock, S. S. The life career game. Personnel and Guidance Journal, 1967, 46, 328-335.

Borrow, H. (Ed.). Career Guidance for a New Age. Boston: Houghton Mifflin, 1974.

Boy, A. V., & Pine, G. J. Evaluating the school counselor. Counselor Education and Supervision, 1968, 7, 107-113.

Boyd, J. D., & Walter, P. B. The school counselor, the cactus, and supervision. The School Counselor, 1975, 23, 103-107.

Brewer, J. M. Education as Guidance. New York: Macmillan and Company, 1935.

Brown, D. Trends in educational administration: Impact upon the guidance administrator. Counselor Education and Supervision, 1967, 6, 191-196.

Calia, V. F. Organizational theory and research: Some implications for guidance practice. Personnel and Guidance Journal, 1965, 43, 757-763.

Cantrell, J.; Aubrey, R. F.; & Graff, F. A dialogue: Where do we go from here? The School Counselor, 1974, 21, 266-279.

Carkhuff, R. R. The Development of Human Resources. New York: Holt, Rinehart and Winston, 1971.

_____. The development of systematic human resource development models. The Counseling Psychologist, 1972, 3, 4-30.

Carkhuff, R. R., & Berenson, B. G. Beyond Counseling and Therapy. New York: Holt, Rinehart and Winston, 1967.

Carlson, J. The future of school counseling. Focus on Guidance, 1973, 5, 1-10.

_____. (Ed.). Special issue: Consultation. Elementary School Guidance and Counseling, 1972, 7, 81-149.

Cohen, N. Must teaching be a prerequisite for guidance?
Counselor Education and Supervision, 1961, 1, 69-71.

Cook, D. R. (Ed.). Guidance for Education in Revolution.
Boston: Allyn and Bacon, 1971.

Cramer, S. H. (Ed.). Pre-service and in-service preparation of
school counselors for educational guidance. Monograph
prepared by the ACES-ASCA Committee on Preparation for Pre-
College Guidance and Counseling, American Personnel and
Guidance Association, Washington, D. C., 1970.

Crites, J. O. Career counseling: A review of major approaches.
The Counseling Psychologist, 1974, 4, 3-23.

Davis, J. B. Vocational and Moral Guidance. Boston: Ginn,
1914.

Delaney, D. J. A behavioral model for the practicum supervision
of counselor candidates. Counselor Education and Supervision, 1972, 12, 46-50.

Dietz, S. C. Counselor role, function, and job satisfaction.
Counselor Education and Supervision, 1972, 12, 150-155.

Dinkmeyer, D. Developing Understanding of Self and Others, I &
II. Circle Pines, Minnesota: American Guidance Services,
1970-73.

Dinkmeyer, D., & Carlson, J. Consultation: A Book of Readings.
New York: John Wiley, 1975.

Dinkmeyer, D., & Carlson, J. Consulting: Facilitating
Humaneness and Change Processes. Columbus, Ohio: Charles
E. Merrill, 1973.

Donigian, J., & Wellington, A. M. Leadership behavior of guidance directors related to counselors' expectations.
Counselor Education and Supervision, 1971, 10, 146-152.

Doverspike, J. E. Neophyte, nexus, nirvana or how are things
in the field? Counselor Education and Supervision, 1972,
11, 231-235.

Dowell, C. R. Adolescents as peer counselors: A program for
psychological growth. Unpublished doctoral thesis.
Harvard University, 1971.

Dunlop, R. S. Counselor competence: Some proposals in search
of advocacy. Personnel and Guidance Journal, 1968, 46,
655-660.

Dustin, R. Training for institutional change. _Personnel and Guidance Journal_, 1974, 52, 422-427.

Dworkin, E. P., & Dworkin, A. L. The activist counselor. _Personnel and Guidance Journal_, 1971, 49, 748-753.

Eckerson, L. O. White house conference on children: Implications for counselors as change agents. _Elementary School Guidance and Counseling Journal_, 1972, 6, 239-244.

Eisenberg, S., & Delaney, D. Using video simulation in counseling for training counselors. _Journal of Counseling Psychology_, 1970, 17, 15-19.

Erickson, V. L. Psychological growth for women: A cognitive-developmental curriculum intervention. Unpublished doctoral thesis. University of Minnesota, 1973.

Experimental Designs Committee of the Association for Counselor Education and Supervision. _Research Guidelines for High School Counselors_. New York: College Entrance Examination Board, 1967.

Faust, V. _The Counselor-Consultant in the Elementary School_. Boston: Houghton Mifflin, 1968.

Filbeck, R. W. Perceptions of appropriateness of counselor behavior: A comparison of counselors and principals. _Personnel and Guidance Journal_, 1965, 43, 891-896.

Flanders, N. A. Some relationships among teacher influence, pupil attitudes, and achievement. In B. J. Biddle and W. P. Ellena (Eds.), _Contemporary Research on Teacher Effectiveness_. New York: Holt, Rinehart and Winston, 1964.

Fullmer, D. W., & Bernard, H. W. _The School Counselor-Consultant_. Boston: Houghton Mifflin, 1972.

Gazda, G. M. _Group Counseling: A Developmental Approach_. Boston: Allyn and Bacon, 1971.

Gelatt, H. B. Confronting the status quo. _Focus on Guidance_, 1971, 4, 1-8.

_____. School guidance programs. _Review of Educational Research_, 1969, 39, 141-153.

Gelatt, H. B.; Varenhorst, B.; & Carey, R. _Deciding_. New York: College Entrance Examination Board, 1972.

Gelatt, H. B.; Varenhorst, B.: Carey, R.; & Miller, G. P. *Decisions and Outcomes*. New York: College Entrance Examination Board, 1973.

Ginzberg, E. *Career Guidance*. New York: McGraw-Hill, 1971.

Griffin, A. Teaching counselor education to black teen-agers. Unpublished doctoral thesis, Harvard University, 1972.

Guttman, M. A., & Haase, R. F. Generalization of microcounseling skills from training period to actual counseling setting. *Counselor Education and Supervision*, 1972, 12, 98-108.

Hansen, J. C.; Niland, T. M.; & Zani, L. P. Model reinforcement in group counseling with elementary school children. *Personnel and Guidance Journal*, 1969, 47, 741-744.

Hansen, J. C., & Warner, R. W. Review of research on practicum supervision. *Counselor Education and Supervision*, 1971, 10, 261-272.

Hansen, L. A. A learning opportunities package. Minneapolis: University of Minnesota Department of Counseling and Student Personnel Psychology, 1970.

Hemphill, J. K.; Griffiths, D. E.; & Frederikson, R. *Administrative Performance and Personality*. New York: Columbia University Press, 1962.

Herr, E. L. (Ed.). *Vocational Guidance and Human Development*. Boston: Houghton Mifflin, 1974.

Hill, W. F. *Learning Through Discussion*. Beverly Hills, California: Sage Publications, 1969.

Hoppock, R., & Stevens, N. S. High school courses in occupations. *Personnel and Guidance Journal*, 1954, 32, 540-543.

Howard, W., & Zimpfer, D. G. The findings of research on group approaches in elementary school guidance and counseling. *Elementary School Guidance and Counseling*, 1972, 6, 163-169.

Hoyt, K. B. *Career Education*. Salt Lake City, Utah: Olympus Publishers, 1975.

Hudson, G. R. Counselors need teaching experience. *Counselor Education and Supervision*, 1961, 1, 24-25.

Humes, C. W. Solution to school counselor role: Administrative change. *Counselor Education and Supervision*, 1970, 10, 87-90.

Humes, C. W., & Lavitt, J. A. Counselor attitudes toward administrative practices: Massachusetts and Connecticut. Counselor Education and Supervision, 1971, 10, 153-157.

Hummel, D. L., & Bonham, S. Pupil Personnel Services in Schools: Organization and Coordination. Chicago: Rand McNally, 1968.

Ivey, A. Microcounseling: Innovations in Interviewing Training. Springfield, IL.: Charles C. Thomas, 1971.

Jacobs, A., & Spradlin, W. The Group as Agent of Change. New York: Behavioral Publications, 1974.

Joint ACES-ASCA Committee on the Elementary School Counselor. Preliminary statement, joint ACES-ASCA Committee on the Elementary School Counselor. Personnel and Guidance Journal, 1966, 44, 658-661.

Joseph, E. A., & Drury, W. R. Ohio counselors evaluate their formal preparation. Counselor Education and Supervision, 1971, 11, 56-61.

Kagan, N. Multimedia in guidance and counseling. Personnel and Guidance Journal, 1970, 49, 197-205.

Katz, M. R. Accountability of counselors and evaluation of guidance. Focus on Guidance, 1973, 6, 1-11.

Kaufman, J. J., & Lewis, M. V. The Potential of Vocational Education: Observations and Conclusions. University Park, PA.: The Institute for Research on Human Resources, Pennsylvania State University, May 1968.

Kehas, C. D. Administrative structure and guidance theory. Counselor Education and Supervision, 1965, 4, 147-153.

_____. Guidance in education: An examination of the interplay between definition and structure. In V. F. Calia and B. D. Wall (Eds.), Pupil Personnel Administration. Springfield, IL.: Charles C. Thomas, 1968, 21-35.

_____. Toward a redefinition of education: A new framework for counseling in education. In B. Shertzer and S. C. Stone (Eds.), Introduction to Guidance: Selected Readings. Boston: Houghton Mifflin, 1970, 59-71.

_____. What research says about counselor role. Focus on Guidance, 1972, 9, 2.

Kehas, C. D., & Morse, J. L. Perceptions in role change from teacher to counselor. Counselor Education and Supervision, 1970, 9, 248-258.

Kemp, C. G. Counseling responses and need structure of high school principals and of counselors. Journal of Counseling Psychology, 1962, 9, 326-328.

Kohlberg, L.; LaCrosse, R.; & Ricks, D. The predictability of adult mental health from childhood behavior. In B. Wolman (Ed.), Handbook of Child Psychopathology. New York: McGraw-Hill, 1970.

Krumboltz, J. D. An accountability model for counselors. Personnel and Guidance Journal, 1974, 639-646.

_____. Changing the behavior of behavior changers. Counselor Education and Supervision, 1967, 6, 222-229.

Limbacher, W. Dimensions of Personality. Dayton, Ohio: George Pflaum Publishers, 1969.

Lindberg, R. E. PPS director: Administrator or counselor educator? Personnel and Guidance Journal, 1972, 51, 195-198.

Linden, J. D., & Linden, K. W. Modern Mental Measurement: A Historical Perspective. Guidance Monograph Series. Boston: Houghton Mifflin, 1968.

Lister, J. L. Counselor experiencing: Its implications for supervision. Counselor Education and Supervision, 1966, 5, 55-60.

Lortie, D. C. Administrator, advocate or therapist? Alternatives for professionalization is school counseling. In R. Mosher, R. Carle, and C. Kehas (Eds.), Guidance: An Examination. New York: Harcourt, Brace, 1965, p. 138.

Lowenstein, N., & Hoppock, R. Teaching of occupations in 1952. Personnel and Guidance Journal, 1953, 31, 441-444.

Lucio, W. H., & McNeil, J. D. Supervision: A Synthesis of Thought and Action. New York: McGraw-Hill, 1962.

Mackie, P. Teaching counseling skills to low achieving high school students. Unpublished doctoral thesis, Boston University, 1974.

Mahler, C. A. Group Counseling in the Schools. Boston: Houghton Mifflin, 1969.

Marland, S. P. Career Education: A Proposal for Reform. New York: McGraw-Hill, 1974.

Mathewson, R. Guidance Policy and Practice. New York: Harper and Row, 1962.

Mezzano, J. A survey of the teaching of occupations. Vocational Guidance Quarterly, 1969, 17, 275-277.

Mosher, R. L., & Sullivan, P. Moral education: A new initiative for guidance. Focus on Guidance, 1974, 6, 1-12.

Mosher, R. L., & Sprinthall, N. A. Psychological education: A means to promote personal development during adolescence. The Counseling Psychologist, 1971, 2, 3-82.

Mosher, R. L., & Purpel, D. E. Supervision: The Reluctant Profession. Boston: Houghton Mifflin, 1972.

Munson, H. L. Guidance and instruction: A rapprochement. In D. R. Cook (Ed.), Guidance for Education in Revolution. Boston: Allyn and Bacon, 1971, 335-355.

Noble, F. C. Why don't counselors counsel? The School Counselor, 1968, 16, 94-98.

O'Hara, James M. In-service education for school counselors - a point of view. Counselor Education and Supervision, 1968, 7, 211-215.

Ohlsen, M. M. (Ed.). Counseling Children in Groups. New York: Holt, Rinehart and Winston, 1973.

_____. Group Counseling. New York: Holt, Rinehart and Winston, 1970.

Peterson, B. H., & Brown, D. Does teaching experience matter? Personnel and Guidance Journal, 1968, 48, 893-897.

Pietrofesa, J. J., & Van Hoose, W. H. Participant change during an EPDA institute: Personality, attitudinal, and learning dimensions. Counselor Education and Supervision, 1971, 11, 147-152.

Pinson, N. M. Supervision: The silent S of ACES. Counselor Education and Supervision, 1974, 14, 157-159.

Pulvino, C. J., & Perrone, P. A. A model for retooling school counselors. Counselor Education and Supervision, 1973, 12, 308-313.

The role of the secondary school counselor. The School Counselor, 1974, 5, 380-386.

Rose, S. D. _Treating Children in Groups_. San Francisco: Jossey-Bass, 1972.

Ruben, A. G. Will counselors ever be consultants? _The School Counselor_, 1974, 5, 376-378.

Ryan, T. A.; Baker, R. D.; Fitzpatrick, G. M.; & Hosford, R. E. Commitment to action in supervision: Report of a national survey of counselor supervision. Committee on Counselor Effectiveness, Association for Counselor Education and Supervision, 1969.

Schultz, M. W. Strengthening supervisory practices for directors of guidance. _Counselor Education and Supervision_, 1969, 333-334.

Schwartz, L. J., & Sherman, R. The action counseling workshop: An intensive teaching-learning model. _Counselor Education and Supervision_, 1975, 15, 144-148.

Shertzer, B. _Fundamentals of Guidance_. Boston: Houghton Mifflin, 1971.

Shertzer, B., & Stone, S. C. _Fundamentals of Counseling_. Boston: Houghton Mifflin, 1968, p. 31.

Shoemaker, J. T., & Splitter, J. L. A competency-based model for counselor certification. _Counselor Education and Supervision_, 1976, 15, 267-274.

Sinick, D.; Gorman, W. E.; & Hoppock, R. Research on the teaching of occupations. _Personnel and Guidance Journal_, 1966, 44, 591-610.

Spivack, J. D. Critical incidents in counseling: Simulated video experiences for training counselors. _Counselor Education and Supervision_, 1973, 12, 263-270.

Sprinthall, N. A. _Guidance for Human Growth_. New York: Van Nostrand Reinhold, 1971.

Sprinthall, N. A., & Erickson, V. L. Learning psychology by doing psychology: Guidance through the curriculum. _Personnel and Guidance Journal_, 1974, 52, 396-405.

Stiller, A. Presenting: The consultant to counselors. _The School Counselor_, 1974, 5, 342-349.

Stintzi, V. L., & Hutcheon, W. R. We have a counselor problem - can you help us? _The School Counselor_, 1972, 19, 329-334.

Sullivan, H. J., & O'Hare (Eds.). Accountability in pupil personnel services: A process guide for the development of objectives. California Personnel and Guidance Association, Monograph Number 3. Fullerton, California, 1971.

Sugar, M. The Adolescent in Group and Family Therapy. New York: Brunner/Mazel, 1975.

Super, D. E. Transition: From vocational guidance to counseling psychology. Journal of Counseling Psychology, 1955, 2, 3-9.

Tamminen, A., & Miller, G. Guidance programs and their impact on students: A search for relationships between aspects of guidance and selected personal-social variables. St. Paul, Minneapolis: U. S. Department of Health, Education and Welfare and Minnesota State Department of Education, 1968.

Tiedeman, D. V. Predicament, problem, and psychology: The case for paradox in life and counseling psychology. Journal of Counseling Psychology, 1967, 14, 1-8.

Trotzer, J. P. Do counselors do what they are taught? The School Counselor, 1971, 18, 335-341.

Tyler, L. The methods and processes of appraisal and counseling. In A. S. Thompson and D. E. Super (Eds.), The Professional Preparation of Counseling Psychologists. New York: Columbia University Press, 1964.

Vriend, J., & Dyer, W. W. Counseling Effectively in Groups. Englewood Cliffs, New Jersey: Educational Technology, 1973.

White, A. J., & Parsons, B. M. An alternative approach to the teaching experience requirement for school counselors. Counselor Education and Supervision, 1974, 13, 238-241.

Wicas, E. A., & Mahan, T. W. Characteristics of counselors rated effective by supervisors and peers. Counselor Education and Supervision, 1966, 6, 50-56.

Winefordner, D. W. Career Decision Making Program. Charleston, W. Virginia: Appalachia Educational Laboratory, 1974.

Chapter **9**

SUPERVISING

COUNSELORS

IN

PREPARATION

Daniel J. Delaney, Director
Outpatient and Outreach Services
Community Mental Health Center
Norfolk, Virginia

SUPERVISING COUNSELORS-IN-PREPARATION: A FRAMEWORK

Editor's Notes

Historically, supervision has been prominent in counselor preparatory programs. Counselors-in-preparation need supervisory feedback regarding their performance in order to improve skills, and their counseling must be monitored so that client welfare is insured. Supervision thus has always been an indispensable facet of counselor education, and remains so today.

Supervising counselors as they complete a preparatory program is in some ways an easier task than post-degree supervision in helping-service settings. Student-counselors expect supervision and generally offer less resistance than practicing counselors, and preparatory programs usually provide technical facilities that are not available to field supervisors. But as Dr. Delaney explains, supervision in a counselor education program can be as demanding as the supervision of practicing counselors.

The following Chapter offers a view of supervision unique in two regards. First, Dr. Delaney's idea of supervision as a helping process which parallels that of counseling is virtually synonomous with the editor's conceptualization in Chapter 1 and the behavioral approach in Chapter 3; supervision is described as a skill-focused consultation process utilizing training, evaluation, and counseling. Second, Delaney views supervision within training institutions as a process constantly influenced by situational variables. Through graphic display and narrative these variables are identified, and described.

To summarize, this Chapter offers readers a broad environmental perspective on supervision within training institutions, combined with a skill-based approach to supervision practice. Dr. Delaney's social learning theory orientation is translated into a supervisory position that is palatable to supervisors of other theoretical persuasions.

Daniel J. Delaney

Daniel J. Delaney (Ph.D.) is Director of Outpatient and Outreach Services, Community Mental Health Center, Norfolk, Virginia. In addition to the more traditional outpatient services, his responsibilities include resocialization and after-care programs in a comprehensive community mental health center and in seven outreach facilities located throughout the City of Norfolk. He is also Professor and Director of Continuing Medical Education, Department of Psychiatry and Behavioral Sciences, Eastern Virginia Medical School, a sister institution of the CMHC, both of which are organizational components of the Eastern Virginia Medical Authority.

Dr. Delaney was Professor of Educational Psychology at the University of Illinois, Urbana, before coming to Norfolk. He is a licensed psychologist in Illinois and Virginia and has extensive experience as a consultant in the fields of corrections, education and mental health services. He holds an A.B. degree from Stonehill, College, a M.Ed. degree from Massachusetts State at Bridgewater and received his Ph.D. degree from Arizona State University in 1966. He resides with his wife and six children in Virginia Beach.

SUPERVISING COUNSELORS-IN-PREPARATION: A FRAMEWORK

Daniel J. Delaney

Supervision is a process involving the influence of one
person on another. This process takes place across a span of
time and has certain identifiable stages, as well as beginning
expectations of those involved in the process. The setting in
which the process occurs, the purpose of the process, prior
preparation of those involved, and where the process occurs in
relation to broader organizations are all intervening variables.
The purpose of this Chapter is to look at these variables,
expectations, process stages and influencing methods in the
context of educational preparation programs designed to
graduate competent professional counselors prepared to work in
a variety of settings.

The first task in this Chapter will be to sort out some of
the more obvious dimensions of supervision and to offer practical suggestions for the enhancement of their efficacy.
Following this task, a recommended framework for counseling
supervision will be presented along with steps for its development within a college or university.

The dimensions of supervision to be examined prior to
building a framework are as follows: scope of supervision,
expectations of the supervisory relationship, the settings in
which supervision occurs, supervision models, and the supervisory paradigm which includes the supervisor, the characteristics of effective supervisors, the ethical responsibilities
of the supervisor and the supervisee.

SCOPE OF SUPERVISION

Specific material relevant to this discussion is briefly
reviewed to set the stage for studying the supervision of
counselors-in-preparation. The three points reviewed here are

from previous Chapters in this book and are the major aspects
that determine the scope of supervision. The three points are
as follows:

1. Counselor supervision has been defined as the function
   of overseeing the counselor's work for the purpose of
   facilitating personal and professional development,
   improving competence, and promoting accountability in
   counseling and guidance. To accomplish these purposes
   the supervisor employs the four activities of consultation, counseling, training and instruction, and
   evaluation. Consultation is the supervisor's predominant activity in which the objectives and strategies
   of supervision are established. Strategies may allow
   the supervisor to remain in the consulting activity,
   or may involve the activities of counseling and
   training/instruction in which the supervisor leaves
   the consultant stance. Evaluation is another major
   activity of supervision that is often a companion to
   consulting and training/instruction.

2. Counselor supervision involves multiple activities.
   The activities employed are those of consulting, counseling, training and instructing, and evaluating as
   presented in Figure 9.1.

3. Four broad models of supervision were articulated in
   Chapters 2 through 5: the psychotherapeutic model,
   the behavioral model, the systems model, and the integrative approach. These models are not mutually
   exclusive, but rather, they suggest that the comprehensive counselor supervisor have competency in all
   approaches. The parallels of these models and the
   activities of the supervisor noted previously, are
   obvious.

Competency in the implementation of these models requires
a certain set of conceptualizations of counseling supervision.
Such a set of conceptualizations would include the supervisor
as a counselor, a teacher, and a consultant. The supervisor's
work as a counselor can be viewed as the enactment of a helpgiving process for the student (counselor-in-preparation) where
aspects of a therapeutic relationship are experienced. The
goals of this process would be to aid the counselor-in-
preparation in developing the necessary conditions for counseling: empathy, nonpossessive warmth, openness and genuineness.
The counselor-in-preparation learns these as he experiences
them, the supervisor modeling these as a counselor.

The supervisor-teacher approach treats counselor supervision in a fairly straightforward teacher-student relationship.
Information concerning aspects of counseling is to be

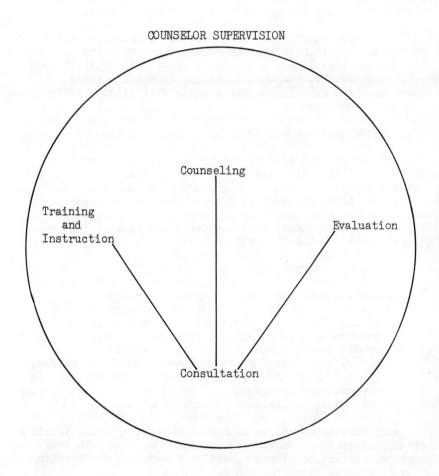

COUNSELOR SUPERVISION

Counseling

Training
and
Instruction

Evaluation

Consultation

Figure 9.1.   Counselor Supervision: Multiple Activities.

learned by the student counselor. This information is
followed by the supervised practice of the counselor-in-preparation and appropriate feedback is made by the supervisor. The
supervisor-consultant approach considers the student counselor
as a professional who has acquired a specific set of skills and
who is not in an inferior position to that of the supervisor.
The supervisor functions as a resource person and one who helps
the student counselor to reflect more on the dynamic process of
counseling and on the counselor-client relationship.

These approaches certainly are not mutually exclusive.
The synthesis of these approaches within a supervisor's activities is the most likely criteria of the truly competent counseling supervisor, one who is able to synthesize these
approaches and activities into a style that is most efficacious.

EXPECTATIONS OF THE SUPERVISORY RELATIONSHIP

After making a cursory review of the literature (ACES,
1969; APGA, 1961, 1967; Delaney & Moore, 1966; Patterson, 1964;
Truax & Carkhuff, 1964) one might draw the conclusion that the
supervisor is an instructor, a consultant, a counselor, and one
who critiques the counsel performance. These perceptions seem
to match the expectations that supervisees have of the supervisor's roles in the following vein:

> . . . as a person who is to: direct the work of the coun-
> selor, instruct the trainee, provide counseling infor-
> mation, demonstrate counseling and techniques of
> counseling, provide for the support and the security of
> the counselor . . . . instruct and demonstrate clerical
> procedure, act as an administrator-instructor, direct the
> counselor while supporting him or providing for his
> support, . . . carry a regular case load of counselees,
> . . . emphasize the supervisee's responsibility for his
> own growth and development, (and to be) available for con-
> sultation . . . (Delaney & Moore, 1966, pp. 15-16).

Supervisees expect to learn new behaviors, to be helped to
strengthen desired behaviors, to accept the responsibility for
their growth and development, and they expect the supervisor to
help make these things possible.

A considerable amount of "supervisory influence" exists
in this role and these functions. As a practicing counselor,
the supervisor has developed an approach to working with
persons that is viewed as the most effective and efficient, and
obviously the supervisor acts to influence the supervisee
toward this counseling orientation. An important point is that
both must recognize the nature of this orientation. Also

important is the recognition that this influence exists not only from the supervisor but also from the very nature of the supervisory relationship. Therefore, the author stresses that supervisory "assignment," that is, a supervisor being assigned a counselor-in-preparation for the purpose of supervision, is a very poor administrative practice. However, to the credit of counselor education, this practice does not seem to be widely employed. The solution to the difficulty of assignments poses no additional problems and is right at hand. Supervisors as counselor educators have other duties and responsibilities, one of which is the teaching of courses. In this manner, counselors-in-preparation become familiar with instructors, and instructors' biases, bases of operation, belief systems, and other notions and hunches about humans and their behavior. Ample opportunities exist for counselors-in-preparation to become acquainted with educators and vice-versa. The author's proposed solution, then, is to allow the natural grouping of students (counselors-in-preparation) with a counselor educator for the purpose of supervision.

From this perspective, the expectations of the supervisors and supervisees (counselors-in-preparation) seem to be quite similar. The supervisor should be aware of his or her own orientation to counseling, and, through interactions with supervisees, help them to recognize this orientation by being open and explicit about hunches, biases and prejudices. A mutual selection of student supervisees and supervisors for counseling supervision should be implemented. Only in this manner will the potential for growth and development of both be assured.

SETTINGS IN WHICH SUPERVISION OCCURS

Certainly much supervision goes on in any setting in which education and training are expected to occur. Along with didactic instruction (the explaining how to do something) and modeling (the demonstration of the focal behavior by an expert), some process is used to give learners feedback as to their progress, especially in the area of performance of acquired skills. This process of feedback is one of influence, whether used to aid learners to strengthen selected behaviors, or to weaken and thereby modify other behaviors. This process of influencing supervision--is therefore an integral part of any well-formulated learning paradigm.

Of particular focus are those areas in which counselors are provided feedback regarding their counseling skills. In many ways counselor education and training should be directed to this feedback, concerning both acquired skills, and a perception of counselors as persons who appreciate the personhood of others as well as the environment in which all must exist. Specifically, particular learning experiences exist in counselor preparation programs where the task is to provide students (counselors-in-preparation) with concrete feedback concerning their demonstrated behavior as counselors. The most common nomenclature used to describe these experiences include field experiences, practica, and internships. A differentiation needs to be made among these terms because of a considerable lack of clarity and consistency and because often the terms are used interchangeably.

Field experiences are used to refer to experiences received by students (counselors-in-preparation) in specific settings outside of the counselor education institution. The field settings include elementary and/or secondary schools, community agencies, jails, and so forth. These experiences usually are well controlled and supervised, and although contact and interaction with a client population is encouraged, counseling may not be. Goals are that the students (counselors-in-preparation) will become familiar with the setting, its operations, systems, organization, and idiosyncrasies, as well as the population that is served.

Practica and/or supervision are conducted often within the counselor education institution. Practica seem to imply certain laboratory constructs and are much more directly related to counseling performance than are field experiences. The supervisor observes performances by using one-way glass mirror systems, and audio and video recordings. The goals are that students will develop and strengthen those behaviors that are appropriate for competent professional practice.

The third specific supervised experience offered in counselor education programs is the internship. Usually internship refers to experiences that follow the formal educational and preparation program. At this point field experiences, practica and, indeed, the whole preparation program come together and the student experiences more independence and freedom. Internships themselves however do entail supervision, by both the educators and those professionals from the internship environment itself (Gust, 1970).

What is being addressed in this Chapter is the process of supervision offered through the counselor education program that leads to the preparation of professional counselors. Although the total preparation process assumes supervision, as in any well implemented educational program, the specific areas upon which focus is made are field experiences, practica, and internships.

348

SUPERVISION MODELS

In recent relevant literature is revealed an increase in activity in the study of supervision (Hansen, Pound, & Petro, 1976). This trend may be interpreted as general agreement by counselor-educators that commonly agreed upon models for conducting supervision of counselor-in-preparation are open further to study and development. Also another interpretation may be valid: little is known about the specific elements of the counseling supervision experience that facilitate counselor-in-preparation growth and effectiveness and this accounts for the increase in research activity.

Goldman (1972), in a paper presented at the 1972 APGA convention, was critical of the "storehouse theory," and advocated a combination of the theoretical and practical: "Most people learn things best, and can retrieve them best, when they learn them in a setting of application...that is, in a practical, functional, applied manner" (p. 3). The applied practice tacked on after a series of didactic courses may not be the best solution. Jakubowski-Spector (1969) pointed out some drawbacks of the emphasis on theoretical counseling models followed by a supervised experience. Lack of preparation, the building up of expectations, and the retrospective nature of counseling supervision are mentioned as limitations. She proposed that "the process of assisting the student-counselor /counselor-in-preparation/ in developing confidence, a personally effective counseling style, and a greater understanding of theory needs to be accelerated through pre-practicum simulated counseling experiences" (p. 3).

Didactic-Experiential Model

Research on the relative effectiveness of different modes of supervision is limited and inconclusive. Birk (1972) examined the importance of the supervision method and the students' (counselors-in-preparation) preferences for supervision method in a supervision analogue. Her results were that, while supervision preference was not significant in affecting the criterion measure (empathic understanding), a significant effect was shown for supervision method and for the interaction between supervision method and supervisor. Specifically, the group receiving supervision using a didactic, rather than experiential, model scored significantly higher on the criterion measure. Spice and Spice (1976) described a triadic method of helping counselors-in-preparation to learn to function alternately in three roles--supervisor, critical commentator, and facilitator of open communication and dialogue.

Developmental Model

This supervision model may be described along dimensions
other than didactic/experiential. Tarrier (1971) presented a
developmental view of supervision--"generations" that may
include elements of didactic and experiential supervision. Very
briefly, the five generations he presented were the following:
First Generation--consultation; Second Generation--audio
recording; Third Generation--one-way mirror viewing; Fourth
Generation--audio-video recording; Fifth Generation--coached
clients and simulated experience. Tarrier commented:

> As the supervisor moves through the generations, the
> emphasis shifts from counseling techniques to personal
> involvement and reaction...It becomes more and more likely
> that the supervisor trainee meeting will focus on personal
> attitudes and values aroused by the stimulus (tape or
> client) rather than strictly techniques of counseling.
> This emphasis is not traditional (institutional) (p. 9).

Tarrier's generations provide for increasing amounts of
information in the supervisory session, and also (in the Fifth
Generation) for individualization in the design of the
counselor-client interaction.

Practice-based Models

In addition to the input of the supervisor, counselor,
preparation programs may offer a variety of practice-oriented
experiences. One such model was developed by Cormier and Nye
(1972). These authors presented an individualized discrimination preparation program focusing on three areas: (1) self-
development of the counselor, (2) skills, techniques, and
strategies, and (3) consequences of counselor behavior on
client behavior. This program utilizes written self-tests,
rating charts, and accuracy checks with observers; the
counselor-in-preparation, rather than the supervisor, is
required to initiate the self-controlling responses as well as
the responses to be controlled. Video tapes, coached clients,
and video simulation tapes are utilized.

Lifton (1971), in order to broaden student-counselors'
experiences, discussed the advantages of placing counselors-
in-preparation in other than educational settings. Placements
in various agencies provide students a more realistic view of
the limits and functions of the various agencies and allow
students to interpret experiences for their educational value.

THE SUPERVISORY PARADIGM

The three persons involved in the counseling supervision process are the supervisor (S), the counselor-in-preparation (CP) and the client (Cl). The supervisory paradigm is presented in Figure 9.2.

The supervisor has dual responsibilities: (1) to help the counselor-in-preparation through the supervisory process and (2) to provide careful guard and assurance for the welfare of the client. These responsibilities seem quite obvious and in nearly all occasions the dual responsibilities are, in practice, a one-and-the-same supervisor obligation.

Counselors-in-preparation, while primarily involved in their own preparation, have the direct responsibility for the welfare of the clients with whom they are working. These counselors-in-preparation should be aware of the supervisor's responsibility for client welfare and should be able to understand the supervisor's ethical and professional position if difficulties arise.

The suggestion is for the selection of supervisors and supervisees to be a mutual process, probably the result of contact both have made in other areas of the counselor education program. Both these groups understand the ethical and professional implications and responsibilities of the supervisor as these relate to the client with whom the supervisee will be working.

THE SUPERVISOR

Most supervisors of counselors-in-preparation are counselor educators who have many other duties and responsibilities, only one of which is counselor supervision. Certain other characteristics of this group have been mentioned in Chapter 1. However, some additional remarks should be made. The supervisory skills possessed by counselor educators seem to be the result of incidental learning or self-instruction. While this unplanned learning process often produces positive results, general agreement exists that more formal preparation of supervisors can improve the field of counselor preparation in a significant manner.

The supervisor of counseling in graduate preparatory programs is likely to hold a doctoral degree, to function in a curriculum that involves supervision of many student activities, to be actively involved as a counselor, and to supervise counseling behavior in experiential courses such as field experiences, practica, and internships. As an educator, he/she has many other duties in addition to supervision, and as a

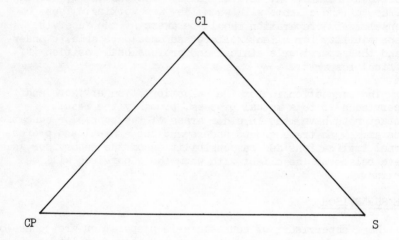

Figure 9.2. The Supervisory Paradigm: Supervisor (S),
             Counselor-in-Preparation (CP), and Client (Cl).

counselor this professional has undoubtedly developed a broad orientation and a personalistic style to the helping of persons through counseling activities. In general, the supervisor is expected to act as a dynamic consultant, able to provide supervisees with training, instruction, counseling, and evaluation.

Many attempts have been made to assess and evaluate counselor supervision, but this is no easy task. Without a formal way to describe the supervisory process, preparation in supervision has taken on a "master supervisor" approach, that is, a watch-how-I-do-it system of modeling. This approach appears to be somewhat successful, in that good supervisors do become available to the profession as a result of preparation programs. This is no doubt analogous to the field of counseling before any identifiable principles were formulated on which to base the operationalization of counselor education programs.

One other often-raised concern worth mentioning is whether or not the truly competent supervisor need be a currently practicing counselor. The criticism has been raised that the nonpracticing counselor cannot be a good supervisor, and this criticism applies to most counselor educators. Once again, the master-counselor/supervisor model is the one most often employed, although "master" sometimes implies "not now practicing." Whether counseling and supervision are seen as arts and/or sciences, continual practice has to be an essential variable in being able to deal adequately with these processes. As in other such human endeavors, whether playing a musical instrument, doing laboratory research in chemistry, or diagnosing an automobile engine, practice is required for competent performance. Therefore the strong suggestion is that to be a competent supervisor an active program in the practice of counseling must be followed.

Characteristics of Effective Supervisors. (The following material reflects content from S. Eisenberg and D. J. Delaney, The Counseling Process, Second Edition, Chicago, Ill: Rand McNally, 1977.) Supervisors are helpers and the factors that characterize effective helpers are the same factors that characterize effective supervisors. The author believes that these factors include the following abilities and characteristics:

Effective supervisors are able to reach in as well as to reach out. They are able to help supervisees think openly and non-defensively about themselves because supervisors are not afraid to participate in these experiences themselves.

Effective supervisors communicate caring and respect for the supervisees being helped. Supervisors believe that the persons with whom they work are capable of learning, of overcoming obstacles to growth, and of maturing into responsible, self-reliant individuals.

Effective supervisors like and respect themselves and do not use the supervisees they are trying to help to satisfy their own needs.

Effective supervisors have special knowledge in counseling that will be of value to their supervisees.

Effective supervisors attempt to understand, rather than to judge, the behavior of the supervisees they are trying to help.

Effective supervisors are able to reason systematically and to think in systems terms. They realize that supervisees' concerns and problems are influenced by many complex factors that must be identified and understood as an inherent part of the helping effort.

Effective supervisors are contemporary and have a world view of human events and an awareness of how these events affect their lives as well as the lives of others.

Effective supervisors are able to identify behavior patterns that are self-defeating and to help supervisees change these to more personally rewarding behavior patterns.

Effective supervisors are skillful at helping supervisees look at themselves, and to respond non-defensively to the question, "Who am I?"

Ethical Responsibilities of the Supervisor. (The following material reflects content adapted from: Ethical Standards for Research with Human Subjects. Washington, D. C. American Psychological Association, 1972). Ethical problems associated with the supervision of counselor candidates in the counseling situation are many, but it is virtually impossible to identify them. Ethics are more adequately approached by becoming aware of principles and guidelines to be followed, some of which are as follows:

The supervisor has the personal responsibility of making a careful evaluation of both the level of counselor competence and the level of client need for expert help.

The final responsibility for the welfare of the client rests with the supervisor.

The client should be informed of the level of counselor competence if this is a feature that reasonably could be expected to influence the outcome of counseling.

Openness and honesty should characterize the relationships between supervisor, counselor (supervisee), and client as regards the involvement of the supervisor, covert observation of private sessions (disguised windows and audio or video equipment) and any other features that may be broadly considered as an invasion of the client's privacy.

The counselor (supervisee) and supervisor should respect the client's right to choose not to participate in the supervised counseling process at any time and they should be prepared to offer other more private counseling processes.

A clear and fair agreement should exist between and among the supervisor, counselor (supervisee), and client as to the responsibilities of the former two to the latter and an obligation of the professionals to honor all commitments in that agreement.

Supervisors should protect clients from all discomfort, harm, danger, and stress that could result from the counseling process as offered by the counselor-in-preparation.

After counseling has been terminated, if the client requests feedback from the supervisor, the supervisor should consider this and do what is needed to assure that no damaging consequences have occurred to the client as a result of these processes.

Where counseling procedures may result in undesirable consequences for the client, the supervisor has the responsibility for employing appropriate measures to detect and remove or correct these consequences, including where relevant, long-term after effects.

The supervisor and counselor (supervisee) should keep in confidence all information received about any client. When any known possibility exists that others may obtain access to such information, this possibility, together with the plans for protecting confidentiality, should be explained to the client as part of the procedure for obtaining informed consent.

The Counselor-in-Preparation (Supervisee)

The persons being supervised in counselor education programs are difficult to describe in any statistical fashion (Webb & Rochester, 1969; Felker & Brown, 1970). More importantly, these persons have gravitated in their career development to the area of helping professions and specifically to professional counseling. From various social, economical, racial, and educational backgrounds, these men and women are interested and committed to preparing themselves to help others. The reasons for this commitment are many, not the least of which must be the satisfying of one's own needs, that is, a self-fulfillment through helping others to grow, develop and find their own fulfillment.

Supervisees are people from various and diverse backgrounds who have expressed a commitment to the field of counseling, and are interested in a total educational program including preparation in the necessary skills to function as competent counselors. They expect to learn these skills through the process of supervised counseling activities. They also expect the supervisor to teach, direct, demonstrate, and provide information to help them learn counseling skills, while at the same time, supporting and protecting them during this process.

Counselors-in-preparation are willing to follow a counselor education program which includes academic and personal development. The programs in which they are involved offer many courses and experiences, the more traditional academic areas being organization and administration, counseling theories and techniques, career development, research, use of tests and measurements, principles and practices of personnel services, group work, and child and adolescent development. Almost all of these areas are at the graduate level of education. Part of the preparation program is in supervised counseling practice, whether conducted in a field setting, a training laboratory (practicum), or an internship placement. In these three settings, particularly, counselors-in-preparation become part of the supervisory system.

Counselor education programs are mainly graduate education programs, although a slight trend may be occurring for undergraduate curricula with both terminal and professional characteristics. These graduate programs are either masters degree level, post master/predoctoral level, or doctoral level. In that practices of supervised counseling cut across all degree levels, supervision is supervision and is to be viewed as such regardless of the level of functioning or educational attainment of supervisees.

In summary, supervisees are graduate students in counselor education programs which are designed and implemented to prepare them to become competent professional counselors. Actual supervision of counselor behaviors is likely to be performed in courses and experiences such as field experiences, practica, and internships, although supervision, broadly conceived, is an essential component of any well formulated preparation program.

BUILDING A FRAMEWORK

What is needed in this area of concern is a framework within which a supervisor can integrate the four supervisory activities that have been identified. This framework should act as a foundation on which to build a comprehensive structure that would encompass various supervision preparation models, determine procedures for the evaluation of supervision practices, while offering some clearer conceptualizations of counselor supervision. This substructure and framework also should help to facilitate the establishment of parameters for needed research in supervision and in training programs for supervisors. The remainder of this Chapter is an attempt to build such a framework, but first there seems to be another important and quite relevant consideration to be made: the relationship of counseling to supervision.

Certainly a strong similarity exists between the processes of counseling and of supervision, and this fact explains why master-counselors respond so well to supervision preparation. Rather than checklist the similarities between these two, the following dimensions will be used to describe how each parallels the other: supervision and counseling as processes, supervision and counseling as interventions stressing the influence of the supervisor on the counselor and the counselor on the client, and the inherent interaction of the activities of counseling on counseling supervision and vice versa.

Human Interaction Processes

Counseling, and the supervision of counseling, are processes that seem to be based on similar systems of knowledge, means, and skills. Both the competent counselor and supervisor have a broad background of knowledge and understandings in psychology, educational psychology, education and other related fields. This knowledge has been synthesized into a working model, or at least a model in which the professional can reflect his activities. One needs not review commonalities in this area as they simply reflect the standards of preparation of the professional organizations (e.g., APGA, 1967).

In addition to possessing knowledge in related fields, one must have a _means of helping_, based upon principles of human behavior acquisition. These elementary principles as described by Eisenberg & Delaney (1977) may be stated as follows:

1. People learn new behaviors by receiving verbal instructions from significant others.

2. People learn to behave in new ways by imitating the behavior, beliefs, values and attitudes of significant others.

3. The reinforcement contingencies in a person's environment influence the way he/she behaves in that environment. Changing the reinforcement contingencies can be expected to influence a change in behavior.

4. Some people learn to function more effectively by becoming aware of certain characteristics about themselves or their environments.

5. Some people learn to function more effectively by acquiring a specific method for decision making.

6. Some people learn to function more effectively by acquiring a more favorable sense of self-worth.

Whether involved in attempting to help a person to modify behavior in some meaningful manner for personal self-fulfillment (counseling) or for professional self-development (supervision), these principles seem to be the means for helping to initiate behavior change.

The third component to these processes are the _skills needed to actualize the knowledge and means in a human relationship: human interpersonal interaction skills_. Some of these skills, whether understood in a theoretical and/or applied manner, are the use of accurate empathy, active listening, concreteness, genuineness, professionalism, appropriate verbal responses and other attentive behaviors.

The relationship between the processes of counseling and supervision are presented in Figure 9.3, using the system of knowledge, means and skills, as described. The two processes, though rooted in the same basics, have at least one discernible difference: The counseling process must be, in some way, a component of supervision, in that the latter is a further extension of the means, skills, and knowledge of the former.

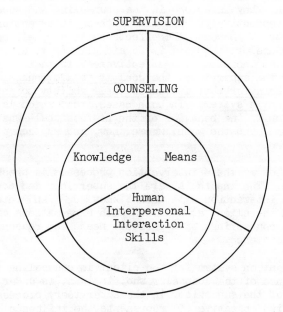

Figure 9.3.   Counseling and Supervision: Human Interaction
              Processes.

Counseling and Supervision as Intervention

Both the counselor and the supervisor are influencers, and as such, they intervene in the counseling and supervisory processes respectively. The aim of these interventions is to help persons to increase the effectiveness of their behavior. For the counselor, the goal is to aid clients to engage in behavior that increases the effectiveness in their style of living for the supervisor, the goal is to aid counselors to engage in behavior that increases their ability to intervene in the client's system. In both cases, that which is used as intervention is the behavior of the professional--what is communicated, and the when, where, how, and why communications are employed.

The flow of these intervention processes is presented in Figure 9.4. The inputs (A) are the supervisor and counselor as persons in interaction with means, knowledge, and interaction skill, and the client as a person with expectations of the counselor, counseling, with personal needs and reasons for seeking assistance.

The intervention system for the client is counseling (B) under the influence of the counselor who, in turn, is under the influence of the supervisor in the supervisory process (C). The specified objective (D) represents the influence of counselor behavior on client behavior. For example, the counselor skill of communicating empathic understanding helps the client to engage in further self-exploration. The client alone comprises the client system (E) which exists, for the most part, outside of the counseling process. Evaluation and feedback (F) are responsibilities of the counselor to the client and the supervisor to the counselor. The goals, skills employed, persons involved, and processes used in supervision are so fundamentally entwined in counseling that the former (supervision) may only be understood by knowledge and appreciation of the latter (counseling).

Interaction of Counseling and Supervision Processes

Four relative, though identifiable, stages are pertinent to the counseling process:

1. the establishment of a facilitative relationship,

2. the identification of the goals of the counseling process,

3. the employment of counseling interventions to achieve the stated goals, and

360

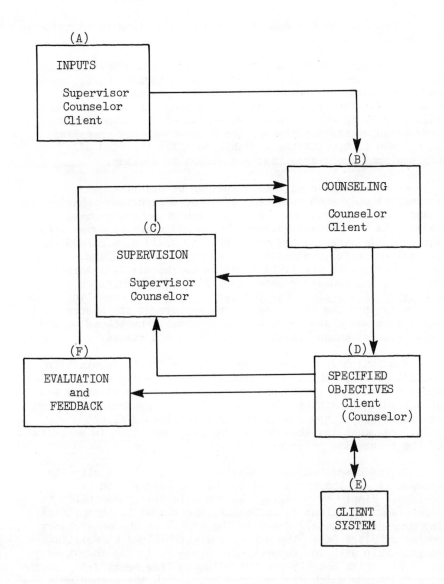

Figure 9.4. Counseling and Supervision as Interventions.

4. termination and follow-up of the interventions as well
   as the process itself (Delaney & Eisenberg, 1972).

Outlining these stages to compare counseling to supervising
can be helpful.

The relationship stage of counseling can be best described
in terms of the process goals of empathic understanding, warmth
and acceptance, genuineness and honesty, and professional
competency. The product goal of this stage is to establish a
relationship in which the client learns of the counselor's
understanding and acceptance, and learns that the counselor
is one who is trustworthy and able to offer the kind of
professional assistance that the client is seeking.

Because successful counseling can be described as
successful only when some kind of observable client behavior
change has occurred, the identification of behavior-change
targets is the process goal of the second stage of counseling.
The client's target behavior (a product goal) also serves as
the criterion for evaluating the outcome of counseling.
Concurrently with the identification of the client's target
behavior, the counselor maps out a plan of intervention for
achieving this goal. Thus the second stage of counseling leads
naturally into the third stage, the employment of intervention
strategies which are based on the previously mentioned
principles of human behavior acquisition and change.

The fourth and final stage of counseling is termination
and follow-up of the intervention. Process goals of evaluation
and feedback help the counselor determine if the strategy was
effective in attaining the product goals of generalization and
stabilization of newly acquired or strengthened client
behaviors, that is, the outcome goal as identified in stage two
of the counseling process.

Having described the counseling process, the similarity
between it and the process of counseling supervision is
obvious. Simply by changing the nomenclature of counselor to
supervisor and client to counselor, the stages in the counseling process adequately describe the stages in the supervisory
process. Stage One: The supervisor establishes a facilitative
relationship with the supervisee. Stage Two: Together they
set goals which usually consist of counseling behaviors, though
personal needs which may be interfering with the counselor's
effectiveness are appropriate targets for intervention. Stage
Three: evaluation by the supervisor encompasses the counsel-
or's evaluation of the counseling process. The development of
successful counseling behaviors is the goal of the supervisory
process and as such is the outcome goal of supervision. The
criterion for success of these counseling behaviors is that the

client achieves his/her outcome goals as a result of the counseling process. The evaluation feedback system presented in Figure 9.4 suggests that counseling and supervision are two similar processes in a state of constant interaction.

While stressing the similarities and common elements of the counseling and supervision processes, no implication is made that they are identical. Lambert's (1974) research has emphasized this point by revealing a significant difference between the levels of genuineness and respect in the capable practice of counseling and supervision. In his study competent therapists offered significantly higher levels of empathy and specificity in counseling than in supervision. Lambert (1974) stated:

> In fact, the results of (his) study indicate a significant and consistent tendency for therapists to offer lower levels of empathy and specificity in supervision than they do in counseling... . In other words, the trainee may learn to appreciate and understand the feelings of the client without having had his own feelings of uncertainty and inadequacy recognized or acknowledged and without having experienced high levels of empathy himself. (p. 59)

THE FRAMEWORK: A SPIRAL MODEL OF COUNSELING SUPERVISION

The purposes of this text, as set forth in Chapter 1, are

1. to develop clearer conceptualizations of counselor supervision;

2. to develop further the distinct properties of, and commonalities in, different models for preparing supervisors of counseling;

3. to determine the parameters of effective supervision amenable to evaluation; and

4. to reinforce the need for adequate research in the area of supervision practices and related activities.

Applying these goals to the specific area of counselor supervision in educational preparation programs, and in light of remarks made to this point in this Chapter, the complexity of this task is seen readily. One also should recognize easily that this present work is to be received as a starting point rather than as a finished product. In light of these considerations, if the result of this Chapter is the presentation of a framework upon which can be built subsequent development in this area of concern, then its objectives will have been met.

The basic structure for developing a better understanding of the supervisory process should encompass all of the components of a preparation program that can be identified and described. Such a structure is presented in Figure 9.5, a Spiral Model of Counseling Supervision. The model is viewed as a spiral, to symbolize the dynamism of supervision as a process tied to environmental properties while constantly undergoing refinement, redirection, evaluation and evolution. The model will be explained by following the spiral through one revolution and making some brief comments on its various components. The total supervisory process is involved and at the same time, some light is shed by the model on the processes for involving supervisor trainees (counselors-in-preparation) as part of their educational and experiential programs. For supervisor trainees to have a system upon which to reflect their learnings can only aid in their perception of supervision as they become employed in various settings.

MODEL COMPONENTS

Program Need Assessment. Every counselor education program has a certain uniqueness as the result of interactions among staff, students, curricula and environment. The same is true, of course, for the program components of practica, field experiences and internships. To design these components for maximum efficiency necessitates planning based on the identification of needs. Such planning and need identification are based on the answers to questions represented, in part, by the following: What positions do counselors-in-preparation enter upon graduation? What is the academic and experiential backgrounds of counselors-in-preparation? Where do program components best fit into the curriculum, for example, is practicum offered throughtout the student's program or after the completion of certain academic courses? What is the best staff/student ratio for supervision? Is laboratory training in counseling used as a prerequisite for supervised practice in counseling? Are separate programs planned for preparing counselors for differing educational levels, agencies, and institutions? Does the staff view their programmatic thrusts as being aimed at a particular level of graduate education, such as a doctoral program? Obviously these need assessment procedures take a good deal of staff and student time, energy and effort.

Establishment of site needs. Following from program assessment is identification of the needs of sites to be used for supervised practice. The establishment of site needs would take into consideration the site itself, site physical plant, site population, problems of this population that can be

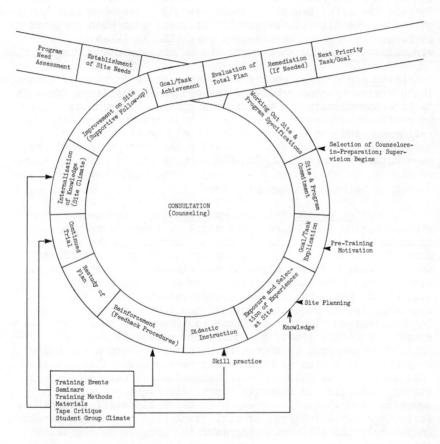

Figure 9.5. Spiral Model Of Counseling Supervision.

365

expected to be presented in counseling, and the ethical, professional, and administrative arrangements necessary for personnel to work together effectively.

Working out site and program specifications. This task is an interfacing process between the program and the site. In such processes it should be noted that compromise is very often the byword. At times what is desired by the counselor education staff places too much of a burden on the site staff. Cooperative efforts such as these usually place more additional duties on the site staff than is realized, even when the work performed by the counselors-in-preparation is taken into consideration.

Site and program commitment. This stage is no more than the contract agreement between the program and site staffs. It is probably unrealistic to expect any final program that will work effectively and efficiently without continuous monitoring, refinement and evaluation. There should be at this point, however, a commitment for cooperation that is specified in as much detail as possible. This commitment should identify those procedures to be used to change any of the items that have been developed between the two parties.

Selection of counselors-in-preparation. The selection process begins long before this point in time. Screening students for the graduate program in counseling, the development of programs to fit the students' needs and backgrounds, and the continued evaluation of the students' progress are all part of this selection process. Some procedure for staff evaluation should be devised whereby evaluations of students are collected at regular intervals and some composite is made. This evaluation might be a simple continuum or Likert-type scale ranging from "Absolutely not counselor material" through "Highly recommended as counselor material." Such a composite of staff evaluations probably would be the most valid instrument available on which to base judgments. Final decisions on student admission to supervised practice might be made at a counselor educator staff meeting in which all staff participate. Following such selection, or concurrent with it, students make mutual selections of each other for the purpose of counselor supervision.

At this stage in the model, actual supervision begins. Although the model is suggested for all supervised practices, some modifications would have to be made in the differentiations of field experience, practica and internships. These modifications are minor and probably more of intentions and expectations than in practices. For these reasons it would help, and suffice for this presentation, to select one area on which to focus--counseling practicum. This focal point is added to that of supervision so that the model will henceforth operate on a dual track system reflecting both the operation of the practicum itself and the development and refinements of counselor skills. One can see that the remaining stages of the spiral may be employed to describe the functioning of the practicum itself as well as to describe supervision and the interaction of these two processes.

At the very center of the spiral is the supervisor's main function of <u>consultation</u>. This main function facilitates the student trainees' movement through the evolutions of the spiral. The counseling function is placed in a central location, though secondary to consultation, in that counseling is viewed as facilitating consultation. <u>The supervisor is always a consultant, sometimes a counselor, a provider of instruction, and an evaluator for the counselor-in-preparation.</u>

<u>Goal/task explication.</u> To begin supervision the supervisor identifies some particular counselor behavior on which to focus. This behavior is identified and described in detail. Initially, this focus is likely to be some target behavior that is essential to the early stages of the counseling process and is usually a behavior that can be studied and strengthened by most students in the practicum group. An example might be counselor attentive behaviors. See Chapter Three for an extended treatment of the analysis and assessment of counseling skills.

<u>Pretraining motivation.</u> This component involves the use of instructional techniques to help students realize the importance of acquiring the focus behaviors. In the example used previously, a technique might be that of negative practice in role-playing situations to determine what happens to clients' behavior if the counselor-in-preparation acts fidgety or unconcerned. If the target of "attentive behavior" is too subtle try substituting the establishment of facilitative relationship, diagnostic practices, systematic desensitization, verbal conditioning, premature termination or any one of the hundreds of behaviors or sets of behaviors needed for successful counseling practice.

<u>Exposure and selection of experiences at site.</u> This stage involves not only the selection of learning experiences at the site but also the evaluative criteria to be used for determining success. Attention is paid not only to the target behaviors but also to their applications with various clients at different times and under varying circumstances. Experiences may include seminars, process groups, observations of counseling both live and video/audio taped, assignments and discussion of selected relevant literature, and peer review and critique of counseling sessions.

Site Planning. To insure that the counselor is able to gain the most from learning experiences, planning at the site is essential. This planning is the continued responsibility of the supervisor and includes the preparation of site personnel for the arrival of counselors-in-preparation, the coordination of client assignments to counselors with appropriate levels of training, scheduling of counselors' and supervisors' time, and provisions for the feedback of counselor effectiveness.

Didactic Instruction. No academic program, including prepracticum laboratory experiences, can possibly prepare fully the counselor candidate as a professional counselor or as a truly competent counselor in practicum. Some of the crucial learnings for a counselor-in-preparation cannot occur until the need is recognized by the counselor and/or supervisor during supervision of counseling. When a need is recognized, didactic instruction from the supervisor within a seminar-like meeting may become an essential accompaniment to supervision, the desired result being knowledge, skill development and implementation. A list of learnings (Shoemaker & Splitter, 1976) would include demonstrations of effective use of:

Minimal encouragement to talk

Silence

Open-ended questions

Focus on client's content

Paraphrasing content

Reflection of feeling

Summarization of content

Summarization of feeling

Respect for client

Understanding and accepting cultural differences of clients

How the counselor's values influence the counseling process

Knowledge of decision making

Ability to explore actions and reactions of the immediate environment and larger society

Ability to focus on client content

Understanding of the psychological basis for a theoretical rationale

Knowledge of learning theory strategies in counseling

Knowledge of perceptual-phenomenological strategies in counseling

Knowledge of career-development strategies in counseling

Other methods used to increase the knowledge, psychological awareness, and skills of the counselor-in-preparation are the following: (a) Training events, (b) Seminars, (c) Training methods, (d) Materials, (e) Tape critique sessions, and (f) Student group climate--the maintenance of an atmosphere in the practicum group that may be characterized as a facilitative relationship. This atmosphere facilitates counselors' behavior trials as in-skill practice, for example. The whole notion is one of "Tell me what to do, let me try, and help me to feel free to make my mistakes here in practicum so I may learn from these mistakes."

Reinforcement. Throughout the spiral model, procedures for feedback must be developed and maintained. This seems to be an appropriate time in the model to make reinforcement procedures concrete. These procedures apply to the whole practicum experience, and especially to individual members of the practicum and the result of their endeavors in learning the necessary understandings and skills as expressed in some target behavior. If the feedback identifies the goals and processes as being on target, their Continued Trial is in order. If problems are identified, then there should be restudy of the supervision/practicum plan and modifications made. This step addresses the questions:

Is the counseling experience appropriate for the counselor-in-preparation candidates both individually and as a group?

Is the site the appropriate setting for providing the expected counselor experiences?

Has the supervisory/practicum goal, or specific task expected as a result of the supervisory process, been made explicit and is it satisfactory?

Do the selection of, and exposure to, selected experiences have a point-for-point correspondence with the stated goal?

Has the need for practical and theoretical knowledge
and understandings been adequately assessed and
effective interventions designed to meet these needs?

Is additional skill practice required?

In general, is the total experience worthwhile for
the counselor, and if so, is it worthwhile enough to
warrant a continuation of the supervisor-counselor
counseling processes?

If the total experience is not worthwhile and
productive, where did it break down? In the site
selection? Planning stages? Lack of readiness on
part of the counselor-in-preparation? Inappropriate
or irrelevant training events? What is salvageable
and how many steps backward need to be taken in order
to correct the errors and to redirect activities
along more successful lines?

Internalization of knowledge. When target counselor
behaviors have been internalized and the atmosphere at the site
location (including counselor/client relationship) is seen as
receptive to the acquired behaviors, then the counselor-in-
preparation is ready to incorporate these behaviors into the
counseling process. This incorporation should lead to improvement on site which again includes the counselor facilitating
development of process goals in his counseling relationship.

Goal/task achievement refers to the acquisition and
competent use of a professional behavior or set of behaviors.
The task to be achieved was identified during the Goal/Task
explication stage of the model. The behavior was identified
and described in detail at that time and, subsequently, became
the focus throughout a single revolution of the spiral. The
goal/task achievement stage is that point in time when the
identified task, the target behavior, whether developed or
strengthened, is achieved.

The evaluation of the total supervisory/practicum plan
recognizes the importance of all of the components in the model.
These evaluative procedures should lead to refinements in, and
modifications of, the total supervisory process, including
those training events, materials, etc., that have been
identified. If difficulties are uncovered, or problems identified, there is still time for remediation before moving on to
a new task. In rating the interview behavior of the counselor-
in-preparation, the supervisor may want to focus on the
following dimensions of the counselor-in-preparation:

Awareness and itellectual insight into the nature of the
client's problem and the dynamics of the relationship with
the client.

Courage to explore with the client the various feelings of
the client in a caring and accepting manner.

Non-defensiveness and openness of self.

Ability to understand the internal frame of reference of
self.

Ability to be seen by the client as an authentic, genuine
and real person.

Independence from the client's personality and manipulative behavior.

Capacity to establish and maintain a facilitative
relationship with the client.

Ability to project a reasoned and logical organization of
thought to the client.

Ability to accurately reflect client feelings and meaning.

Over-all effectiveness in interviewing skills.

Next priority task/goal. This goal is the beginning of
the next loop in the continuing spiraling model. The next task
may be a specific new target behavior for the counselor-in-
preparation to focus on, or in the broader context, a refinement of the supervisory model itself.

To suggest that such a goal as an in-depth study of the
supervisory process be a priority for counselor evaluation
seems fair. Whatever form the research model takes, it should
be tied to the environmental properties of supervision.
Emphasis must be placed on those involved in the supervisory
paradigm, the counseling process and its relationship to
supervision, the roles and functions of the supervisor, and the
site in which all of these processes take place. The spiral
model presented is a suggestion, and maybe even a starting
point, for further action/field research.

SUMMARY

The author's suggestion is that investigations of counselor supervision, especially in educational preparation
programs, attend to the many factors and variables that, as
components, comprise the total model of supervision.

Descriptions of practica should include all of the elements
identified in the "Spiral Model of Supervision." Research in
this area also should identify all of these elements in
addition to the research variables that are manipulated.
Important as it is to identify the research dependent variables,
it is as important to the broad understanding of supervision
to identify the following factors: the site in which counseling practicum takes place; any unusual contractual
arrangements between the site and the graduate education
program; the selection process of students into supervised
practice experiences and the assignment or selection of
counselors-in-preparation to supervisors; the educational/
experiential backgrounds of supervisors; whether supervision
models stress consultation, counseling, or instruction;
the methods for evaluation of students; the training events,
methods, materials and critique methods employed; on-going
modifications made during practicum while research is being
conducted; counselor-in-preparation group climate both
on-campus and at the site; methods for supportive follow-up
practices; and other factors both identified in the spiral
model as well as to be identified by counselor educators and
supervisors.

These same variables should be part of the study of
counselors-in-preparation in supervision experiences. Focus
on the actual supervisory process is needed, but as this
process is so interrelated with all of the other factors,
conceptualizations of supervision should pay attention to all
of the environmental properties in which supervision occurs.
More descriptions of training events are needed not only to be
studied and understood but to be researched. Evaluation
procedures of counselor candidates, including the assigning
of grades for practica courses carrying graduate credit, need
to be shared.

One supervisory model may be more efficacious than others.
Presently, however, there are insufficient data available to
make this decision or to approximate such a conclusion.
Research can supply this data, but before building designs, a
large body of literature is needed describing current supervisory practices in counselor education programs. Out of this
literature would come the parameters of supervisory practices
from which researchable questions could be constructed.

REFERENCES

American Personnel and Guidance Association. A statement of
    policy: Standards for the preparation of school
    counselors. Personnel and Guidance Journal, 1961, 40,
    400-407.

American Personnel and Guidance Association. Standards for the
    preparation of secondary school counselors--1967.
    Personnel and Guidance Journal, 1967, 46, 97-106.

Association for Counselor Education and Supervision. Committee
    on Counselor Effectiveness. Commitment to Action in Super-
    vision: Report of a National Survey of Counselor
    Supervision. 1969.

Birk, J. M. Effects of Counseling Supervision Method and Pref-
    erence on Empathetic Understanding. ERIC. Microfiche.
    No. ED 063 873/HE 003 125. Urbana, University of Illinois.
    1972, p. 17.

Cormier, W. H., & Nye, L. S. Discrimination Model for System-
    atic Counselor Training. ERIC. Microfiche. No. ED 082
    100/CG 008 278. 1972, p. 56.

Delaney, D. J., & Moore, J. C. Student expectations of the role
    of practicum supervisor. Counselor Education and Super-
    vision, Fall, 1966, 6, 11-17.

Delaney, D. J., & Eisenberg, S. The Counseling Process.
    Chicago, Ill: Rand McNally, 1972.

Eisenberg, S., & Delaney, D. J. The Counseling Process,
    Second Edition. Chicago, Ill.: Rand McNally, 1977.

Felker, D. W., & Brown, D. F. Counselor candidates and graduate
    students in education: A comparison of characteristics.
    Counselor Education and Supervision, 1970, 9(4), 286-291.

Goldman, L. Critical Concerns in Counselor Education. ERIC
    Microfiche. No. ED 066 690/CG 007 405, 1972, p. 56.

Gust, T. Extending counselor supervision. Counselor Education and Supervision, Spring, 1970, 9, 157-161.

Hansen, J. C.; Pound, R.; & Petro, C. Review of research on practicum supervision. Counselor Education and Supervision, December, 1976, 16, 107-116.

Jakubowski-Spector, P. A. An Application of the Behavior Change Principles of Role Playing and Shaping to the Training of Counselors. ERIC. Microfiche. No. ED 043 040/CG 005 785, 1969, p. 10.

Lambert, M. J. Supervisory and counseling process: A comparative study. Counselor Education and Supervision, 1974, 14, 54-60.

Lifton, W. Improving the Reality Index of Counseling Practices in an Urban Setting. Experience vs. Inexperience: The Story of Counselor Sophistication. ERIC. Microfiche. No. ED 059 512/CG 007 015, 1971.

Patterson, C. H. Supervising students in counseling practicum. Journal of Counseling Psychology, Spring, 1964, 11, 47-53.

Shoemaker, J. T., & Splitter, J. L. A competency-based model for counselor certification. Counselor Education and Supervision, June, 1976, 15, 267-274.

Spice, C. G., & Spice, W. H. A triadic method of supervision in the training of counselors and counseling supervisors. Counselor Education and Supervision, 1976, 15, 251-258.

Tarrier, B. Five Generalizations of Supervision. ERIC Microfiche. No. ED 051 511/CG 006 439, 1971, p. 11.

Truax, C. B., & Carkhuff, R. R. Toward an integration of the didactic and experiential approaches to training in counseling and psychotherapy. Journal of Counseling Psychology, Summer, 1964, 11, 240-247.

Webb, L, & Rochester, D. E. A descriptive survey of counselor education students. Counselor Education and Supervision, Summer, 1969, 8, 308-312.

Chapter **10**

COUNSELOR SUPERVISION

FROM THE

STATE DEPARTMENT

OF EDUCATION

Neil C. Gunter, Director
Student Support Services
Department of Education
State of Georgia
Atlanta, Georgia

COUNSELOR SUPERVISION

FROM THE STATE DEPARTMENT OF EDUCATION

Editor's Notes

A vast array and number of helping services are offered to the American people through federal, state, and local community channels. Counselors usually find themselves working in the community/service-delivery channel, and being supervised from local, state, and national levels. For example, school counselors are employed by local school systems and are supervised at the primary level by the system's supervisor(s), at the secondary level by state department of education supervisors, and from a tertiary position by the U.S. Office of Education. These same three levels, although from different sources, exist for counselors in mental health, social welfare, and related levels.

Dr. Gunter exposes the reader to a supervisory point of view and setting (state department) that has not been covered in the preceding Chapters. Supervision from the state department is treated as a leadership function, and the state department supervisor is depicted as a "developer, planner, and implementer of programs and activities"--a role which sharply contasts the "regulatory role" of the past. Among the many activity avenues suggested for the supervisory leader are needs assessment and competency-based counselor preparation, guidance management from contemporary theories, program evaluation, counselor in-service training and personal development, and the development of resources and materials. Supervisor action within these avenues, and from Gunter's leadership role model, call for the activities (see Chapter 1) of consultation, training and instruction, evaluation, and the technical methodology from Section Two. The result of this confluence is a state-level supervisory function which is forward looking and action-oriented.

Neil C. Gunter

Neil Gunter (Ed.D.) throughout his career has served as a practitioner and leader in counselor supervision at the state and national levels. He has been the Supervisor of Guidance, Counseling, and Testing Services in the Georgia Department of Education (1964-69), and he presently serves as Director and Supervisor of Student Support Services in Georgia. These two positions have placed Dr. Gunter in state-level supervisory contact with public school practitioners in the specialities of guidance, school psychology, school social services, health services, and testing.

Leadership and professional service is a prominent characteristic of Dr. Gunter's supervisory career, evident in his past professional service as president of the Georgia Personnel and Guidance Association, and the Georgia Association for Counselor Education and Supervision. Regionally and nationally he is a leadership force as exemplified by serving as president of the Southern Association for Counselor Education and Supervision (1970-71), and president of the National Association for Counselor Education and Supervision (1975-76). From his stance as a state-level supervisor and nationally known leader Dr. Gunter continues to be a most significant figure in the field of counselor supervision.

COUNSELOR SUPERVISION
FROM THE STATE DEPARTMENT OF EDUCATION

Neil C. Gunter

Many state department of education guidance units are not what they used to be--guardians of the school subsidy accounts, enforcers of outmoded regulations, and keepers of the archives. Quite the contrary, some state department guidance units are assuming viable roles of leadership in curriculum, guidance and counseling, vocational-technical education, and in the complex process of facilitating educational change in our schools (Gibboney, 1967; Hollis & Wantz, 1977). State Department guidance components can no longer be regarded as outmoded; they have become vigorous, lively agencies with appropriately selected, well-trained personnel who are responsive to educational needs and demands. Past modes of operation cannot be projected into the future role of state guidance units. The state department guidance unit has more contributions to make to education than has been demonstrated in the past.

A heightened consciousness and awareness of the need for expanded school guidance programs exists in the populations served by the schools. With the many needs and restrictions impinging upon our professional practice from the populations served, guidance and counseling must respond in an effective manner, or risk becoming a profession of the past.

Education in the 70's has sounded an awakening cry for accountability. Demands for accountability have come from various populations--school boards, administrators, parents, the community-at-large, and even students. But external pressures not withstanding, the impetus for accountability should come from within. As professionals, our responsibility is to seek continually more effective and efficient means of delivering those skills which we have to give. More effective guidance and counseling programs are needed in modern schools with their increasing technological and emerging humanistic orientation. Guidance and counseling staff must be sensitive to the constantly changing philosophies of our societal

structure and must work with communities and their existing
institutions to construct innovative models and devise
alternative strategies for meeting human needs. Traditionally
prescribed roles and functions are no longer acceptable.

FUNCTIONS OF STATE GUIDANCE PERSONNEL

While societal changes continue and public education
struggles to keep pace, state departments of education are
also in a progressive change stage. Historically, state
department of education guidance units have not assumed
aggressive roles in implementing guidance and counseling
directions. A study of the role of the state director of
guidance services reported by Duncan and Geoffroy (1971)
revealed little data to substantiate the functions of state
guidance personnel other than the traditional ones. The
majority of functions reported were related to information-
giving, record-keeping services, administration within the
guidance unit, financial management and similar activities.
There was a conspicuous absence of innovative leadership and
service functions. Somewhat similar functions have been
reported in other studies (Riccio, 1961; Gade & Zaccaria, 1966;
Fitzpatrick, 1967; Geoffroy, 1968; Johnson, 1968; Knowles,
1968; Riccio, 1968).

Hollis and Wantz (1977) in a study of state department
units in fifty states and four territories reported data from
forty-six of the fifty-four units regarding areas of responsibilities for the state unit. "Consistency in five areas
/of responsibilities/ is present in over 80% of the states
(p. 461)." The consistent areas were as follows: career and
life planning; agency liaison (working with community agencies
other than schools); demonstration, pilot, and/or exemplary
programs; evaluation of counseling and guidance programs; and
vocational guidance (p. 461).

Hollis and Wantz also studied the services offered and
they reported that the overall time spent among consultation,
in-service, and administration and/or supervision was somewhat
evenly divided (pp. 462-463). They reported the following
which may be significant in viewing the change for the 1950's
and 60's to the last half of the 70's:

Consultation was the service requiring the greatest
amount of time overall from the 37 State Departments
supplying data. Consultative service was defined as
expertise of staff used in assisting others (p. 462).

In-service was the second highest percentage of time spent
of the services offered by counseling and guidance staffs

in State Departments. In-service was defined as
training of others, systematic encouragement of growth
activities for counselors, and conducting in-service
programs. Since in-service receives a high percentage
of the service time and since counselors received the
majority of the in-service as revealed in "Clientele
Served by In-Service Programs," then State Department
staffs potentially have a significant impact on the
professional development of counselors after employment
(p. 462).

The overseeing of programs and/or supervision was third
highest in time spent among the services offered. The
time was not much different from consultation and in-
service (p. 463).

In most states the inception of guidance and counseling
services at the state department level occurred in the late
1940's or early 1950's. Some states did not establish units
until state and federal financial support was given to
guidance and counseling with the passage of the National
Defense Education Act (NDEA) of 1958. Through the decades of
the '40's and '50's, state department guidance units were
primarily charged with tangentially overseeing guidance programs and applying state and/or federal regulations in the
administration and utilization of modest fund allocations.
States generally witnessed expansion and growth in guidance
and counseling programs as a result of the passage of NDEA.
This growth was accompanied however by a significant time
demand on state department guidance personnel for the application of federal and state regulations regarding fund expendi-
tures and basic program development. Relatively little time
was left to devote to comprehensive and innovative program
expansion within local school system guidance units.

Because of the state department guidance work created by
NDEA, counseling practitioners and other local school district
personnel began to view state department supervision as the
management and control of education through directives and
derived powers resulting from funds controls. Subsequently,
and to the present, they have not expected much more than
general regulatory functions from state departments. Local
systems traditionally have not perceived state departments as
assuming much bona fide responsibility for educational innovation and creativity. State department activities have been seen
as relating primarily to organization, regulation and gover-
nance, fiscal support, and maintenance of minimum standards
in guidance.

Current demands for functional accountability and for
meeting the needs of transitional communities and populations

place state education departments in a precarious yet strategic position. State departments are beginning to respond by becoming developers, planners, and implementers of programs and activities which clearly call for leadership roles. Gust (1970), in discussing extended guidance and counseling supervision, proposed that one stage of a complete continuum of supervisory experiences for counselors necessitates that state agencies assume leadership in providing on-the-job direction of counselor functions. This action means that state department guidance units should be expected to become directly involved in the practice of meeting needs, developing models and strategies, and following through in effecting totally functional programs within all local education agencies.

> As the extension of supervisory experiences is considered and attention focused upon counselor supervision in the on-the-job setting these may render a more complete impact upon the provision of quality counseling services to the public and the "professional" upgrading of the counseling profession (Gust, 1970, p. 160).

Evidence is increasing that state department guidance units are emerging from traditional role expectations and are assuming sound leadership functions in serving local school system guidance programs.

MODELS FOR DELIVERING PUPIL PERSONNEL SERVICES

Traditionally, the services delivery system within the typical education setting essentially has been limited to a professional didactic model. This model has employed instruction or teaching in dispensing guidance and counseling services to students. The didactic model lends itself basically to one-way communication, either one-to-one instruction or group instruction. Students have not been involved in planning activities or participatory exercises, and consequently, they have not responded enthusiastically to the potential impact of guidance and counseling services because of the delivery system. The didactic model has been restrictive in that students have been exposed to such a model throughout the educational career. Only minimal flexibility has been possible with the model; therefore, students have to a great extent viewed guidance and counseling as just another course or an information-giving system.

Although the didactic model has been a prevalent mode of performance for state department guidance units in the past, the practice need not continue in the future. Innovative ideas which shake the traditional model are presently being discussed by state department guidance personnel. Some of these ideas are as follows:

1. utilization of students or clients in helping each other (peer guidance and counseling relationships);

2. parent involvement in planning the services and subsequent delivery of the services;

3. team arrangements involving curriculum personnel, community and business people, et al. (role playing, game theory, modified human relations skills);

4. organization of guidance centers, providing a variety of resource personnel and maintaining materials collections which clientele can draw upon as needed;

5. development of area or regional "diagnostic centers" appropriately staffed which can move expeditiously to assist students/clients in difficult situations--who might be experiencing special problems; and

6. arrangement for offering consultation and services for crisis situations (drugs, pregnancies, runaways).

Gunter (1972) developed a model for team strategy in delivering pupil personnel services (Figure 10.1) which was presented for discussion to the school social workers in the state of Georgia. This model is a systematic way of focusing human energy on human needs from problem and/or crisis "input" through "evaluation" and "follow-through" phases. The team model is predicated upon the availability of guidance personnel assigned to specific schools.

Such innovative ideas are not unrealistic, and the pupil personnel services delivery model proposed and partially implemented in the state of Georgia is an illustration. This particular model (Gunter, 1972) is based on a team strategy for service delivery, and its components are graphically presented in Figure 10.1. The pupil personnel services team model represents an effort to coordinate the numerous resources of human energy directed toward meeting human needs. Many functions and services are being duplicated without coordinating efforts. The model proposes a systematic way of pulling together a collection of existing student support services to meet needs of greater numbers. An explanation of the model follows.

Input Phase

The input phase involves providing initial referrals or basic information to the team members. Input could represent an immediate crisis of one or more individuals, anticipated problem situations, or other types of information relating to

PHASE	PURPOSE (GOALS)	PERSONS INVOLVED
INPUT	Provision of Initial Referrals and Basic Information to Team Members	Teachers Students Principals Parents Agencies
INTAKE	Collection and Basic Analysis of Data Preliminary Classification or Diagnosis Initiation of Involvement of Specialists in Planning Team Strategy	In-House Team PPS (Counselor, Visiting Teacher, Psychologist)
ANALYSIS and TEAM STRATEGY	In-Depth Analysis of Specific Information Decision Making For Methods of Therapy/ Treatment/Disposition Involvement of Specialists	Strategy Team (Visiting Teacher, Psychologist, Teacher, Principal, Health Personnel) Family Other Agencies
OPERATION "Attack and Solution"	Individual and Group Strategy Performed Collection of Additional Data Interaction With Student(s) Utilization of Resources in Community	Strategy Team Other Agencies Family Student(s)
FEEDBACK	Review/Analysis of Findings, Suggested Solutions, Therapy/ Treatment Plans Input From Individual Team Members, Family, Student(s), Community	Strategy Team Parents Other Agencies Student(s)
EVALUATION/ FOLLOW-THROUGH	Evaluation of Delivery System Team Action "Post Mortem" Follow-Up on Problem Area Planning For Preventive/ Developmental Activities	Entire PPS Team Outside Agencies Parents Student(s)

Figure 10.1. Pupil Personnel Team Model--A Systematic Way to Focus Human Energy on Human Needs.

crises prevention or developmental needs of populations served as well as many other areas. The input phase can be initiated through clients, family, teachers, non-school agencies and other sources.

Intake Phase

The intake phase of the team effort is initially handled by the building counselor. Other members of the team are consulted and/or utilized in such activities as: analysis of basic data on referral, preliminary classification or diagnosis of the situation, initiating the involvement of other specialists in planning team strategy to deal with the problem/ situation.

Analysis and Team Strategy Phase

This phase represents an in-depth analysis of the total situation surrounding the specific individual referred or the problem area(s) presented. Decisions are made as to methods of therapy, treatment or disposition of the problem(s). Team members other than the pupil personnel specialists should include those who can make contributions for maximum impact upon the situation. The team will focus upon a variety of alternative delivery systems in dealing with the input information, utilizing the expertise of individual team members.

Operation - "Attack and Solution" Phase

At this juncture, decisions have been made as to the role each team member will perform and how total team efforts will be employed in attacking the situation, seeking possible solutions. At this phase all team members demonstrate cooperative efforts and collective expertise when total energy is focused on human need.

Feedback Phase

This phase offers the team members and all parties involved an opportunity to review and further analyze the findings, suggested solutions, therapy or treatment plans and other information. This phase serves as a checkpoint to determine team involvement and impact to a given point as determined by the total team.

Evaluation and Follow-Through Phase

The total effort of the pupil personnel services team is evaluated to determine effectiveness. The team makes decisions as to most productive activities and decides additional approaches or efforts.

AN INTEGRATED FUNCTION: COMPREHENSIVE NEEDS ASSESSMENT
AND GOAL SETTING FOR GUIDANCE SERVICES AND COMPETENCY-
BASED COUNSELOR CERTIFICATION

In the remainder of this Chapter, a selection of contemporary guidance functions and practices are discussed which place the state department guidance unit in a firm position of leadership. One of the most influential functions on statewide guidance practice from the state department is the assistance given to school guidance programs in the establishment of goals. This function sets the direction for guidance throughout the state. Recently, many state departments have operationalized the notion that guidance should derive its goals from the developmental needs of students rather than from a prescribed set of services. The procedure of reference is termed needs assessment and the setting of behavioral objectives.

No less important to statewide guidance practice than needs assessment and behavioral objectives is the state department function of establishing criteria for counselor certification. This function enables the state department guidance unit to influence significantly what kind of professionals are entrusted with the responsibility of implementing effective guidance programs and services. A contemporary approach to the certification function is through the competency-based method. Counselors are asked to present evidence of having attained a required set of competencies in order to gain certification.

Less apparent than the importance of needs assessment and competency-based certification to statewide guidance is the implicit relationship between these two functions. Suggestions are that state department leadership and involvement in one of these functions necessitates similar influence on the other. Guidance goals derived from the needs assessment procedure should serve as the basis for developing a list of process-related competencies required of counselors to function effectively within the framework of a needs-based guidance system. The goals and their related counselor competencies can then be used for the development of a modular delivery system for use during counselor preparation and for the development of a competency-based program for the certification of guidance personnel.

The schematic illustrations which are depicted in Figures 10.2 through 10.5 (Ware, 1973), help convey the ideas which are expressed in the preceding paragraph. In the illustrations are suggested tentative models revealing the interrelated components of guidance needs assessment and competency-based training and certification for counselors.

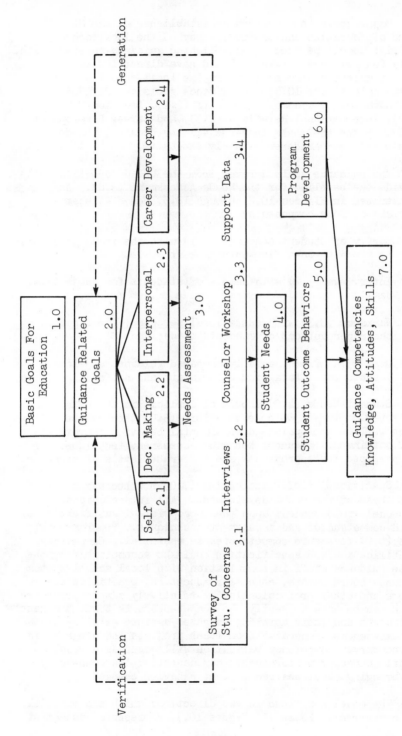

Figure 10.2. Needs Assessment, Phase I, Foundation.

Major goals in education as established by the State
Board of Education and the philosophy of the local school
district should be used in establishing guidance-related goals.
Goals for guidance services should have direct implications
for the guidance personnel within the local school district.
As shown in Figure 10.2, the guidance goals are divided into
four domains. The domains are Self (2.1), Decision-Making
(2.2), Interpersonal Relations (2.3), and Career Development
(2.4). Since the goals traverse all the domains, the domains
should not be considered mutually exclusive.

The guidance goals derived from the broad education goals
provide the baseline for the Needs Assessment (3.0). As
illustrated in Figures 10.2 through 10.5, Needs Assessment
consists of four components:

Survey of Student Concerns (3.1) with the items presented
to students on a five-point Likert scale.

Interviews (3.2) with sample of students for subjective
data.

Workshop (3.3) with educational personnel for input on
their perceptions of students needs; and

Data (3.4) from specially prepared guidance services
inventories. Data from other state and national projects.

Student Needs (4.0) should be implicit in the data
collected. Student Outcome Behaviors (5.0) then can be written
which reflect appropriate developmental behavior approximating
goal attainment. Student behavior assessment techniques can
be developed for appropriate age and grade levels of students.

Specification of Competencies (7.0) now becomes a significant phase of the model development. All future components of
the model are dependent upon the appropriate identification of
valid competencies and assessment techniques. Program Development (6.0) to assure competencies is essential. Competency
identification and specification could be accomplished by the
state guidance staff in consultation with local school system
guidance coordinators, counselor educators, practicing counselors and other professionals. A relatively simple procedure
which can be used to verify the competencies is through a panel
of experts and their opinions weighted against existing lists
of competencies generated from other projects and programs in
the country. Competency validation will occur as a result of
actual counselor performance: demonstrating the competency
and bringing about desired student behavior change.

The model now flows in two directions which are parallel
and concurrent. Phase II, Figure 10.3, represents assessment

388

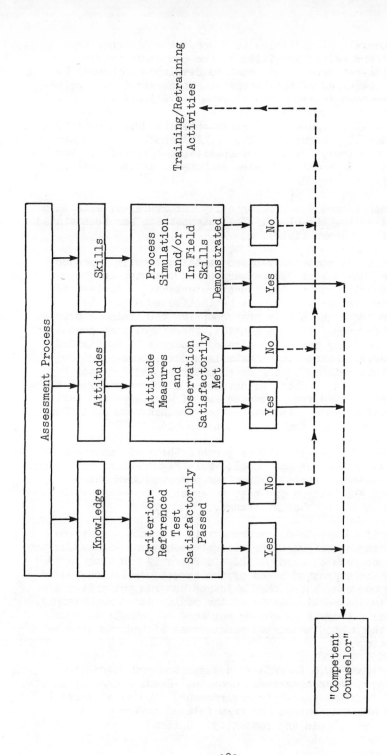

Figure 10.3. Competency Assessment Of Counselors, Phase II.

of the counselors' abilities to demonstrate the knowledge, attitudes and skills specified in the competency statements. A criterion-referenced test must be developed to assess the knowledge required of the "competent counselor." The criterion-referenced instrument will require validation.

Phase III, Figure 10.4, represents the development of a modular delivery strategy. The modules should be self-pacing training packages, composed of specific competencies. Modules can be added in knowledge-based components as the model is continually developed.

Phases II and III are logically interrelated, with each phase validating the other. This supposition has been stated quite well by Rosen (1972):

As much as competency-based certification is dependent upon instruments, competency-based training is dependent upon instructional materials. Efficient and effective training cannot be instituted until the knowledges and skills that comprise the training program are defined. It is essential, therefore, that protocol and training materials already underway be maintained. However, instructional materials development must be closely related to the development of instruments. They should in fact, be developed simultaneously or at least derived from the same set of knowledge and skill specifications. In this matter training and certification reinforce and support one another (p. 22).

Phase IV, Figure 10.5, is perhaps the most important and significant aspect of the model. This Figure concerns student behavior change. Phase IV involves comprehensive outcome assessment utilizing a pre-post interaction assessment to determine student behavior change.

Specifically, needs assessment is a simple tool to be used in finding out what the student population wishes for the guidance program to accomplish. In Phase IV one step is to identify the expressed needs of the target population and by so doing one can ensure that guidance program priorities are related to the service needs of the recipients. For example, to conduct a program of career guidance in schools without knowing the stated career interest areas of the students is unrealistic.

In Figure 10.6 is offered a suggested procedure for organizing a needs assessment program. Needs emerge as input obtained from the real-life environment. The total input is recorded and synthesized and then related to the educational goals of the schools and community. Guidance needs emerge as

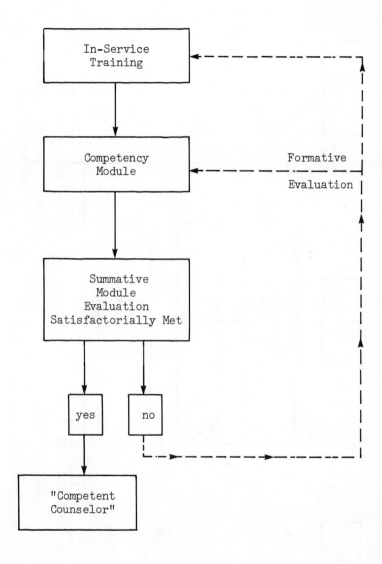

Figure 10.4. Competency Training For Counselors, Phase III.

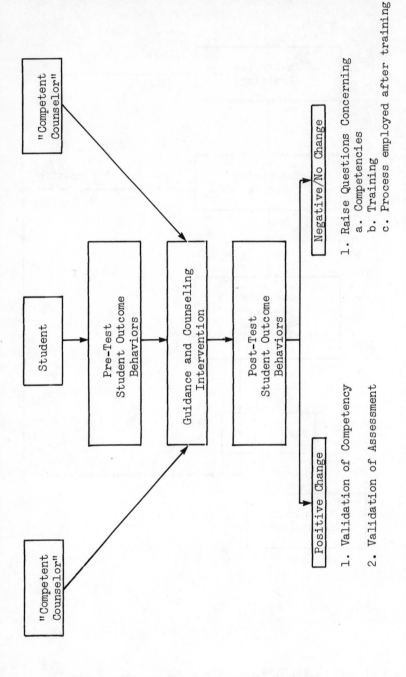

Figure 10.5. Assessment of Student Behavior Changes Due To Guidance And Counseling Intervention, Phase IV.

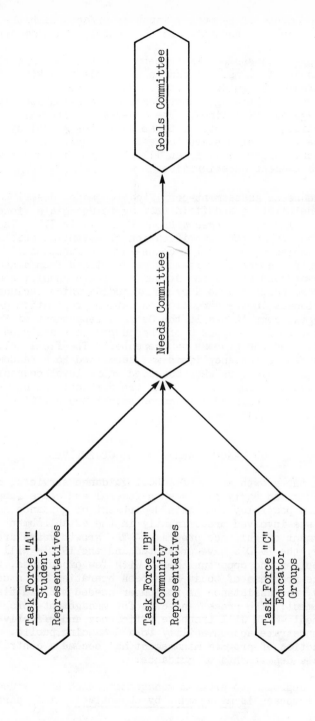

Figure 10.6. Proposed Organizational Structure For A Needs Assessment Program.

the by-products of community input interfaced with the goals and philosophy of education in the schools and community.

A needs assessment instrument and procedure might assume one of several forms. It can be as simple as asking students, "what should our guidance program do for you?" or it can be as complex as a multi-page questionnaire cross-indexed with other multi-page questionnaires. The assessment material can be standardized instruments or those which the school system guidance personnel prepare to meet the requirements of the situation. Figure 10.7 is an illustration of a student needs assessment questionnaire.

The needs assessment-certification model described has undergone piloting and field testing in Georgia's Pioneer Educational Services Agency under ESEA, Title III. The first phase focused on the identification of essential skills and compentencies necessary for counselors to function effectively. The specific competency items were developed from a needs assessment conducted among students. The counselor competency items were submitted to a group of judges which included professionals in the counselor education preparation program in Georgia, consultants in the Georgia Department of Education, and others. The responses of the judges were analyzed and grouped, then the process was repeated. The final collection of counselor competency items was submitted to a random sample of Georgia counselors who possessed entry level counselor certification. The competencies are currently being refined and will be translated into competency-based certification criteria for future use.

GUIDANCE MANAGEMENT BY OBJECTIVES

In the growth years of school guidance services, during the 1950's and early 1960's when federal and state funds made expansion possible, the state department of guidance in most states was involved predominantly in the establishment and development of guidance programs. The growth years are now history; the 1970's have presented and the 1980's will present new problems and opportunities. With few exceptions, the guidance programs of today have been operating for a decade or more, and assistance is no longer needed with initial development. The present need is for management--program management which will increase efficiency and effectiveness, and demonstrate accountability to a demanding public. Thus, the function of program management has become a central one for state departments of guidance.

An approach to program management which has gained widespread advocacy is management by objectives. This particular

```
┌─────────────────────────────────────────────────────────────┐
│                                                             │
│                Hometown Public Schools                       │
│                                                             │
│          GUIDANCE ASSESSMENT STUDENT QUESTIONNAIRE           │
│                                                             │
│                                                             │
│   School_____Male_____Female_____          │
│                                                             │
│   Course of Curriculum (general, college preparatory,        │
│   business, etc.)                                           │
│                                                             │
│   ─────────────────────────────────────────────────────     │
│                                                             │
│   You are assisting in the study of guidance needs for stu-  │
│   dents in this school system. The study should help in      │
│   planning more effective services for students. You should  │
│   be frank and accurate in answering questions. Make any     │
│   comments you wish on the form, using the back if you need  │
│   more space. Please answer all questions.                   │
│                                                             │
│   1. If you have a problem in deciding a particular course   │
│      of study, from whom would you be most likely to seek    │
│      help on this problem?                                   │
│                                                             │
│         _____a. Counselor                                    │
│         _____b. Teachers or Principal                        │
│         _____c. Family                                       │
│         _____d. Other_____                       │
│                                                             │
│   2. If you have a personal/social problem, to whom would    │
│      you go to discuss the problem?                          │
│                                                             │
│         _____a. Counselor                                    │
│         _____b. Teachers or Principal                        │
│         _____c. Family                                       │
│         _____d. Other_____                       │
│                                                             │
│   3. Have you talked with a school counselor? YES____ NO____ │
│                                                             │
│   4. What were (are) your reasons for seeing the counselor?  │
│                                                             │
│   5. Was it helpful to you to visit the counselor? How?      │
└─────────────────────────────────────────────────────────────┘
```

Figure 10.7. Illustration of a Student Needs Assessment
            Questionnaire.

6. Please check on the scale below how helpful you feel the counselor has been to you in any way, whether or not you have had private conferences with him/her. A check at "1" would mean you really have not received any help at all; a check at "7" would mean she/he has been extremely helpful.

1	2	3	4	5	6	7

No Help   Extremely
At All   Helpful

7. Check the following items in ways in which the counselor gives assistance to students and in ways the counselor should give help.

	Gives Help	Should Give Help
a. Gives or helps students get information about colleges	____	____
b. Gives or helps students get information about trade or vocational schools or military training	____	____
c. Explains test scores to student	____	____
d. Helps students get information about jobs in the community	____	____
e. Helps students get to know or get oriented to the school	____	____
f. Helps students decide on and make changes in subjects	____	____
g. Helps students plan their total high school program	____	____
h. Helps student to better understand their own abilities, interests, and aptitudes	____	____
i. Helps students develop better study skills	____	____

Figure 10.7. Continued.

	Gives Help	Should Give Help
j. Works with students trying to decide on a school or college to attend	___	___
k. Helps students find part-time or summer jobs	___	___
l. Helps graduating seniors find jobs	___	___
m. Helps students who are dropping out to find jobs	___	
m. Works with students who have personal or social concerns such as feeling left out, shyness, nervousness, trouble with the family, etc.	___	___
o. Helps students who are in trouble in school	___	___
p. Works with students in trying to decide on a career	___	___
q. Helps students by having visits with their parents	___	___
r. Helps handicapped students	___	___
s. Helps students make the most of special talents or abilities	___	___
t. Discusses dating problems	___	___
u. Discusses drug abuse problems	___	___
v. Helps teachers with classroom problems relating to teacher-student communication	___	___
w. Helps teachers with group activities within the classroom	___	___
x. Helps students in other ways (Please tell how)		

Figure 10.7. Continued.

HELP YOU MOST NEED (Circle Your Needs)

1. To complete my course of study I need help:

   a. Acquiring study skills
   b. Completing course assignments
   c. Earning satisfactory grades
   d. Maintaining satisfactory school behavior
   e. No help needed at this time
   f. Other _____

2. I need the most help with:

   a. Tests that will help me with my career plans and
      decisions
   b. High school course selection
   c. Personal problems
   d. Jobs or occupations after high school
   e. College or college plans
   f. Relationships with teachers
   g. No help needed at this time
   h. Other _____

3. In planning my career, I need the most help with:

   a. Training requirements
   b. Salaries and pay scales
   c. Work and social roles
   d. Job skills and behaviors
   e. Job trends and opportunities
   f. All of the above
   g. No help needed at this time
   h. Other _____

DIRECTIONS: Please check (X) YES or NO to indicate your
            feelings about each question. If you feel
            that you cannot give a definite Yes or No
            answer, please check (X) in the space marked
            ?.

YES NO   ?   QUESTIONS

___ ___ ___   1. Does your school help you to consider
                   information about yourself related to
                   your future educational and vocational
                   plans?

___ ___ ___   2. If you had a personal problem, would you
                   feel free to discuss it with your
                   school counselor?

Figure 10.7. Continued.

398

___   ___   ___   3. Does your school counselor help you to understand the meaning of your test scores? (Examples: School ability, achievement, and aptitude.)

___   ___   ___   4. Has your school provided your parents an opportunity to discuss your educational plans?

___   ___   ___   5. Do you have access to the information you want and need about your and other schools which offer post-high school education?

___   ___   ___   6. When you entered this school, were you helped to learn about your school and how to get along in it?

___   ___   ___   7. Have you had an opportunity to discuss with your school counselor approaches to solving problems with which you have been faced?

___   ___   ___   8. Have your parents ever talked with your school counselor?

___   ___   ___   9. Have you been helped to plan the subjects and activities you need and want to take while you are in high school?

___   ___   ___   10. Can you talk about your real feelings about things with your school counselor?

___   ___   ___   11. Do your teachers discuss the various occupations which are related to the subjects taught by them?

___   ___   ___   12. Have you had an opportunity to participate in group discussions about the concerns of students?

___   ___   ___   13. Has a counselor helped you to examine your abilities, personality traits and interests as they may pertain to your future plans?

Figure 10.7. Continued.

```
YES  NO   ?

___  ___  ___  14. Do you feel that your school experiences
                   have provided you with opportunities
                   to develop self-reliance?
```

Figure 10.7.   Continued.

approach is a recommended model for state departments and guidance personnel for reasons which will be explained in the following pages. Management by objectives rests upon the principle that objectives should serve as the principal guide in a planned approach to individual performance. Objectives are not stated as broad goals, but rather as concrete statements of specific performance outcomes. They are not static, but are continually changing in response to changes in the population served, personnel turnover, organizational modifications, and so forth. Evaluation in the management by objectives approach, as opposed to the traditional method of guidance evaluation which examines process and services, directly and straight-forwardly determines whether previously stated outcomes are achieved (Sullivan & O'Hare, 1971).

As applied by state departments of guidance, management by objectives is operationalized by helping local school guidance and counseling personnel to develop realistic and measurable guidance program objectives. Process objectives, those which assume the form of services or actions taken to attain goals, must consider the feasibility of implementation and means of measuring attainment. Product objectives are to be stated as discernible student behavior changes.

An efficient method for state departments of guidance to promote the management by objectives approach is through training workshops which prepare counselors to organize objective-based guidance programs. Numerous workshop models could be developed and successfully implemented. Illustrated in Figure 10.8 is a systems model structure which might be used in initial training sessions with counselors. The first block of Figure 10.8 concerns problem identification (1.0), while block 2 moves to the planning phase (2.0) of the suggested model, and block 3 outlines the operational stages (3.0) of the objective-based guidance program.

A sample objective might be conceptualized by counselors and implemented via the example as shown: SAMPLE OBJECTIVE - begin with a basic problem statement: An excessive number of students are not getting to school on time each day. The focal objective for the stated problem: For students to understand why they should get to school on time each day. The population in question is delineated: Seventh grade students who have had three or more referrals to the school administration for tardiness. The guidance activity is then established: Five weekly group counseling sessions with the students. The outcome(s) should be clearly defined: During a subsequent three month period following completion of the activity, school records will reveal an elimination of unexcused tardiness by ninety percent of these students.

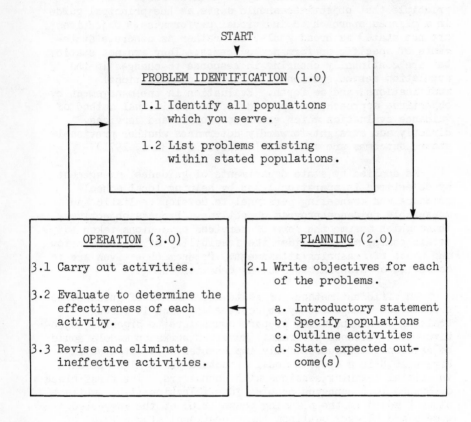

START

PROBLEM IDENTIFICATION (1.0)

1.1 Identify all populations which you serve.

1.2 List problems existing within stated populations.

OPERATION (3.0)

3.1 Carry out activities.

3.2 Evaluate to determine the effectiveness of each activity.

3.3 Revise and eliminate ineffective activities.

PLANNING (2.0)

2.1 Write objectives for each of the problems.

   a. Introductory statement
   b. Specify populations
   c. Outline activities
   d. State expected outcome(s)

Figure 10.8. Systems Model Structure Used in Initial Training Sessions With Counselors For Designing Objective Based Guidance Program.

The previous procedure is a very simple one, but if
implemented consistently it should demonstrate that such
procedures and practices can make guidance efforts more fully
accountable. Chiles (1973) spelled out the need for such
accountability procedures and models by stating:

> There is a need to develop models to tell counselors
> what has worked. We need objective data. The
> practitioner needs to know specific things. These are
> the needs of the clientele. These are the skills I
> have. Thus, based on clientele needs and my skills,
> these programs are possible. They can be evaluated in
> these specific ways (p. 1).

OTHER MANAGEMENT MODELS

Other management models are given attention in the
professional literature and might be considered for guidance
program use. Some are models which lend themselves to program
adaptation in school environments. Each of the management
models presented in this section operates on a planned and
systematic procedure.

Management By Reflection

The "management by reflection" model is a management
approach which requires the manager to assume the place or
role of the client or student. In the educational environment,
this management style has been primarily the work of Leon
Lessinger. Lessinger practiced this approach as a public
school system superintendent to ascertain student needs and
begin assessment on whether or not student needs were being
met via the system. From time to time Lessinger assumed the
place of a student for a day. He would follow that student's
daily schedule and then share his experiences with school
staffs.

Several important advantages of "management by reflection"
are as follows:

1. Focuses upon the students.

2. Provides a means by which guidance services and activities can be made relevant.

3. Provides for direct feedback on the appropriateness
   of the system's activities.

4. Provides a vehicle by which attainable objectives can
   be developed.

Management-by-reflection works most effectively as an integral part of other management styles employed and when treated as a technique. The success of this technique depends upon the specific skills of the manager, such as ability to listen, ability to share, and ability to consider needs and wishes of students in developing a program of services. Guidance units at the local system level are ideal for the practice of management by reflection since counselors have skills which enable them to work effectively with both individuals and groups, and to assess overall student needs. Unfortunately, this approach is not always present or at least not systematically employed in the management of guidance services, but it can be easily integrated.

Futures Management

Another interesting management model which is gaining increasing attention in the literature and is obviously being practiced in many programs is "management by futures." This approach is a combination of basic concepts in management and selected techniques. The primary utility of the "futures management system" is that it serves to explore current changes and allows managers to calculate determinations of change implications for future operations. The manager needs appropriate research skills when utilizing the management by futures system. Farmer (1969) has delineated five fundamental steps in the management by futures model:

1. Perception of a problem or opportunity

2. Development of a general plan

3. Actions to meet goals

4. Information feedback as a check for actions

5. Modification of plans in terms of results

The implementation of Farmer's five procedural steps requires a host of activities and management techniques. Lessinger (1972) has suggested six procedures which might be employed:

1. Delphi Principle--to enact the Delphi Principle one employs successive rounds of questions or statements to attain consensus. Supervisors can use this procedure to determine goals and objectives for a guidance program. Example: A guidance committee could enumerate a broad list of projected goals and objectives for a school system guidance program. A series of questions or statements could be developed to be used in making decisions on the importance and significance of each goal or objective listed. The material

might be submitted to the entire professional staff
of the school system, thereby eliciting their individual responses and utilization of the questions or
statements in making judgements about the broad goals
and objectives listed. Following initial responses,
the process could be repeated to gain consensus.

2. Cross-Impact Analysis--This procedure is one which has
   potential for assessing the impact of events through
   the use of computer potential for analysis of a cross-
   impact matrix. Management of guidance objectives by
   this process provides insight into effectiveness and
   impact of present practices or events, and an opportunity to analyze the potential effectivenss and impact
   of future events upon anticipated guidance outcomes.
   Cross-impact analysis requires appropriate research
   skills by the program manager.

3. Scenario Writing--Through scenario writing the supervisor describes "pieces of the future," indicating
   sequences of events leading to a future situation.
   In guidance management the technique may be employed
   to simply explore future needs and projections.
   Example: A guidance program manager or guidance
   committee might explore the future needs of students
   in "life-coping skills." The manager, the committee,
   and students could research trends for the future
   in the specified area and begin writing "pieces of the
   future," with each individual or team developing a
   particular cell, developing sequences of events for a
   given cell or unit, and then putting the puzzle
   together to get a view of the projected future
   situation in terms of "life-coping skills."

4. Trend Extrapolation--This procedure involves making
   predictions of future directions from current trends.
   Guidance management can be enhanced through thorough
   analysis of existing trends and movements in guidance
   practice, and looking to the future in terms of the
   momentum and force of the current trend.

5. Intuitive Reasoning--This procedure is one which
   utilizes individual training and experiences to
   hypothesize future conditions and situations. Effective guidance management will employ the expertise and
   experience of all resources in projecting future
   guidance programs and activities. Involved would be
   the school professionals, students, parents, and the
   total community for the input phase of future planning.

6. Historical Analogy--A historical analogy is simply a comparison of an incomplete sequence of events with a completed sequence of similar events. Application to guidance management takes the form of review and critical analysis of existing practices and looking to future practices.

Futures management has strong implications for guidance administration. Students in schools are voicing their feelings that school experiences are too far removed from real life to be meaningful, and the total education environment is changing because of such criticism. Toffler (1970) has emphasized that incidence of change is increasing, and the rate at which changes are occuring has increased even more. The protective aura of permanence which has surrounded education in the past has been shattered.

If management by futures had no other specific utility for guidance, its orientation would be worth the basic investment. Demands placed upon guidance services are changing constantly as student needs change. Therefore, if we continue to limit the orientation of guidance personnel to the traditional therapeutic models and one-to-one relationships, the justification for guidance programs based upon identifiable outcomes is already doomed.

Change-Agent Model

Another approach to positive results in guidance and counseling programs which may be viewed as a mangement model is the "counselor as an agent of change." This "model" has been given much verbal support but has not actually been implemented as frequently as perhaps it could be. State department guidance units could provide leadership in renewing and implementing the model, and it has the breadth to constitute the foundation of the overall guidance program within a school.

In essence, the "counselor as a change agent" model focuses on the counselor as a person, and also on the object of the counselor's concern--the student or client. There are basically three dimensions by which the counselor may view profitably the student: from the student's self perception, as the student really is, and as the student can become. This process involves knowing the student, gaining insights into the self-concept of the student, as well as understanding how the student sees him/herself as a social object. Logically what follows is that before change can be effected in an individual, the individual first must have an accurate self perception. Therefore the counselor needs to possess the skills to be able to induce realistic self perceptions.

Furthermore, the counselor must be able to view the student as he/she can become; thereby allowing the student to explore, evaluate, and "try out" for what he or she becomes. The counselor encourages the student to develop and set realistic basic life goals.

What are some prerequisites of the counselor who would operate as an agent of change? One is the counselor's belief in the change that he is trying to effect. A fundamental belief in the essential dignity and worth of every human being, and living this belief, are essential for effective change agents. The belief is to be practiced, as the philosopher Kant considered it, in such a way that one's action could become eternal law. The counselor, as an agent of change, must be prepared to recognize the strengths as well as the weaknesses of clients. Imperatively the counselor, as an agent of change, must question and reject some of society's "givens" which do not yield an equal opportunity or chance to all.

Essentially, the worth of the "counselor as a change agent" model is contingent upon the moral caliber of the individuals employed as counselors. Counselor preparation institutions, state department guidance units, and local school system administrations must give greater attention to the assessment of the personalities and basic life styles of would-be counselors. The inflexible, narcissistic person with an overly developed superego may not become a very effective counselor.

Management By Participation

The final management model to be presented relates to "management by participation," a management style developed by Kurt Lewin for the incorporation of recipient participation into managed programs. This model is predicated upon the assumption that if given the opportunity to participate in the shaping of guidance program goals, students will be more willing to accept and work effectively toward meeting the specified goals. Utilization of such a system or model requires confidence on the part of the local system guidance coordinator.

Management by participation considers students as human beings rather than as cogs in a machine, moving as they are directed. Some of the advantages in the use of this style of management for administration and supervision of guidance services are as follows: goals established by participants are accepted overtly and covertly; motivational levels are high, with favorable attitudes which provide powerful stimulation to implement goals; communications channels are open and well integrated--allowing for decisions to be made on more accurate information; performance is high; and control is achieved through widespread responsibility for review and final decisions.

The "management by participation" model requires careful planning by the local school system managers, and a time period of perhaps two years is needed to introduce the model. Successfully implemented, the system should yield better morale among the population served, higher productivity with a sense of contribution by all, increased and expanded responsibility among students, and a new reservoir of ideas generated. This model might be integrated with other models discussed in developing useful systems or strategies for service delivery within any given guidance program.

Summary and Synthesis

State department guidance supervisors can assist local school system guidance units in the planning and implementation phases of the models discussed. Assistance also is needed for adapting the models to the characteristics of local system programs. No single management approach should encumber a guidance program. Each of the management approaches presented has valid contributions to sound and viable management practice. An important point is that common and unique features of many styles of management be utilized. A synthesis of the management models presented in the foregoing section suggests several characteristics of sound management, which are as follows:

1. Is dependent upon practical, operational goals and objectives expressed in measurable terms.

2. Is established upon knowledge and information of past and present activities and events, and upon projections of future trends and movements.

3. Encompasses plans for the implementation of goals and objectives, decision-making and procedural closure, and measuring performance.

4. Is based upon continuous feedback of information to appropriate sources for determining usefulness of the system, methods, procedures, techniques, and so forth.

5. Emphasizes the use of a variety of models/systems which have been demonstrated to have practical utility.

GUIDANCE PROGRAM EVALUATION

Many guidance programs throughout the country have been developed and continue to be based on "assumed effect" rather than demonstrated results. Only a minimal assessing of accomplishment has occurred, perhaps because guidance personnel have been taught to think of effectiveness in nonquentifiable terms. This condition must be reversed; we need to redefine the rules of the game.

Evaluation and accountability have high priority for the present decade, and perhaps even higher priorities in the 1980's. All subsystems that constitute the educational system, including guidance and counseling services, must be sound in respect to evaluation and accountability. All educators will be held accountable for their products. Education, and in particular guidance and counseling activities, can no longer be regarded as an unquestionable process in one's journey to maturity (Page, 1970).

Guidance processes and outcomes must be subjected to evaluation using a systems approach if guidance programs and services are to be meaningful. Starr (1970) viewed evaluation as a subsystem and saw no value for it if evaluation does not become a part of the total planning effort; he referred to this as an Evaluation-Program Planning Cycle. Starr listed five important points to use in implementing a systems approach to evaluation. The five points are recounted as follows:

1. The evaluation problem should be defined in terms of the purposes and expected outcomes of evaluation.

2. A conceptual model should be developed which articulates evaluation with program planning procedures.

3. An information-measurement system should be formulated to provide particular data required for evaluative decisions about program outcomes.

4. Feedback mechanisms should be provided to permit monitoring of the effectiveness and efficiency of the information system in providing significant data for decision making.

5. Since the evaluation system is only one part of a total program-planning system, the evaluation system must be capable of articulation with other components of a larger program-planning system.

Wellman (1970) offered the following recommendations regarding the use of a system approach to the development and evaluation of guidance programs:

1. The system model provides a framework for the conceptualization of the programs.

    a. In terms of pupil outcomes and objectives. . .
    b. In terms of program objectives and outcomes. . .

2. The flow of activities must move from the general to the specific.

3. The following components should be included in the system.

    a. Needs
    b. Goals
    c. Developmental objectives
    d. Behavioral objectives

4. The specification of meaningful objectives and the use of appropriate criteria to estimate the achievement of objectives are essential for adequate evaluation.

Wellman obviously placed strong emphasis on using properly stated objectives in a systematic approach to evaluation. He has developed a taxonomy of guidance objectives for the National Study of Guidance Programs. In the national study, Wellman outlined three major categories of objectives. The categories are the following: Perceptualization, that is, the development of awareness and differentiations of relevant environmental and self variables; Conceptualization, the process of analyzing relationships, making predictions, evaluating consequences, and taking actions relevant to educational, vocational, and social goals; and Generalization, the development of behavior patterns typified by consistency, commitment, effectiveness, and autonomy. A flowchart of the Wellman systems model is shown in Figure 10.9.

The Wellman material was used as a general "systems model" in designing and developing a format for guidance evaluation in Georgia school systems. The Georgia planning committee and those who ulimately developed the final instrument to be used in the evaluation process translated general concepts into operational processes and procedures. Thus, the evaluation instrument developed and currently used in Georgia is unique in design and approach, incorporating ideas and concepts from a variety of sources.

The Guidance and Counseling Unit of the Curriculum Leadership and Pupil Personnel Services Division in the Georgia Department of Education in 1969 began initial planning for comprehensive evaluation of guidance programs in all local school systems in Georgia. The first phases of planning

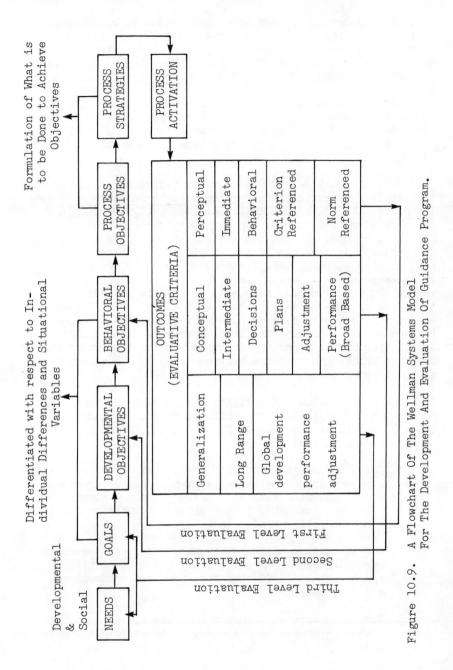

Figure 10.9. A Flowchart Of The Wellman Systems Model For The Development And Evaluation Of Guidance Program.

411

focused on determining what questions needed to be answered
by the evaluation and what criteria would be employed to
answer them. Once these were determined, the design and
development of an evaluation instrument was begun. The final
product, the Georgia Guidance Services Inventory (Vail, et al,
1969), was designed to be used with students, teachers,
counselors, administrators and other professionals. The format
of the instrument lends itself to Likert responses to "what
counselors actually do compared to what counselors should do."
Also a section of the instrument yields a personality profile
of the counselor.

During the 1971-1972 school year, twelve school systems
in Georgia were evaluated using the Georgia Guidance Services
Inventory, and an indepth interpretation was given within those
school systems evaluated. Approximately 30,000 students,
teachers, counselors, and administrators responded to the
instrument. As a result of the findings, counselors began to
work on strengthening weak areas found in their respective
guidance programs. During the 1972-73 school year, approximately 100,000 students, teachers, counselors and administrators from twenty-one local school systems responded to the
inventory. Results again were interpreted to the personnel
in each of the participating local school systems. Additional
school systems have been added each year with the intent to
continue until each guidance program in Georgia has been
initially evaluated which will occur in 1978.

The major evaluation activities involving programs,
procedures and objectives as performed by the Guidance and
Counseling Unit of the Georgia Department of Education are
summarized as follows:

1. The original item pool for the Georgia Guidance
   Services Inventory was established using four open-
   ended questions with a statewide sample of over 2,000
   students, teachers, counselors and administrators in
   schools housing grades 7-12.

2. The first form of the instrument was field tested in
   seven different schools housing grades 7-12 with
   approximately 1,800 students, teachers, counselors,
   and administrators.

3. Revisions were made in the instrument, based on
   frequency counts by response, by those completing the
   inventory.

4. A second form was field tested in five different
   schools in grades 7-12 with approximately 1,200
   students, teachers, counselors, and administrators.

5. Interpretations based on frequency data were made for four of the schools.

6. Factor analysis was performed on the data rendering five major factor loadings under which school guidance activities were grouped. Frequency counts by response and by items also were accomplished.

7. Using the factor analysis data and frequency data from the administration of the second form, a third revision was drafted.

8. The third revision was used in twelve school systems in Georgia during the 1971-72 school year. Following analysis of data an in-depth interpretation was provided to the personnel in these schools. This involved following analysis of data administration to more than 30,000 students, teachers, counselors, and administrators.

9. After extensive analysis, a fourth revision was accomplished, and this revised form was administered to 100,000 students, teachers, counselors, and administrators during the 1972-73 school year.

10. The Georgia Guidance Services Inventory was administered to 10,000 students in the DeKalb County School System in 1973-74. The Inventory was applied in a pretest and post-test arrangement. State department guidance consultants interpreted the data to school personnel.

11. For the school years 1974-75 through 1977-78 the evaluation has been carried out in all local school systems in Georgia. The Georgia Department of Education has assumed financial responsibility for scoring and reporting services.

Guidance program evaluation is vitally essential if services are to be provided commensurate with the expressed needs of populations served. School systems must rely upon systematic procedures and systems to arrive at objective evaluations of program content and processes. Guidance program critics feel that the guidance and counseling profession has relied too heavily for too long on inappropriate subjective evaluative procedures. The profession must demonstrate the need for programs and the viability of services via sound evaluation approaches.

413

COUNSELOR DEVELOPMENT AND IN-SERVICE TRAINING

State departments must assume more direct and involved leadership in facilitating the personal growth and development of counselors. Specific activities and program design for personal growth and development can be effectively introduced and fully implemented through statewide in-service training. If counselors are to be change agents and become more involved in the lives of their clientele, then they must be involved in personal growth and developmental experiences which free them to be maximally effective in meeting needs of others.

Only a minimum of effort has been made by state departments to organize and implement personal growth through in-service workshops for all guidance personnel under state jurisdiction. Some individual counselors have taken advantage of personal growth workshops offered through colleges or universities, professional organizations, and commercial enterprises. If a small sample of counselors avail themselves of such training opportunities and profit personally from their investment, then state department guidance personnel should investigate the feasibility of providing in-service personal growth workshops for all counselors. Sufficient information in professional literature and multiple personal growth guides and materials on the commercial market can be used to generate state department planning for statewide programs in counselor personal growth.

State department guidance units have a vital function to perform in establishing training modules for counselor in-service. The issues and concerns expressed throughout this Chapter lend themselves to areas of counselor in-service training which would normally be provided through the state department. Many counselors fail to return to formal training programs once they have reached a given plateau. Thus, they will rely upon state department guidance units to provide appropriate in-service programs and activities to meet a variety of needs.

The state department guidance unit must be prepared to deal effectively with an extensive array of guidance program needs. Some needs can be met only through personal or program contact. Other needs can be met through group contacts on a regional statewide basis. The following areas are representative of the concerns which state departments must address in planning counselor in-service training:

--student assessment techniques and instrumentation

--personal and professional development of counselors

--ethical and legal issues in guidance

--state and federal legislation in guidance

--career awareness, career development, career planning

--job placement skills for counselor

--alternate strategies in services delivery systems

--guidance management models

--computer-assisted guidance programs

--human relations training/skills development

--writing/application of objectives in guidance

--guidance program evaluation

--needs assessment (students, teachers, parents)

--development of parent consultation skills

--development of mini-guidance unit courses

--extending skills in crises counseling (drugs, venereal disease, teenage pregnancies)

--student behavior management skills

--structuring/utilizing accountability teams in guidance

--developing strategies for guidance/counseling outside the school walls

State department guidance units are in a position to have access to current literature, audio-visual materials, computer-assisted programs, and the basic means through which to gain additional access to many other sources and resources. The information and materials accessible to state departments personnel must be synthesized and processed into useful media for local school system personnel.

DEVELOPMENT OF RESOURCES AND RESOURCE MATERIALS

State departments of education must exercise leadership in assisting local system guidance personnel with the development, organization and delivery/utilization of resources and resource materials. A sound and functional guidance program is dependent upon the types and quality of resources and materials available within a community and/or throughout the state. Exercising expertise in identifying and organizing resources and materials, and applying skills in appropriate utilization of resources and materials is vitally essential in successful guidance program development. A list of available guidance resources and materials would be inexhaustive; however, some significant areas will be briefly reviewed in this section of the Chapter.

Resource Handbook

In making provision to assure the availability of a current directory of resources and materials, the state department might take appropriate measures in mandating that local system guidance units prepare an annual planning and operational plan. Such a plan would reflect the requirement that local, regional and statewide resources and materials be enumerated and detailed in a handbook. In addition to reviewing local system plans and checking for compliance, the state department has an obligation to provide consultive assistance in identifying resources and materials, and assisting in delineating the utility and delivery of resources and materials. A multitude of resources and materials go unidentified year after year, causing some guidance programs to collapse.

Many small local school systems with one-counselor guidance programs or few-counselor guidance units cannot accomplish some things which larger school systems are able to accomplish because smaller systems have fewer personnel and financial resources. The state department can be of invaluable support to these small local systems by filling those gaps with expertise and manpower from the state level. One of the most significant contributions the state department can provide is the development of a common handbook for counselors which generally could be used by all guidance personnel within the state regardless of the size of the school system and/or the geographical location. The handbook can be developed basically by the state staff, utilizing a representative group of guidance personnel from throughout the state. A suggested outline for a handbook developed by Roseberry (pp. i-ii, 1972) follows:

I. Position Statement - broad statements of policy and procedure

1. length of day and year for counselors
2. administrative responsibilities and general school duty
3. pupil/counselor ratios
4. clerical assistance

5. school policies development and procedural operations
6. guidance program supervision
7. confidentiality
8. salaries

II. Philosophy and Objectives of Program

1. assisting students in self-understanding
2. assisting students in decision making
3. assisting students in adjusting to school
4. providing appropriate information to students
5. assisting teachers in better understanding students
6. assisting teachers in relating educational program to students
7. coordinating community resources available to teachers and students
8. assisting parents in better understanding of children
9. assisting parents in understanding school functions

III. Counselor Job Description
Responsibilities of the counselor as related to foregoing objectives are as follows:

1. orientation (list activities with each category)
2. information service
3. counseling
4. appraisal services
5. program coordination
6. follow-up and follow-through
7. placement
8. research and evaluation
9. services to the school staff
10. registration and scheduling

IV. The Pupil Personnel Team

1. descriptions of other respective services
   a. psychological
   b. social work
   c. health
   d. exceptional children

2. chart depicting contrasts of specialty services' operations in re clientele, mode of operation, methods of changing behavior, and so forth

V. Guidance Services (general)

1. counseling
2. testing program (including types of tests with limitations, testing schedule, tips on testing procedure and data utilization, test terms)

417

V. Guidance Services (general)

1. counseling
2. testing program (including types of tests with
   limitations, testing schedule, tips on testing
   procedure and data utilization, test terms)
3. pupil placement
4. referral and resource agencies
5. use of cumulative records and suggested forms
   and formats
   a. records security
   b. ethical use of records
6. research, evaluation and follow-up

VI. Suggested Guidance Program Calendars

1. elementary school program (month-by-month)
2. middle school program (suggested month-by-month
   activities)
3. senior high school (month-by-month)

VII. Suggested Specific Guidance Activities

1. group activities with students
   a. educational planning--study skills, testing
   b. vocational planning--job opportunities, career
      areas
   c. personal-social development--peer group relations,
      parent and child relations
2. in-service activities with parents and teachers
   a. parent-child relationships
   b. parent-teacher relationships
   c. teacher-child relationships
   d. educational and career planning of students
      (detailed listing and description of other
      activities, Gasda and Folds, 1968)

VIII. The Counselor in the Elementary School

1. coordinating activities and responsibilities
   a. assessment
   b. career awareness
   c. research and evaluation
   d. public relations
2. consulting activities and responsibilities
   a. liaison between school and home
   b. leads parent discussion groups on child
      behavior
3. counseling activities and responsibilities
4. role-playing techniques
5. the unfinished story

6. sentence completion
7. sociogram uses

IX. The Guidance, Counseling and Testing Services, State Department of Education

1. organizational chart depicting arrangement/delivery of services
2. program development consultation
3. guidance materials--collection and distribution
4. in-service programs and activities
5. professional conferences
6. evaluation and research
7. funds administration
8. program interpretations to profession/lay groups

X. Counselor Certification Requirements and Procedures

1. general course requirements
2. experience requirements

XI. Professional Organizations

1. national
2. regional
3. state
4. local

XII. Recommended Resources Materials

1. print and non-print
2. other video and audio materials
3. general commercial publications

XIII. Innovative Programs and Concepts

Computer-Based Information Systems

Local school system guidance units need access to guidance information systems which offer local programs instant information relating to student needs. State departments can develop computer potential to structure and maintain a system of instant information which could be quickly and easily transmitted to local system guidance programs. Computer terminals could be installed at strategic centers throughout the state which would be convenient to every guidance unit within the state. Some states are offering modified computer-based guidance information systems, and a few other states have plans on the drawing board. The survival of effective guidance programs might well be contingent upon the availability and/or accessibility of instant information and resources.

Workshops for Resource and Materials Dissemination

Collection and maintenance of printed and non-printed materials (guidance services handbooks, films, filmstrips, tapes) constitute a portion of state department leadership responsibility. Such materials can be used effectively to enhance the achievement of outcomes in guidance programs. State department guidance personnel must develop systems through which the materials collection is properly advertised, appropriately distributed, and adequately utilized. A responsibility of the state guidance staff revolves around developing appropriate uses of both printed and non-printed materials. The state staff will need to plan and conduct workshops to enhance and improve materials utilization skills of local system guidance personnel.

State department guidance units that fail to provide competent leadership in the utilization and application of multiple resources and resource materials are not fulfilling basic obligations to local school systems--to improve and expand guidance programs, to meet student needs, and to enhance the instructional program. Workshops in the development of resources and utilization of resource materials are too frequently viewed as unimportant in terms of priorities of state department guidance units. Student needs assessments reveal that resources and resource materials comprise significant components of a sound functional guidance program.

APPROACHES IN FUNCTIONAL GUIDANCE LEADERSHIP

What direction will guidance supervision and leadership take in the balance of the 1970's and the decade of the 1980's? A mounting feeling is that guidance must touch the lives of many more people, and touch them more deeply. Students in our schools seem to be asking--through their actions, if not through their words--for help; many seem to feel they have somehow lost control of the direction and management of their lives. Widely acknowledged is that guidance and counseling services in the years ahead must move in new directions and devise a variety of procedures for delivering services and reaching the lives of a maximum number of students. Therefore, a crucially important activity of the state department guidance units is to provide high quality leadership to local school system guidance units. To fulfill the leadership role state department personnel should be in touch with current innovative and exemplary programs around the country. A knowledge of such programs and activities provides a base for responding positively and effectively to future educational trends and movements which have implications for guidance.

A number of trends are emerging on the horizon for innovative and exciting activity in guidance. These trends must be analyzed carefully in order that maximum benefits might accrue to the major recipients of guidance services--students in our schools. Incumbent upon state department guidance units is to weigh the potential value and subsequent use and application of significant trends for local school system guidance programs. The degree to which state department guidance personnel are abreast of educational trends and can integrate the best of these trends into state department management is reflected in the level of quality of statewide guidance programs. Some of the foremost general educational trends which have implications for guidance are discussed in the remainder of this section.

Experimentation With and Expansion of New Procedures and Techniques

Even though behavior modification techniques are utilized fairly extensively and quite effectively in many guidance programs, in other programs such approaches have never been attempted. Many unexplored and unused techniques and possibilities exist in the broad area of behavior modification. A variety of modification techniques have proved effective in changing and improving the behavior of disruptive students in school guidance clinics in Sacramento, California. The state department personnel might explore the feasibility of establishing pilot clinics, teaching behavior modification techniques, and establishing in-service program schedules which would provide opportunity for all local system guidance personnel to receive training. McQueen (1973) reported an experiment in Seattle, Washington, in which behavior modification techniques were introduced to solve problems of student disrupters, before they became unmanageable. Teachers followed through by awarding one point at the end of each class period to all students who had not broken any agreed-upon roles. Each Friday, the points could be invested in a self-selected activity.

Reality therapy techniques which Glasser (1965) espouses have useful implications for guidance programs. The major applications of the reality therapy methods rest on guiding students to constructive action rather than probing the student's innermost feelings, so that students eventually see how to solve their own problems. Guidance personnel should be able to reach a greater number of students when using the reality therapy approaches.

The Intelligent Use and Adaptation
of Systems Technology in Guidance Services

Technology has met considerable resistance in education because many educators tend to associate technology exclusively with equipment and hardware. Technology too often has been equated with aversive consequences attributed to the use of equipment and machinery, as in technological unemployment and technological pollution. Komoski (1969) noted that

> our present understanding of "technology" itself is still so influenced by the machine-centered, mass-producing, man-reading technology of the first industrial revolution that most talk about the "impact of technology on education" still precipitates an emotionally charged atmosphere, inhospitable to effective communication. (p. 70)

Komoski further stated that "technology refers to any man-made device, process or logical technique designed to systematically produce a reproducible effect." (p. 74). Silverman (1968) distinguished between technology as method and technology as application when he stated ". . .technology as method is an approach to problem solving and to the creation of new programs, methods and machines that is rational and orderly. . . Technology as application uses the results of technology as method."

The idea of "systems" in guidance program planning currently is being investigated, and in some programs a variety of models is being applied. Systems concepts, like technology, are too often misunderstood, and sometimes associated exclusively with detailed diagrams and complicated charts. Corrigan and Kaufman (1967) defined system as

> . . . a closed-loop analytic and developmental process which can be utilized to continuously: (1) assess the results of performance; (2) maintain sensitivity to performance requirements; and (3) provide for the self-correction of performance in order that the specified objectives can be achieved.

Perhaps the major advantage in using some arrangement of systems thinking is the increased probability of achieving desired outcomes from established objectives. The design and operation of a functional guidance system necessitates the statement of precise outcomes, the designation of specific activities to implement each outcome, and assessment of the degree to which each outcome is achieved. Campbell, et al., (1971) indicated that the systems procedures are outcome-oriented.

Systems models show relationships and flow start to finish and facilitate the management and monitoring of a program. Problems and impediments to achieving the goal can be spotted, modifications installed, resources shifted, and deadline adjusted. The systems approach identifies alternative methods for achieving a goal, creates a searching attitude, insures "backup" plans if the primary plan breaks down, and has procedures for determining the success of the program built into the system. Through trial installation, monitoring, and feedback, a program is continuously assessed to determine the degree to which it is achieving its initial goal. (p. 3)

An application of systems concepts in guidance has been proposed at the Center for Vocational and Technical Education at the Ohio State University. The proposal includes four basic components: specifying program objectives, generating alternate methods, designing program evaluation, and implementing planned changes. The four components form the base for developing a ten-phase procedural model for guidance programs:

1. context evaluation
2. assigning program goal priorities
3. translation of goals to student behavioral objectives
4. input evaluation: method selection
5. input evaluation: selection of techniques
6. diffusion: trial implementation
7. process evaluation
8. product evaluation
9. adaption
10. recycling

A system which shows promise for effective planning, implementing, and monitoring of guidance programs, is the written Activity Description and Task Schedules, as described by Sullivan and O'Hare (1971). The Activity Description might be used to clarify initial planning, provide a basis for review and approval, and denote resources, broad objectives and constraints. A sample follows:

Activity Description

Problem: The guidance programs of X School System have never operated with a written plan for guidance services to the student population. The individual schools within X School System have operated independently. There has been little or no effort to unify the individual programs

423

via a comprehensive operational plan of
guidance services delivery systems for
X School System.

Objective: To develop a system-wide operational plan
for guidance services and services
delivery for X School System.

Plan of Attack: Each school with a guidance program in
X School System will select representa-
tives as a part of the system-wide task
force to assist in developing a system-
wide comprehensive guidance plan. The
individual school representatives will
present respective plans for existing
operations of programs. The system
director of guidance will chair the task
force committee. The final draft of the
guidance plan will be written and presented to the local system superintendent
and board of education within sixty days
from the initial planning meeting.

Resources: Each school representative will be given
one day of release time each week until
the plan is completed. The director of
guidance will provide sample guidance
plans from other school districts. Other
system-wide personnel will be utilized
by the committee as needed.

The Task Schedule goes a step beyond the Activity Description to provide specific detail for this particular guidance
system. A sample Task Schedule is shown in Figure 10.10.

The use of systems technology in guidance is essential
if new developments in the field are to become more than mere
attachments to existing programs. O'Hare (1974) stated that
new sensational developments may even divert attention from
the more critical guidance problems if systems approaches are
not used.

Multi-Media in Guidance

Thousands of multi-media selections are released annually
which have potential use for guidance purposes. Information
relating to availability and use of much of this material never
reaches the counseling practitioner. State department personnel
are in a strategic position to assist local school systems in
obtaining and effectively integrating multi-media materials into
guidance and counseling; extensive media research results are

	Program:	Development of a Guidance Plan for X School System		
	Responsibility:	Director of Guidance (X School System)		

Event	Start date	Completion date	Responsibility
1. Select individual school representatives for Task Force committee	9/01	9/03	School Administrator in consultation with Guidance Director of System
2. Initial orientation and planning--full committee	9/04	9/04	Guidance Director
3. Individual school representative presenting existing respective school guidance program plans	9/05	9/09	School Representatives
4. Open discussion on systemwide guidance plan composition	9/20	9/30	Guidance Director
5. Individual Task Force assignments (conduct needs assessment)	10/5	10/25	System Superintendent and Guidance Director
6. Task Force members report	11/1	11/15	Individual Task Force members
7. First draft of system-wide guidance plan	11/20	11/30	Representatives and Guidance Director
8. Submit first draft to administration and faculties	12/3	12/10	Guidance Director
9. Review of plans with suggested amendments	12/11	12/20	Guidance Director
10. Second draft of system-wide guidance plan	1/03	1/15	Guidance Director and school representations
11. Submit to administration, faculties, student group	1/17	1/23	Guidance Director
12. Revise plan based on revision	1/30	2/12	Guidance Director and committees
13. Approve final plan	2/15	2/25	Administration, School Principals, faculties, students

Figure 10.10.   Sample Task Schedule for X School System.

available which state department guidance personnel could synthesize and channel to local system guidance directors. Such research findings should provide local systems a base for selecting and making appropriate applications of existing media in guidance.

Since guidance services exist to enhance and support the instructional program, guidance personnel need to be knowledgeable concerning media usage as related to the overall instructional program. DeKieffer (1969) found that based on media research over the past fifty years the primary advantages resulting from the use of media are as follows:

1. effectiveness in presenting factual information;

2. clarity in meaning by using visuals as well as audio;

3. permanence of learning by re-creating lifelike situations and involving pupils in the learning process;

4. effectiveness in improving attitudes, emotions and other behavioral responses; and

5. gaining and holding attention.

A brief listing and synopsis of some of the familiar and perhaps unique applications of guidance media follow.

Filmstrips, slide-audio tapes, filmstrip-audio tapes. Numerous materials are available in these categories. The Ohio Vocational Education Division and Ohio State University have produced excellent materials in the vocational and career information areas. Many state departments are developing their own materials and adapting them for use in local school system guidance programs. The American Personnel and Guidance Association has promoted the development and use of appropriate materials in guidance programs.

Television, films, video recordings, audio recordings. Some state departments are engaged in exploring the uses of these multi-media devices to provide innovative and exemplary activities, model programs, and in-service training for local school system guidance personnel. Career information, on-the-job interviews, and therapeutic counseling tapes are examples of materials available for guidance programs personnel. The Georgia Department of Education has done extensive productions in occupational information films which are aired on regular schedules on educational television. Similar uses of this area of multi-media are reported in the Delaware Department of Education, the Atlanta (Georgia) City Schools, Dade County in Florida, and Washington County Schools in Maryland.

426

Microforms. Guidance-related uses of microfilm/microfiche have focused on record keeping and career guidance materials. In view of the fact that guidance personnel have maintained considerable responsibility for student records, the potential contribution of microfilm/microfiche is significant. This area of media can be most valuable in the collection, evaluation, and dissemination of career and vocational information. Two programs which have utilized microfilm successfully in career development are VIEW (Vocation Information for Education and Work), planned by the San Diego County Schools and VOGUE (Vocational Guidance for Education) developed by the New York State Education Department and the New York Employment Services, The VIEW system provides information on jobs and VIEW scripts containing an aperture card which includes a 35mm microfilm frame. VOGUE employs printed job descriptions in binders and aperture cards.

Computers and computerized materials. This area of technology holds considerable promise for guidance systems, but funding has limited extensive investigation and subsequent application of computers. The state department staff is in a position to generate computerized materials and distribute to local guidance personnel, e.g., test data usage, college admission programs, dropout studies, guidance program evaluation studies, and identification of learning problems. The computer can be a useful device in course scheduling for students. Even personality inventories can be interpreted through the computer.

Computer information systems have been developed which allows the individual student to interact with computer programmed information. Considerable career and vocational information has been linked to computer systems. The Computerized Vocational Information System (CVIS) developed in Villa Park, Illinois, offers tremendous potential for guidance programs. Other computerized programs are developed at Pennsylvania State University; Computer-Assisted Career Exploration system (CACE), the Total Guidance Information Support System (TGISS), developed in Oklahoma through the Bartlesville School System; and the Computer-Based Automated Counseling Simulation System for Vocational Decision (ISVD), developed by Tiedeman, et al. (Peatling & Tiedeman, 1977) of Harvard University.

Many logistical problems and considerations are to be worked out before the computerized materials and programs in guidance can reach maximum benefit for local school system guidance. However, state department personnel must maintain a high level of support and interest in such systems because of the potential value and use of such technology. Educational functions can be accomplished more effectively at faster rates with computer assistance, freeing guidance and instructional personnel to devote more personal time to individual students and small groups of students who need personal attention.

Counseling and Guidance Activities Outside School

Some state department guidance leadership personnel have begun to plan for moving guidance and counseling beyond the walls of the school. The implementation of a model for "beyond school guidance and counseling" will perhaps require a reorganization of the entire educational enterprise. Furthermore, for such a reorganization to proceed with optimal effectiveness it will become important that all those presently in a school become aware of the implications of a "beyond school guidance and counseling" model, and prepare to reconceptualize their roles and functions accordingly. The state department will play a decisive role in staff development as concern is generated for new roles and functions to fully implement the proposed model.

Student needs and problems cannot always be met and solved inside the confines of the school community. The life of the student relates also to the home and to the total community. Subsequently, it is imperative that strategies and models be conceptualized which can be applied in a guidance and counseling framework to clientele in the community whenever needs arise or problems exist.

Guidance Related to Crisis Issues

Drug use, the new morality or sexual freedom, racial problems, venereal disease, and other social issues have catapulted our schools into the position of reassessing goals, objectives and processes of the entire education enterprise. It is incumbent upon educators, and particularly guidance and counseling personnel, to deal immediately and effectively with the problems that students face in the throes of a social revolution.

The state department must help structure the motif of training and retraining models in order that school counselors and related professionals can stem the tide of the social revolution which is having a significantly negative impact upon the students and the schools. Local school system staff development program planning arranged in consultation with the state department appears to be a viable procedure in preparing for crisis issues.

Utilization of Paraprofessionals in Guidance

Some state departments have developed certification standards for paraprofessionals in education, including

428

guidance services. Some of the state departments have assisted counselor education training institutions in establishing programs to train guidance paraprofessionals. Other state departments have themselves assumed responsibility for the training of paraprofessionals. State guidance units should be instrumental in implementing in-service workshops with local school systems in the effective utilization of guidance paraprofessionals.

Use of Guidance Accountability Teams

States might give consideration to encouraging local school systems by offering technical assistance to school system guidance units in the area of forming "guidance accountability teams." Since traditional guidance and counseling procedures have reached a relatively small percentage of school populations, alternate approaches and procedures to reach greater numbers of students need to be considered.

The team might include paraprofessionals, specially trained students and teachers, interested community individuals and perhaps parents, along with the counselor as the team leader (see Figure 10.1 as a suggested structural framework). Such a model should enhance the overall guidance and counseling program of a school district. The quantity and quality of student referrals should improve. Students should develop appropriate leadership qualities, and there should be better communications between school, students, home and community.

COORDINATION OF GUIDANCE PROGRAM AND SERVICES

Because of the mass of information available, the numbers of students involved, and the transitional character of education programs and services aggressive coordination is necessary for guidance and counseling services to succeed and continue to be relevant. If less is done, major omissions and unnecessary duplications will occur in a vertical learning program that cannot afford to waste time or resources (Hatch, 1974). In many school systems program components are found which lend themselves to direction or supervision by more than one specialty area. For example, career education and/or career guidance might be coordinated through a given instructional component of education. In this event, guidance and counseling personnel acting in a role of assisting with career education and career guidance might be confronted with serious administration obstruction, since there would be division of responsibility. Such situations are unfortunate, and remedies must be found if programs are to be viable and significant. State department guidance staffs can assume active roles in promoting program coordination efforts within local school systems. Coordination planning and organizational skills can be taught through workshop in-service activities.

A number of administrative models exist (some presented in this Chapter might possess conversion utility) which may have transferability to the coordination of interdisciplinary educational programs. The following set of questions suggested by Hatch (1974) (from original material by Jean Busfield, Michigan State University) might be helpful to local school systems in coordinating services and programs--in this particular case, career education:

1. Is a particular staff member responsible for the coordination of the instructional program? If the answer is "yes," the individual assigned to coordinate the career educational program should become a member of his/her staff.

2. Is there an individual responsible for the coordination of the guidance and counseling program? If the answer is "yes," a plan must be adapted that permits maximum cooperation between these two components in planning, implementing, and evaluating the career education program.

3. Is an individual available who has both administrative and guidance competencies? If the answer is "none in the system," it may be necessary to go outside the district to obtain in a qualified person, since nothing would be more detrimental to the success of the program than to have leadership that could best be described as the "blind leading the blind."

4. Is there an individual in each building who has the interest and ability to serve as coordinator of career education in that building? If the answer is "no," a way should be found to obtain such a person, since the demands of an efficient program require constant liaison between all facets of the district. The person selected may perform these duties on a part-time basis, provided adequate time is available for the coordination of responsibilities.

5. Will the school district have a model for career education which designates an emphasis on careers at certain levels of the school program? If the answer is "no," then some model such as "career awareness" for the primary grades, "career exploration" for the middle grades, and "career preparation" for the high school should be adopted. A model usually results in easier definition of responsibility by teachers at the various levels and permits a program to evolve in proper sequence, minimizing omission and duplication.

Coordination problems virtually can be solved if appropriate answers to the foregoing questions can be worked out. Coordination of programs and services depends greatly upon professionals in the various disciplines coming to the conference table to agree upon how the coordination is to be accomplished. Students are the losers when professional educators do not plan appropriate arrangements for coordination of programs and services.

Numerous other trends in guidance and counseling leadership exist, but limitations of space and the overall purpose of this Chapter preclude the continuation of what possibly might be an impossible enumeration. Guidance and counseling will continue to occupy a unique role and leadership responsibility in the areas of dissent and discontent of minority groups. Issues and concerns surrounding minority groups remain to be resolved and guidance should be in the forefront in leadership development. The changing role of women is gaining considerable attention in our world. Again, guidance and counseling personnel must assume positive leadership roles in facilitating the desirable role changes sought by women. A revolutionized effort should be directed toward more involvement with total instructional staffs in the guidance efforts of a school system. The role of the instructional staff is too frequently taken for granted by the guidance and counseling personnel. The basic foundation for a sound program of guidance services resides in the classroom and under the direction of the instructional staff. These and many other issues and trends are highly significant and worthy of discussion. The reader may wish to review the current literature which deals more forcefully and at greater length with current issues/trends focusing on guidance and counseling

SUMMARY

The information presented in this Chapter is representative of a plethora of contemporary ideas and thoughts which are emerging in state department guidance supervision and leadership. Guidance personnel at local school system levels have the right to expect state department guidance personnel to be prepared to provide necessary leadership, supervision, and services commensurate with local program needs. When the state department fails in its responsibilities to provide competent leadership and supervision, no adequate justification remains for continued existence of the state unit.

State department leadership has been presented in a variety of dimensions including the historical perspective of supervision and leadership of guidance through state departments. Following the introductory treatment of state department supervision, the author discussed selected areas of legitimate concern appropriate to state department of education supervision. The major areas included guidance program needs assessment, competency-based counselor certification, guidance management by objectives, guidance program evaluation, counselor in-service training, development of resources and resource materials in guidance, innovative approaches in guidance leadership, and coordination of guidance services.

The ancient adage, "a chain is only as strong as its weakest link," appropriately expresses the status and quality of local school system guidance programs in proportion to viable leadership and supervision provided through the state department. Historically, the local systems have expected the state department to establish the general pace of program movement. This pace must accelerate if local systems, in the future, will continue to perceive the state department as the pace-setter. Moreover, without supervision and leadership from the "expected source," guidance programs may become dormant, leading to eventual extinction.

REFERENCES

Campbell, R.; Dworkin, E.; Jackson, D.; Heoltzel, K.; Parsons, G.; & Lacey, D. The systems approach: An emerging behavioral model for vocational guidance (Center for Vocational and Technical Education, the Ohio State University, January, 1971).

Chiles, D. A counselor's perspective. Guidepost, 1973, 15(18), 1.

Corrigan, R., & Kaufman, R. A system approach for solving educational problems. Operation PEP, Office of the San Mateo County (California) Superintendent of Schools, October, 1967.

DeKieffer, R. Implications of new educational media. Chapter 12 in Planning for Effective Utilization of Technology in Education, edited by E. L. Morphet and D. L. Jesser. New York: Citation Press, 1969.

Duncan, J., & Geoffroy, K. A factor analysis of the role of the state director of guidance service. Counselor Education and Supervision Journal, Fall, 1971, 10, 251-261.

Farmer, R. N. Management of the Future. Belmont, California: Wadsworth Publishing Company, 1969.

Fitzpatrick, G. M. State supervisors and the professional literature. Counselor Education and Supervision, 1967, 7, 78.

Gade, E. M., & Zaccaria, J. S. Topical entries and institutional sources in counselor education and supervision, Vol. 1-4, 1961-65. Counselor Education and Supervision, 1966, 5, 221-225.

Gazda, G., & Folds, J. Group Guidance: A Critical Incidents Approach. Parkinson Division, Follett Educational Corporation, 1968.

Geoffroy, K. E. A factor analysis of the role of the state supervisor of guidance services. A paper presented at the APGA Convention, Detroit, Michigan, April, 1968.

Geoffroy, K., & Duncan, J. A factor analysis of the role of the state supervisor of guidance services. Counselor Education and Supervision, Winter, 1971, 10, 138-145.

Gibboney, R. The role of the state education department in educational change. Chapter 6 in Perspectives on Educational Change, edited by Richard J. Miller. New York: Appleton-Century-Crofts Publishers, 1967.

Glasser, W. Reality Therapy. New York: Harper and Row, 1965.

Gunter, N. Pupil personnel services team model. Curriculum Leadership and Pupil Personnel Services Division, Georgia Department of Education, Atlanta, Georgia, 1972.

Gust, T. Extending counselor supervision. Counselor Education and Supervision Journal, Spring, 1970, 9, 157-160.

Hatch, R. The Organization of Pupil Personnel Programs--Issues and Practices. Michigan State University Press, 1974.

Hollis, J. W., & Wantz, R. A. Counselor Education Directory 1977: Personnel and Programs. Muncie, IN.: Accelerated Development, 1977.

Johnson, J. A. Membership in ACES. Counselor Education and Supervision, 1968, 7, 137-142.

Knowles, R. T. Attitudes of ACES members. Counselor Education and Supervision, 1968, 7, 305-314.

Komoski, P. The continuing confusion about technology and education of the myth-ing link in educational technology. Educational Technology, November, 1969.

Lessinger, L. M. Competency-based professional accountability. A paper presented at Georgia State University, Atlanta, Georgia, April, 1972.

McQueen, M. Trends in guidance and counseling. The Education Digest, March, 1973.

O'Hare, R. Technology in pupil personnel services. Chapter 4 in Organization of Pupil Personnel Programs--Issues and Practices, edited by Raymond N. Hatch. Michigan State University Press, 1974.

Page, R., et al. A master plan of research, development and exemplary activities in vocational and technical education. Springfield, Illinois, State of Illinois, Bulletin No. 11-670, 1970.

Peatling, J. H., & Tiedeman, D. V. Career Development: Designing Self. Muncie, IN.: Accelerated Development Inc., 1977.

Riccio, A. C. The counselor educator and graduate supervisor: Graduate training and occupational mobility. Counselor Education and Supervision, 1961, 1, 10-17.

_____. Counselor educators and guidance supervisors: A second look at graduate training. Counselor Education and Supervision, 1966, 5, 73-79.

Roseberry, J. Model for Objective-Based Guidance Program. Georgia Department of Education, Pupil Personnel Services, 1972.

Rosen, D. The Power of Competency-Based Teacher Education: A Report. Boston: Allyn, Bacon, 1972.

Silverman, R. Two kinds of technology. Educational Technology, 1968, 8(1), 3.

Starr, H., et al. A System for State Evaluation of Vocational Education. Columbus, Ohio: The Ohio State University, 1970.

Sullivan, H. J., & O'Hare, R. W. (Eds.). Accountability in pupil personnel services: A process guide for the development of objectives. Chaps. 1, 5-6. California Personnel and Guidance Association. Fullerton, California, 1971.

Toffler, A. Future Shock. New York: Random House, 1970.

Vail, P.; George, M.; et al. Georgia guidance services inventory. Guidance and Counseling Unit, Curriculum Leadership and Pupil Personnel Services Division, Georgia Department of Education. Atlanta, Georgia, 1969.

Ware, W. The development of a model comprehensive needs-based guidance system and modular instructional strategies. ESEA, Title III, Guidance Project. Pioneer Cooperative Educational Service Agency, Cleveland, Georgia, 1973.

Wellman, F. Systems model for guidance program development and evaluation. A paper presented at the 64th Annual Vocational Convention, New Orleans, Louisiana, December, 1970.

Chapter **11**

A

RELATIONSHIP APPROACH

TO

COUNSELOR SUPERVISION

IN

AGENCY SETTINGS

Harold A. Moses
Associate Professor
Edcuational Psychology
University of Illinois
Urbana, Illinois

John T. Hardin
Family Therapist and Consultant
Southside Area Mental Health
Services
12 East Tabb Street
Petersburg, Virginia

A RELATIONSHIP APPROACH

TO COUNSELOR SUPERVISION IN AGENCY SETTINGS

Editor's Notes

The authors of Section Four (Chapters 8 through 11) have voiced somewhat distinctive views of supervision as they believe it should be practiced in their respective settings, and each author has indicated how his particular setting determines, to some extent, the form of supervision practiced within that setting.

Drs. Moses and Hardin take a new tack regarding the supervision of agency counseling; they suggest that the supervision setting does not contain the most important factors in supervision practice. In their opinion the essence of counselor supervision is in the relationship between the supervisor and supervisee, and the conditions of this relationship are the instrumental factors which lead to its success or failure. Following the therapeutic approach of Robert Carkhuff, these authors define two sets of relationship conditions, facilitative and action-oriented, which predominantly but not exclusively determine supervision effectiveness. Through these two sets of conditions within the supervisory relationship, as expressed during supervision activities, the therapeutic process of supervision flows.

Supervisors in agency settings, or any setting, may find the relationship approach to be refreshing, particularly if they are or have been indoctrinated with a strong emphasis on "clinical technique." One's faith in self and the human condition is reaffirmed by the author's implied message that a "fully functioning" individual as counselor is just as vital to helpgiving as contrived clinical techniques. Through the relationship approach, the agency supervisor can release and/or facilitate the supervisee's natural therapeutic potential, which in turn will enhance technical expertise.

Harold A. Moses

Harold A. Moses (Ph.D.) is one of the nation's foremost spokesmen for counseling and counselor supervision in agency settings. He has co-authored or edited four books, has published many articles in professional journals, and through-out his career has been active in professional organizations. Dr. Moses, an Associate Professor of Educational Psychology at the University of Illinois, is listed in Who's Who in the Midwest.

As a counselor educator and registered psychologist in the State of Illinois Dr. Moses is continually involved in the practice of counseling and supervision. During the last decade he has personally supervised over one hundred counselors.

John T. Hardin (Ph.D.) co-authored this article as a doctoral candidate at the University of Illinois.

John T. Hardin

John T. Hardin (Ph.D.) is a psychologist at Southside Area
Mental Health Services, Petersburg, Virginia, where he func-
tions as family therapist and consultant with other agencies.
Prior to this position, he was a psychologist in Decatur,
Illinois, Mental Health Center, psychiatric ward of St. Mary's
Hospital, and Adolph Meyer Zone Center (a state psychiatric
residential treatment center in Illinois).

John, after completing his doctorate, backpacked throughout Mexico, Central America, and South America for over a year.
His military service was as an officer in the United States Air
Force. During the study on the doctorate, he had an extended
period of involvement with supervision of both individual and
group counseling.

In 1975 he did a study to determine what counselors and
supervisors in community mental health agencies perceive to be
the ideal role of a supervisor of counselors. From the information obtained a model was developed for the supervision of
full-time, practicing counselors in a professional setting.

A RELATIONSHIP APPROACH

TO COUNSELOR SUPERVISION IN AGENCY SETTINGS

Harold A. Moses and John T. Hardin

In recent years growth has occurred not only in the type
and number of helping agencies which employ counselors but also
in the number of counselors needed to fill the increasing open-
ings in existing agencies. Among the agencies that have
experienced either a significant increase in the number of
counselors or an increased consciousness of professionalization
are those in the areas of mental health, employment service,
vocational rehabilitation, career guidance, industrial employee
counseling, and family and marital counseling. Although
specialized knowledge is required of the counselor to function
effectively in providing the specialized services offered by
these various settings, this Chapter proposes that the fundamental principles of counseling and of supervision in each
setting are essentially the same.

Every indication is that the growth trend for agency
counseling will continue, and while this growth creates a need
for an increased number of trained counselors, by far the
greater need is for more effective helpers. This emerging need
for effective agency counselors challenges not only our counselor educators in graduate schools to consider ways of improving
their preparation programs, but also are challenged to consider
ways of contributing to the continued learning and development
of their supervisees.

General agreement seems to be that the supervision of
counselors in their work with clients should play a central
role in their in-service training. Altucher (1967) considered
supervision to be "one of the cornerstones of the training
process, if not its foundation" (p. 166). And yet, as
Gladstein (1970) pointed out, while much consideration has been

given to the role and function of supervision in graduate counselor education programs, relatively little attention has been accorded to the supervision of full-time, practicing counselors.

Lambert (1974) stated that although supervision is considered critical to training, most of the material on supervision is theoretical because the supervisory process has not been studied by many researchers. Pinson (1974) lamented the fact that so little has been written by actual on-the-job supervisors. Miller and Roberts (1971) observed that there was no model for supervision within a state agency.

Several articles have emphasized the need for supervision in on-the-job settings for counselors. Biasco and Redfering (1976) stressed the need for continued supervision or consultation of group counselors. Dunlop (1968) observed that counselors new to the profession often complain that their preparation did not equip them fully for the work they are expected to do. Goldin (1965) in his study of rehabilitation counselors found that two-thirds of those studied reported dissatisfaction with their preparation. Hays (1968) suggested that:

> The nurturing of a budding counselor begins with his entrance into a well defined counselor education program under the leadership of a qualified counselor educator. It should continue, at least, through the first year the counselor is on the job (p. 51).

Kaplan (1964) pointed out that first-year school counselors who participated in a number of personal supervisory conferences reported fewer professional problems. Even though Dunlop, Hays, and Kaplan were considering counselors in public school settings, the generalization of these observations to other settings seems appropriate.

Supervision of the practicing counselor appears, then, to be a significant though neglected area of vital concern in the helping profession. Hansen and Stevic (1967) called attention to the fact that little emphasis is placed on the supervisory process in counselor education programs. "This is true even though most of these persons will be expected to supervise" (p. 205).

THE NATURE OF SUPERVISION

General agreement has been reached on the importance of a supervisory experience for the counselor-in-preparation as well as for the counselor in the field, but much less agreement exists on the nature of what this experience should be. Davidson and Emmer (1966) pointed out that while many researchers have spent considerable time investigating and discussing supervisory behaviors, no substantial agreement regarding the theoretical nature of the supervisory process has been reached. The greatest divergence of opinion seems to be between what Truax, Carkhuff, and Douds (1964) identified as the "didactic" and the "experiential" approaches. Didactic supervisors (Krasner, 1962: Krumboltz, 1967) have stressed the counselor's need for feedback regarding his/her performance and the counselor's need for reinforcement to shape the behaviors necessary for successful work. On the other hand, experiential supervisors (Rogers, 1957; Arbuckle, 1963; Patterson, 1964) view the didactic approach as primarily objective, impersonal, technique-oriented, and mechanical. These authors stressed a more subjective, personal, nontechnique-oriented emphasis with attention given to the counselors' need for security so that they may explore their own feelings and learn from their own experiences.

While some of the learnings that occur within the supervisory relationship may involve the more cognitive elements of information giving, especially in areas in which the supervisee lacks certain specific kinds of information, the greater portion of the learnings will often be of a more personal, self-explorative nature. Patterson (1964) stated that supervision is neither teaching nor therapy but falls somewhere between these two processes. More often than not, supervision, could be viewed as therapeutic rather than didactic.

Hansen et al (1976) concluded that, according to their research review, didactic training was more effective than experiential; but Lambert (1974) suggested that, day-to-day or immediate effects may be greater for the didactic approach but future research could well indicate the experiential approach to have more long-term effectiveness. Perhaps, instead of viewing supervisors as either teachers or therapists, a more appropriate view might be as Kaplowitz (1967) suggested, "persons in whom the qualities characteristic of the two roles are fused and used according to the specifics of the situation."

Dangers can exist in the supervisor adopting and operating totally from either extreme. As Miller and Oetting (1966) pointed out, supervisees resist and resent the supervisor who approaches them primarily as a therapist. Such attitudes could well have an interfering effect on the learnings which might occur in the supervisory relationship. Furthermore, an exclusively psychotherapeutic approach to supervision could easily focus totally on the self of the supervisee without considering the interactions of this self with the client.

Conversely, in a number of studies indications are that, while students anticipate and welcome instruction, direction, and structure from the supervisor, an overemphasis on the didactic often will lead to a corresponding underemphasis on the counselor's self. Combs and Soper (1963) have written that effective counseling is not just a matter of technique, but can depend upon how well the counselor uses his/her unique self as an instrument in the helping relationship. If the supervisee's self is not considered at all by the supervisor the effect might be the acting out of therapeutic behaviors as an attempt to fill a role, to "play the part" so to speak, rather than the natural expression of the supervisee's self.

The self or person of the counselor is his/her most important asset--the only asset the counselor takes into the therapy session. When the counselor enters into interaction with clients, though he/she hopefully has had the learnings and experiences necessary to function professionally, these assets are present only to the degree to which they have become personally meaningful, that is, the degree to which they have been integrated into the self or person of the counselor. Such integration is not likely to take place at a highly rational, intellectual level within a structured, didactic, supervisory relationship. In such a relationship the supervisee often becomes an extension of the supervisor rather than an independently functioning helper.

The ultimate goal of supervision is not simply a more knowledgeable and skilled technician but rather a more human self-actualizing person. Supervision should provide an extending experience in which the supervisee can blend professional knowledge and personal qualities, becoming ever more capable of being effective help to others in realizing more fully the potentials of their true selves. While part of supervision is instructional, it goes beyond instruction to focus upon the person or self of the supervisee. Ideally, supervision is the continuous and harmonic blending of an increasingly developed theorectical structure with a deeper and fuller appreciation of the self of the counselor. As was stated previously, another way of conceptualizing this ultimate goal of supervision is the supervisee's ability to translate these supervisory experiences into client benefits.

Are the differences between these apparently contradictory approaches so great that, as a supervisor, one must choose between them? Or, is it perhaps possible to reconcile these

seemingly inconsistent orientations and develop a more
integrated base for supervision? Rogers (1961) suggested that
these two divergent currents only seem irreconcilable because
we have not yet developed the larger frame of reference that
would contain them both.

SUPERVISION: A RELATIONSHIP

Research evidence in the area of helping relationships
has been accumulating, especially in the last ten years, to
suggest that the most effective element contributing to the
personal growth of the client is the nature of the therapeutic
relationship established by the counselor. That is, the
crucial element of a counselor's effectiveness is not the use
of a given technique or the adoption of a particular theory;
rather, effective therapeutic interaction is more dependent on
the quality of the therapeutic relationship. While all of the
evidence is not yet in, research has indicated that
relationship variables are much more important in influencing
outcome than has been generally accepted. Hanse, et el
(1976) concluded from their five-year review of practicum
supervision research that "the supervisor who directly or
indirectly models facilitative behavior will be more effective"
and that the effectiveness of such modeling is supported in the
literature. Wolpe (1958) conceded that as much as sixty
percent of his effectiveness with counter-conditioning may be
because of "nonspecific relationship factors." Thus,
considering the supervisory process within the frame of
reference of the relationship, the distinction between a
didactic and an experiential approach and a comparison of their
respective merits are no longer seen as the major issues in
supervision. The nature of the supervisory relationship itself
has now become a more meaningful consideration.

As Patterson (1964) pointed out, supervision is primarily
a relationship, and, like all good human relationships, it
should be therapeutic. In describing the supervisory
relationship, Margulis (1970) stated:

> For me, the optimal supervisor-supervisee
> relationship is no different than that which occurs
> between the therapist-patient at the times when
> growth is allowed to occur. This is the same
> connectiveness that occurs between lovers, between
> parents and child, between persons at moments of
> genuine encounter (p. 54).

The supervisory relationship is thus seen to be an encounter,
a genuinely personal interchange between supervisor and supervisee, a sharing interactive process based on mutual respect.

The immediate goal of the supervisory process becomes the establishment of such a therapeutic relationship with the supervisee, a relationship which will set in motion and facilitate the supervisee's continuing personal and professional growth. Within this relationship, the process of growth occurs.

Supervision contains many of the same elements as counseling and psychotherapy, the most essential aspect being the relationship. Another aspect of the helping process which also appears to be essential to supervision as well as to counseling and psychotherapy is the client's--or, in this case, supervisee's--self-exploration. That self-exploration is related to the growth and development of the client has been demonstrated in a number of studies (Truax & Carkhuff, 1967; Carkhuff & Berenson, 1967). While the relationships examined were not on such a level as to indicate the possibility of other significant variables relating to outcome, the importance of self-exploration within those relationships was nevertheless unquestionable. Supervisee self-exploration then is seen as the major thrust of the supervisory process.

Such self-exploration should be directed toward developing in counselors an openness to their own experience--how they experience the client and themselves in relation to the client--and an awareness of the nature of their interaction. After counselors have developed an openness to, become aware of, and developed an understanding of their "inner experiencing," the supervisor should help counselors explore how they might use this inner experiencing as an effective helping instrument. As counselors develop increasing openness to their own experiencing and greater understanding of themselves, their clients, and their interactions, they will see more clearly the different courses of action open to them. The supervisor can then support and work with the supervisee in considering the short- and long-term implications of each course of action, in developing ways of accomplishing that course, and, most importantly, in acting on those decisions.

The _intermediate goals_ of the supervisory process may then be defined as exploration, awareness and understanding, and action. Achievement of these intermediate goals will continue and facilitate the process of growth set in motion by the establishment of the supervisory relationship. The supervisee's continuing attainment of higher degrees of both personal and professional growth and his/her development into an effective, independent, and fully-functioning helper is the _ultimate_ goal of the supervisory process. Another way of conceptualizing the ultimate goal of supervision is the supervisee's ability to translate supervisory experiences into client benefits.

The relationship provides both a setting for and sets in motion the intermediate goals which define the growth process and leads to this ultimate goal. Consideration of those core conditions which constitute a facilitative supervisory relationship thus becomes essential in examining the supervisory process.

CONDITIONS OF SUPERVISORY INTERVENTION

Carkhuff (1969), in discussing the dimensions of a therapeutic relationship, proposed that all effective interpersonal processes, of which supervision is but one form, share a common core of conditions conducive to facilitative human experiences. After examining a substantial body of evidence he concluded the most effective experiences in developing effective helpers, as well as effective persons, are those which occur within a relationship based on what he identified as the "facilitative" and "action-oriented," or "core," conditions.

Facilitative Conditions

During the early phase of the supervisory relationship, the supervisor should give full attention to the supervisee, and should do all he/she can to listen, to understand what the supervisee is saying or trying to say, and to respond to the supervisee in such a way as to communicate this understanding. The supervisor's responses will be most effective when they are based on the "facilitative" conditions, which include empathy or understanding, respect or unconditional positive regard, and concreteness or specificity of expression. These facilitative conditions may be described as follows.

Empathy, or understanding. Empathy is seeing the world through the supervisee's eyes. Rogers' definition, found in Patterson (1973), perhaps described empathy as well as any: "....the state of perceiving the internal frame of reference of another with accuracy, and with the emotional components and meanings which pertain thereto, as if one were the other person, but without ever loosing the 'as if' condition" (p. 384). The central aspect of empathy is adopting the supervisees' points of view, their internal frames of reference, and experiencing their world as they do. As the lawyer Atticus Finch said to his children in Harper Lee's To Kill a Mockingbird, "You never really understand a person until you consider things from his point of view--until you climb into his skin and walk around in it" (p. 51).

Empathy involves a distinction between "knowledge about" the supervisee and an "understanding of" the supervisee. Knowledge about the supervisee is an understanding from an external frame of reference and is based on the objective observable facts; an understanding of the supervisee involves empathically experiencing the supervisee from his/her own internal personal frame of reference and is based on the subjective facts, beliefs, values, attitudes, feelings, and perceptions of the supervisee. The latter are the real "facts" in supervision.

As Patterson (1974) pointed out, many barriers to understanding another person result from differences in their experiences. He went on to point out that it is not necessary to understand or empathize with another fully, that in really trying to understand others and in communicating these efforts, individuals are helped to explore, express, experience, and understand themselves. Such a process is seen as a "shared journey."

Respect, or unconditional positive regard. Respect includes acceptance, interest, concern, warmth, liking, and caring for the supervisee. It is nonjudgmental, a caring without conditions. The essential communication is, "With me you are free to be who you are." This acceptance is not however a blind acceptance of attitudes and behaviors of the supervisee, whatever they might be. Rather, it is an acceptance of the supervisee as a person, regardless of certain specific attitudes or behaviors which, to the supervisor, may be unacceptable or unlikeable. In the early stages of the supervisory relationship, the communication of respect may well involve the suspension of feelings, attitudes, and judgements on the part of the supervisor that might have a restrictive effect on the communications of the supervisee. Later, as the supervisor enters into the supervisee's frame of reference and comes to develop an understanding of the supervisee, the supervisor will begin discovering attributes which can be responded to positively. If not, as Carkhuff (1969) pointed out, there may be no basis for continuing the relationship, since, in a relationship based on a lack of respect, it is unlikely that the supervisee can come to respect his/her own capacities for making appropriate discriminations and acting on them. Respect also involves a belief that, under the appropriate conditions, supervisees are capable of assuming responsibility for themselves, that they can work through difficulties which may arise, making the 'right' or best decisions for themselves. Respect is expressed in the supervisor's listening to the supervisee, trying to understand, and communicating this understanding to the supervisee. There is, then, a direct relationship between respect and understanding, with respect increasing as understanding increases.

Concreteness, or specificity of expression. Concreteness is dealing with the specific feelings, behaviors, and experiences of the supervisee. Concreteness is the opposite of vagueness or ambiguity. Supervisees are kept close to their own experiences and feelings which fosters accuracy of understanding on both the part of the supervisor and the supervisee. The focus of the supervisee's explorations should be material that is personally meaningful, with the supervisor helping search out the significant aspects from those which are not significant. Concreteness is especially critical in the early stages of the supervisory relationship in helping the supervisor understand the supervisee's perceptual systems which form the basis for his/her behavior.

Action-Oriented Conditions

During the later phase of the supervisory relationship, the supervisor uses what has been learned from the supervisee's explorations as a basis for initiating further discussion. The supervisor becomes more active in helping the supervisee develop a deeper experiential understanding and to act on this understanding. The supervisor's increasingly more active involvements will be most effective when they are based on the "action-oriented" conditions, which include genuineness or congruence, confrontation, and immediacy. These action-oriented conditions may be described as follows.

Genuineness or congruence. Genuineness is simply being real in a relationship with the supervisee. The supervisor is not thinking or feeling one thing and saying another but is honest, open, and sincere in his/her interactions with the supervisee. The supervisor's actions are congruent with his/her experiencing. Genuineness however should not be confused with free license for supervisors to do what they will. As Carkhuff and Berenson (1967) noted, a difference between a construct of genuineness and a construct of facilitative or therapeutic genuineness exists. As was the case with respect, the supervisor should inhibit potentially destructive responses, in spite of their genuineness. Genuineness does not require supervisors to share their feelings always; but does require that whatever the supervisor expresses be real. Genuineness necessitates that the supervisor "be" a supervisor, not "play the role" of one. In striving to be genuine when interacting with the supervisee, the supervisor should focus on understanding the supervisee's communications and be guided by what is effective for the supervisee, rather than allowing a dominance of spontaneity to detract.

Confrontation. Confrontation, essentially is, telling the supervisee what you've been experiencing as you've been listening. The purpose of confrontation is to reduce the ambiguities and incongruities in the supervisee's experiencing and communication. It is directed at discrepancies between the supervisor's and supervisee's perceptions in an attempt to

bring out, into the open, possible incongruence in the supervisee's feelings, attitudes, and behaviors. For example, confrontation might involve supervisors' pointing out that they
experience the supervisee differently than the supervisee does,
that they experience differences between what the supervisee
says and actually does, or that they experience differences in
the supervisee at different times. The sharing of these
perceptions, however, is not enough. Also the supervisor and
supervisee work through these differences of perceptions in a
climate of increasing supervisee self-understanding and
acceptance of personal responsibility. However, it may become
necessary to gauge the supervisee's readiness for such
confrontation, perhaps by encouraging further exploration of
the issue at hand. If unready, a supervisee not only may be
demoralized but even immobilized by premature confrontation
(Carkhuff, 1969). Again, at all times, the supervisor should
be guided by what is effective for the supervisee.

   Immediacy. Immediacy is focusing on what's going on
between the supervisor and the supervisee. This focus is
concerned with feelings and experiences that grow out of their
current interaction in the present, the "here and now." Whenever the supervisee is having recurrent problems with clients,
often a corresponding difficulty in supervision occurs. Thus,
whenever a supervisee brings a problem with a client to the
supervisor, the supervisor should begin to at least wonder what
its counterpart is in the supervisory relationship. As Cudney
(1968) pointed out, the way the supervisee related to the
supervisor may be a snapshot of how he/she relates to others,
especially clients. Kell and Mueller (1966), in their
discussion of the process of counselor supervision, suggested
that counselors often attempt to create a relationship with
their supervisor that is similar in some significant
dimensions to the relationship they have with one or more of
their clients. Supervision then can become an arena for
playing out the supervisees' difficulties with their clients.
Patterson (1974) suggested that perhaps it would be appropriate to focus on immediacy when the supervisory process seems
to be stalled.

LEVELS OF SUPERVISORY INTERVENTION

   While much of the substantiating evidence relating level
of helper functioning to constructive or deteriorative consequences for the helpee involves parent-child, teacher-student,
and counselor-client interactions, there is no reason to doubt
its generalization to supervisor-supervisee interactions.
Thus, supervision may be for "better or worse," depending not
only on the relationship variables or core conditions offered
but also on the level of functioning of the supervisor on
these core conditions.

At high levels of the core conditions, the supervisor is
sensitive to the feelings of supervisees and communicates this
understanding (empathy), accepts supervisees as persons
capable of growth without evaluating their feelings and
behavior (respect), and helps them to explore their feelings,
behaviors, and experiences in specific terms (concreteness).
The supervisor is honest, open, and sincere when interacting
with the supervisee (genuineness), strives to reduce
discrepancies in the supervisee's feelings, attitudes, and
behaviors (confrontation), and brings the supervisee's
problems with clients into the context of the supervisory
relationship whenever appropriate (immediacy). Thus, high-
level functioning supervisors not only respond more accurately
to the feelings and meaning of the supervisee's expressions but
their responses are related to the statements of the supervisee.
In contrast, at low levels the supervisor ignores even the most
obvious feelings, is judgmental and does not see the supervisee's worth, and deals with him/her at an abstract level.
The supervisor is not real with the supervisee in their
relationship. Thus, low-level functioning supervisors are not
only inaccurate in responding to the feelings and meanings
experienced by the supervisee, but their responses are
unrelated to what the supervisee has shared.

Some examples to help clarify differences between low-
level detractive responses, and high-level additive responses
are the following:

Facilitative Responses	Empathy
Supervisee Statement:	Sometimes I feel that I can't be of help to anyone. Sometimes I wonder if I'll ever be a good therapist.
Low-level, Detractive Supervisor Response:	Everybody gets discouraged sometimes. Don't sit around and feel sorry for yourself.
Minimally Facilitative Supervisor Response:	Sometimes you feel as if you don't have any impact at all on your clients, and you wonder if you ever will.
High-level, Additive Supervisor Response:	Sometimes you get discouraged because you feel you aren't helping your clients change. But even more, you get discouraged because you feel you can't help yourself change.

Respect

Supervisee Statement:	I just couldn't help it. She made me so mad I told her I didn't want to see her again.
Low-level, Detractive Supervisor Response:	I don't care how you feel. It's the client that's important. Aren't you ever going to learn?
Minimally Facilitative Supervisor Response:	She made you so mad you just didn't see how you could continue to work with her?
High-level, Additive Supervisor Response:	You seem as if you were exasperated not only by your client's behavior but also by your own behavior. I wonder if you felt frustrated because you felt you weren't getting anywhere with her.

Concreteness

Supervisee Statement:	I don't know why I don't want to work with elderly clients. I guess it's because they're so much older than I am.
Low-level, Detractive Supervisor Response:	It seems that this may be a problem with people you see as authority figures. I wonder what your relationship has been with older authority figures in your life--for instance, your parents.
Minimally Facilitative Supervisor Response:	I wonder if what you're feeling is not so much that these clients are older, but that you are younger.
High-level, Additive Supervisor Response:	I get the feeling that it's not that you don't want to work with older clients, but it's that you don't want to work with clients who you don't believe will respect you--in this case, because of the age difference.

Action-Oriented Responses

Genuineness

Supervisee Statement:

I want to know--Am I handling this case properly? Am I operating in the client's best interests? Or are my values entering in too much?

Low-level, Detractive Supervisor Response:

Yeah...Those are good questions. But I think I'll let you answer those questions yourself. I don't want to add my opinions to your confusion.

Minimally Facilitative Supervisor Response:

You seem to be questioning how well you're handling the case and are looking to me for some answers.

High-level, Additive Supervisor Response:

Hey, I've had lots of doubts about some of my cases too, and I know how important another person's impressions of "how I'm doing" can be. While I think that most of the time you are with your client, there do seem to be times when you try to force your values on her. For instance...

Confrontation

Supervisee Statement:

Of course, I believe it's important to be honest at all times with my clients. Don't you think I have been?

Low-level, Detractive Supervisor Response:

Er umm...Maybe we need to go over your tapes again. Perhaps then you can answer your own questions.

Minimally Facilitative Supervisor Response:

You're wondering if I perceive you as being honest at all times with your clients.

High-level, Additive Supervisor Response:	While you believe it's important to be honest with your clients, I sense that you have doubts about whether you are as open and honest as you could be.

Immediacy

Supervisee Statement:	I'm not sure whether I should continue with our supervision sessions. You--they don't seem to be helping me. They seem so impersonal.
Low-level, Detractive Supervisor Response:	You feel like calling it quits.
Minimally Facilitative Supervisor Response:	It's important for you to work with someone you feel is concerned with you.
High-level, Additive Supervisor Response:	You're telling me you feel $\underline{I}$ don't really care about you as a person.

METHODS OF SUPERVISORY INTERVENTION

In Chapter 1, Boyd wrote about the four main activities which comprise supervision: <u>consultation</u>, <u>counseling</u>, <u>training and instruction</u>, and <u>evaluation</u>. Other writers also have sought to define supervision in terms of its component activities. The relationship approach differs from this conception of supervision as the sum of its component activities; the supervisory process is defined, not in terms of certain activities, but in terms of the relationships provided. These relationships are expressions of supervisors' attitudes, with their specific responses, techniques, and activities flowing from these attitudes. Thus, the activities of consultation, counseling, training and instruction, and evaluation are forms or methods of supervisory interventions rather than defining entities. These activities will be considered methods of supervisory intervention within the relationship approach.

Consultation

Consultation is the act of providing advice and counsel to the supervisee on both personal and professional problems. Traditionally, the consultant's role has been to determine the needs of the supervisee and, after careful deliberation, to recommend or direct what to do. While on the surface this action may seem to be both an efficient and an effective way of helping the supervisee, at a deeper level such an approach is seen to be more of a growth-inhibiting than a growth-enhancing intervention. Such an approach suggests that the supervisor does not believe in the supervisee's ability to search for and find his/her own answers and that the supervisor, rather than the supervisee, is responsible for the supervisee's growth and development. This approach, obviously, is incompatible with helping supervisees become independent and self-reliant, assuming responsibility for and directing their own learnings. The emphasis should not be on solving supervisees' difficulties for them but on helping them to work with these problems through themselves. Thus, supervision is seen to be a shared rather than a directed journey.

The supervisor needs to guard against being seduced into becoming a problem solver for the supervisee. While there is a certain seductive quality in finding the answer to a problem which is troubling the supervisee, the danger inherent in such activity is that solving the specific problem becomes an end in itself rather than helping supervisees develop to the point where they can solve such problems themselves. Such an approach manifests a lack of personal and professional respect for supervisees and detracts from their developing a professional identity separate from that of the supervisor. The supervisee is apt to become or remain dependent on such a supervisor and may well become no more than an extension of the supervisor. One should note that such consulting or advice-giving more often satisfies the needs of the supervisor for ego-gratification or self-esteem, rather than the needs of the supervisee.

The authors are not suggesting that counsel should not be given. Rather, the question becomes the context in which such consultation should occur. Instead of advocating or urging a particular solution, the supervisor should share his/her perceptions of the supervisee's situation for the purpose of stimulating deeper self-exploration on the part of the supervisee. For instance, suppose the supervisee is having difficulty in determining how to approach a particular client differently in order to be of more help. The supervisor might offer perceptions of the supervisee's difficulties in the context of "Here's what seems to me to be going on. . . I wonder what your reaction to this is." The emphasis in this response does not lie in suggesting or directing the supervisee to implement a particular course of action but in encouraging the supervisee to initiate self exploration in a direction which he/she had not considered. The supervisee should be further encouraged to explore what caused him/her to overlook this particular course as a possible alternative. If such a course is eventually selected, it should be selected because the supervisee found it to be meaningful, not because the supervisor found it so, nor because the supervisee was dependent, yielding to authority, unsure, desperate, or just not giving clients the attention they deserved.

Counseling

Counseling is a helping process, the aim of which is to enable the client to better utilize available resources to more effectively cope with the challenges of daily living. Within the supervisory process the aim of counseling is to enable the supervisee to better utilize the resources available in order to more effectively cope with the challenges of professional work. Thus much similarity exists between counseling and supervision. Both are therapeutic experiences that occur within a relationship, with self-exploration as the essential process. The characteristics of a good supervisory relationship are identical to those of a good counseling relationship. Both supervision and counseling begin where the person is in the present and continue as far as he/she is able or willing to go. But while supervision and counseling are both helping processes with similar goals, methods, techniques, and basic processes, there is nevertheless a difference in focus. Where counseling is primarily focused upon the personal problems of the client, the focus of supervision is primarily the professional problems of the supervisee.

While there are some professional problems that are cognitive, dealing with a lack of information, knowledge, or skill, the greater portion of professional problems involve the persons or selves of the supervisees, their own intrapersonal dynamics and the interpersonal dynamics of their relationships with their clients. Becoming a more fully-functioning helper often involves becoming a more fully-functioning person. The supervisor must maintain a dual perspective, moving between the personal and professional aspects of the supervisee in assisting in the development of an effective helper.

In supervision, the supervisee's personal problems are considered only as they relate to professional functioning. For consideration of those personal problems apart from his professional functioning, the supervisee should be referred. Or, if mutually acceptable, such consideration could occur in a relationship between the supervisor and supervisee, either in sessions apart from supervision or, if not requiring extensive work, in the supervisory sessions. However, consideration of such personal problems should supplement, not replace, consideration of the supervisee's professional functioning. Thus, the line between the personal and professional growth of the counselor, between counseling and supervision, may become so fine that, for most practical purposes, the differentiation is often meaningless. The most meaningful observation is that supervision and counseling contain many of the same elements.

Training and instruction

Instruction is the act of imparting specific information or knowledge to the supervisee, while training is the act of helping the supervisee to develop a particular skill or set of skills. Training and instruction are both seen to be aspects of the teaching process, with instruction helping the supervisee to develop a factually supported basis from which to operate, and training helping the supervisee to translate this factual basis into effective helping skills. For example, a counselor in a mental health center may lack sufficient knowledge of the various kinds of psychological tests and may require training in their administration and interpretation for use in psychological evaluations. Or, a counselor in a rehabilitation center might need both instruction to fill gaps in knowledge concerning the effects of the many kinds of physical and mental impairments on client functioning, and training to develop the skills involving the use of such technical information in the counseling process. Or, a counselor in a vocational counseling agency might need to acquire a greater command of occupational information and develop skill in using this information to help a client make the most appropriate vocational and career decisions.

The amount of training and instruction the supervisor will need to provide the supervisee will depend on the level of the supervisee's knowledge, experience, and skills, as well as on the specific requirements of the particular work setting. The focus of such training and instruction initially should be on the supervisee's knowledge of and communication of the facilitative and action-oriented relationship variables and then on the supervisee's command of and provision of various modes of treatment. Hopefully, the greater portion of training and instruction would have been accomplished in the supervisee's formal preparation program. However, this is often not the case. Further, with the increasing employment of untrained or only partially trained sub- or para-professionals in the many and varied mental health related agencies, an increased responsibility is placed on the supervisor to help supervisees acquire the necessary knowledge and develop the necessary skills to be of maximum help to their clients.

Although training and instruction primarily focus on content rather than feelings, on activities or techniques rather than attitudes, these interventions are nevertheless not incompatible with the relationship approach to supervision.

In the teaching area there is evidence to indicate that the level of functioning of the teacher on the relationship conditions is related to the learning achievement of the student (Aspy & Hadlock, 1969). The effective supervisor, then, is not simply a knowledgeable person who communicates knowledge and insight to a supervisee. Rather, the effective supervisor is a person who offers expertise in a relationship based on high levels of the facilitative and action-oriented dimensions.

In providing training and instruction, the supervisor should be aware of and strive to avoid those pitfalls which would detract from the supervisee's developing into an independent and fully-functioning helper.

1. The supervisor should guard against allowing the supervisee to become dependent upon the supervisor as the monitor and director of learning. Instead, the supervisor should encourage the supervisee to assume as much responsibility as possible for his/her own growth. Rather than simply answering questions the supervisee might raise, the supervisor should encourage and help the supervisee to search for answers. For example, suppose the supervisee approaches the supervisor regarding the various sources of occupational information. The supervisor might suggest certain resource material--e.g., Hoppock's Occupational Information and Hollis & Hollis', Personalizing Information Process--and offer to discuss the supervisee's readings when he/she feels ready. Such an approach would leave the primary responsibility for directing learning with the super- visee. Thus, while demonstrating a willingness to help, the supervisor would not be assuming full responsibility for the growth of the supervisee. Rather, this approach would be sharing in the responsi- bility for supervisee learning while leaving the greater share of this responsibility with the super- visee. The supervisor's function would be to supple- ment what the supervisee had learned and to explore how this material might be utilized in work with clients. Thus, whenever possible, the supervisor should put the supervisee in touch with resource material rather than serve as a source. However, such might not always be possible, in which case the super- visor will necessarily have to assume greater responsi- bility for presenting material and/or programs.

2. A second tendency supervisors need to guard against is providing training and instruction based on what they think is important rather than on what the supervisee thinks is important.

The danger here is that the supervisor, in directing the learning of the supervisee, may base decisions regarding the areas in which the supervisee needs training or instruction on his/her own theoretical approach to helping rather than on the supervisee's. In such a situation, the supervisor would not be dealing with the supervisee from where he/she was but from where the supervisor felt the supervisee should be. Such an attitude results from the supervisor's operating from an external rather than from an internal frame of reference and communicates a lack of both personal and professional respect for the supervisee's search for ways of helping. This approach could result in the supervisee becoming little more than an extension of the supervisor rather than a self-reliant professional helper.

Whenever differences of opinion as to what is important for the supervisee to know or to practice arise, these differences should be discussed openly in an atmosphere characterized by deep levels of the core conditions. Such an interchange might well bring the supervisee to a more intimate encounter with his/her theoretical position by forcing the giving of a more detailed clarification, resulting in a deeper level of understanding for the supervisee of this approach to helping. As a result of such an interchange based on acceptance and respect, the supervisee would feel less threatened, lower defenses, and begin to consider objectively his/her theoretical basis or bias. Or, it might be that the focus of the interchange should shift away from content to the feelings of the supervisee's apparent tendency to become defensive and rigid when disagreement occurs. In such circumstances the supervisor must be especially sensitive to the difference between honest disagreement and defensiveness. Possibly the supervisor is the one being defensive and rigid. If this were the case, it would suggest that supervision was being conducted from the supervisor's own perspective rather than from that of the supervisee. It is most essential that, at the outset of supervision, the theoretical position of the supervisor be stated clearly and concisely so that the supervisee will know from where the supervisor is coming. Thereafter, interactions with the supervisee should be based on the relationship conditions, which include acceptance and respect, and should flow from the supervisor's adoption of the supervisee's frame of reference.

If the supervisor is unable to accept and respect the theoretical basis from which the supervisees are operating, it is extremely unlikely that he/she will provide them with the kind of relationship necessary for them to explore and experience themselves and their work and to use this experience to grow. Supervisees need to feel that they have meaningful input into the supervisory process, that their relationship with their supervisor is based on mutually shared acceptance and respect rather than on authority. If training and instruction arbitrarily are imposed, likely sufficient resentment and defensiveness will be generated as to make the effect of such learning negligible. If this be the case, arrangements should be made for the supervisee to work with a supervisor who can provide the acceptance and respect necessary.

3. A third tendency against which the supervisor needs to guard is allowing the temporary adoption of a didactic strategy to overshadow what is primarily a relationship approach to supervision. The supervisor needs enough self-discipline to be able to move in and out of the specific role of trainer or instructor without detracting from the more general and pervasive role of supervisor.

Evaluation

Evaluation is the process of assessing the effects of the supervisee's professional performance on clients. Traditionally, evaluation has been conceptualized as an end in itself, a single event that takes place at a specified point in time, as required by the agency or decided by the supervisor. In these instances, evaluation often takes the form of a formal written judgment of the "goodness" or "badness" of the supervisee's efforts to be of help to clients. Evaluation, however, should be more a means than an end, more of an ongoing, continuous process than a single event. The goal of evaluation should be supervisee growth. The focus of evaluation should be the effect of the supervisee on clients. The process of evaluation should both involve and require the supervisor to share perceptions of the supervisee's work and to confront the supervisee with this assessment of the supervisee's efforts to be of help. However, whether such confrontations are seen as challenges to be met or as threats to be avoided depends on whether the supervisee feels adequate or capable enough to meet such confrontations and whether they are approached defensively or nondefensively. The authors suggest that such confrontations be introduced within the framework of a non-threatening, supportive, and caring relationship, one

460

characterized by the six core conditions. The supervisor should be constructive and positively oriented in evaluations, focusing on the supervisee's strengths as well as weaknesses. Further, the supervisor should avoid being general, vague, or ambiguous in evaluations and be as specific, concise, and to the point as possible.

Evaluation should not be simply a reactive judgment of the supervisor to the supervisee; instead, evaluation can be an active effort to promote the supervisee's growth. The supervisor must therefore go beyond simply pointing out the supervisee's strong and weak areas and provide an opportunity for supervisees to react to those evaluations, encouraging them to explore how they might utilize their strengths in overcoming their weaknesses. Evaluation thus is seen to be a shared process in which the supervisor and supervisee work together for the growth of the supervisee.

Evaluation should be not only _of_ the supervisee but _with_ him/her, as well. The supervisee should have the opportunity always to introduce personal input into the evaluation process. The ongoing informal assessments that take place throughout the supervisory sessions could be in the form of free and open interchanges between the supervisor and supervisee. The formal and often required evaluations that take place at specified times could be in the form of jointly submitted written evaluations, one by the supervisor and one by the supervisee. In such an arrangement the supervisee would come to feel more like a colleague than a subordinate. In experiencing the respect of the supervisor, the supervisee would not only experience increased self-respect but also develop a sense of professional identity.

The supervisor should encourage the supervisee to go beyond simply reacting to his/her assessments. He/she should encourage the supervisee to assume increasingly more initiative in evaluating his/her own professional performance. This task could be done on a scheduled basis, with self-evaluations being either informal interchanges with the supervisor or formal written self-assessments. Thus, as the supervisory process unfolds, the focus of evaluation would shift from the supervisor to a more mutually shared process in which supervisees would become more and more responsible not only for their own growth but also for their own assessment. Only in this way can supervisees ever become independent, self-reliant, and able to direct and monitor their own progress.

The authors do not suggest that the supervisor should eventually transfer ultimate responsibility for evaluation to the supervisee. While it is important for the supervisee to share in this process as much as possible, ultimate responsibility for evaluation nevertheless rests with the supervisor, who has a responsibility to the profession, to the agency, to the supervisee, and most importantly the client, to monitor the services provided and to insure that under the circumstances the best possible services are being provided. Given that the supervisee is probably not a master therapist, perhaps the most practical and meaningful criterion for exercising this responsibility and intervening is where the client is obviously being hurt and the supervisee refuses to accept this possibility. Otherwise, the supervisor should allow his/her supervisees as much responsibility as possible for directing and monitoring their own efforts.

One should note that the criteria for such an intervention must necessarily be based upon the supervisor's theoretical approach; consequently, the supervisor and supervisee should be closely aligned in their theoretical approaches. There might otherwise emerge a situation in which the supervisee has certain criteria for helping while the supervisor has different, perhaps opposite, criteria for judging the effect of the supervisee's effort to help.

Since evaluations are based on the perceptions of the supervisor, these evualuations are subjective in nature and should be recognized as such. Supervisors need to guard against becoming overly arbitrary or biased in their assessments because of their own theoretical rationale for helping. Their evaluations should primarily be based on an understanding of and acceptance of a supervisee's theoretical framework, even if supervisors don't agree with it. And it is within this framework that assessment should occur. Otherwise, the supervisee would be evaluated on criteria other than that on which he/she operates. If supervisors find it impossible to accept the theoretical framework of a supervisee, then the responsibility is to find the supervisee someone who could accept his/her theoretical rationale with whom to work. It also is essential that, whatever the criteria, the supervisee should know the bases of evaluation. Whether or not the supervisor's theoretical rationale differs from the supervisee's, the essence of the evaluative criteria used should be the supervisee's ability to offer clients a relationship built upon the core relationship conditions, since these have been demonstrated to be basic and essential to all approaches to helping. Additional criteria then should be mutually negotiated between the supervisor and supervisee.

An apparent dilemma in supervision is: How can the supervisory session be nonthreatening if evaluation is an integral and ongoing part of the process? As Patterson (1964) pointed out, threat cannot be entirely removed in the supervisory relationship any more than in many other situations. While threat cannot be completely removed, it can be reduced to generally acceptable limits. Reduction of fear or anxiety is accomplished by approaching evaluation as a shared process occurring within a facilitative relationship with the goal of helping the supervisee's growth rather than, as is traditional, approaching evaluation as an arbitrary impersonal judgment of the worth of the supervisee, that judgment occurring as an isolated event, devoid of acceptance, respect, and caring. Accepting that evaluation is always threatening to some degree, the question then becomes whether or not the supervisee is overwhelmed by minimized threat. It may become necessary to help the supervisee work through a difficulty in dealing with minimally threatening situations as part of the supervisory process.

MODELS OF SUPERVISORY INTERVENTION

The supervisory process has been viewed in terms of two phases, corresponding to the two categories--facilitative and action-oriented--of core conditions. During the initial phase, the goal is supervisee self-exploration and self-experiencing, both at a personal and professional level. During the later phase, the goal is to help the supervisee establish and operate in a constructive direction. The supervisor helps supervisees to return to the realities of their professional environment after having effectively explored and realized a deeper and more functional appreciation of themselves. The issue now becomes, "What are you going to do with these new understandings?" The answer, of course, lies in considering the various alternative courses of action, their long- and short-term advantages and disadvantages, and in choosing the best approach available.

To a greater or lesser degree, all of the core conditions can be present throughout the supervisory process. Action-oriented conditions may not be unique, or separate from, but are actually extensions of the facilitative conditions, where genuineness is born of respect for the supervisee, confrontation is a striving for concreteness, and immediacy is empathy in the present. It might therefore be more appropriate to consider the supervisory experience as a single, continuous, developmental process in which certain conditions are implemented at deeper and deeper levels, with a differentiation into two stages more conceptual than actual.

The relationship approach to the supervisory process is based on extensive research demonstrating that the helper's effectiveness can be accounted for independent of his orientation and technique, based on the level of the core conditions offered. One should not assume that systematic

attention to these core conditions excludes the employment of
other additional modes of therapeutic intervention. While
increasing evidence demonstrates the necessity of the helper
providing high levels of core conditions, there nevertheless
exists a good deal of controversy concerning the sufficiency
of these conditions. Within the relationship, all potential
modes of therapeutic intervention should be considered which
might contribute to the supervisee's, and ultimately the
client's, change or gain beyond the provision of a relationship
built around the core conditions offered at increasingly higher
levels.

A simple model, utilizing the three facets of supervisory
intervention, has been developed by the authors to show the
three-dimensional relationship of supervisor-supervisee interaction. This model illustrated in Figure 11.1 demonstrates how
each facet-the level of intervention, its conditions (facilitative and action-oriented), and the methods used to accomplish
each stage in counselor growth-is related to the other two.

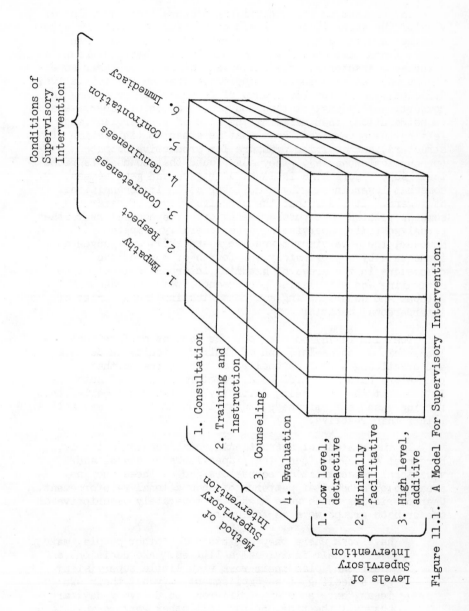

Figure 11.1. A Model For Supervisory Intervention.

465

SUPERVISION: THE SUPERVISEE'S VIEW

In considering the supervisory process from the point of view of the supervisee, it would be helpful to consider just how the supervisee views the supervisor. Smits and Aiken (1969) found that counselors in vocational rehabilitation agencies characterized the leadership behavior of their supervisors more as allowing the supervisee freedom for initiative, decision, and action (tolerance of freedom) and regarding the comfort, well-being, status, and contribution of supervisees (consideration) than defining the role of a supervisor and letting the supervisees know what is expected (initiation of structure) and applying pressure for productive output (production emphasis). They also found that counselors rated their supervisors high in level of regard and genuineness, somewhat lower in empathy, and lower still in unconditionality of regard. It seems that the perceived level of regard is somehow related to counselor behavior. The counselors further perceived their supervisors to be generally competent. However, the supervisor's knowledge and skill was judged as inadequate by approximately one-fourth or more of the counselors in the areas of handling interpersonal relations, motivating and stimulating performance, teaching casework methods and understanding and communicating the dynamics of interpersonal behavior.

Donigian (1974) pointed out the lack of professional leadership of counselors and of their difficulty in defining and practicing a professional role. He indicated that counselors have been trained as reactors instead of actors. In somewhat the same vein, Smith (1976) stated the belief that, for increased effectiveness, supervision should be more active rather than reactive.

In their study of occupational reinforcement patterns, Borgen et al (1968) found that supervisors of school and vocational rehabilitation counselors judged these two job areas to offer similar patterns of occupational reinforcement. Characteristics which were highly or moderately descriptive of one or both groups were as follows:

> have work where they do things for other people, make use of their individual abilities, make decisions on their own, plan their work with little supervision, get a feeling of accomplishment, try out their own ideas, have something different to do every day, are busy all the time, do not tell other workers what to do

(p. 61). Rosen et al, (1972) found that supervisors of counselors in private employment agencies believed this job area to have most of these same characteristics, also. Fay and Moses (1972) carried this line of investigation one step

farther and compared the perception of vocational rehabilitation counselors with those of their supervisors. An
extremely high correlation was found which indicated, at
least for their population, that there is significant
agreement between supervisors and counselors as to what
aspects of the job constitute occupational reinforcement. They
also found substantially high agreement between vocational
rehabilitation supervisors of two different states as to what
needs were being satisfied by the job and what reinforcers were
present.

Smits and Aiken (1969) also found a significant relationship between supervisee assessment of supervisory behavior and
supervisee job satisfaction. Muthard and Miller (1966)
regarded supervisee job satisfaction as an important criterion
in personnel management. Smits (1971) suggested that the
supervisor is influential in contributing to supervisee morale.
"In short, if the counselor is the direct link between the
agency and the client, the supervisor is the direct link
between the counselor and the agency" (p. 7).

Ronan (1970) suggested that supervisory behavior is the
link between the supervisee's job satisfaction and job
performance. While supervisory behavior cannot be termed the
causal explanation for either supervisee job satisfaction or
job performance, it may provide a link in translating satisfaction into performance and vice versa. If, then, supervisee
job satisfaction is related to job performance, logic suggests
that the key person in most attempts to increase supervisee
job satisfaction would be the supervisor. Thus, as Smits
(1971) suggested:

> To the supervisor will fall the challenge of
> keeping counselors emotionally involved in
> their work; in helping them progress in their
> professional development; of teaching them
> how to deal with difficult assignments so that
> the executive aspects of the job are seen as
> a challenge rather than a burden; and of
> giving them performance objectives, emotional
> support, accurate feedback and praise when
> they perform well (p. 60).

SUGGESTIONS FOR SUPERVISORS

A number of writers have offered some very practical
suggestions for supervisors, Hall and Warren (1956) and the
Joint Liaison Committee (1963) being two such sources. The
following list of suggestions is based on a combination of
these references and suggests a number of objectives which
the supervisor should consider and strive toward in working
with supervisees.

1. Help the counselor experience the realities of the counselor-client and the supervisor-supervisee relationship.

2. Enable the counselor to organize and consolidate his/her philosophy and attitudes.

3. Help the counselor acquire greater proficiency and confidence in applying theoretical knowledge and in integrating skills.

4. Enhance the formulation of an identification with a professional role and incorporate high standards of professional ethics.

5. Provide for an awareness of the process of community organization in meeting the needs of the client.

6. Help the counselor to work cooperatively with the supervisor, fellow workers, and cooperating personnel.

7. Help the counselor recognize that he/she provides an essential service not performed by other related professional persons.

8. Acquaint the counselor with organizational structure, protocol, relationships, processes, and working conditions of the employing agency.

9. Help the counselor and supervisor to identify areas of specialization for which the counselor may have particular interest or aptitude.

10. Provide an opportunity for the counselor and supervisor to evaluate the strengths and weaknesses of the counselor as well as the agency itself.

11. Enable counselors to try out knowledge and techniques under conditions which are less likely to be injurious to the client.

Problem Areas

Stotsky (1963) talked about various difficulties, tensions, and impasses which might arise within the supervisory relationship and divert attention from the problem the supervisor and supervisee are trying to solve. He (1963, pp. 2-3) suggested the following problem areas:

1. Gratification of one's own needs for self-aggrandizement by keeping client dependent upon counselor, or counselor on supervisor.

468

2. The wish to play God or omnipotent, beneficent father.

3. Fear of taking or encouraging others to take risks lest failure reflect unfavorably on your self-esteem.

4. Overidentification with client or counselor.

5. Imposition of one's own personal values on others or on the situation itself. As it is, the client often identifies with the values of the counselor.

6. The client or the counselor may remind the supervisor favorably or unfavorably of some affectively important person in his life. Supervisor may react to client or to counselor as he would to this significant figure.

7. Counselor or supervisor may entertain stereotype attitudes or prejudices to the group of which the client is a member. These may in turn influence the latter's response. Reactions may occur both ways to the stereotype rather than to the true person.

8. Supervisor may pursue certain points raised by client with counselor in a compulsive manner, regardless of their appropriateness to the problem. The supervisor may ride his own hobby horses and pet projects in a similar manner.

9. Having achieved a level of stability in his relationship with the client, the counselor may be unwilling to disturb the equilibrium of the patient. The supervisor may feel it to be unwise to disturb the equilibrium even though no progress is being made to resolve the dependency impasse.

10. Situational factors in the counselor's or supervisor's life, e.g., domestic difficulties, may influence his thinking and actions in a manner unsuitable to the present relationship.

11. Ethical, moral, and religious questions, which may not be applicable in this particular situation, may influence the counselor's or supervisor's judgment and behavior. In some instances, they may also restrain him from confronting the client with evidence that he is resisting change.

12. Fear of loss of the patient's respect or approval may prohibit or inhibit the counselor's work.

13. Excessive identification with the underdog regardless of the merits of the latter's position.

14. The manner by which the counselor structures his role as representative of the agency-social agent, giver or withholder, etc. View of client as helpless, social orphan or a deceitful person, intent on fooling the agency. This category is less applicable to the supervisor-counselor relationship, but even there the role prescriptions are not so fixed that deviations or distortions do not occur.

15. Degree of interest in objectivity may be low. This again demonstrates the need for a detached observer, a view by a third man into the relationship.

16. Conflict within counselor or supervisor as to whether he is a "company" man or advocate for the client. Role may tend to become marginal and with the loss of objectivity comes the temptation to move in one or the other direction. The supervisor in particular may have strong inhibitions against enforcing the rules and policies of the agency if, in doing so, he loses the "nice guy" self-image.

17. Seeing counselor as a threat or rival. This is accentuated if supervisor has doubts about his own capacity or wonders if his counselor is more knowledgeable than he.

18. Just as the client may delight in playing on the counselor's weaknesses and anxieties, so may the counselor do the same with the supervisor.

19. The question may arise of the relative importance of the dependency problem in the client's, counselor's and supervisor's thinking. Question of differences in point of view regarding positive and negative incentives, roundabout versus direct methods--all these may contribute to the impasse.

20. Ambivalence of counselor and supervisor about terminating a case.

Communication

Effective communication between supervisor and supervisee is essential if an optimum working relationship is to be developed and maintained. Growthproducing communication requires that it occur in an atmosphere of minimal threat where each party feels free to be open and receptive to the other. It is an interchange of ideas, thoughts, and feelings--a two-way process based upon mutual respect and consideration. Dooher and Marquis (1965) indicated ten points to consider to maximize effective communication. They were as follows:

--seek to clarify your ideas before communicating;
--examine the true purpose of each communication;
--consider the total physical and human setting whenever
   you communicate;
--consult with others, where appropriate, in planning
   communication;
--be mindful of the overtones, as well as the basic
   content of your message;
--take the opportunity, when it arises, to convey
   something of help or value to the receiver;
--follow up your communication;
--communicate for tomorrow as well as for today;
--be sure your actions support your communication;
--and seek not only to be understood, but to understand--
   be a good listener.

Morgan (n.d., p. 2) has developed a list of "Points to
Ponder" which contain a number of valuable hints which the
supervisor should consider when interacting with supervisees.
Suggestions were that these hints also might be considered by
the supervisee when interacting with his/her supervisor.

1. Be exceedingly wary of using and thinking in terms of
   absolutes, i.e., always, never.

2. Don't intimate solutions or make promises that can't
   reasonably be kept.

3. Perhaps the most acid test of our maturity is the way
   we react to immaturity in others. Do we act or react?

4. A concentrated effort to organize one's time is
   essential. Delegate when possible and feasible.

5. You can never know all the facts. Obtain those you can
   and act within those that are known.

6. To an extent, each man has his own language. Meaning
   lies not in words, but in individuals.

7. Because we understand something when we express it, it
   does not mean the other person does. Usually,
   anything that can be misunderstood will be misunderstood (Murphy's Law).

8. Just because you are who you are may be both a bane and
   a blessing. Certain factors about you--age, height,
   sex, accent, background--may make it difficult (or may
   facilitate) your work with another.

9. First of all, we are all people. Too often we treat
   others as if they were laborers, professionals, saints,
   sinners, rather than as persons.

In addition to communication problems, which are
potentially present in all forms of relationships, a number of
other problems must be guarded against. Since to be forewarned
is to be forearmed, some of the more common ones will be noted.

The supervisor must not do the work for the supervisee.
Sometimes this is easier than getting the supervisee to do it.
"If you want something done right, do it yourself" may be
feasible in many situations, but in the long run it is
inefficient and contraindicated in a supervisor-supervisee
relationship.

Making Corrections

Many supervisors may find it difficult to correct supervisees. Fair (1969, p.3) offered the following suggestions
which should facilitate this process.

1. Pick the right time to make even the most unimportant
   correction. Make it soon after the event, but not so
   soon that any hurt feelings are still raw.

2. Select the right setting. Privacy is best.

3. Recognize the emotional feelings of the individual.
   Not all people respond to some set formula.

4. Avoid surprise: it is best to drop a hint of what is
   coming.

5. Keep your own reactions under control and in proper
   perspective. The mistake may be familiar to you, but
   it may be that particular employee's first.

6. Keep emotion out. Bad humor tends to feed and build
   upon itself.

7. Be sure of all the facts involved. One error of fact
   can ruin what follows.

8. Keep the individual's personality out of the
   discussion.

9. Don't compare one person's performance with another's.
   This tends to build staff discord, and to alienate the
   one being held up as an example.

10. Close with an effort to restore the individual's
    confidence in himself.

SUPERVISEE GAMES

Kadushin (1968) wrote an amusing, yet interesting and
useful article on the games people play in supervision.
Although he admitted that they are caricatures and that
supervisors also play games in supervision, he emphasized the
games played by the supervisees.

One set of games is designed to manipulate demand levels
imposed on the supervisee. One such game, called "Two Against
the Agency" is seduction by subversion while another, "Be Nice
to Me Because I Am Nice to You" is seduction by flattery.

Another set of games is designed to redefine the relationship. The game called "Protect the Sick and Infirm" or "Treat
Me, Don't Beat Me" is one in which the supervisees expose
themselves rather than their work. "Evaluation Is Not For
Friends" is a game designed to convert the relationship into
a social one. "Maximum Feasible Participation" is another
game which puts the supervisory relationship on a peer basis,
thus allowing the supervisee to call the shots.

Reduction of the power disparity is the goal of another
series of games which the supervisee can play. "If You Knew
Kostoyevsky Like I Know Kostoyevsky" is a game which puts
the supervisor on the defensive and may actually reverse the
roles of supervisor and supervisee. "So What Do You Know About
It" is similar; in this game the supervisee capitalizes on the
fact that the supervisor has not had the benefit of the supervisee's experiences. "All or Nothing at All" is a game
designed to make the supervisor feel guilty for compromising
or going along with the power structure.

Other games developed by the supervisee to control the
supervisory session include "I Have a Little List." This game
enables the supervisee to structure the session by posing
questions to the supervisor. "Heading Them Off at the Pass"
takes the form of severe self-criticism by the supervisee.
"Little Old Me" is a game in which the supervisee acts
dependent and helpless and shifts the responsibility onto the
supervisor. The sequel to this game is "I Did Like You Told
Me" which places the blame for the failure on the supervisor.
"It's All So Confusing" is a frequently used alibi, meaning,
since authories don't agree, how can one say for sure just
what is the most desirable course of action?

473

Fear of personal change may cause resistance in the supervisory relationship (Bauman, 1972). Some of the forms that resistance may take are submission, turning the tables, an "I'M no good" approach, helplessness, and projection. The supervisor should recognize that, regardless of the type of behavior the supervisee exhibits in the supervisory relationship, it is probably the same type of behavior that has been used effectively in similar situations. Some of the techniques which the supervisor may use to counteract supervisee resistance are: interpretation, feedback, generalization, ignoring, role playing, the alter-ego technique, and audiotaping.

Supervisors should be aware of the games that supervisees play. They should be equally aware of the games supervisors play on their supervisees and try to establish a relationship wherein neither feels the need for gamemanship.

SUMMARY

In proposing a relationship approach for supervision, the authors suggested certain necessary dimensions or conditions on which any supervisory intervention should be based. These dimensions were defined as the facilitative dimensions of empathy, respect, and concreteness and the action-oriented dimensions of genuineness, confrontation, and immediacy. Next, suggestion was that these dimensions could be offered at different levels. These levels were defined as low-level detractive, minimally facilitative, and high-level additive. Finally, suggestion was that certain basic forms or methods could be used in supervisory interventions. These forms were defined as consultation, counseling, training and instruction, and evaluation. These four concepts, when taken together and integrated define the supervisory relationship approach, one that is appropriate to any setting in which counselor supervision occurs. No differences should occur in the application of this model from one setting to another.

While most writers in the area of supervision tend to stress the role of the supervisor, suggestions were that perhaps too little attention has been given to the role of the supervisee. Since supervision is a two-way process, its success or failure depends on the supervisee as well as the supervisor.

Supervisees should be interested in the following:

1. Self-improvement and believe in the potential value of supervision.

2. Have confidence not only in the supervisory process but also in their supervisor.

474

3. Involve themselves in the process in an open, sincere, and nondefensive manner, and should be willing to explore themselves both personally and professionally with a self-critical attitude, searching out their weaknesses as well as their strengths.

4. Should not only want to increase their knowledge and sharpen their skills but be willing to put forth the necessary effort.

5. Need not be yielding but certainly should be receptive to their interactions with their supervisor.

6. Should not just want to grow, they should be willing to change.

If these are the qualities the supervisees need to bring into the supervisory process, what are the qualities which need to be developed through the supervisory process? Indeed, much has been written about the qualities of an effective counselor. While there is much agreement among authorities as to what makes for an effective helper, major differences all exist. Again, the problem consists of reconciling these differences in order to develop an integrated approach to supervision.

General agreement seems to be that the counselor must believe that, given the "right" conditions, the client is capable of positive change. General agreement also exists that the counselor must have a philosophy of helping and an integrated theory of human behavior in order to guide him/her in providing these conditions to the client. The authors suggest that the counselor who has never really developed a theory of behavior and a philosophy of helping will be influenced by every current of thought that comes along and will be unable to maintain consistency and continuity in relationships with clients. However, equally successful counselors may have quite different approaches to helping, the obvious consideration becomes which one of the many orientations to helping the supervisor should focus to help the supervisee become an effective facilitator of client growth. The supervisor's? The supervisee's? A combination of the two? Some suggest that a reasonable approach would be to take the best from all theories. Often however what one winds up with is not eclecticism, a meaningful combination of features from various sources into a harmonious whole, but syncretism, a hodge-podge of concepts and ideas without any attempt at unification or integration.

As was stated previously, there is substantial evidence that the crucial element of a counselor's effectiveness is not the adoption of a particular theory or the use of a given technique, but the ability to offer a therapeutic relationship based on the facilitative and action-oriented conditions. The ability of the counselor to offer empathy, respect, concreteness, genuineness, confrontation, and immediacy to clients then becomes both the goal of supervision and the criteria for assessing its success. As the supervisee develops skills in offering these conditions at deeper and deeper levels, the supervisor then may begin to consider and explore with the supervisee the many potential modes of therapeutic intervention. Though the sufficiency of a relationship based on the core conditions has yet to be satisfactorily established, such a relationship is unquestionably necessary for client growth. Whether these conditions are sufficient or not, they are necessary and thus must be present in any approach to helping and, as such, should be emphasized in supervision.

REFERENCES

Altucher, N. Constructive use of the supervisory relationship. Journal of Counseling Psychology, 1967, 14, 165-170.

Arbuckle, D. S. The learning of counseling: Process not product. Journal of Counseling Psychology, 1963, 10, 163-170.

Aspy, D. N., & Hadlock, W. The Effects of High and Low Functionary Teachers Upon Students' Academic Performance and Truancy. Unpublished study, in R. R. Carkhuff, (Ed.) Helping and Human Relations, Volume II. New York: Holt, Rinehart, & Winston, 1969.

Bauman, W. F. Games counselor trainees play: Dealing with trainee resistance. Counselor Education and Supervision, 1972, 11, 251-256.

Biasco, F., & Redfering, D. L. Effects of counselor supervision on group counseling: Client's perceived outcomes. Counselor Education and Supervision, 1976, 15, 216-220.

Borgen, F. H.; Weiss, D. J.; Tansley, H. E. A.; Dawis, R. V.; Lofquist, L. H. Occupational reinforcer patterns. Minnesota Studies in Vocational Rehabilitation, 1968b, 24.

Carkhuff, R. R. Helping and Human Relations. New York: Holt, Rinehart, & Winston, 1969. 2 vols.

Carkhuff, R. R., & Berenson, B. G. Beyond Counseling and Therapy. New York: Holt, Rinehart, & Winston, 1967.

Combs, A. W., & Soper, D. W. The perceptual organization of effective counselors. Journal of Counseling Psychology, 1963, 10, 222-226.

Cudney, M. R. The use of immediacy in counseling. In J. C. Hesten and W. B. Frick (Eds.) Counseling for the Liberal Arts Campus. Yellow Springs, Ohio: Antioch Press, 1968, 135-136.

Davidson, T. N., & Emmer, E. T. Immediate effect of supportive and non supportive supervisory behavior on counselor candidates' focus of concern. Counselor Education and Supervision, 1966, 6, 11-17.

Donigian, J. What counselors need: Professional leadership. Counselor Education and Supervision, 1974, 13, 316-317.

Dooher, M. J., & Marquis, V. Effective Communication on the Job. New York: American Management Association, 1965.

Dunlop, R. S. Pre-practicum education: Use of simulation program. Counselor Education and Supervision, 1968, 7, 145-146.

Fair, W. W. Making staff corrections smoothly. The Office Economist, 1969, 51, 3.

Fay, F. A., & Moses, H. A. Occupational reinforcer patterns of vocational rehabilitation. Rehabilitation Research and Practice Review, 1972, 3, 2, Special Spring Issue.

Gladstein, G. A. In-service education of counseling supervisors. Counselor Education and Supervision, 1970, 9, 183-188.

Goldin, G. J. A study of factors influencing counselor motivation in the six New England state rehabilitation agencies. Northeastern Studies in Vocational Rehabilitation, Boston: Northeastern University, 1965.

Hall, J. D., & Warren, S. H. (Eds.). Rehabilitation Counselor Preparation. Washington, D. C.: National Rehabilitation Association, 1965.

Hansen, J., & Stevic, R. Practicum in supervision: A proposal. Counselor Education and Supervision, 1967, 6, 205-206.

Hays, D. G. A need for dialogue. Counselor Education and Supervision, 1968, 7, 150-152.

Joint Liaison Committee. Studies in Rehabilitation Counselor Training: Guidelines for Supervised Clinical Practice. Minneapolis: Joint Liaison Committee, 1963.

Kadushin, A. Games people play in supervision. Social Work, 1968, 13, 23-32.

Kaplan, B. A. The new counselor and his professional problems. Personnel and Guidance Journal, 1964, 42, 473-478.

Kaplowitz, D. Teaching empathic responsiveness in the super-
    visory process of psychotherapy. American Journal of
    Psychotherapy, 1967, 21, 774-781.

Kell, B. L., & Mueller, W. J. Impact and Change: A Study of
    Counseling Relationships. New York: Appleton-Century-
    Crofts, 1966.
Krasner, L. The therapist as a social reinforcement machine.
    In H. H. Strupp and L. Luborsky (Eds.) Research in
    Psychotherapy. Volume II, Washington, D. C.: American
    Psychological Association, 1962.

Krumboltz, J. D. Changing the behavior of behavior changers.
    Counselor Education and Supervision, 1967, 6, 222-229.

Lambert, M. J. Supervisory and counseling process: A compara-
    tive study. Counselor Education and Supervision, 1974,
    14, 54-60.

Margulis, M. Growing the therapist. Voices: The Art and
    Science of Psychotherapy, 1970, 6, 52-55.

Miller, D. C., & Oetting, E. R. Students react to supervision.
    Counselor Education and Supervision, 1966, 6, 73-74.

Miller, L. A., & Roberts, R. R. Understanding the Work Milieu
    and Personnel in Developing Continuing Education for
    Rehabilitation Counselors. Report no. 2, Iowa City:
    University of Iowa, 1971.

Morgan, C. Points to Ponder. Unpublished Manuscript, Oklahoma
    State University, n.d.

Muthard, J. E., & Miller, L. A. The Criteria Problem in
    Rehabilitation Counseling. Iowa City: University of Iowa,
    1966. (a)

_____. Perceptions of rehabilitation counselor
    counselor behavior. Personnel and Guidance Journal, 1966,
    44, 517-522. (b)

Patterson, C. H. Supervising students in the counseling prac-
    ticum. Journal of Counseling Psychology, 1964, 11, 47-53.

_____. Theories of Counseling and Psychotherapy.
    (Second Ed.) New York: Harper & Row, 1973.

_____. Relationship Counseling and Psychotherapy. New
    York: Harper & Row, 1974.

Pinson, N. M. Supervision: The silent "S" of ACES. Counselor Education and Supervision, 1974, 14, 157-159.

Rogers, C. R. The necessary and sufficient conditions of personality change. Journal of Consulting Psychology, 1957, 21, 95-103.

_____. Two divergent trends. In R. May (Ed.) Existential Psychology. New York: Random House, 1961, 85-93.

Ronan, W. W. Individual and situational variables relating to job satisfaction. Journal of Applied Psychology Monograph, 1970, 54, 1.

Rosen, S. D.; Weiss, D. J.; Hendel, D. D.; Dawis, R. V.; & Lofquist, L. H. Occupational reinforcer patterns. Minnesota Studies in Vocational Rehabilitation, Volume II, 1972, 29.

Smith, E. J. Issues and problems in the group supervision of beginning group counselors. Counselor Education and Supervision, 1976, 16, 13-24.

Smits, S. J. Leadership Behaviors of Supervisors in State Rehabilitation Agencies. Atlanta: Georgia State University, 1971.

Smits, S. J., & Aiken, W. J. A Descriptive Study of Supervisory Practices as Perceived By Counselors in State Vocational Rehabilitation Agencies. Bloomington: Indiana University, 1969.

Stotsky, B. A. Understanding the motivation of counselors and supervisors in breaking barriers of dependency. In R. J. Margolin and F. L. Hurwitz (Eds.) Report on a Motivation and Dependency Workshop. Boston: Northeastern University, 1963.

Truax, C. B., & Carkhuff, R. R. Toward Effective Counseling and Psychotherapy: Training and Practice. Chicago: Aldine, 1967.

Truax, C. B.; Carkhuff, R. R.; & Douds, J. Toward an integration of the didactic and experiential approaches to training in counseling and psychotherapy. Journal of Counseling Psychology, 1964, 11, 240-247.

Wolpe, J. Psychotherapy by Reciprocal Inhibition. Stanford: Stanford University Press, 1958.

APPENDIX A

COUNSELOR COMPETENCY SCALE

For The Analysis And Assessment Of Counselor Competencies

This scale is an altered version of the "Survey of Counselor
    Competencies," developed by Dennis B. Cogan, Department of
    Counselor Education, Arizona State University, Tempe,
    Arizona 85282.

COUNSELOR COMPETENCY	ANALYSIS Skill Value to Interview			ASSESSMENT Proficiency	
	Non-Essential	Important	Critical	+	−

PERSONAL CHARACTERISTICS

1 SOCIAL RESPONSIBILITY - the counselor states, and his/her past experiences show, that he/she is interested in social change.
— — — — —

2 PEOPLE ORIENTED - the counselor is people oriented as demonstrated by his/her past experiences and by his/her present social interactions.
— — — — —

3 FALLIBILITY - the counselor recognizes that he/she is not free from making errors.
— — — — —

4 PERSONAL PROBLEMS - the counselor's personal problems are kept out of the counseling session.
— — — — —

5 MODELING - the counselor models appropriate cognitive processes, behaviors, and feelings during the counseling session.
— — — — —

6 NON-DEFENSIVE - the counselor gives and receives feedback to and from his/her clients, peers, and supervisor without making excuses or justifications.
— — — — —

Other _____
— — — — —

Other _____
— — — — —

Other _____
— — — — —

PHILOSOPHICAL FOUNDATIONS

7 EVALUATION - the counselor's theoretical frame of reference includes a means for describing the cognitive, behavioral and/or affective change (s) that take place in determining the effectiveness of the selected counseling strategy.
— — — — —

8 DIAGNOSIS - regardless of his/her theoretical orientation, the counselor can identify maladaptive symptomology consistent with his/her theoretical frame of reference.
— — — — —

9 THEORY - the counselor states his/her assumptions about human behavior, through which he/she will incorporate or abstract his/her empirical findings and through which he will make predictions concerning his/her client.
— — — — —

10 THEORY - the counselor explains human behavior from at least two theories of personality.
— — — — —

11 PRIORITIZING - the counselor decides on which problem, when presented with more than one, to deal with first according to his/her theoretical frame of reference.
— — — — —

12 INTERPRETATION - the counselor provides the client with a possible explanation for or relationships between certain behaviors, cognitions, and/or feelings.
— — — — —

	ANALYSIS Skill Value to Interview	ASSESSMENT Proficiency
COUNSELOR COMPETENCY		

Philosophical Foundations (continued)	Non-Essential Important Critical	+	−

13 PROGNOSIS - the counselor can make an evaluation of the client's potential for successful treatment consistent with theoretical frame of reference.

     — — — — —

14 INTERACTIONS - the counselor describes the interactions that take place between the counselor and client consistent with his/her theoretical frame of reference.

     — — — — —

15 DEFENSE MECHANISMS - the counselor is aware of the defense mechanisms used by the client, the purpose they serve, and can help the client substitute more appropriate ones for less appropriate ones.

     — — — — —

16 CATHARSIS - the counselor understands the concept of catharsis.

     — — — — —

17 NATURAL CONSEQUENCES - the counselor understands the concept of "natural consequences."

     — — — — —

18 ENVIRONMENTAL MANIPULATION - the counselor understands the concept of environmental manipulation.

     — — — — —

19 TEST SELECTION - the counselor selects an appropriate test (s) according to his/her theoretical frame of reference.

     — — — — —

20 INFERENCE - the counselor provides an explanation for and the functional use of the client's behaviors, cognitions, and/or feelings consistent with his/her theoretical frame of reference and how they might influence the counseling process.

     — — — — —

Other _____   — — — — —

Other _____   — — — — —

Other _____   — — — — —

COMMUNICATIONS

21 OPEN-ENDED QUESTION - the counselor asks the client a question that cannot be answered by a yes or no, and the question does not provide the client with the answer.

     — — — — —

22 MIMIMAL VERBAL RESPONSE - the counselor uses "mmmh, oh, yes" to communicate to the client that he/she is listening, without interrupting the client's train of thought or discourse.

     — — — — —

23 GENUINENESS - the counselor's responses are sincere and appropriate.

     — — — — —

24 POSITIVE REGARD - without interjecting his/her own values, the counselor communicates respect and concern for the client's feelings, experiences, and potentials.

     — — — — —

	ANALYSIS	ASSESSMENT
COUNSELOR COMPETENCY	Skill Value to Interview	Proficiency

Communications (continued)	Non-Essential Important Critical	+ −

25 LANGUAGE - the counselor uses terminology that is understood by the client.
— — — — —

26 CLARIFICATION - the counselor has the client clarify vague and ambiguous cognitions, behaviors, and/or feelings.
— — — — —

27 PARAPHRASING - without changing the meaning, the counselor states in fewer words what the client has previously stated.
— — — — —

28 SUMMARIZES - the counselor combines two or more of the client's cognitions, feelings, and/or behaviors into a general statement.
— — — — —

29 RESTATEMENT - the counselor conveys to the client that he/she has heard the content of the client's previous statement (s) by restating in exactly or near exact words, that which the client has just verbalized.
— — — — —

30 EMPATHIC UNDERSTANDING - the counselor's responses add noticeably to the expressions of the client in such a way as to express feelings at a level deeper than the client was able to express for himself/ herself.
— — — — —

31 REFLECTION - from non-verbal cues the counselor accurately describes the client's affective state.
— — — — —

32 PERCEPTIONS - the counselor labeled his/her perceptions as perceptions.
— — — — —

33 CONFRONTATION - the counselor confronts the client by stating the possible consequences of his/her behaviors, cognitions, and/or feelings.
— — — — —

34 SUPPORTIVE - the counselor makes statements that agree with the client's cognitions, accepts the client's behavior, and/or shares with the client that his/her feelings were not unusual.
— — — — —

35 PROBING - the counselor's statement results in the client providing additional information about his/ her cognitions, behaviors, and/or feelings.
— — — — —

36 DISAPPROVAL - the counselor makes a statement that conveys disapproval of one or more of the client's cognitions, behaviors, and/or feelings.
— — — — —

37 ADVICE GIVING - the counselor shares with the client which alternative he/she would select if it were his/her decision to make.
— — — — —

Other _____
— — — — —

Other _____
— — — — —

Other _____
— — — — —

		ANALYSIS		ASSESSMENT	
COUNSELOR COMPETENCY		Skill Value to Interview		Proficiency	

COUNSELOR COMPETENCY — Skill Value to Interview — Proficiency

COUNSELING SKILLS

	Non-Essential	Important	Critical	+	−
38 VOICE - the counselor's tone of voice and rate of speech is appropriate to the client's present state and/or counseling session.	—	—	—	—	—
39 EYE CONTACT - the counselor maintains eye contact at a level that is comfortable for the client.	—	—	—	—	—
40 INITIAL CONTACT - the counselor greets the client in a warm and accepting manner through some accepted form of social greeting (handshake, nod of head, etc.)	—	—	—	—	—
41 ACTIVITY LEVEL - the counselor maintains a level of activity appropriate to the client during the counseling session.	—	—	—	—	—
42 PHYSIOLOGICAL PRESENCE - the counselor's body posture, facial expressions, and gestures are natural and congruent with those of the client's.	—	—	—	—	—
43 COUNSELOR DISCLOSURE - the counselor shares personal information and feelings when it is appropriate in facilitating the counseling process.	—	—	—	—	—
44 SILENCE - the counselor does not speak when appropriate in facilitating client movement.	—	—	—	—	—
45 ACCENTING - from the client's previous statement, behavior, and/or feeling, the counselor repeats or accentuates the same, or has the client repeat or accentuate the statement, behavior, and/or feeling.	—	—	—	—	—
46 OBJECTIVITY - the counselor has sufficient control over his/her feelings and does not impose his values on the client.	—	—	—	—	—
47 PROBING - the counselor avoids bringing up or pursuing areas that are too threatening to the client.	—	—	—	—	—
48 RESISTANCE - the counselor is able to work through the client's conscious and/or unconscious opposition to the counseling process.	—	—	—	—	—
49 VERBOSITY - the counselor speaks when it is necessary, does not inappropriately interrupt the client or verbally dominate the counseling session.	—	—	—	—	—
50 ATTENDING - the counselor's attention is with the client's cognitions, behaviors, and/or feelings during the counseling session in accord with his/her stated theoretical frame of reference.	—	—	—	—	—
51 TRANSFERENCE - the counselor is able to work through feelings directed at him/her by the client which the client originally had for another object or person.	—	—	—	—	—
52 COUNTER-TRANSFERENCE - the counselor is aware of and is able to correct his/her placing his own wishes on the client.	—	—	—	—	—

COUNSELOR COMPETENCY	ANALYSIS Skill Value to Interview			ASSESSMENT Proficiency	
Counseling Skills (continued)	Non-Essential Important Critical			+	−
53 MANIPULATION - the counselor recognizes the client's attempt at influencing the counselor for his/her own purpose.	—	—	—	—	—
54 FACTORS - the counselor explores and is aware of socio-economic, cultural, and personal factors that might affect the client's progress.	—	—	—	—	—
55 DEPENDENCY - the counselor encourages the client to be independent, does not make decisions for the client or accept responsibility for the client's behaviors, cognitions, and/or feelings.	—	—	—	—	—
56 THEORY - the counselor can work with clients from at least two theories of counseling.	—	—	—	—	—
57 ALTERNATIVE EXPLORATION - the counselor, with the client, examines the other options available and the possible consequences of each.	—	—	—	—	—
58 IMPLEMENTATION - the counselor helps the client put insight into action.	—	—	—	—	—
59 DISTORTIONS - the counselor explains to the client his/her previously distorted perceptions of self and the environment.	—	—	—	—	—
60 MOTIVATION - the counselor can verbally confront the client with his/her lack of goal directed behavior.	—	—	—	—	—
61 CASE HISTORY TAKING - the counselor obtains factual information from the client that will be helpful in developing a course of action for the client consistent with his/her theoretical frame of reference.	—	—	—	—	—
62 INSIGHT - the counselor helps the client become more aware of his/her cognitive, behavioral, affective, and spiritual domain.	—	—	—	—	—
63 STRUCTURE - the counselor structures the on-going counseling sessions so there is continuity from session to session.	—	—	—	—	—
64 INCONSISTENCIES - the counselor identifies and explores with the client contradictions within and/or between client behaviors, cognitions, and/or affect.	—	—	—	—	—
65 RE-FOCUSING - the counselor makes a statement or asks a question that redirects the client to a specific behavior, cognition, or feeling.	—	—	—	—	—
66 GOALS - the counselor, with the client, establishes short and long range goals which are congruent with societal goals and are within the client's potential.	—	—	—	—	—

COUNSELOR COMPETENCY	ANALYSIS Skill Value to Interview	ASSESSMENT Proficiency

Counseling Skills (continued)

	Non-Essential	Important	Critical	+	−
67 REINFORCEMENT - the counselor identifies and uses reinforcers that facilitate the identified client goals.	—	—	—	—	—
68 FLEXIBILITY - the counselor changes long and short term goals within a specific session or during the overall counseling process as additional information becomes available.	—	—	—	—	—
69 BEHAVIORAL CHANGE - the counselor can develop specific plans, that can be observed and/or counted, for changing the client's behavior (s).	—	—	—	—	—
70 STRATEGY - the counselor's course of action is consistent with the counselor's stated theory of counseling.	—	—	—	—	—
71 TERMINATION - the counselor resolves the client's desire for premature termination.	—	—	—	—	—
72 EMERGENCIES - the counselor can handle emergencies that arise with the client.	—	—	—	—	—
73 TERMINATION - the counselor ends each session and the counseling relationship on time or at a point at which the client is comfortable with the issues that have been explored.	—	—	—	—	—
74 TERMINATION - the counselor advises the client that he/she may return in the future.	—	—	—	—	—
75 PERIODIC EVALUATION - with the client, the counselor periodically evaluates the progress made toward the established goals.	—	—	—	—	—
76 FANTASY - the counselor has the client use his/her imagination to gain insight and/or move toward the client's established goals.	—	—	—	—	—
77 HOMEWORK - the counselor appropriately assigns work to the client that is to be completed outside the counseling session.	—	—	—	—	—
78 PROBLEM SOLVING - the counselor teaches the client a method for problem solving.	—	—	—	—	—
79 TEST INTERPRETATION - the counselor interprets test (s) according to the procedures outlined in the test manual.	—	—	—	—	—
80 ROLE PLAYING - the counselor helps the client achieve insight by acting out conflicts and/or situations unfamiliar to him/her.	—	—	—	—	—
81 DESENSITIZATION - the counselor can apply a purposeful technique to reduce the level of anxiety that the client is experiencing.	—	—	—	—	—

COUNSELOR COMPETENCY	ANALYSIS Skill Value to Interview	ASSESSMENT Proficiency

Counseling Skills (continued)

Non-Essential | Important | Critical → ↓ ↓ ↓ | + − ↓ ↓

82 DREAMS - the counselor works with client's dreams in a manner consistent with his/her stated theoretical frame of reference.
— — — — —

83 CONTRACTS - the counselor makes a contractual agreement with the client.
— — — — —

Other _____
— — — — —

Other _____
— — — — —

Other _____
— — — — —

ADJUNCTIVE ACTIVITIES

84 CASE NOTES - the counselor is able to communicate in writing in a clear and concise manner initial, ongoing, and summary case notes.
— — — — —

85 STAFFING - the counselor can staff a case in a clear and concise manner by presenting an objective description of the client, significant information, goals for the client, strategy to be used, and a prognosis for the client.
— — — — —

86 TEST ADMINISTRATION - the counselor can administer test (s) according to the procedures in the test manual.
— — — — —

87 DIAGNOSIS - the counselor identifies cognitions, behaviors, and/or feelings in the client important in making a diagnosis according to the Diagnostic and Statistical Manual of Mental Disorders II.
— — — — —

88 APPOINTMENTS - the counselor is on time for his/her appointments with clients, peers, and supervisors.
— — — — —

89 INFORMS - the counselor provides the client with factual information.
— — — — —

90 ORGANIZED - the counselor effectively organizes and completes the assigned work within the prescribed time limits of the setting in which he/she is employed.
— — — — —

91 DRESS - the counselor's attire is appropriate to the client population and work setting being served.
— — — — —

92 RESPONSIBILITIES - the counselor can clarify the role and responsibilities he/she and the client have in the counseling relationship according to his theoretical frame of reference.
— — — — —

93 ATMOSPHERE - within the limits of his/her work setting, the counselor provides an atmosphere that is physically and psychologically comfortable for the client.
— — — — —

COUNSELOR COMPETENCY	ANALYSIS Skill Value to Interview			ASSESSMENT Proficiency	
	Non-Essential Important Critical				

Adjunctive Activities (continued)

94 CANCELLATIONS - the counselor notifies the client as soon as possible when he/she will be unable to keep an appointment.
— — — — —

95 COMPETENCY - the counselor is aware of and does not go beyond his/her counseling abilities.
— — — — —

Other _____
— — — — —

Other _____
— — — — —

Other _____
— — — — —

ETHICAL STANDARDS

96 PROFESSIONALISM - the counselor maintains a professional relationship with the client in accord with APA and/or APGA ethical standards.
— — — — —

97 ETHICS - the counselor adheres to the ethical standards outlined by the APA and/or APGA.
— — — — —

98 CONFIDENTIALITY - the counselor adheres to the ethical standards of confidentiality as outlined by the APA and/or APGA.
— — — — —

Other _____
— — — — —

Other _____
— — — — —

Other _____
— — — — —

APPENDIX B

INSTRUMENTS FOR THE ANALYSIS AND
ASSESSMENT OF COUNSELOR PERFORMANCE

BEHAVIORAL INTERACTION DESCRIPTION SYSTEM
    R. C. Rank

A system which rates the verbal behavior of the counselor
dichotomously on five dimensions: delivery mode, content
(affective-cognitive) process (process-other), and focus
(self-other). Can be used as a descriptor of group inter-
action-was originally designed as such.

Rank, R. C. Counseling competence and perceptions. Personnel
    and Guidance Journal, 1966, 45, 359-365.
Rank, R. C.; Thoreson, C. E.; & Smith, R. M. Encouraging
    counselor trainees affective group behavior by social
    modeling. Counselor Education and Supervision, 1972, 11,
    270-278.

CHECKLIST OF COUNSELOR SUBROLES
    A. E. Hoffman, Marshfield Road, Cleveland, Ohio

The checklist consists of descriptions of fifteen subroles
assumed by counselors and instructions for classifying the
subroles which include: Friendly Discussion, Information
Gathering, Diagnosing, Information Giving, Supporting,
Listening, Asking for Elaboration, Reflecting, Participating,
Structuring, Relationship, Focus of Topic, Advising, Rejecting,
Tutoring, Unclassifiable, and Other.

Hoffman, A. E. An analysis of counselor subroles. Journal of
    Counseling Psychology, 1959, 6, 61-67.

CLIENT EXPECTANCY INVENTORY (CEI)
    Ernest G. Thro and Joseph W. Hollis, Accelerated
    Development Inc., P.O. Box 667, Muncie, Indiana 47305.

An instrument designed to measure the client's expectations at
or near the beginning of counseling process. Scoring keys
permit determining expectations within the cognitive and
affective domains separately or by four separate diagnostic
scales including personal-social, vocational, information
utilization, and internal recognition.

COUNSELING EFFECTIVENESS SCALE
    A. E. Ivey (University of Massachusetts), C. D. Miller,
    W. H. Morrill, and C. J. Normington

The scale is a twenty-five item semantic differential form
filled out by the client which purports to measure the
effectiveness of the counseling.

Ivey, A. E.; Normington, C. J.; Miller, C. D.; Morrill, W. H.; & Hasses, R. F. Microcounseling and attending behavior: An approach to prepracticum counselor training. _Journal of Counseling Psychology_, Monograph Supplement, 1968, 15(2).

Ivey, A. E.; Miller, C. D.; Morrill, W. H.; & Normington, C. J. The counselor effectiveness scale. Unpublished report, Colorado State University, 1967, (Mimeo).

Hasse, R. F., & Dimattia, D. J. The application of micro-counseling paradigm to the training of support personnel in counseling. _Counselor Education and Supervision_, 1970, 10, 16-22.

COUNSELOR ACTIVITY INVENTORY
R. R. Stevic, State University of New York, Buffalo, New York.

A sixty item inventory of time usage with a five-point Likert-type response format. Items cover six areas: providing service to individual students, providing service to groups of students, establishing and maintaining community relationships, promoting the general school program, establishing and maintaining staff relationships and accepting professional responsibilities.

Stevic, R. R. The school counselor's role: commitment and marginality. Unpublished doctoral dissertation, Ohio State University, 1963.

Hansen, J. C. Job Satisfactions and job activities of school counselors. _Personnel and Guidance Journal_, 1967, 45, 790-793.

COUNSELOR CANDIDATE VERBAL BEHAVIOR SCALES
J. S. Dilley, (University of Wisconsin) and D. E. Tierney

A method of scoring responses to the Wisconsin Counselor Education Selection Interview (WCESI) based on counting words and phrases in a typescript of the selection interview. Scores are derived on six scales: verbosity, fluency, judgmentalness, counselee focus, assumptiveness, and flexitility.

McCreary, W. E. An empirical derivation of hypotheses related to indivual characteristic approaches to school counseling situations. Unpublished doctoral dissertation, University of Wisconsin, 1962.

Wasson, R. M. The Wisconsin Relationship Orientation Scale as a unique variable in the assessment of applicants for counselor education. _Counselor Education and Supervision_, 1965, 4, 89-92.

Dilley, J. S., & Tierney, D. E. Counselor candidate verbal behavior and relationship orientation. Counselor Education and Supervision, 1969, 8, 93-98.

COUNSELOR EFFECTIVENESS RATING SCALE
    J. C. Hansen (State University of New York, Buffalo) and G. D. Moore

An instrument for the rating of counselor effectiveness based on activity descriptions adapted from the Counselor Activity Inventory (Stevic, 1966), and with a nine-point Likert-response format. Ratings are made by supervisors and co-workers of the counselor for each activity.

Stevic, R. A new strategy for assessing counselor role. The School Counselor, 1966, 14, 94-97.
Hansen, J. C., & Moore, G. D. The full-time--part-time debate: A research contribution. Counselor Education and Supervision, 1968, 8, 18-22.

COUNSELOR EVALUATION RATING SCALE
    Robert D. Myrick (University of Florida, Gainsville) and F. D. Kelly

The Counselor Evaluation Rating Scale (CERS) is composed of twenty-seven items which enable a respondent to rate a counselor's performance in counseling and supervision. The instrument yields three scores: (a) counseling; (b) supervision; (c) total. Thirteen items are designed to assess an individual's work in counseling, while another thirteen items appraise the counselor's work and progress in supervision. When the items in these two sub-categories are totaled and the final items on the CERS, "Can be recommended for a counseling position without reservation," are included, the composit score is a measure of an individuals performance in a supervised counseling experience. The CERS is a self-administered measure which can be used by a supervisor or by the counselor himself.

Myrick, R. D., & Kelly, F. D., Jr. A scale for evaluating practicum students in counseling and supervision. Counselor Education and Supervision, 1971, 10, 330-336.
Myrick, R. D., & Kelly, F. C. A scale for evaluating practicum students in counseling and supervision. Counselor Education and Supervision, 1971, 10, 330-336.
Myrick, R. D.; Kelly, F. D.; & Wirrmer, J. The sixteen personality factor questionnaire as a predictor of counselor effectiveness. Counselor Education and Supervision, 1972, 11, 293-301.

Jones, L. K. The counselor evaluation rating scale: A valid criterion of counselor effectiveness. *Counselor Education and Supervision*, 1974, 14, 112-116.

COUNSELOR FUNCTION INVENTORY
   G. F. Shumake, 4268 Rocking Chair Len, Stone Mountain, Georgia

The CFI consists of seventy-seven statements of functions in seven areas of counselor services: placement, counseling, follow-up, orientation, student data, information, and miscellaneous. Responses are made on a five-point scale from "The counselor should personally perform this function" to "The counselor should have no direct responsibility for this function."

Shumake, G. F., & Oelke, M. C. Counselor function inventory. *School Counselor*, 1967, 15, 130-133.
Maser, A. L. Counselor function in secondary schools. The *School Counselor*, 1971, 18, 367-373.

COUNSELOR PERFORMANCE RATING SCALE
   J. W. Kelz (Pennsylvania State University)

The CPRS requires that the rater directly observe the interview or a filmed interview to rate the counselor on eight categories of counselor effectiveness: appearance, expression, relationship, communication, knowledge, perception, interpretation and termination. The counselor is rated on a five-point scale from unsatisfactory to outstanding.

Kelz, J. W. The development and evaluation of a measure of counselor effectiveness. *Personnel and Guidance Journal*, 1966, 44, 511-516.
Johnson, R. W., & Frederickson, R. H. Effect of financial renumeration and case description on counselor performance. *Journal of Counseling Psychology*, 1968, 15, 130-135.
Ryan, D. W.; Johnson, E. G.; Folsom, C. H.; & Cook, K. E. The evaluation of an instrument to measure counselor effectiveness. *Measurement and Evaluation in Guidance*, 1970, 3, 119-124.

COUNSELOR RATING SCALE
   A. A. Dole (University of Hawaii, Honolulu, Hawaii)

Supervisors rate counselors on a five-point scale on eight characteristics: personal characteristics, counselor-staff relationships, counselor-student relationships, guidance

organization and administration, skills in guidance, general
school services, professional growth and counselor-community
relations. Raters also indicate their degree of confidence
in the rating on a five-point scale.

Dole, A. A. A rating scale for school counselors. Counselor
    Education and Supervision, 1964, 3, 137-144.

COUNSELOR RATING SCALE
    S. H. Osipow and W. B. Walsh (Ohio State University)

Scale used to assess specific counseling behaviors by a
supervisor. Scores may be obtained in the following areas:
counselor communication skills, counselor understanding of
client, ability to help clients with problems, counselor
sensitivity, and general.

Osipow, S. H., & Walsh, B. W. A behavioral rating scale for
    judging counselor performance. (Experimental Form 2)
    Columbus, Ohio: Department of Psychology, Ohio State
    University, 1968.

COUNSELOR RATING SCALE
    J. M. Whitely (University of California, Irvin), N. A.
    Sprinthall, R. L. Mosher and R. T. Donaghy

The CRS consists of eight subscales, arranged in three broad
categories (overall rating of competence, flexibility in the
counseling process and response to supervision) designed to
catetorize counselor-behavior as cognitively rigid or flexible.
Descriptions of flexible and rigid behaviors are supplied as
markers for each subscale and a seven-point rating procedure is
used.

Whitely, J. M.; Sprinthall, N. A.; Mosher, R. L.; & Donaghy,
    R. T. Selection and evaluation of counselor effective-
    ness. Journal of Counseling Psychology, 1967, 14, 226-234.

COUNSELOR RESPONSE SCALE
    D. W. McKinnon, Oregon College of Education, Monmouth,
    Oregon.

The scale purports to measure the counselor's verbal behavior
during an interview. Judges rate counselor on a five-point
scale on these continua: responses are freezing to
controlling, acceptant to judgmental, client-centered to coun-
selor-centered, affectively-oriented or cognitively-oriented.

McKinnon, D. W. Group counseling with student counselors.
  Counselor Education and Supervision, 1969, 8, 195-200.

COUNSELOR SITUATION ANALYSIS INVENTORY
  G. R. Walz (University of Michigan) and E. C. Roeber

A series of thirty-four counseling situations are presented,
followed by alternative counselor responses or actions. The
respondent indicates his/her agreement with each alternative
in each situation on a five-point Likert scale ranging from
"Strongly Agree" to "Strongly Disagree."

Walz, G. R., & Roeber, E. C. Supervisors' reactions to a
    counseling interview. Counselor Education and Supervision,
    1962, 2, 2-7.
Havens, R. I. Changes in counselor candidate response during
    the introductory practicum. Counselor Education and
    Supervision, 1968, 8, 23-31.

COUNSELOR VERBAL RESPONSE SCALE
  N. Kagan (Michigan State University), D. Kratwohl, and
  G. Griffin

A set of descriptions with which to rate the counselor's
communications on five dimensions: affective-cognitive,
understanding-nonunderstanding, specific-nonspecific,
exploratory-nonexploratory, and a summarizing-effective-
noneffective, to provide a global rating of the adequacy of
each counselor response.

Kagan, N.; Kratwohl, D.; & Griffin, G. Interpersonal process
    recall: Stimulated recall by video-tape in exploratory
    studies of counseling and teaching-learning. East
    Lansing, Michigan, 1966.
Boyd, J. Microcounseling for a counseling-like verbal response
    set: Differential effects of two micromodels and two
    methods of counseling supervision. Journal of Counseling
    Psychology, 1973, 20, 97-98.

CRITICAL BEHAVIOR SCALES INVENTORY
  J. E. Muthard (University of Florida) and L. A. Miller

The CBS Inventory consists of eighteen vignettes describing
specific counselor behavior. Each vignette is responded to on
a six bipolar semantic differential-type of scale.

Jacques, M. E. Critical Counseling Behavior in Rehabilitation
    Settings. College of Education, University of Iowa, 1959.

Muthard, J. E., & Miller, L. A. Perceptions of rehabilitation
counselor behavior. _Personnel and Guidance Journal_, 1966,
_44_, 517-522.

EMPATHY RATING SCALE
P. A. Payne (University of Cincinnati) and D. M. Gralinski

A carefully defined, one item, seven-point scale of empathy,
defined as: "the tendency of a person to perceive another's
feelings, thoughts, and behavior as similar to his/her own.
When another has empathy toward you, he/she understands exactly
how you feel and what you mean. At a low level of empathy the
person indicates that he/she is not interested or is interested
but unable to be aware of your feelings. At a high level of
empathy the message 'I am with you' is clear. The person's
remarks fit in just right with what you are feeling at the
moment."

Payne, P. A., & Gralinski, D. M. Effects of supervision style
and empathy upon counselor learning. _Journal of
Counseling Psychology_, 1968, _15_, 517-521.

FIELD PRACTICE CHECKLIST
J. S. Dilley, University of Wisconsin

The checklist consists of thirty statements of employee
qualities selected from a list of 724 standardized by Uhrbrock
(1950) which the author sees as having usefulness in the
evaluation of counselors in training and in employment
statement values are based on mean item values assigned by a
group of professors, college students and factory foremen. The
high- and low-valued items are alternated in order, followed
by neutral items.

Dilley, J. S. Rating scale statements: A useful approach to
counselor evaluation. _Counselor Education and
Supervision_, 1965, _51_, 40-43.
Uhrbrock, R. S. Standardization of 724 rating scale
statements. _Personnel Psychology_, 1950, _3_, 285-316.
Dilley, J. S. Decision-making ability and vocational maturity.
Personnel and Guidance Journal, 1965, _44_, 423-427.

INVENTORY OF FULFILLMENT OF CLIENT EXPECTANCY (IFCE)
Ernest G. Thro and Joseph W. Hollis, Accelerated
Development Inc., P.O. Box 667, Muncie, Indiana 47305.

Since many clients come to counseling by their own choice and
since they attend with the expectations of certain outcomes,
one measurement of counseling effectiveness would be the extent

to which the client's expectations are fulfilled. The IFCE is
designed to measure extent of satisfaction in the cognitive and
affective domains separately or in the diagnostic scales.

MEASURE OF COUNSELOR VERBAL BEHAVIOR
     N. R. Gamsky (University of Wisconsin) and G. F. Farwell

The measure is used to rate counselor verbal behavior and is
a revision of Bales (1950) System of Interaction Process
Analysis which is a general purpose framework for describing
social interactions. The fourteen categories of verbal
behavior are: (1) gives reassurance (2) shows approval
(3) shows tension release (4) shows agreement (5) gives
suggestions (6) gives interpretation (7) reflects (8) gives
information (9) asks for information (10) asks for elaboration
(11) disagrees (12) avoids (13) shows disapproval (14) shows
antagonism.

Bales, R. R. Interaction Process Analysis. Cambridge, Massa-
     chusetts: Addison-Wesley Press, 1950.
Gamsky, N. R. Effect of client demeanor and focus of hostility
     upon the verbal responses of school counselors.
     Unpublished doctoral dissertation, University of
     Wisconsin, 1965.
Gamsky, N. R., & Farwell, G. F. The effect of client demeanor
     upon the verbal responses of school counselors. Personnel
     and Guidance Journal, 1967, 45, 477-481.

Q-SORT OF COUNSELOR RESPONSIBILITIES
     L. D. Schmidt, Ohio State University, Columbus, Ohio.

A Q-sort of fifty statements covering five areas of counselor
responsibilities: assistance to students, assistance to
teachers, assistance to administration, assistance to parents
and research assistance to the school. The statements are
sorted as either appropriate or not appropriate.

Tennyston, W. W. An analysis of the professional guidance
     positions of certified secondary school counselors in
     Missouri. Unpublished doctoral dissertation, University
     of Missouri, 1956.
Schmidt, L. D. Concepts of the role of secondary school
     counselors. Personnel and Guidance Journal, 1962, 40,
     600-605.

RATING SCALE OF COUNSELOR ACTIVITY
Susan G. O'Leary, Kings Park State Hospital, Kings Park, New York.

The scale consists of a fifteen-item rating scale of counselor activity which is scored by trained raters (for scoring procedure see O'Leary, 1969). The items were: (1) supplies test information (2) supplies other information (3) expresses his/her opinion (4) asks student for information (5) asks student to express his/her self (6) expresses disagreement (7) expresses agreement (8) recognizes student's potential (9) talks of high goals (10) tells student he/she is capable (11) suggests plan (12) asks student for plan (13) is expressive (14) is concrete (15) changes.

O'Leary, Susan G. Counselor activity as a predictor of outcome. Personnel and Guidance Journal, 1969, 48, 135-139.

RATING SCALE OF COUNSELOR ROLES
J. R. Tomczyk, Wisconsin State University, Superior, Wisconsin.

The scale defines twelve counselor verbal roles (listening, rewarding, questioning, working together, persuading, information giving, improving study habits, defining counseling, approving--reassuring, nonaccepting, focusing on topic, and promoting friendly discussion). Client is asked to indicate on a seven-point rating scale, ranging from "Always" to "Never," the degree to which each verbal role was used in a twenty minute session with a counselor.

Tomczyk, J. R. Determinants and effects of counselors' verbal roles. Personnel and Guidance Journal, 1968, 46, 694-700.

ROLE BEHAVIOR SCALE
G. M. Gazda (University of Georgia) and W. C. Bonney

Descriptions of role behaviors for nineteen roles (opinion seeker, interpreter, etc.) adapted from Bales (1950, Benne and Sheats (1948), and Gorlow, Hoch, and Teleshow (1952) with modifications and additions by Ohlsen (1962).

Benne, K. D., & Sheats, P. Functional roles of group members. Journal of Social Issues, 1948, 4, 42-47.
Bales, R. F. Interaction process analysis. Cambridge, Massachusetts: Addison-Wesley Press, 1950.
Gorlow, L.; Hoch, E. L.; & Teleshow, E. F. The Nature of Nondirective Group Psychotherapy. New York: Bureau of Publications, Teachers College, Columbia University, 1952.

Gazda, G. M., & Bonney, W. C. Effects of group counseling on role behavior of counselors in training. Counselor Education and Supervision, 1965, 4, 191-197.

APPENDIX C

Counselor Self Assessment

COUNSELOR SELF ASSESSMENT

This self-assessment form is to be completed shortly after listening to a recording of your counseling interview. The assessment questions are intended to facilitate awareness of important aspects of the interview that may be discussed in supervision.

Go beyond these questions and add any comments about the interview which are important to you. Please make your answers and comments brief, and indicate those you wish to discuss with the supervisor.

1. How did you feel as you entered the interview - do you recall any emotions or thoughts that may have affected how you behaved in the interview?

2. What kind of a relationship developed between you and the client?

3. What aspects of the client's personality and interview behavior were attractive to you? What were aversive to you?

4. Identify the strengths and weaknesses in your counseling performance during the first fifteen minutes of the interview.

5. Did any notable patterns of interpersonal behavior develop between you and the client during the interview?

6. Identify the strengths and weaknesses in your counseling performance during the middle portion of the interview.

7. How did you feel as you closed the interview?

8. Identify the strengths and weaknesses in your closing.

9. As the client looks back on the interview, what do you feel are his/her thoughts and feelings about you and the counseling session?

10. How would you like the supervisor to help you during supervision? (If you want to review specific taped segments, please identify these on your tape.)

APPENDIX D

Counseling Interview Summary

COUNSELING INTERVIEW SUMMARY

CLIENT_____DATE_____

COUNSELOR_____TIME: BEGAN_____ENDED_____

CASE NUMBER_____   INTERVIEW NUMBER_____

REASON FOR CONFERENCE

DESCRIPTION OF THE CLIENT AND PRESENTING CONCERN

PARSIMONIOUSLY DESCRIBE WHAT HAPPENED IN THE INTERVIEW, WHAT
COUNSELOR WAS TRYING TO ACCOMPLISH, AND COUNSELOR'S METHODOLOGY

ON THE BACK OF THIS PAGE WRITE YOUR PROGNOSIS AND FUTURE PLANS
FOR COUNSELING, AND ANY ADDITIONAL COMMENTS.

APPENDIX E

CASE STUDIES OF COUNSELING SUPERVISION

FROM A PSYCHOBEHAVIORAL APPROACH

Supervision Case Study: Counselor A. . . . .Louis V. Paradise

Supervision Case Study: Counselor B. . . . . .Angelo Gadaleto

Supervision Case Study: Counselor C. . . . . . .John C. Dovel

SUPERVISION CASE STUDY: COUNSELOR A

Louis V. Paradise, Ph.D.
Catholic University
Washington, D.C.

Editor's Note: The psychobehavioral supervision process described transpired between Louis V. Paradise and Counselor A during one-semester practicum. At the time of supervision Lou was a doctoral student enrolled in a course on counselor supervision. Counselor A was a Master's degree candidate in a counseling practicum course. The report which follows was written by Lou and edited for inclusion in this text.

Precounseling Supervision

In advance of Counselor A's (CA) initial counseling session, two supervision sessions occurred. CA had requested that I serve as his supervisor partly because I was in another class of his at the time and he was somewhat familiar with me. This previous acquaintance certainly contributed initially to establishing a favorable atmosphere.

The first two supervision sessions were primarily directed toward getting to know one another and discussing the supervision process. Questions and procedures were discussed and the point was quite apparent that CA was very interested in the availability of a supervisior and was cooperative in terms of what we would be doing together. I attempted, during these early supervision sessions to establish an atmosphere conducive to counselor trust, acceptance, encouragement, and so forth, and to maintain a positive relationship with CA, especially during this critical period prior to seeing his first client.

One of the first things we did was to role play a counseling session, giving me the opportunity to observe his entry-level counseling skills. We used the tape for discussing some of the problems a neophyte counselor encounters in counseling and focusing on the positive elements of his performance.

CA appeared very eager to learn and discuss aspects of his counseling, and our early sessions were usually about two hours in length. He appeared to be eagerly awaiting his first practicum client and did not manifest any reservations or anxiety. We discussed his expectations at some length during these first sessions, and I was careful to specifically discuss

what my function was to be and what kinds of activities we'd
be engaged in during the supervision process. We established
a friendly and cooperative supervisory relationship.

After two supervision sessions I had learned that CA was
experienced in dealing with people (he was formerly in business
as well as having some broadcasting experience). I felt that
this background had taught him to relate to people in a
nonanxious and open manner, over-riding any initial fears or
anxiety that most beginning counselors experience. After our
role playing I did have some initial indications of certain
counseling behaviors which needed supervisory focus, but these
were reserved until after CA's first actual counseling session
with a client.

We agreed to have weekly supervision sessions regardless
of whether CA had seen a client that week. He felt very
strongly that this action would be an excellent way to gain
feedback on a regular basis. Rather than state what happened
during each supervision session, the supervision process with
CA will be illustrated by presenting significant and relevant
events within a generalized time perspective of their
occurrence.

Psychobehavioral Analysis and Assessment

The first two counseling sessions for CA served as a
performance baseline for an analysis and assessment of his
skills and dynamics. We met together after each of these
sessions, critiqued the tapes, and set immediate and long-range
goals for supervision. The supervision goals included dynamics
and skills, and these will be presented later.

Our procedure for analyzing and assessing skills was to
informally chart CA's performance frequency for a list of
twenty-two communication techniques. We focused on strengths
and weaknesses, and I was careful not to overwhelm CA with the
technical aspects of charting. However, I did conduct a
thorough analysis and assessment on my own and the data are
presented in Figure E.1.

As CA and I charted his skills we gradually made a gross
evaluative assessment. Each skill of importance to the interview was judged as being in one of three categories:
(1) inappropriate - should be extinguished or reduced,
(2) desirable - should be increased, (3) desirable - performed
satisfactorily. I was careful to give ample positive reinforcement to CA for satisfactory performances as they occurred
because I did not want him to become discouraged.

A dynamic analysis and assessment was also conducted on
CA's first two interviews and the results corresponded to some

	Session			
	One[a]		Two[b]	
	#	%	#	%
1. Ordering, directing	0	0	0	0
2. Warning, threatening	0	0	0	0
3. Moralizing, preaching	1	1	0	0
4. Advising, suggesting	1	1	2	2
5. Teaching, lecturing	0	0	0	0
6. Judging, criticizing	0	0	0	0
7. Praising, agreeing	7	9	2	2
8. Name-calling, labeling	0	0	0	0
9. Interpreting, analyzing	7	9	6	7
10. Reassuring, sympathizing	5	7	0	0
11. Questioning, probing**	32	43	53	64
12. Withdrawing, distracting	0	0	0	0
13. Noncommittal (oh, I see)	12	16	8	10
14. Door openers (open ended?)	4	5	3	4
15. Mirroring	0	0	0	0
16. Feedback	2	3	2	2
17. Reflection of feeling**	0	0	1	1
18. Paraphrasing**	2	3	2	2
19. Summarizing**	0	0	1	1
20. Attending to nonverbal cues	0	0	0	0
21. Eliciting client summarization	0	0	0	0
22. Clarifying	1	1	3	4
Total	74	98	83	99

* frequency
** selected behavioral goals
a. a 50-minute counseling session
b. a 60-minute counseling session

Figure E.1. Frequency And Percentage Of Counselor-Initiated
Communications For Baseline Period Counseling
Responses.

thoughts I had during our early role-playing session. CA seemed to be uneasy about handling client feelings and appeared to circumvent affective exploration. He justified his avoidance by saying he "goes directly to the heart of the client's problem." The skill-assessment results supported my hypothesis of affect avoidance by showing no instances of counselor initiated reflections of feeling. Although CA was not enthusiastic about choosing affect avoidance as a dynamic goal to work on he did agree that it was a worthy target for supervision.

Supervision Goals

Based on the analysis and assessment presented in Figure E.1, the following skill goals were established: (a) the counselor will increase appropriate use of paraphrasing responses in order to verify his perceptions of what is being said and to demonstrate to the client that he is "with him"; (b) counselor will increase appropriate use of reflection of feeling in order to facilitate the client's self-exploration; (c) counselor will decrease use of questioning responses, e.g., interrogating, by replacing those responses with other verbal interaction techniques such as open-ended questions, clarifying, illiciting client summarization, reflecting, etc.; and (d) counselor will increase use of summarization in order to check verbal following and invite client feedback.

These goals were discussed along with possible strategies to facilitate accomplishment of the goals. We discussed other possible goals that could be established further into the semester, e.g., learning specific techniques that CA could use with certain clients. At this point, CA appeared very interested in improving his counseling skills and he showed a feeling of commitment to becoming more proficient.

We also explored possible dynamic goals for supervision and CA's affect avoidance. Agreement was reached that CA should try to increase the affective component of his counseling, and I explained how "Interpersonal Process Recall" (IPR) was a technique I would use to help CA become more affective. The overall dynamic goal we set was to increase CA's awareness of intrapersonal and interpersonal dynamics in himself and his clients, thereby enabling him to attend to affect in his counseling sessions.

Supervision Strategies

CA had approximately eleven counseling sessions throughout the semester and we conducted from twelve-fifteen supervision sessions. Throughout this time many strategies were used to

facilitate his development, some relating to the initial goals
and others relating to issues or concerns that appeared later.
Several of the sessions were conducted within the framework of
consultation. For example, CA was interested in using a test
with a client to help her see and evaluate some of her self-
perceptions. Since he was dealing with a self-concept concern,
the Adjective Checklist was used and some of our supervision
sessions were devoted to scoring and interpreting this
instrument for use in counseling. These sessions had a
definite consultative tone, with the dynamic elements we had
previously discussed interspersed throughout the sessions. I
felt this was appropriate since the counseling process was
relatively long term (five sessions) and the presenting concern
was affect laden.

Parenthetically, this client had requested that she not be
taped (I did observe the first session) so that for some of
these supervision sessions a consultative role was almost
necessary since I had only CA's recollection of what had
transpired. The absence of recording did, however, force CA to
recall, verbalize, and become aware of his and the client's
feelings/perceptions because we could not listen to a tape.
Therefore, the process greatly facilitated dynamic supervision
while not lending itself to behavioral supervision (which at
this point did not seem as crucial to CA's growth and development as a counselor). Much of the dynamic supervision used
during this later stage of the counseling practicum consisted
of helping CA learn how to therapeutically utilize his
experienceing process.

However, not to get too far ahead of myself in discussing
strategies, I should back up to those strategies that were used
to accomplish the initial skill and dynamic goals. Behavioral
supervision strategies used for skill goals included
instruction, modeling, role playing and considerable positive
reinforcement. Going over tapes and having CA suggest possible
summarizations and clarifications at various points in the tape
was very helpful with skill goals "a" and "b." Since the fact
was determined in assessment that CA's knowledge of these
techniques was present but had to be performed and applied to a
greater extent, this method proved to be effective for demonstrating technique application.

The same approach was used for increasing the use of
reflective responses. Additionally, a checklist of feelings
that people have but fail to identify was used to help CA
identify and differentiate various feelings that were present
on the tape. Role playing and modeling to suggest possible
ways to reflect feeling without the monotonous use of "you
feel. . ." were also utilized in conjunction with the tapes.

517

Other skills that were performed satisfactorily, such as establishing goals and evaluating antecedents and consequences of actions and feelings, were refined by instruction and modeling. That CA could use these techniques adequately seemed apparent, the only problem being that of timing, i.e. he would immediately get into behavioral analysis and goal setting without sufficient time for client self exploration. A supervision effort was made to focus on this problem and discuss possible ways to facilitate sufficient self exploration prior to goal-setting.

Psychotherapeutic supervision strategies used for dynamic goals were discussing the tapes and CA's perception of what was occurring in the affective domain as well as the use of IPR. The IPR approach was not too successful partly because a time-lag existed between the counseling session and the IPR session, and partly because CA had a very difficult time recalling feelings from audio tapes. After a consultation with Dr. Boyd the decision was made that perhaps an efficacious strategy to lower any possible defensiveness would be to reflect CA's dynamics instead of forcing his recall, and to dispense with directive methods which seemed to raise his performance anxiety. This process proved to be effective in "loosening-up" CA and he was able to recognize some of his difficulties in handling the affective modalty. Part of this difference could be due to his participation in concurrent counseling sessions at the University Counseling Center. This counseling primarily dealt with affective elements, as he later recollected to me.

Evaluation of CA and Supervision

A brief evaluation of two skill goals is presented in Figure E.2. The evaluation is cautiously made because it is based on data that were gathered in a manner which does not conform to the guidelines of experimental research, and the data were drawn from "initial" interviews and cannot be generalized to later interviews in the counseling process. In global terms, however, the slopes of the data suggest that desired changes were occurring in CA's counseling responses during psychobehavioral supervision. CA was increasing the use of reflections and decreasing questions.

Other noticeable changes occurred for which no supporting data exist. CA seemed to be appreciably improved in terms of our initial skill objectives in many of his later interviews. When specific techniques and strategies were discussed and modeled his verbal feedback about application was knowledgable. Also, a greater attention on his part to the affective components of counseling and a greater willingness to discuss them seemed to be present. He repeatedly demonstrated an

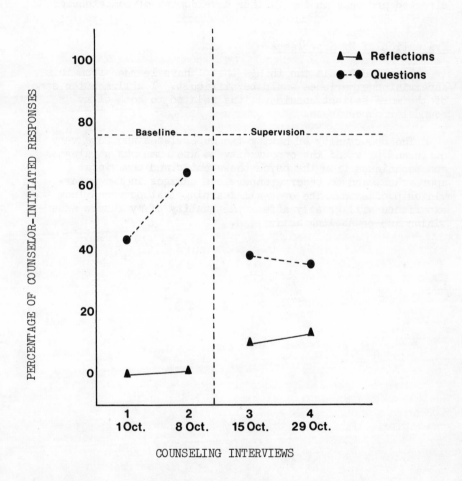

FIGURE E.2.   Comparison of Two Skill Goals Prior to
and During Supervision.

519

increased awareness of his intrapersonal dynamics and an understanding of how they influenced his counseling behavior.

To summarize, CA has developed a strong set of basic counseling techniques and strategies, and he can competently apply them. CA also has a realistic perception of his strengths and weaknesses and I believe he will continue self-directed progress in the further development of competencies.

Evaluation of My Experience

To put down all the things that I have learned from this supervision experience would be difficult. I will mention some of the more salient considerations related to both of my counselor supervisees.

The opportunity of having two supervisees who were very different provided the opportunity to use numerous strategies and techniques from the psychotherapeutic and behavioral approaches, and to observe supervisee changes in two supervision processes. The over-all learning that occurred from the experience will greatly affect the quality of my future supervision and counseling activities.

SUPERVISION CASE STUDY: COUNSELOR B

Angelo Gadaleto, Ph. D.
Associate Director
Counseling Center
Radford College
Radford, Virginia

Editor's Note: This case study was prepared by
Angelo Gadaleto while he was a doctoral student in a
counselor supervision course. His supervisee,
Counselor B, was a Master's degree candidate enrolled
in a counseling practicum. Angelo's report has been
edited for publication.

Initial Assessment and My Proposed Method of Supervision

My initial assessment of Counselor B is as follows: CB is
a strong, attractive, approximately twenty-two year old male
who has had no previous experience with counseling. His career
goal is somewhat undefined but a tendency exists toward high
school counseling. He seemed of average intelligence and had a
somewhat defensive style of interaction. He was anxious to
learn yet unable to take much in the form of criticism. CB is
not extremely verbal and had a tendency to slip into response
sets.

My initial supervision plan was to establish a safe,
secure relationship that would enable me to slip through his
defense so that he could internalize constructive criticism.
I proposed to use a strong operant-reinforcement model to
effect an increase in counseling skills. Other methods of
supervision intervention included teaching, role playing, role
reversal, modeling, readings, homework, and continuous feedback.

Process of Change

I spent the first supervision session developing rapport
with CB and setting the stage for constructive change. My
general approach might be called psychobehavioral since I
performed nearly an equal balance between psychotherapeutic and
behavioral methods. After a very poor first counseling session,
I gave what positive feedback I could and took the approach of
microcounseling. The tools of attending behavior were, one by
one, talked about, explored, modeled, and role played. CB
responded very well to the modeling, followed by role playing
which was used extensively throughout our supervision process.

Although I gave CB a dynamic form of feedback on his
skill accomplishments during the first five counseling
sessions, behavioral base lines were also established and
improvement on the designated skills were recorded. After the
necessary basic counseling skills (attending behaviors) were
mastered, more counseling skill topics were systematically
introduced. We concentrated on developing all of the following
skills: forming a relationship, beginning an interview,
interpretation, use of silence, referral, and termination.

The last third of our weekly supervision sessions dealt
with methods of increasing CB's understanding and effectiveness.
At one point Interpersonal Process Recall was used to help CB
understand to a greater degree (1) his feelings and needs;
(2) the client's feelings and needs; and (3) the effect of 1
and 2 on the counseling relationship. The technique of fantasy
exploration was explained as a method for coming in contact
with one's own feelings. Several counseling methods or
techniques were explored and role played: decision theory as
applied to practice, behavior modification, goal setting with
the client, and cognitive restructuring.

Our last session stressed the need for continual self
improvement and evaluation. Procedures for monitoring one's
performance were discussed and also the value of peer
supervision.

Final Assessment and Recommendations

I feel CB has a good grasp of the basic skills necessary
for counseling. He is capable of effectively working with
counselees having developmental concerns, though I recommend
more supervised experience before permitting him to
independently counsel with serious personal problems. A field
practicum with close supervision would be very beneficial for
CB's competency development, and this experience should be
completed before he enters independent practice.

SUPERVISION CASE STUDY: COUNSELOR C

John C. Dovel
Doctoral Candidate
School-Child Psychology Program
University of Virginia

Editor's Note: In this case study a supervisor-
candidate, John C. Dovel, examines his longitudinal
supervision process with a Master's degree student in
a counseling practicum course. Although John does
not describe his methodology in detail, choosing
instead to study the supervisory relationship and
dynamics, his approach includes techniques from
the psychotherapeutic and behavioral approaches to
supervision. The case study has been edited, and
names have been changed to protect the anonymity
of supervisees.

The presentation of this case study will perhaps be in a
somewhat unorthodox form. A need exists to report on the
counselor's personality and skill development, supervision
techniques, interpersonal and intrapersonal dynamics, and so
forth. But I also feel the need to assess the overall
development of myself in the supervisory role and my relationship with the supervisee. I fear that by compartmentalizing
this development into segments or topical areas, the process of
growth that myself and my supervisee experienced may be
obscured. From my consultation sessions with Dr. Boyd I have
an awareness of the supervision process I experienced, but to
put it all together I plan to review all eight of my supervision tapes and recapture the experience as it happened.

On this I am about to embark, simultaneously reliving and
hindsighting the supervision process. After listening to each
tape I will record my reactions.

THE SUPERVISEE

Counselor C (CC) was thirty-nine-year-old public school
teacher with a Master's degree in his teaching field and
several years teaching experience. He was pursuing a career in
school counseling. We met for the first time one week prior to
our initial session. During this meeting we exchanged
information about our professional histories and goals and
superficially about ourselves. I remember being struck by his
projection of an image that portrayed a great deal of
competence. He seemed to regard himself as somewhat more
experienced and astute than his classmates, as sort of a
"natural helper." I was unsure how much of this was due in
fact to relatively greater experience and how much might be
coming from a need to disarm any impending criticism.

SUPERVISION SESSION I

CC's first client presented a history of problems and
indeed seemed somewhat confused during the counseling session.
Throughout most of the subsequent supervision session we
focused on the client's presenting concerns, her disorgani-
zation, her obsession with detail, the severity of her problems,
and so forth. This exploration was in a fair amount of depth.
I played back some of the counseling session, asked directed
questions, and paraphrased and/or summarized CC's answers. By
the middle of this supervision session the fact is evident that
we seemed to be forming some kind of an alliance by focusing
solely on the client's problems. I cannot help but wonder
about the nature of this comradery. By restricting ourselves
to the difficulties of the counselee, do we not skirt one of
the real purposes of supervision? Do we not sidestep the
general issue of how CC counseled? I submit that a trade off
might have occured here. CC avoids any assessment or message
that he has done a less than perfect job. I yield to my
reluctance to do anything that could possibly create a rift in
our newly-forming relationship. I was perhaps also responding
to a feeling that he may easily become defensive. He did tend
to somewhat overrate his performance.

At this time CC's skills seemed definitely advanced over
the typical Master's level student. During the initial
counseling session he seemed confident and demonstrated a good
ability to explore concerns, listening actively, paraphrasing,
and summarizing effectively. His reflections on the whole were
good and his comments during supervision about the client's
intrapersonal dynamics were insightful. However, during
counseling, a hint existed of CC wanting to lord power over the
counselee, to have complete control over the session. He
seemed to have a need to be right, telling the client what was
wrong with her and tending to be argumentative.

At one point during this session I focused on CC's admission of having experienced some anger toward his client. I was making a rather meager attempt to facilitate dynamic awareness of his need to be right and be in control. I now find interesting seeing how he shifted the focus back to the client. I moved it back to him, and he back to the client again. I am also struck by my extreme reluctance to reapproach the issue, using a host of qualifiers which obscured my points.

I remember now being left with the feeling of having thoroughly and satisfactorily explored the client's problems. But I wondered about what appeared to be a confrontive, argumentative style in CC and how his apparent need to be right might lead to resistance in supervision.

SUPERVISION SESSION II

During the second counseling session CC did a good job in helping his female client clarify a presenting concern - that of wanting to be more spontaneous with men and to talk about her feelings more freely. His pervasive style, however, was inpatient, confrontive, and judgemental. I saw as my delimma in supervision trying to get him to look at this without "turning him off." To me his style in counseling was fore-shadowing what his resistance could be in supervision.

In reviewing this tape I am hit with what occurred during the first of the supervision session. CC immediately announced how the client liked the counseling, how he felt about it, and how that was more important than what anyone else said. He essentially was telling me I had better not say anything critical.

We focused again on the client a great deal as I supported CC in having clarified a presenting concern. We talked extensively about what kind of affinity the client was develop-ing for him and how she might be playing through some of her concerns in the counseling relationship. Also, techniques of history taking were discussed somewhat didactically and the necessity of getting a history in a case such as this. In listening to this part I am hearing my style become smoother. I am not as overly cautious with word selection as before.

CC brought up that his class was critical of him for being "too pushy." This provided me with the opportunity to focus on his anger at classmates and on what they might be trying to communicate. The maneuver was oblique and it missed my objective. Later in the supervision session CC communicated a great deal of impatience with his client's intellectualization. I clarified this for him and asked if this might have been communicated to the client as well. This was a decent inroad.

But I am struck with how I quickly backed off, providing CC with excuses for anything he might have said when counseling. The fact is now fairly evident that my fear of CC's defensiveness was as much or more of a problem in this part of supervision as was his personality style.

With a combination of forethought and frustration, I had us listen to and analyze tape segments from the counseling session. This is probably one of our most important episodes in terms of supervisory objectives. By asking CC what he might be communicating to the client I tried to focus on his impatience, confrontation, and arguing. After some slight resistance initially, CC began to examine his dynamics and counseling behavior. In fact, he began to recognize a pervasive style and provided his own word of "authoritarianism." An inroad had been made and the process was not as catastrophic as I had anticipated.

SUPERVISION SESSION III

CC's third counseling session with this client on the whole went very well. He helped the client focus on her relationship with a current boyfriend and her fear of rejection. CC's confrontive style was significantly tempered but present. An excess of "you" and "why" statements existed as well as a bombardment of questions. On a couple of occasions the client seemed to become slightly irritated with CC.

As I begin listening to this supervision session I notice that both of us seem much more comfortable with each other than before, perhaps because some of our earlier agenda was out of the way. Initially, I wanted to give CC many strokes for a job well done and did so by talking about the client. But I still needed to get at his argumentative, "what's wrong with you" style which at times seemed to shift the focus from the client's concerns to a power struggle in the counseling session. My dilemma was getting him again to look at this style without disrupting our relationship or totally negating the good things he had done in counseling. Further, as CC presented himself to me so positively, to shift to how he might have done something differently without creating confrontation was difficult.

I played back a segment of the counseling tape and asked CC what he could be communicating to the client. We moved from this to his talking about how he tends to argue and try to "be right." He then began to totally down himself so I alternated between noting difficulties and supporting effective skills.

We parted on a good note that day. CC now seemed to be making a concerted effort to objectively look at his style, without excessive defense or self flagellation. I think he was also overcoming the fear of me evaluating him negatively as a person, and was beginning to understand that we were working together.

SUPERVISION SESSION IV

CC saw a new client prior to this supervision session, a young man who was having marital difficulty, generally feeling that his wife belittled him. I remember observing the counseling and being struck with how CC failed to explore the client's concerns. Exploration had been one of his strongest points, yet he repeatedly sidestepped the major issue of the client's commitment to the marriage. I also noticed how he made a number of self-referent statements.

In reviewing the first part of this supervision session I am seeing what a mutual understanding we now seem to have formed. The fact is obvious in the way we tackle the counseling session together. CC no longer gives me warning signs of "watch out or I'll be defensive." He openly and honestly assesses himself and looks to me for some guidance.

We looked at the issue of commitment and how to get at it by role playing. CC was the "client" and I the "counselor." As we proceeded into role playing CC somehow looked as if he was having a negative reaction to the "skit." Soon he leveled with me and disclosed that he was currently dealing with a similar situation in his own marriage. Following CC's disclosure I can see a slow transition in my role from that of instructor and consultant to one of counselor. From this new position we dealt with two main issues: (1) How CC's current personal situation might interfere with his effectiveness with this particular client - i.e. should he make a referral?, and (2) CC questioning his own competence, thinking that a good counselor is effective in all settings regardless of personal situations. CC talked freely and emotionally about his marriage and how it has been interfering with other endeavors.

I would not decide for CC about making a referral. I wanted him to make his own decision. So we met for lunch a few days later prior to his scheduled second session with this client. CC was squemish with me, somewhat embarrassed with our last session. I noted the uneasiness and we talked about how he wanted to deny what had happened or at least tone it down. Interestingly enough, the discussion pointed out a parallel for the relationship between CC and his client. Because the client had never before talked about his marriage, we speculated that

he now may also want to tone things down. CC decided to
continue with the second counseling session and seemed
comfortable with that choice.

SUPERVISION SESSION V

Indeed the client did tone things down. In fact he seemed
to be terminating from the beginning of the session. He
nervously said that his marital problem was not nearly as
troublesome as it had seemed in the first interview, and the
second interview was spent backing off of his previous
disclosures.

The supervision session seemed to go the smoothest of any
yet. CC showed a great deal of insight into the client's
intrapersonal dynamics. Perhaps this fact is due in part to
the similarity of CC's life with the client's. But I am also
thinking that, having weathered well the friction CC and I
were experiencing in our own relationship, we could now focus
more efficiently and effectively on counseling and skill
development.

At one point in the second interview CC essentially told
the client that more existed to his problem than what he was
revealing. We looked at how this created an impasse and
implied an attack on the client's credibility. CC nondefensively assessed this aspect of his performance and seemed
very comfortable. And I am hearing myself be more direct,
using far fewer qualifiers.

SUPERVISION SESSION VI

CC saw another new client this time. The young woman was
late and for the first twenty minutes just "chitchatted." CC
did not "push" in the least but gradually moved into a problem
area. I was ecstatic! This was so different from what his
previous style had been. The client's concern was not being
assertive when perhaps it was appropriate, and subsequently
feeling angry with herself.

In supervision I found myself with not much to say except
to comment on the counseling process and support CC in what he
had done and how he had done it. I wanted to make sure that
CC recognized the difference in style and saw it as an
accomplishment. I also wanted him to see how he and the client
explored the problem together; CC noted his improvement and
"patted himself on the back". Most of the supervision session
was spent in brainstorming what kinds of dynamic contingencies
have been going on for the client and what could be brought out
next time.

SUPERVISION SESSION VIII

During the second session with this client CC took some history which helped clarify the client's concerns about assertiveness, and she explored situations during the past two weeks in which she was and was not assertive, and why. CC also helped the client look at her irrational self blaming for other people's actions.

Again, I found little to add during supervision. This was an easy, open client and CC shined. Only one thing I might have looked at: the point was unclear whether the client was making the distinction between goal-directed assertion and angry outbursts. CC and I freely talked about this issue.

SUPERVISION SESSION VIII

This was a light-hearted yet close exchange. CC had not seen another client before today so we spent the period taking a general overview of our experience together. In this we compared and contrasted clients and again looked at CC's development. We both expressed much enjoyment over having worked together and our parting was touched with a little bit of sadness.

EVALUATION

As I mentioned earlier, CC came into the practicum course somewhat ahead of his classmates. He had already established a sense of professional identity and seemed for the most part confident. His strong points were in problem exploration and active listening. He seemed to excise and hone in on the essence of problems.

We needed to work through major dynamic hurdles. One was CC's tendency to be defensive (perhaps partly due to my style) including my fear of his defensiveness. The second was getting him to see how his style can at times be argumentative. We seemed to work through these dynamics simultaneously, and when these were resolved we could focus more effectively on counseling process and skills. At that point CC seemed to blossom as a counselor. He demonstrated a better than average understanding and sensitivity to intrapersonal and inter-personal dynamics, his empathy level rose to above minimal levels, and supervisory feedback helped him refine basic skills.

CC is at a point now where advanced study and supervised practice would be of utmost benefit. Reading in therapeutic techniques, psychopathology, and learning theory would be very

529

helpful in extending his knowledge base from which to practice.
Overall, working with CC has been a rewarding and enjoyable
learning experience for me.

Index

ACES, See Assn for Counselor
  Education and Supervision
APGA, See American Personnel
  and Guidance Assn
Abeles, N 83
Accountability
  counselor activities 205, 206
  counselor services 205, 206
  performance objectives of 203
Accountable relationship,
  facets of 16
Action-oriented conditions 449
Action plan implementation 269
Activity descriptions 423, 424
Administrative patterns of
  supervision 335
Administrative performance,
  assessing 314
Affective Sensitivity Scale 71
Agency
  referral 23
  settings 438
  supervisors 8
Aiken, W J 466, 467, 480
Alschuler, A 303, 314, 329
Altekruse, M K 107, 124
Altucher, N 37, 39, 44, 51, 82,
  441, 477
American Personnel and Guidance
  Assn xv, 7, 140, 178, 188,
  346, 349
  Standards for the preparation
    of school counselors 373
  Standards for the preparation
    of secondary school coun-
    selors 373
American Psychological Assn xv,
  354
American School Counselor Assn
  95
Analysis phase 385
Anchor, K N 70, 84

Anger 237
Anti-evaluation syndrome 25
Anxiety
  attacks 65
  confrontation 54
  control 116
Appleton, G M 329
Apprenticeship
  function within 8
Approaches, Differentiated 31-
  212
Arbuckle, D S 37, 82, 107,
  124, 443, 477
Archer, J 48, 71, 82
Armor, D J 304, 313, 329
Arndt, G M 112, 126
Arnold, D L 13, 28, 143, 166
Asking recall questions 242
Aspy, D N 477
Assessing counselor competen-
  cies, skill model for 305-
  306
Assessment
  categories 94
  of dynamic awareness 43-44
  student behavior changes 392
Assn for Counselor Education
  and Supervision xv, 7, 8, 18,
  19, 24, 26, 28, 171, 193,
  292, 312, 346
  Committee on Counselor
    Effectiveness 7, 373
Attitudes, reflection of 101
Aubrey, R F 292, 295, 299,
  312, 329, 330
Audio recordings
Audiotaped performance 250
Audiotapes 426
Austin, B 107, 124
Authier, J 114, 124, 139, 166,
Aversion 237
Avery, A W 138, 139, 166
Awareness treatment 116